N

LAHAINA
WAILUKU

MAUI

HANA

KAHOOLAWE

D1474291

WAIPIO

KAWAIHAE

HILO

HAWAII

KAILUA

ALSO BY PAUL BAILEY

FICTION

For Time and All Eternity
Ghost Dance Messiah
For This My Glory
Type High
The Gray Saint
Song Everlasting
The Claws of the Hawk

MYSTERY FICTION

Deliver Me From Eva

HISTORY AND BIOGRAPHY

City in the Sun (the Japanese Concentration Camp at
  Poston, Arizona)
Concentration Camp, U.S.A.
Polygamy Was Better Than Monotony
The Armies of God
  (the Mormon Militia on the American Frontier)
Sam Brannan and the California Mormons
Fabulous Farmer (the Story of Walter Knott and His
  Berry Farm)—with Roger Holmes
Walkara, Hawk of the Mountains
Wovoka, the Indian Messiah
Grandpa Was a Polygamist
Jacob Hamblin, Apostle In Buckskin
The Mormons In California (Ed.)
  (Pioneer Journal of William Glover)

THOSE KINGS AND QUEENS
OF OLD HAWAII

A Mele to Their Memory

THOSE KINGS AND QUEENS OF OLD HAWAII

by

PAUL BAILEY

WESTERNLORE BOOKS ... 1975 ... LOS ANGELES 90041

Library of Congress Catalog No. 75-259
ISBN No. 0-87026-035-9

PRINTED IN THE UNITED STATES OF AMERICA BY WESTERNLORE PRESS

To Evelyn . . .

*so steadfast and
so understanding*

ACKNOWLEDGMENT

To THOSE scholars of Hawaiiana who for years have recorded island history through the research and publishing facilities of the University of Hawaii, Hawaiian Historical Society, and the Bernice P. Bishop Museum, and who have so patiently answered the questions, this author is forever indebted. To the Bishop Museum especially, who furnished the many rare historical photographs, and whose librarians and staff members—Judith Reed, Lynn Davis, and Edwin H. Bryan particularly—proved so constantly and so generously attentive to my search and my wants — a very special *mahalo*.   — PAUL BAILEY

CONTENTS

ILLUSTRATIONS

HAWAIIAN PRONUNCIATION

Three simple rules are an invaluable guide to Hawaiian pronunciation:

(1) Pronounce each vowel.

(2) Never close a syllable with a consonant.

(3) Sound the vowels as follows:

a — a as in *water*
e — ey as in *they*
i — i as in *king*
o — o as in *noble*
u — oo as in *pool*

PART ONE

Kamehameha — Lonely Warrior

I

THE EIGHT islands of Hawaii, a series of basalt peaks whose tips emerge above water, are part of an underwater mountain range built by millions of years of volcanic eruptions. Their offshore depths plunge eighteen thousand feet to ocean floor. On some of the islands, particularly the big island of Hawaii, there are volcanic cones towering thirteen thousand feet above the sea line—some of them still active. If ever these islands were born according to Hawaiian mythology, their births must have been fiery ones.

For Hawaiian animism and tradition argues that the people and the islands are one; that both are products of the omnipresent realm of the spirits. Legend and genealogy declare their spiritual birth. Parents of all, as Malo records it, were Pa-pa, the earth—and Wa-ke-a, the sky, sun, great restless, passionate father of space. The primal concumbence of Wakea brought the big island—Hawaii—as firstborn. And the womb of the earth mother likewise spawned the island of Maui.

In conformance with Polynesian concept of royal matings, Wakea was a polygamist at heart and in practice. While the fertile but weary Pa-pa returned to Tahiti to recuperate, Wakea seized the opportunity to incestually impregnate their daughter. This younger god-woman bore him the islands of Lanai, and Molokai.

When the true earth mother heard of the sexual peregrinations of Wakea, and her "womb became jealous at its partnership" with her daughter, she returned, angrily and vengefully. Again she mated with Wakea. From this union was born the island of Oahu—an untidy and anxious spawn.

With this godly family tiff finally settled, the earth mother more willingly became pregnant—this time delivering the island of Kauai. Then, to Wakea, she bore Niihau and Nihoa.

But that did it. After this last issue, she was barren. Kahoolawe was delivered as a red rock. And, wearied by his monumental studship,

Wakea too had lost the urge. He took no more godwomen to wife. The islands were complete — a great, beautiful, tangled family. And Hawaii's honored genealogy goes directly back to Wakea and his matings.

The honored genealogy, of course, is the royal genealogy. The first parents of the Alii*—the ruling or privileged class—were these same gods. Along with their islands, the Alii were reputedly born of the gods. Common Hawaiians, over whom they despotically ruled, were never allowed to forget that fact. After a thousand years, royal Hawaiians still looked and walked like gods. It was kapu (tabu) to mongrelize with common blood. By continuous and vigilant interbreeding, their six foot stature was maintained—apparent down to the last king and queen. For any runty or ordinary Hawaiian to look into the face, or stand in the shadow of one of the Alii, was to earn cruel and certain death.

Nothing on earth is quite comparable to Hawaii's royalty. Their genealogy served as an untrammeled code of conduct regulating their lives, their outlook, and their comportment. To keep the blood line pure and untainted, polygamy, polyandry, and incest were openly practiced. Brothers married sisters, fathers married daughters, mothers married sons—until the kinship pattern of the Alii resembles a conjugal nest.

But in genealogy the Alii point straight line back to the gods who bred and birthed the islands. Unhesitatingly they declare that the islands and themselves are one—born of common parents. Hawaiian peasantry, under their rule, had no share to such honor or acclaim. They served their masters.

Racially, such deliberate interbreeding through generations should have been disastrous. In the case of the royal Hawaiians, it just was not so. Instead of the warty runts which geneticists would have predicted, they emerge as kings in stature as well as practice. Instead of insanity and feeble-mindedness, one would be hard put to find a more alert and intelligent segment of mankind. As a ruling class, they were bred to rule. As men and women, they walked with dignity and pride—sure of themselves; sure of their standing.

Every member of the Hawaiian royalty turns out to history as an interesting person—whether he or she be despot, opportunist, warrior, or genial monarch. None of them were ordinary. And the only racial disaster that struck down the Alii came from the white man—the foreigner—the *haole**.

*A-li-i: Ah-*lee*-ee.
*Ha-o-le: Hah-oh-lay (more common usage, how-*lay*).
Vowels in Hawaiian words are given the Latin pronunciation—each vowel pronounced separately. Every syllable ends in a vowel. There are no silent letters.

These kings and queens ruled over an island paradise—almost completely free of disease. When Captain James Cook opened paradise to the world, and the ships brought in the white man—the Alii, in trying to accommodate, destroyed themselves. Disease, Christianity, exploitation—whalers, missionaries, mercenaries—in that order—wiped out the Hawaiians.

With their subjects no longer tractable, possessions totally vanished, the Alii had no further reason to exist. In 1893, when the Americans finally toppled Queen Liliuokalani* from the throne of Hawaii, the most amazing monarchy in the world toppled with her.

But the islands themselves—cutting diagonally across the Tropic of Cancer, and two thousand miles seaward from North America—have weathered under tropic sun and gentle rains into verdant havens of green and sand. They are interlaced with some of the world's most startling upland scenery. As gem-string prizes they have, from the beginning, been instantly appreciated—and just as inevitably coveted and claimed.

*   *   *   *   *

Before the time of the first Kamehameha* they were ruled by chiefs and kings, many interrelated, governing by the strength of kinship, pugnacity and intrigue. It was Kamehameha the Great, master of these ingredients, who conquered all, and extended his dominance over the entire island chain. His climb to immortality is a tale of violence and unrelenting will.

The date, the place of birth, and even the parentage of Kamehameha the Great, remain something of an historical guessing game. Whether or not he was a true son of Keoua* and nephew of Kalaniopuu* or was grafted to the royal stem by Kahekili's assignation, is still a tantalizing mystery. Only the fact that he was highborn, and Alii, can be declared with assurance and certainty.

Keoua was younger half brother to Kalaniopuu, rightful heir to a vast feudal chunk of the island of Hawaii—the kingdom of his father, Keeawe. But Keeawe was destroyed by the interloper, Chief Alapai,* who held the young sons in subjection, had added their mothers to his harem, and had set himself up as supreme Mo'i of the big island—with court and palace at Kailua, on the Kona coast. As sop to infamy, King Alapai allowed Kalaniopuu to rule the province of Kau, to the south, and made the handsome Keoua a favorite at court. Secretly, Keoua detested his rapacious stepfather.

*Lili-u-o-ka-la-ni: Lee-lee-*oo-oh*-kah-lah-nee.
*Ka-me-ha-me-ha: Kah-*may*-hah-*may*-hah.
*Ke-o-u-a: *Kay*-oh-oo-*ah*.
*Ka-la-ni-o-pu-u: Kah-lah-nee-*oh*-poo-oo.
*A-la-pa-i: *Ah*-lah-*pah*-ee.

Keoua's marriage to Kekuiapoiwa* had meant much at Kailua. The beautiful chiefess, niece of Alapai, had strengthened the young chief in favor, and had marked him with highest promise. But, more important, he had truly loved this bride.

The nuptials had accepted the traditional niceties and the royal customs. To assure Alii paternity, the bride had been kept isolated by the priests until she had provided natural evidence she was totally without child. Then up the mountainside, among the pili grass and shaggy pandanus trees, the tent of newly-made kapa cloth had been erected. Priests had consecrated the ground where it stood. Royal staffs had been set at its four corners because, within the shelter, would be consummated a union of the *alii-kapu*.

Keoua had approached his *hoomai keiki*, or "sowing a baby," like a strutting cock, preceded by his warrior attendants bearing *kahilis*, and heralding his arrival with the mating moan from the conch-shell horn. In the night the bride had been carried to the tent on the *manele*, toted by her servants. They had placed her on lauhala mats; brushed her long black hair to sheen; dusted her with aphrodisiac pollen from the hala bloom. Her anxious brown body had been bathed with the oil of mountain ginger.

After the eager experience, Keoua had returned, spent and satiated, to the nuptial feast at the court of the king. They had carried his bride, by *manele*, back to Kailua, to be placed for four months in sacred kapu.

But out of the *hoomai keiki* had come no child.

For a year Keoua's bride, at court, wore her black hair free and deep, as badge of childlessness. Vivacious, slender-bodied, conically breasted, she had been a man's real pride. Not until her fateful visit to the neighboring island of Maui, did the weight of Alapai's displeasure fall upon her.

None of the island courts were more lavish and open than that of King Kahekili,* ruler of Maui and lord of two other islands he had conquered. Son of a fighting king, he had come to Maui's throne in 1736. There he had surrounded himself with reckless warriors anxious to do or die in his name. Now, having won every war, he was host to an extravagant circle—at Wailuku, on Maui. Of his many wives, the tempestuous queen, Namahama, maintained a court of her own, almost as sumptuous as that of her husband. An invitation from the King or Queen of Maui, to share their primal whirl, was an honor highly coveted among the Alii.

*Ke-kuia-poi-wa: *Kay*-ku-ee-ah-*poy*-wah.
*Ka-he-ki-li: *Kah*-hay-*kee*-lee.

The request had come directly from Namahama. Keoua long regretted the day he had granted his woman her eager plea for the sea journey to Maui. First had come reports of Kahekili's sudden interest. It had demeaned one to fend off rumors that the, King of Maui was lustfully pursuing the young wife of a Kailua chieftain. But soon after Kekuiapoiwa's return to the Kona coast, she had announced herself *hapai*. Court gossips buzzed. Keoua and his bride had kept themselves head high, and above it.

Even though the baby might have had Maui genesis, Keoua and his woman would have absorbed the thrust. They would have accepted the child under Polynesian pattern of kinship. And, too, there was a great probability the baby could be Keoua's own. But old Alapai was furious. Sensing treachery from his rival on Maui, he allowed a once deep love for his niece to turn to bitter hate.

For years Kahekili had boasted he would someday take the kingdom of Alapai. Now, to plant his own child in the Kailua household, was a subtle form of threat and insult. Legend says that Alapai became obsessed with the idea that some evilish monster had been vulpinely placed in the womb of his niece. Were this child to live, he reasoned, it would doubtless come as a revolutionary—a destroyer. The king, already plagued with senile fears, and under coercion of his kahunas, became as one insane.

Not content with demanding instant death for an unborn child, he turned his fears and his hates upon Keoua, and the girl who once had held such favor. For their own safety, Keoua and his woman went into hiding. Even though Keoua felt most keenly hurt and betrayed, it was Alapai's madness that drove him into rebellious determination to protect his wife and child.

Plans for the accouchement were made with care. In the month of November, in one of those disputed years from 1753 to 1758, a large double-hulled war canoe moved close in to the northern coast of Kohala. Keoua put his wife ashore in the night. Travel by sea was the only sure way to avoid Alapai's hunting parties.

In the grass house at Halawa, a priest and midwife were waiting. The woman's breasts, ready for the new child, were full of good milk. She knew exactly how to aid this girl so abruptly dropped to shore, and so hurriedly brought to her by the tall chief in *mamo* cloak.

When the pains became frequent and urgent, the girl was led out of the hut to the open area beneath the sky and stars. To ease the torment, she squatted over a spread of fresh pandanus leaves. The old woman, from behind, locked hands above the young woman's belly. With rhythmic pressure, Polynesian style, the child was expelled. The midwife severed the foetal cord with her natal cutting stones. And,

while she ministered to the newborn boy-child in the darkness, the girl rested and gathered strength upon the earth.

And, looking up into the skies, Kekuiapoiwa saw—as did her husband Keoua in his canoe far at sea—the strange light with the tail feathers of a bird. Here, to both of them, was indisputable sign that a king had been born. The heavens had declared it. What the young chief and his woman probably saw was Halley's Comet—visible to Hawaiian skies in those November nights of 1758.

Three days later Keoua returned to the Kohala coast. At the grass hut at Halawa he found his woman—alone and distraught. Men had come. They had taken both the midwife and the infant. The mother had howled and fought like a whelping bitch.

Not until Keoua explained that these were not Alapai's killers—that the seizure was according to his own plan, and by his own men, headed by the trusted chief, Naole—would the mother be consoled. He explained that for her to acknowledge, or care for this child, was open invitation to death. The infant, spirited away, was safe, and in good hands. Though she could never herself mother it, she must give her son this chance for life. In returning to Kailua, and in facing court and king, she must, for her own safety, declare that her child had been buried stillborn.

So Keoua and his wife voyaged back to the Kona coast and Kailua. Both of them faced their peers. Observing that Kekuiapoiwa again was slender and trim, even old Alapai accepted the story. In a mood-switch common to dementia, he quickly emerged from his compulsive madness, and subsided into the calmer pattern of senility. In time all scars of suspicion and intrigue were healed. And, when Keoua's wife again became *hapai*, and she delivered a boy baby with no shadows to cloud the paternity, all was forgiven.

Meanwhile the hidden child, named Paiea, lived five years in the secluded Valley af Waipio. No more isolated refuge could be imagined. Narrow, landlocked, wrapped on three sides by perpendicular cliffs, and funneled out to the sands and open sea, Waipio was not only an Eden of dreamy beauty, but had been sanctuary to troubled Alii for centuries. When Paiea came to live in one of its tiny villages, no questions were asked of Naole, his guard and keeper. The care given this boy child, the security surrounding his custody, marked him Alii.

◁ *A HAWAIIAN CHIEF WEARING A FEATHER HELMET*
An engraving after Webber.

—*Bernice P. Bishop Museum, Honolulu.*

The valley possessed ancient holy sites, and was haunted with legend. In habitation its few villages were very small. These, and the more scattered dwellings, clung to the green roots of the "thrust up" mountains. Rain clouds constantly hovered the high peaks, dropping their moisture, to tumble in cascades to the pools below. These fern-clad water basins drained out across the valley's floor in streamlets, sustaining a green and fertile wonder; the water coursing eventually to the sea. The mountain waterfalls, tinted in rainbow colors, made of Waipio a mystic dream.

Waipio's patchwork of taro gardens, fish ponds, palm and banana groves, spoke of moisture and rich soil. Huge breadfruit trees, and the lush circles of habitation, were proof of peace and plenty. The green valley, wedging into the northern Kohala coast, was the place where man could meditate, and the spirits talked.

Naole taught the boy to swim—in Manaue pool. Like all Poly-nesians he had no fear of water. In the sea's rolling surf, Paiea quickly learned every fishlike trick. His attendants saw to it that his body was molded and toughened into physical perfection. By *lomi lomi* massage his flesh was kneaded over the bones to straightness and symmetry. Before his skull plates were hardened, his cranium had been shaped to crown point, high forehead, and straight line to the neck. He was taught to walk erect, with the lithe, sinuous grace that would forever mark him Alii.

It was inevitable that the parents would someday take custody of this lonely, handsome child. At an opportune time, Keoua instructed Naole to bring his son to Kona. By the time Paiea was moved to Kailua, and assumed his rightful place at court, the matter of his threatening and worrisome paternity had been buried.

King Alapai, old and feeble now, sensed no anomaly in his favor-able acceptance of the lad he once had sentenced to death, and whom his warriors had so assiduously shadowed as a malignant threat. The king, noting Paiea's aloofness, gave him the name of Kamehameha—"the lonely one." Though the boy was thoughtful, solemn, and seldom laughed, there was nothing timid or shy about him. Waipio tutors had coached and molded him physically into strength and dignity.

At Kailua the meticulous care and training reserved for Hawaiian highborns was continued and intensified. The mark of the Alii—ever upon this young chief—demanded physical and mental superiority. Family, unassailable genealogy, aristocratic bearing, were not enough. A true leader must excel in all things.

The high goal, of course, was the *alii-aimoku*—a standing and title which must be earned, and never inherited. It was customary to select one promising son from an Alii family—not necessarily the first or

eldest son—for the rigorous training necessary for *alii-aimoku* acceptance. This leadership came not by primogeniture right, but by achievement. And that coveted title could not be family conferred or inherited.
At first sight of Kamehameha Paiea, he had been chosen by the king
and by his high chief father, over the less promising but better known
brother. For seven more years, at Kailua, Paiea was schooled in the
rigorous climb.

Even in childhood this sober youngster seemed to excel in anything
he attempted. In the court of Alapai, young Kamehameha would have
grown into the rights and pattern of his father, had not sudden tragedy
shattered the shelter and security of Keoua's existence at Kailua.

The attempt on the high chief's life was baldly and obviously court
treachery. Whether the flighty and tempestuous old king was responsible, or the jealous court rivalry of the king's ambitious son Keaweaopala,* or some diabolical prompting due to Kamehameha's popularity
or paternity—the slow poisoning of the high chief was undoubtedly the
work of *kahuna ana'ana*. Someone had ordered his death.

In desperation the dying Keoua sent for his brother Kalaniopuu,
high chief of the more southerly province of Kau. Knowing he was
doomed, Keoua begged Kalaniopuu to remove his son from the specter
of Kailua's intrigue and Alapai's treachery before he too was murdered.
His last request was that his brother adopt, guide, and educate the boy.

With the death of his father, and Kamehameha's removal to Kau,
a new world opened for "the lonely one." In Kau, Paiea found another
land of strange and mystic solitude. In Kau stood the great snow-rimmed
Mauna Loa, whose periodic volcanic rampages shook the island, and
whose scorching ashes and vomit of molten lava poured devastation
down the slopes and into the sea. Kau was domain of the fireheaded
goddess Pele, whose whims must be placated, whose favors must be
won—if man were to live and exist anywhere near her fiery temple.

Kau became a strange contrast to the green world of Waipio Valley;
different even than the less lush Kona coast at Kailua. The lava flows
from Pele's mountain had made the coastline precipitous and wildly
alive with color. But up the canyon draws, where time and weather
could reduce the volcanic exudation to mineral-rich and fertile soil,
there were forests of hau trees, vines, and flowering meadows. Here
were the villages, the taro patches, the breadfruit trees, the high-tas-
seled coconut palms. Here were flowered pockets of habitation, whose
streams and green abundance were refuges of peace and beauty—so
long as Pele allowed them to be. Here thrived a special breed of Hawaiians—"children of Kau"—proud, independent, deeply religious,
fierce in battle. Their allegiance was to Pele, and not to man.

*Ke-a-we-a-o-pa-la: *Kay*-ah-way-ah-*oh*-pah-lah.

Once accepted and established at the more modest court of High Chief Kalaniopuu, Kamehameha began Kau's version of military schooling. Under tutorship of Kekuhaupio,* Kau's greatest warrior, began the coachings in wrestling, spear throwing, spear dodging, and the beginning tactics of warfare—both defense and offense.

At Kamehameha's first sexual stirrings, and as a promising candidate for *alii-aimoku*, his retainers taught him all the Polynesian niceties of joyful, carefree, uninhibited intercourse. As Alii perquisite, he was amply provided with willing but carefully selected *wahines*.

Kau's priests taught him astronomy, history, the migrations and omens of fish and birds, and all the circuitous variations of religion and kapu. By oral recitation, and by wailing *mele*, he memorized his genealogy back to the gods themselves. Unaided by books or written language, his mind was crammed with the facts that proved Polynesians the master navigators of the world — bravest, wisest, most favored among humans. Kamehameha, too, was coached in the art of oratory. But in this skill alone did the introspective youth lack achievement.

It was in the physical aptitudes of manhood that no one could match him. His excellence was in anything and everything pertaining to the art of war—spear and hammer attack, proper and effective use of the slingshot, how to kill with fists, club, stone blade, and the lithe and rough tactics of Hawaiian wrestling.

From his Alii elders he learned the honor codes which went with war. The times and seasons the gods had set for battle—the religious necessities one must observe if he were to prevail over his opponent—how to gather and increase one's personal mana, so as to enshroud soul and body with spiritual invincibility. He learned that Hawaiian warfare was never permitted during *makahiki*, or the four months following this festival marking the harvest season. Nor could battles ensue during the three months of growing season prior to *makahiki*. That allowed five months only in each year to start and finish all hostilities.

No attack upon an opponent must be made without due warning. Notification must be made as to place and date for battle, so that even the foe might have time to dedicate a temple or *heiau* so as to woo strength and blessing from his gods. Friend and enemy alike must spend long hours in the holy places, to develop and increase their own mana, and to ally themselves with the celestial power necessary for victory in the strife.

But when Kekuhaupio was finished with Kamehameha Paiea he looked at his handiwork with pride. This protégé surpassed any young chief in the land.

*Ke-ku-ha-u-pi-o: *Kay*-koo-hah-oo-*pee*-oh.

Many a female eye roved this genius out of Kohala and Kona. The beautiful Kanekapolei* admired his grace, strength and litheness—to the point of throwing herself at him. Problem was that Kanekapolei was one of the younger wives of Kamehameha's own uncle and benefactor, Kalaniopuu. But the brash youth, already experienced in plucking choice flowers, unhesitatingly helped himself to his uncle's harem.

His female paramour, age thirty-five, was no maiden—but she was choice. When it was learned that young Kamehameha had raided his uncle's bed, the errant wife was expelled from the chief's *hale noa*. Kamehameha promptly married her, and she mothered his first son, Kaoleioku. The high chief of Kau weathered the incident with Polynesian tolerance, and later accepted the wandering chiefess back to his own household.

Another pair of female eyes, ogling from afar, belonged to the young girl Kaahumanu,* whose, illustrious Alii parents had come from the island of Maui to join the court of Kalaniopuu. This precocious youngster already had made up her mind as to Kamehameha.

Then suddenly came news out of Kailua. King Alapai was dead. The nation had gone to his son Keaweaopala,* the erratic prince whom Kamehameha had suspected of plotting the death of his father, and whose hatred and jealousy had forced Keoua's son out of Kailua. The new king of Hawaii was hated even more than was Alapai. Within months the people of Kona and Kau were in open rebellion.

The civil war was a brief one. Kalaniopuu threw his superb Kau fighters into battle. And, in the decisive two-day struggle near Kealakekua Bay, Kamehameha received his first taste of bloody combat. In the tumult the new King Keaweaopala was killed; his forces swiftly annihilated. Kamehameha led an invasion into Kailua, and had the grim satisfaction of burning the palace of Alapai and his arrogant and despised son. And, while fire wiped out Kailua, and the last vestiges of Alapai's regime, the war captives were duly sacrificed on the *heiau* at Hikiau.

Kalaniopuu now not only controlled both Kau and Kona, but had set his ambition toward unification of every rebellious province on the island of Hawaii. Quickly as the priests proclaimed him king, he moved his capital to Kealakekua*—spurning the once popular Kailua, fifteen miles to the north. His grand palace was built on the beach slopes up from Hikiau Head.

*Ka-ne-ka-po-lei: *Kah*-nay-*kah*-poh-*lay-ee*.
*Ka-a-hu-ma-nu: Kah-*ah*-hoo-*mah*-noo.
*Ke-a-wea-o-pa-la: *Kay*-ah-way-ah-*oh*-pah-lah.
*Ke-a-la-ka-ku-a: *Kay*-ah-lah-*kay*-koo-*ah*.

Kamehameha, strutting in victory, and more than ever in favor, was glad to return to Kona; to again join a court where an uncle was king. He was a young man, but his courage and resourcefulness had been battle-proven. It was a gratifying and heady experience.

With Kamehameha elevated to a prince of the realm, Maui's King Kahekili now made a move that could indicate he claimed Kamehameha as his blood son. To the court at Kealakekua he assigned his twin younger brothers. From Maui the princes were dispatched in state canoes; their mission to remain at the side of young Kamehameha; to advise, guide and direct the favored youth.

King Kalaniopuu outwardly accepted the royal ambassadors as a gesture of goodwill. Inwardly he was not at all pleased. Kahekili was master of intrigue; ambitious; arrogant. Kalaniopuu's first decision, as king, was to again strike at his old enemy from the adjacent island.

A year was spent building enough battle canoes for the invasion of Maui, and to train and season an army. When the time came, and the omens appeared to be right, Kalaniopuu personally led the assault. His son Keoua the Younger, and the eager and anxious Kamehameha, were in direct command.

The war, which for months surged bitterly across the green island, ended only in partial victory. In the end Kalaniopuu gained only the Hana coast of Maui—an unresolved conflict that left him the awkward necessity of maintaining constant garrison at the island's Kauiki fort.

It was during this struggle that, out to sea, the strange moving *heiaus* of the God Lono were first observed. The great Lono, who long ago had voyaged from the islands was, according to kahuna divination, again upon the waters. Lono was moving about the islands. Lono was coming home.

II

THE ROYAL COURT at Kealakekua became ever more ripe and interesting to the tough-minded Kamehameha. It was dominated, of course, by Kalaniopuu. But the king was battle-scarred and aged. His excessive drinking of *awa*, especially after his failure to conquer and dispose of Kahekili, was more than ever physically debilitating. Though still alert and wily, it was apparent that uncle had but few years to live. Again intrigue and trouble dominated a royal compound.

Kiwalao,* the eldest son, was heir presumptive; made additionally secure by the fact that his mother, Kalola, in the king's harem, was the highest born, and carried the greatest mana. In royal line also was

*Ki-wa-la-o: *Kee*-wah-*lah*-oh.

the son, Keoua the Younger—half brother to Kiwalao. And now, to the circle of aspirants, was added the king's grafted-in nephew, Kamehameha Paiea. The inevitable struggle for power quickly surfaced.

A bitter quarrel between the king and Papalani, a high chief of Hilo, gave Kamehameha fortuitous opportunity to ingratiate himself. Eagerly he offered himself to the challenge. Had the king not been weakened by age and excesses, he, of course, would have settled his own affairs in combat. To preserve honor, Kalaniopuu gratefully accepted young Kamehameha's offer to serve as battle proxy.

But when it came to personal combat, the nephew soon discovered that the chief from Hilo was no easy man to kill. In Hawaiian fashion the gladiators faced one another with clubs, stone hammers, and their lethal skills at wrestling. It quickly plunged into fearful struggle. The brash young nephew would wear the scars of this battle to his grave. But the strength and impetuousness of youth prevailed. In killing Papalani, Kamehameha vindicated the honor of his king.

For reward, he was given Lower Hamakua, North and South Kohala, and North and South Kona. But, most important, the high priests of Hawaii conferred to his custody Kukailimoku—the god of war. This act added immensely to Kamehameha's mana. For now, into the keep of this fiery prince went the feathered war emblem of Hawaiian royalty —Kukailimoku—Ku, the Divider—Ku, the Snatcher of Lands.

Recognizing also the necessity for orderly transition of the realm after his death, King Kalaniopuu publicly named his eldest son, Kiwalao, as his successor. To Kamehameha now went second place in the kingdom. Keoua the Younger was furious. A nephew had usurped his rightful place as son of the king.

And by now the Alii maiden, Kaahumanu, was old enough for the menstrual house. She had become the constant haunt of her idol, the cocky and firm-muscled Kamehameha. As daughter of Keeaumoku the Elder, high chief of Maui—the *alii-aimoku* who had deserted Kahekili—this young chiefess was as desirable and as highborn as any man could ask. She was also ambitious, vivacious, passionate and beautiful. When Kamehameha took her to wife, it worried her none that he had previously stolen a mate out of the harem of the king.

To this second marriage Kalaniopuu could really look on in favor. Kaahumanu was highest ranking chiefess in the court. The match was accepted by the people. It enhanced Kamehameha's image. But even beyond that, the marriage was a good one. Kaahumanu was to remain always the true love and confidant of Kamehameha's life. She became his ever-present consort, his closest companion.

*   *   *   *   *

Life in a king's residence had little in common with life throughout the more plebeian areas. At the time of Kamehameha's elevation,
each of the populated islands had its own king, with royal courts similar to the one at Kealakekua. Not only was the royal compound the
personal abode of the ruler, but also housed Alii of all ranks. In this
awkward world of custom and ritual, ordinary Hawaiians, and lower
measured Alii, had to be ever aware and vigilant in preserving the
complicated profusion of kapus constantly surrounding personages of
rank and mana.

Supplies for the royal court were furnished as part of the taxes collected from the subjects under Alii rule. Few goods, and little food,
were produced by Hawaiian royalty. The women of Alii rank demanded their kapa cloth and edibles under the system of taxation.

The king maintained an alert retinue. He was constantly attended
by those of rank high enough to gaze into his face and hear talk from
his lips without having to grovel, or risk death from the breaking of
one of the immutable kapus. There were those who sat with him as he
ate, those who shared his games and conversation, day and night.
Others, with special skills, told his stories, or recited the dossier of his
battle triumphs or noble genealogy. The king's apparel, and the preparation of his food, were specialized functions delegated to others. Those
with priestly blood were the keepers of his idols. They said his prayers;
they watched over him while he slept. The more talented wives of his
harem composed *meles*, or chants, in his honor. Skills at singing and
dancing, both men and women, were important enough to bring royal
favor.

Because mysticism and sorcery hung close to every move of life,
personal and trusted retainers followed the steps of every man or
woman born to the Alii. Any exudation from the body—spit, nasal
drip, urine or fecal ordure—must be caught immediately in special
gourd pots or dishes, and immediately and secretly buried. The danger
of some kahuna or politically motivated priest getting even a morsel
from an Alii, and thereby gaining psychic control over the life and
acts of this person, was an ever-present danger.

Gods, both good and evil, controlled the destinies. They must be
recognized and constantly placated. The kahunas, or sorcerers, especially the dreaded *kahuna ana'ana,* who could literally pray a man to
death, were part and parcel of the Hawaiian culture. Every Alii's mana
and personal power had to be diligently guarded.

An essential function at the king's residence were the contests and
sports. These served also as an effective training for war. Wrestling,
fist-fighting, pole vaulting and spear throwing were constantly prac-

ticed. Chiefs would pit their best warriors in sham battles, hoping to impress the monarch, and gain his favor. The Alii themselves often fought one another, so the king might visually judge the best and most competent of his subordinates. Kamehameha, whether in mortal combat, or in sham battle, never failed to maintain impressive status.

At this time the islands were divided into four principal kingdoms. The island of Hawaii itself was, by now, totally under the rule of Kalaniopuu—who also held possession of the Hana district of east Maui. Maui, with the exception of the Hana area, but including its three dependent islands, was still ruled by Kahekili. Oahu was now the possession of King Peleioholani. Kauai and Niihau were ruled by King Kaneoneo. All of these four kingdoms had grown out of a stone age culture. Iron, steel, the wheel, were unknown to the aborigines. Weaponry was of the most rudimentary sort.

Though gunpowder and steel were not yet a part of island battle gear, the struggles between kings and chieftains were still lethal and decisive. Their wars, even though fought with slingshots, clubs and spears, were savage and bloody in the extreme. The father of King Kalaniopuu had been slain in mortal combat with the invader and interloper, Alapai. The two sons of the rightful king—Kalaniopuu and Keoua—had seen their father perish at Alapai's hands.

But war and struggle were still a part of the aging Kalaniopuu's existence. In the very hour that the British naval vessels of Captain James Cook sailed past the island of Maui, the armies of Kalaniopuu were battling desperately for that island's conquest.

It was inevitable that a culture grown out of the stone age would collide with the Nineteenth Century—and with mortal effect upon its kings and queens. In their constant preoccupation with the control of paradise, they were soon to face an unexpected negation. Fate had set the pattern. They must now deal with visitors from another world.

It was Captain James Cook's third voyage into the Pacific, and destined to be his last one. Already, in two previous expeditions, he had established himself as the Pacific's greatest explorer. In 1768, commanding the *H.M.S. Endeavour*, he had completed the first scientific excursion into the South Pacific. He had returned to England, in 1771, with amazing stories of warm and tropical islands, peopled with brown-skinned natives who not only smilingly accepted him, but looked to him as a god.

*   *   *   *   *

Next year he was off again to further map and explore the wide reaches of the great sea in which comfortably rested Australia, New Zealand, Tahiti and the Fijis. It was 1775 before he returned to native

CAPTAIN JAMES COOK

Discoverer of the "Sandwich Islands."

—*Bernice P. Bishop Museum, Honolulu.*

England with additional tales of an island world of even greater interest and beauty. His third voyage into the Pacific, begun in 1776, and lasting four years, was to include a determined search for a northeast passage to the Atlantic Ocean. His ships this time were the *Resolution* and the *Discovery*. They had left Plymouth on July 12, 1776, had rounded the Cape of Good Hope, and before the year was out, were again in the familiar Pacific.

Once more the explorer made visit to the lush and inviting atolls of the South Pacific. After leaving Bora Bora, Cook and his ships sailed northward over uncharted seas.

The first island of Cook's new discovery was Oahu—January 18, 1778. But the tantalizing landfall, rising green and brown out of the sea, was out of Cook's reach because of the adverse blow of the trade winds. The islands of Niihau and Kauai were next sighted, but it was not until evening of the following day that the *Resolution* and the *Discovery* were able to anchor off the leeward coast of Kauai, alongside the village of Waimea.

The natives were thrilled and terrified. Their kahunas divined that the masts and sails of the British ships were trees moving about on the sea, and that the ships themselves were the *heiau*, or altar, of the great god Lono. It was useless to fight the gods, they declared. The shouts were born of excitement. The mood was acceptance and reverence. It was fortuitous and miraculous that Lono should again come, in this day, and be mindful once more of his people.

It was morning of January 20 when the Englishmen stepped to the soil of Waimea. Destiny had set an inexorable hand upon the turbulent kingdoms of the islands.

Captain Cook was tremendously impressed by his new discovery. His circling tour had indicated the amazing scope and spread of this archipelago, thrown up from the ocean floor by the fury of ancient volcanoes. Now the islands stood out of mid-Pacific like green-brown jewels in a spangle of great beauty. His greater astonishment was in the people who greeted his entry. He was struck by the close resemblance of Kauai's inhabitants to the natives he had encountered on Tahiti, Easter Island and New Zealand. He was first to anticipate their common lineage with the peoples of islands much farther to the south and west. It was James Cook who correctly pronounced Polynesia "the most extensive nation upon the earth."

On this first landfall at Kauai, Captain Cook named the string of islands in honor of the Earl of Sandwich, First Lord of the Admiralty, and one of Cook's patrons. The natives of Kauai impressed and delighted him with their happy and utterly frank welcome to himself and his men. Their immaculately clean villages of thatched pili grass, the health and beauty of the bronzed-skin inhabitants, the elegantly feathered cloaks and helmets of their chieftains, all were noted and recorded. The fields they tilled with skill and diligence, their fishing prowess, both in open water and the diked ponds of the sea, did not go unnoticed. Neither did the utter willingness of the comely maidens to service the members of His Majesty's Fleet. In the Sandwich Islands, Captain Cook knew he had made a major discovery.

But his happy experience was a brief one. He was on greater errand. After a short visit to the Island of Niihau, the *Resolution* and the *Discovery* hoisted anchors and set their sails for the northwest coast of America. It was a reluctant leave for Cook and his men, but their task was to chart the supposed northeast passage into the Atlantic. Impressed and delighted with the Sandwich Islands, Cook vowed that he would return.

A year later, almost to a day, Cook was back in the islands. There had been no northern passage. He'd had no desire to put his ships and men through another frigid and paralyzing winter. But again he found it hazardous and difficult to heel his vessels to anchor against the prevailing winds and the shallow and atolled island harbors—harbors so simply and easily navigated by the great double-hulled and outrigged canoes of the natives. Frustrating weeks were spent off the shores of Maui and Hawaii, while his navigator, Captain William Bligh, master of the *Resolution*, and recording artist of the expedition, endeavored to work the ships safely to shore.

It was at Kealakekua, under the snowy mountains of "Owyhee," that Bligh finally found anchor for the ships and the utterly exhausted crews. This time Cook and his sailors were overwhelmed by the welcome. He'd had little intimation that he was considered as Lono, the god returned. The very bay of Kealakekua was sacred to Lono's memory. From there, centuries ago, Lono had departed from his people, with the promise to return. It was winter when Cook and his men set foot to Hawaii's shore. It was also the season of *makahiki*, commemorative to Lono, his gifts and his promise. From every part of the big island, the people had assembled, not only for *makahiki*, but to view the actual and positive return of Hawaii's god. Oddly, the god-sign of Lono-makua was always a high staff with crosspiece from which hung long sheets of white kapa; carried by priests to the people, for their veneration, and as reminder that harvest taxes were due and payable. Had not the real Lono now come—in floating *heiaus*—with high masts, from which hung immense white shrouds?

"I had no where, in the course of my voyages, seen so numerous a body of people assembled at one place," Cook wrote. He was still innocent of the fact that he was considered divine, and that his men were looked upon as sub-gods mysteriously assigned to serve him. "Besides those who had come off to us in canoes, all the shore of the bay was covered with spectators, and many hundreds were swimming round the ships like shoals of fish."

King Kalaniopuu, with Princes Kiwalao, Kamehameha, and Keoua the Younger, and those of the Alii possessing enough mana to share the royal party, led the more formal parade of war canoes. Slowly, and in stately fashion, they circled the British ships. The great tall men, especially in the king's canoe, and those immediately following containing high priests, chiefs, and lower members of the royal retinue, were resplendent in feathered capes and helmets. Other canoes followed, bearing the sacred idols, their attendant priests, and canoe after canoe loaded with Alii women, and heaped offerings of gifts and food.

Cook and his officers stepped ashore, convinced that no discoverer could ever have been more fortunate. The Hawaiian king, his armies, and his people, instead of resisting invasion, met him with the obsequious reverence worthy of the returned god.

Once the crews were lightered ashore, the bartering began for supplies to fill the empty holds of the ships. When the sex-starved sailors commenced their less than godlike advances on the pretty girls of Hawaii, King Kalaniopuu began to sense these visitors were something less than the great and generous dieties he and his Alii had so eagerly welcomed ashore. Nevertheless Kalaniopuu and his people did everything in their power to make Cook and his men contented and satisfied.

Food and women were freely tendered, and without the asking. There were festivals of singing, dancing, and athletic prowess. There were state visits by the royalty, both ashore, and to the magnificent ships. About one of these formal affairs, Lieutenant James King, of the *Discovery*, recorded that one of the principal attendants of King Kalaniopuu "was Maiha-maiha [Kamehameha], whose hair was now plaisted over with a brown dirty sort of paste or powder, & which added to as savage a looking face as I ever saw, it however by no means seemed an emblem of his disposition, which was good natur'd & humorous, although his manner shewd somewhat of an overbearing spirit, & he seemed to be the principal director in this interview."

The twenty-five-year-old Kamehameha, at the time of Cook's visit, had already risen high in royal stature, and certainly in the esteem of Kalaniopuu. And he, intuitively, had reached the conclusion that Captain James Cook and his avaricious men were a good deal less than gods.

In the beginning, the natives were much too eager. They strove in every way to satisfy the earthy appetites of the men they had considered diety. An English sixpenny nail, in the first tradings, easily purchased two Hawaiian hogs. A bead, a mirror, or a button would buy a turbulent session with a hot-blooded maiden. And these were moments no sailor ever forgot. Sexual confrontation with a Polynesian *wahine* was always a frantic fulfillment, in which the girls clawed catlike at the faces and flesh of their paramours. No button or bead could ever have bought more.

But as the market became glutted with baubles and nails, the natives became more covetous; more demanding. As the empty holds of the ships began filling with Cook's and Bligh's cheaply won provisions, the prices rose to knives, daggers, hats, and shirts. These too were paid by the Englishmen for their desperately needed supplies. Soon the island was literally stripped of food. Everything for miles around had been hauled to Kealakekua, and at the king's insistence lightered out to the ships. But now, for the first time, the chiefs and Alii were armed with steel weapons. Many warriors now carried British navy daggers in place of the stone age fighting tools they had possessed only a month ago.

But each day of Cook's sojourn grew more irksome—especially when the food was gone, and the men had grown surfeited with the pleasures so cheaply won. The Hawaiians, by now, had experienced quite enough of English avarice. Cook had become short-tempered and angry about the natives crawling up the sides and through the portholes of his ships. He roared out at the petty pilfering that had taken the place of such willing giving.

Hawaiian hospitality, of course, had been wantonly misused. The people too were wearied of the weeks of attempting to placate the constant wants of the men they had mistaken for gods. When, on February 4, 1779, the *Resolution* and the *Discovery* set sail from Kealakekua, everyone from the king down were glad to see them go.

But fate was not through with Cook and the Hawaiians. No sooner were the ships at sea, when a gale broke with such ferocity that the *Discovery's* rotten main mast was rendered useless. The ships all but broached before the savagery of the storm. Cook and Bligh were forced back to Kealakekua.

This time the return of the ships was no occasion for reverence and glee. No sooner were the men again on shore than trouble erupted.

On the night of February 13, a group of Hawaiian chieftains decided to try out one of those beautiful and coveted English boats. In the darkness, they borrowed the large cutter from the *Discovery*.

Cook was furious. Next morning he took ashore with him a guard of nine marines, all heavily armed, with the avowed intent of seizing King Kalaniopuu as hostage until the cutter was returned. The natives still seemed friendly, until the Englishmen decided to enter the royal compound. Even then Kalaniopuu met Cook and his men with an obsequious attitude still worthy of a god—or at least an equal in the Alii.

The king quickly indicated he knew nothing about the theft of the cutter. He was not at all pleased with Cook's surly attitude, but he did reluctantly agree to return to the ship with Cook. This time, however, the princes and the chieftains were suspicious. They grew increasingly annoyed at the boorishness of the British commander. It was not like Lono to enter a royal compound brandishing muskets, pistols and steel daggers. When the king was marched down to the beach under guard, there were cries of anger and betrayal.

The king's favorite wife Kanekapolei, and princes Kiwalao, Kamehameha, and other chiefs, surrounded the king and begged him not to place himself in jeopardy. Instantly all signs of native friendliness vanished. Warriors commenced gathering; many of them armed with new English steel. At the water's edge, the king, sensing the true intent of his captors, sat down on a rock, and refused to go aboard the pinnace. Angry warriors, intent on rescuing their monarch, closed in.

Cook, realizing his party was vastly outnumbered, with an hostility he had never before experienced, decided against any further attempts to haul Kalaniopuu out to the *Resolution*. His plain job now was to get himself and his marines aboard the pinnace, and out of reach of the angered and threatening natives. At Cook's command, the guards aligned themselves along the rocks, muskets trained on the warriors.

At this point, one of the chieftains raised a spear. He lunged at the commander. Cook fired the first barrel of his pistol at the warrior, wounding him. The second barrel killed one of the natives. Seeing the commander in mortal peril, the marines commenced shooting. But, before Cook could get himself aboard the pinnace, he was knocked down with a club. One of the new English daggers was plunged into his back.

Four marines were soon dead, along with their captain. What remained of the British shore party were lucky to reach the ship alive.

As far as the Hawaiians were concerned, Lono was forever dead. He would return no more to their shores. While the British, from the ships and small boats, poured deadly fire upon their erstwhile friends, Cook's body was repeatedly pierced by the stone and steel weapons of the Alii. The king, unharmed, was hurried back to his thatched palace by Prince Kiwalao.

It was Kamehameha's task to restore some semblance of order. He commanded the people to retreat from the shore, out of reach of the lethal fire from the British. He ordered the priests, now that Cook was dead, to treat the fallen white chieftain as an Alii; to give him death treatment worthy of an Alii, if not of a god. The fallen sailors could be taken away. Their bodies could be handled or cannibalized in the manner of any other conquered enemy.

In the days that followed there were battles, reprisals, and uneasy peace overtures by the king and his people. The stolen cutter was returned. But the Hawaiian monarch never again went aboard an English ship.

Captain James Cook had not been Lono, but he was given funeral treatment worthy of a king. According to Alii custom, the priests stripped the flesh from his bones. The bones were sewn into a finely woven sennit death sack. The only divergence from royal custom was that, instead of secret burial, out of reach of the sorcerers, the remains of Captain Cook were delivered back to the Englishmen. They—instead of the priests and kahunas—buried what was left of the great British explorer—on the Kona coast of the island of Hawaii.

When the *Resolution* and the *Discovery* again put to sea, it was with sorrow for the loss of a great and brave leader. The British, however, departed with a new respect for the strange people of these little known islands.

III

AFTER FINAL DEPARTURE of the British, King Kalaniopuu resumed his lifetime efforts to conquer the neighboring and hostile island of Maui. His only major success against Maui's King Kahekili had been the uneasy possession of the Hana district on Maui's east coast. Now, with new resolve, and armed with British steel, Kalaniopuu landed a formidable army at Maalaea Bay. Victoriously it pushed across the lowlands and sandy isthmus of central Maui to face the full force of Kahekili's men near Wailuku. The encounter proved disastrous. The ten-day battle was as costly as it was decisive. Not only were the invaders utterly defeated, in spite of their new weaponry, but Kalaniopuu's forces were practically annihilated.

Kahekili now had regained complete possession of his beloved Maui, including the long lost Hana district. And, by his clearcut victory, he had made certain the finish of old Kalaniopuu, and the disintegration of Kalaniopuu's rule of Hawaii.

At a council of chiefs, held in the sacred valley of Waipio, Kalaniopuu now solemnly and publicly conferred the kingship on his eldest son Kiwalao. And, not only did he name Kamehameha as second in line to royal succession, but gave him final and complete custody of Ku, the war god of Hawaii's kings. Such citation carried more than the necessity of attending to the services of the god, and maintaining the *heiaus* dedicated to him. It was public acknowledgment that Kamehameha was war chief of the kingdom.

To end his final days on a note of glory, the old king headed an expedition to the southern part of the island, to deal with a rebellious chief. The recalcitrant chieftain was captured in battle, was victoriously hauled by Kalaniopuu to the *heiau* of Pakini in Kau, to be publicly sacrificed to Ku. As delegated head of the nation, Prince Kiwalao accepted the responsibility of dispatching the rebel chief. While preparations were being made at the altar for the rite, the impetuous Kamehameha stepped forward. He seized the captive. Without hesitance, before the assembled priests and witnesses, Kamehameha performed the sacrifice.

This affront to Kiwalao was something the heir apparent never forgot—an estrangement between the two cousins never to heal. Kamehameha justified his act by maintaining that he alone had been given custody of Ku, the war god, and he alone had the right to conduct sacrifice in Ku's name. Jealousy and hatred between the two men erupted with such ferocity that the position of Kamehameha at court was no longer tenable.

The old king, fearing for Kamehameha's life, advised him to leave Kealakekua. Reluctantly, Kamehameha retired to Kohala, his home—taking along his wife Kaahumanu, his growing retinue, and the idols, altars and traps of the war god Ku. There, for a time, he busied himself in the development of his own baronial lands.

When old Kalaniopuu finally died, in 1782, in the province of Kau, almost the entire island lay between the throne and Kamehameha. Kiwalao, the young king, quickly proved a vacillating weakling. He stepped immediately under the spell and guidance of his ambitious uncle Keawemauhili,* head chief of Hilo. This chief's Alii blood was unassailable. He was a man of proven ability. The redistribution of lands, customary at death of a king, was his golden opportunity to aggrandize himself and his friends.

Hawaiian mourning at death of a king was nationwide and all encompassing. Kapus, imposed by the priests, were many and drastic—reaching down to food, celibacy, and assemblage. While the rites were extended many days—to give time to strip the meat from the dead

*Ke-a-we-ma-u-hi-li: *Kay*-ah-way-*mah*-oo-*hee*-lee.

king's bones, carry on the elaborate funeral rites, and allow enough human sacrifice at the *heiaus* to appease the gods and gain favor in rulership for the future—there were phases of it that were equally barbaric and violent.

One evidence of contrite sorrow for the departed were for those of the Alii, who had lived in close association with the king, to augment their wailing by self-mutilation. A most evidential sign of sorrow was for the mourner to knock out one or more of his own teeth. But the ones who paid most utterly in public lament were those chosen for human sacrifice—usually war prisoners, or those who had come under royal displeasure.

During this orgiastic period, High Chief Keawemauhili of Hilo was feverishly laboring to seduce the new king, and grasp for himself everything available in crown lands. The chiefs of western Hawaii were forced to hastily set up an alliance to protect themselves against the king's avaricious uncle, and to counter the ambitions of this sudden menace. Kamehameha, already at loggerheads with Kiwalao, was persuaded to head the new alliance.

Greatest of all public spectacle was when King Kiwalao, with his half-brother Keoua, and his uncle and chief counsellor Keawemauhili, put the royal barge to sea—bearing the bones of the departed monarch. The paddlemen, to the *mele inoa,* or genealogical name-chant of the dead ruler, pushed the funeral craft on to Hale-o-Keawe, the mausoleum of Hawaii's rulers, situated a little south of Kealakekua Bay.

Kamehameha and his allied sub-chiefs, as public duty, assembled also at Kealakekua. There Kamehameha joined King Kiwalao and Prince Keoua in wailing for the departed Kalaniopuu. Dutifully they knocked out a tooth or two, as they went through the complicated ritual as prescribed by the priests and kahunas. Nevertheless, affairs in the royal family were strained. Even at mourning there were incidents which widened the breach between the three young men most intimately involved.

On the distribution of lands which followed, the counselor-uncle to the king was victorious in everything to which he had set his grasping hand. The affair ended in a three-way dispute, in which the short-changed younger brother, Keoua, emerged warlike and irrational. His first move was directed toward Kamehameha—long a target of jealous hate. Keoua and his men invaded Kamehameha's province, cut down coconut trees, and killed Kamehameha's defenders—a most blatant invitation to war.

In an equally devious plan to eliminate one phase of opposition, and to vent his own smoldering hates, Kiwalao allied himself and his warriors to the cause of his angry half-brother. The plan was to defeat Kamehameha and his chiefs in battle; strip them of their possessions as royal prerogative. The impetuous Keoua, and his disputatious claims, could later be dealt with after eliminating this nephew-pretender from the north.

The war was fought at Mokuohai in the summer of 1782—a desperate and vicious one. Kamehameha and his sub-chiefs emerged victorious. King Kiwalao was killed. But the struggle at Mokuohai had split the island into three kingdoms. Kamehameha now held Kona, along with Kohala and the northern part of Hamakua. Keoua was allowed Kau and a portion of Puna. The uncle retained Hilo, and some adjacent areas carved out of Hamakua and Puna. Now, instead of one, there were three kings of Hawaii.

The chiefs who had allied themselves with Kamehameha remained loyal to the end of their days. With their help, Kamehameha lost no time in launching a campaign against his rivals in power.

The battles which followed were frequent, costly, and availed nothing to Kamehameha. For years he suffered either defeat or stalemate in his stubborn effort to gain control of all the island of Hawaii. However uneasy and turbulent, the big island still remained under rulership of three quarrelsome kings.

While Hawaii seethed and festered with its own problems, Kahekili, king of Maui, launched a war of his own. By 1786 he had conquered Oahu, and had moved his seat of government to Waikiki. With both Maui and Oahu now fully his, Kahekili soon had control of every island but Hawaii. For four years the four kings—exhausted by their bloody power struggle—rested uneasily upon what they had gained, and what they now held. For a brief respite, the natives could farm, fish, and tend to their families without being forced into battle, or see their villages, coconut palms and taro patches ravaged by war and reprisal.

In these four years, and following Captain Cook's last tragic appearance, came a steady stream of ships to take advantage of the British discovery and evaluation of the new "Sandwich Islands." Here was an invaluable mid-Pacific landfall. Here were lush green islands where ships could fill their casks with the purest water, replenish their supplies at a fraction of mainland cost, and where their crews found joys unequaled in all the world.

Kamehameha had been impressed with the British warriors serving Captain Cook. Their guns, cannon, and sharp-edged steel made them invincible in battle. He coveted everything they possessed—from gold braid to gunpowder. These were the things he desperately needed.

From the visiting ships the Hawaiian kings and chiefs made every frantic effort to obtain firearms and bladed weaponry. Any wandering vessel could fill holds with foodstuffs by trading a tenth of the value in muskets, pistols, cutlasses and gunpowder. Kamehameha, at Hawaii's port of Kealakekua—and Kahekili, at Maui and Oahu—were in the best positions to gain from the Islands' armament race. But Kamehameha coveted more than just the tools of war. He needed foreign mercenaries to direct his ambitions under the war god Ku; to advise in his government; to train his warriors in the disciplines and skills he so admired.

In this struggle for power, and the possessions of the white man, there came ugly incidents between the natives and the crews and masters of the visiting ships. Captain Simon Metcalfe, an American trader, had put into Honaula, Maui, with his China-bound schooner *Eleanora*. While he traded for supplies, he waited for his other ship, the smaller brig *Fair American*, commanded by his son Thomas Metcalfe. On a January night of 1790, a small boat, tied to the stern of the *Eleanora* was stolen by Maui natives, in an incident similar to Cook's loss. In the nocturnal appropriation, a sailor in the boat, as guard, was killed.

Metcalfe's reaction to the theft and death was merciless. He fired his cannon into the village, killing natives, and demolishing their grass dwellings—only to discover that these townsmen were not guilty of the theft. Too late, he learned that the boat had been stolen by natives from the village of Olowalu. Without hesitance he hoisted anchor, and sailed the *Eleanora* to that village. When Captain Metcalfe's shore party returned with the news that the stolen boat had truly been brought to Olowalu, and was now a wreck, the captain was furious. To all appearances the *Eleanora* was friendly trader. The crafty Metcalfe invited the natives out to the ship. By crossed planks on the port side, in an instantly recognized kapu symbol, Metcalfe was able to keep the fleet of visiting canoes completely to starboard. When the happy, singing people were targeted in at cannon range, the *Eleanora* fired broadsides directly into the closely grouped mass of humanity. It was unspeakable slaughter. More than an hundred islanders were murdered, and many more wounded by the lethal blasts. The "Olowalu massacre" speedily became the topic of conversation at every village.

The hated *Eleanora* moved over to the island of Hawaii. While anchored there, the *Fair American* also reached the islands—only to find herself becalmed off north Kona. Chief Kameeiamoku, who in a previous visit aboard the *Eleanora* had been lashed and insulted by the bullying Simon Metcalfe, had already sworn revenge on the next foreign ship that came his way. Here now, fortuitously becalmed and handy, was the *Fair American*. Best of all, it was captained by Metcalfe's son, Thomas.

The chief and his warriors, after gaining permission in the guise of friendly trade, swarmed aboard the little ship. At a signal, Thomas Metcalfe was killed, and the entire crew thrown overboard. Only one crewman survived. When young Isaac Davis made it to shore, he was taken, a prisoner, to King Kamehameha.

While the tragedy of the *Fair American* was taking place, Metcalfe's other ship, the *Eleanora*, swung at anchor at Kealakekua. To withhold the knowledge of the *Fair American's* fate from Metcalfe, Kamehameha kept Isaac Davis imprisoned where he could not talk. The boatswain of the *Eleanora*, John Young, because he was an Englishman, felt he could risk coming ashore. He too was made prisoner. Remainder of the ship's crew, knowing the low esteem in which they now were rated among the proud and vengeful Hawaiians, had sense enough to remain aboard.

The *Eleanora* waited several days for John Young's return. Convinced he was a deserter, the captain ordered the crew to set sail for China without the missing boatswain. In resuming his voyage, Captain Simon Metcalfe left Hawaii without ever having known that his son Thomas was dead, or that the *Fair American* was now the nautical prize of King Kamehameha.

With the Metcalfes and the *Eleanora* safely out of the way, the two Anglo prisoners were released to freedom. During incarceration Young and Davis had become good friends. They made one attempt to escape, but with no ships handy, and Hawaii an island, they were quickly hauled back to Kamehameha. Surprisingly, the king offered them every inducement to remain voluntarily in his service. They were treated gently, and with respect. Kamehameha presented them with beautiful and highborn maidens as wives. When these were accepted with alacrity, they were showered with more gifts and greater attention. They were presented with lands, servants; and were solemnly titled as chiefs in court of the king.

In comparison to their former cruel servitude as crewmen on Anglo hellships, the two young men found themselves in paradise. In exchange for their help and loyalty, the king repaid them in luxuries and respect they had never before known. Strangely, and most fortunately, both John Young and Isaac Davis reacted as men of character. Neither of them ever left the service of Kamehameha. They never betrayed his trust. They exerted tremendous influence in building the young and ambitious king to greatness.

In Young and Davis, Kamehameha found precisely what he had long sought. They taught his Hawaiian warriors the niceties of killing with the modern tools of gunpowder, cannon, muskets, and cutlass. They coached the king in the foreign life style, dress, customs, and all the tricks of advantageous trading with the ships that were making the islands increasingly their ports of call. In Kamehameha's ascendancy they were ever present; ever helpful.

In a way Young and Davis were symbolic of the transition that had come upon the islands in one short decade of intercourse with a world the natives had never imagined existed. But with the ships came increasing trouble and violence. With the ships also came ideas, and material things which were to immeasurably alter the economy through the years.

What the foreigners brought were things both evil and good. Besides firearms and gunpowder, the traders introduced cotton, wool cloth, and clothes made from the looms of America. They brought silk and luxuries from China. White man's furniture, steel tools, and household utensils came to the islands. A new breed of pigs, and goats and sheep had been left by Captain Cook. Turkeys, horses and cattle were brought in from America. Fruit trees, plants, and garden vegetables were introduced to please the Alii; to augment their diet of fish, pork, taro, breadfruit and coconuts.

The more tragic aspects of the incursion, the lethal factors that came out of the holds of the ships, were fleas, vermin, mosquitoes, scorpions, and centipedes. Diseases, heretofore unkown to the healthy Hawaiians—spread by breath, contact, and sexual intercourse—swept through the villages like the scourges of hell. The visitors furnished the natives with tobacco and alcohol. They taught them how to smoke. And how to make island rum, by distillation—a drink more heady than *awa* —a drink powerful enough to blow them out of their minds.

The world changed rapidly in the years of Kamehameha's rise to power. He courted the visitors for every device that might be useful to him. Thanks to Young and Davis he had an army that could fight Anglo style; a navy that included the cannon-equipped *Fair American;* and a fleet of immense and efficient shallow-draft and double-hulled war canoes.

In the spring months of 1790, Kamehameha launched his drive for conquest of all the islands.

IV

HIS FIRST MOVE, naturally, was upon Maui—against the kingdom of the hated Kahekili. The old king, in residence now at Oahu, had left his son Kalanikupule* in governorship of the province. Kamehameha—the bastard son, according to Kohala legend, and little aware of the supposed kinship—swept across Maui with devastating suddenness. The last stand of Kalanikupule against the invaders was in the precipitous Valley of Iao. Most of the Maui warriors were slaughtered. The dead and bleeding bodies were stacked high enough to dam the valley's streams. Kalanikupule, and a few companions, escaped over the mountains, to finally reach Oahu with news of the catastrophe.

Kamehameha and his victorious army, after ravaging Maui, repeated the victory on the island of Lanai. He was not challenged on the island of Molokai, and effectively rescued the kapu chiefess Kalola, widow of Kalaniopuu, mother of Kiwalao, and sister of Kahekili—who had fled there after the battle of Mokuohai. Here, on her deathbed, Kalola gave Kamehameha her two granddaughters, Liliha and Keopuolani,* to take back to Hawaii. The firstborn, Keopuolani, possessed the highest possible rank as an Alii—higher than did Kamehameha. When Kamehameha later took her as a polygamous wife, it was to know that any children by her would, by Alii birth and mana, be automatically in line for his throne.

But while Kamehameha was achieving victories and increasing his political sway, his home base of power faced unexpected jeopardy. The impetuous King Keoua had turned suddenly against Keawemauhili. He had invaded Hilo with his armies, defeated his former allies, and murdered his uncle. After annexing Hilo, and doubling the size of his kingdom, he had moved boldly into Kohala, and had begun laying waste the territories of Kamehameha. The new war the returning Kamehameha now faced proved as bloody as the one he had fought in Maui, and far more indecisive. The strong and belligerent Keoua beat off every attack.

While this sanguinary and fruitless struggle went on—for the disputed territory of the home island of Hawaii—Kahekili recaptured

*Ka-la-ni-ku-pu-le: *Kah*-lah-nee-*koo*-poo-lay.
*Ke-o-pu-o-la-ni: *Kay*-oh-*poo*-oh-*lah*-nee.

THE HEIAU AT PUUKOHOLA

*Built by Kamehameha, and dedicated to the War God Ku. Site of
sacrifice of Kamehameha's captives and political enemies.*

—*Paul Bailey Photo.*

44

Maui and Molokai—with the military help of Keoua. The conquering Kamehameha found himself besieged from every direction, and worse off than when he had started his ambitious program. His every effort was now negated. He appealed to the sorcerers and kahunas. Without superhuman help, they persuaded him, his dream of conquest and supremacy would end in failure.

The priests reminded him that he was custodian of the war god Ku. Why had Ku been lethargic about granting him success in his battles? The perplexed and frustrated king listened well to the mystics. Before Ku could successfully act in his behalf, they explained, a great *heiau* must be built. A sacrificial altar, sufficiently imposing to gain and keep the god of war, must be erected. Site of the shrine was carefully chosen. With the help of all priests in his kingdom, every warrior he could spare from battle, and by drafting the entire populace, construction of the *heiau* commenced at Puukohola, near Kawaihae.

Finished, this shrine to Ku was a massive and imposing structure. The great stone platform, 224 feet long, 100 feet wide, with walls 20 feet high, resembled a grim fortress. The altar, and temple enclosure at the top, rested upon tens of thousands of lava boulders that had been belched up out of the earth by the volcanoes which the goddess Pele frequently allowed to blow into eruption. At its dedication, Kamehameha himself officiated at the sacrifice of eleven war captives.

But in the years that the *heiau* to Ku was being built, war continued to rage against Kamehameha. From the leeward islands came an invasion as terrible answer to Kamehameha's ambitious move in that direction. Kahekili, joined by Kaeo, and combining their war fleets, suddenly appeared off the northern coast of Hawaii. With frantic effort Kamehameha confronted the invaders at Waipio.

In Kamehameha's fleet was every war canoe he could muster. Aboard were men skilled in use of modern muskets and rifles. Leading the fleet was the captured *Fair American*. John Young and Isaac Davis commanded its artillery. The battle was joined in April of 1791, and it was long and murderous. But modern weaponry told, and Kamehameha's fleet came out supreme. The defeated Kahekili and Kaeo fled back to Maui to prepare for the return invasion they had every reason to expect.

With completion of the great *heiau* to Ku, and probably realizing that not only did Kamehameha have the Hawaiian war god comfortably on his side, King Keoua decided on a state visit to his victorious cousin. The Kohala upstart now possessed every Anglo skill to plot his wars and direct his gunfire. The time had come to recognize a fact; to

stabilize the two kingdoms of Hawaii. To Keoua it seemed wisdom to
end the battles that so long had ravished the island.

The visit of the rival king was made with pomp and pageantry.
Keoua's war fleet entered Kawaihae harbor with all the bright and
colorful trappings of royalty. Kamehameha, in feathered cape and
helmet, was rowed out in his own state canoe. Before the two rival
kings were even met, gestures of peace and friendship were acknowledged across the calm waters of the bay. The visit wore every indication of alliance and friendship.

Then suddenly, as the two fleets drew alongside, there was a scuffle
of warriors. Before Keoua could reach Kamehameha's barge, and before
the visiting king could set foot to shore, he was murdered by Kamehameha's men. Every dignitary in Keoua's state canoe was dead before
Kamehameha moved to intervene or stop the slaughter.

Kamehameha claimed it as an accidental assassination, and not a
bald act of treachery. Nevertheless, Keoua's body was sacrificed to Ku
atop the altar of the new *heiau* at Puukohola. Whether or not Ku was
now functioning in Kamehameha's behalf, the results were promising.
With King Keoua removed, with Kamehameha wearing the divine
cloak of invincibility, it took but little additional warfare to subdue
Keoua's provinces of Kona, Kau, Puna and Hilo. Before 1791 was finished, Kamehameha was ruler over all of the great island of Hawaii.

The devastating wars and senseless struggle for power had so de-
bilitated and impoverished the islands, that Kamehameha was willing
to rest from the battles long enough for his economy to recover from
the strain. Ships were coming in ever increasing numbers. There was
gain to be had in trade, and much that an ambitious monarch could
learn. Remembering all the good that had come out of Captain Cook's
visits, Kamehameha was more than friendly to the British when they
returned.

Captain George Vancouver had accompanied Cook to the islands as
a junior officer. As head of a new expedition, he had no intention of
allowing incidents with the natives to erupt into the tragedy that had
marred the previous visit. He came among the Hawaiians not as a god
but as a willing and helpful human—all smiles, genial, and understanding. He came with the British frigates *Discovery*, *Chatham*, and
a traveling supply ship, the *Daedalus*.

The officially stated purpose of his expedition was to take from the
Spaniards certain lands at Nootka Sound, on the northwest coast of
North America—wrested by Spain from the British subjects colonized
there. He was also to complete the exploration of that coast, as begun
by the ill-fated Captain Cook. Vancouver had been ordered to winter in

the Sandwich Islands. And subsequent actions would indicate that there were more to his orders than he had first intimated.

Actually his sessions in the islands were made in three visits— March 1792, February-March 1793, and January-March 1794. He deferentially recognized and courted Kamehameha. He had known Kamehameha from the Cook visit as a favored prince of the realm. Now he met him as Hawaii's supreme ruler.

Vancouver also maintained friendly relations with Kamehameha's enemies, the kings of the leeward islands. Always the congenial diplomat, Vancouver went from island to island, preaching peace among the quarreling rulers, and, with the fervor of a missionary, endeavoring to patch the rifts, settle the boundaries, and aid the natives in setting up a stable and prosperous economy.

He was assiduous in promoting the good intentions of His Majesty's Government. He made every effort to build up his image as a sort of benevolent father to the Hawaiians. He knew full well that these smiling and gracious people could, at a command of the Alii, turn with savagery and ferocity upon their guests at least intimation of mistrust or betrayal. It took courage, patience, and diplomatic skill, to remain on the safe side of the warring kings. He firmly refused to furnish or sell arms to anyone. By importing from North America the weapons of peace and prosperity—cattle, horses, sheep, poultry, clothing and utensils—and graciously presenting them to the chiefs and to the kings —Vancouver purchased a short era of peace. His altruistic and unassailable efforts established a bond of friendship with the British that would hold for generations.

In Kamehameha, King of Hawaii, he found a receptive intelligence, and recognized a man of destiny. Kamehameha listened; he acted. Leeward chiefs and kings were less cordial and less cooperative. To buy the friendship of Kamehameha, Vancouver presented him with horned cattle for his island kingdom. His surgeon-naturalist, Archibald Menzies, went among the people, instructing them to plant new seeds, grape cuttings, and the wonderful vegetables and fruits brought to the Sandwich Islands to elevate and enrich the people.

For hours on end Vancouver counseled Kamehameha, and answered the king's questions on every subject from government to the unique marriage patterns of his subjects. Alii born, proud and autocratic, Kamehameha was too solidly Hawaiian to ever emerge as a pseudo white man. But there can be no question Vancouver shaped the thinking of an aggressive war lord into that of a wise and understanding sovereign.

He even patched up a marital rift between Kamehameha and his beloved queen, Kaahumanu. The queen, apparently, had become enam-

ored with a young and stately Alii chieftain by the name of Kaiana.*
Miffed, humiliated and jealous, Kamehameha had banished his favorite
wife—only to pine and suffer with the loss. Captain Vancouver, better
skilled at war than at patching up romances, nevertheless managed
this task with the thoroughness and concern he managed everything
else. As intermediary, he arranged for the return of the hot-blooded
Kaahumanu to court. He accomplished this delicate task without jeop-
ardizing the dignity of the monarch, or at the risk of losing royal face.
Kamehameha was grateful to the Englishman. He never forgot the
gracious favor.

Vancouver personally taught close drill to Kamehameha's warriors.
He emphatically advised the king against allowing foreigners to settle
in the islands. The exceptions were, of necessity, John Young and Isaac
Davis, already well established. On these two Anglo ex-seamen, Vancouver had nothing but praise. He agreed with the king. They were
well chosen. They were invaluable.

So thoroughly did Vancouver ingratiate himself with Kamehameha
that the final step was easy. By suggestion, coercion, or a duplicity
probably not fully understood by the king, Kamehameha solemnly
ceded the island of Hawaii to His Britannic Majesty. On February 21,
1794, Kamehameha unprotestingly placed his kingdom under the
British flag, and the protection of King George. The narrow fluke that
saved the Sandwich Islands from forever being under imperial dominance of England, was the fact that somehow Vancouver's government
failed to accept or act on the prize that was laid in its lap.

When Vancouver departed from Hawaii he was recognized as the
"father of the nation." To this day the official Hawaiian flag wears the
pattern of the British Union Jack.

V

With vanishment of the beneficent diplomacy of Vancouver, the internecine strife between the island kings broke out anew. All the
monarchs, and most of the high chiefs, were related by blood and marriage. Kahekili of Maui, even as an old man, was intent upon putting
down the unappreciative upstart Kamehameha. He attempted another

*Ka-i-a-na: *Kah-ee-ah-nah*.

HIGH CHIEF KAIANA
He betrayed Kamehameha—bed (Queen Kaahumanu)—battle (Oahu).
—*Bernice P. Bishop Museum, Honolulu.*

invasion of Hawaii, and in his defeat, Kamehameha carried the war directly to Maui. Again the battles were indecisive, but the obstreperous and defiant Kahekili was killed. After Kamehameha's punitive expedition returned, Kahekili's domain was divided up. To son Kalanikupule went Oahu. To his brother Kaeo went the other islands, including Maui.

Inherited jealousy traveled with the division of Kahekili's island kingdom. Within a matter of months these two new monarchs were at war with one another. In December of 1794, Kaeo invaded Oahu with the former armies of Kahekili. Kalanikupule, in battling his uncle, commandeered the guns and sailors from the *Jackall*, one of Captain William Brown's trading vessels, lying in the harbor at Honolulu. The invaders were successfully beaten, and King Kaeo was killed.

Not satisfied with the fact that he had added Maui to his kingdom, and arrogantly prideful of his victory and prowess in battle, Kalanikupule now decided that he would invade Hawaii. He would add that last and largest prize to his kingdom. He would destroy Kamehameha once and for all.

Instead of gratitude for the *Jackall's* decisive help in battle, Kalanikupule again seized this ship, and with it the *Prince Lee Boo*, another vessel belonging to Captain Brown. In this bold highjacking, Captains Brown and Gordon were murdered, and Kalanikupule ordered the captive British crews to sail him and his warriors to Hawaii.

The ships had barely gotten off Waikiki when the British sailors fought a bloody deck battle with the islanders. Kalanikupule and his men were unceremoniously thrown overboard by the courageous Englishmen. The king and his surprised warriors were forced to swim for the beaches. The ships continued on to Kealakekua, where the Britishers warned Kamehameha of the hostile intent of Kalanikupule.

This time Kamehameha mounted much more than a punitive expedition. With sixteen thousand men, with a fleet armed with modern cannons, with guns, explosives, and the technical know-how of Young and Davis, Kamehameha carried the war directly into Kalanikupule's domain. At Maui he destroyed Lahaina, and ravished the western side of the island. He captured Molokai with little struggle. But, on the way from Molokai, Chief Kaiana, former paramour of Queen Kaahumanu, deserted to Kalanikupule, taking with him all his warriors.

Reduced and crippled by this spiteful treachery, Kamehameha landed his men at Waikiki in April of 1795. The defenders of Oahu battled with fanatical courage. Kalanikupule used well the additional forces which the desertion of Kaiana had provided. But at the base of cloud-piercing Lanihuli, the seasoned fighters under Kamehameha routed the defenders. Kaiana, the deserter and queen seducer, was killed.

Those surviving the awful struggle fled to the end of the valley, to the precipitous Pali of Nuuanu. Some, like Kalanikupule, sought safety in the mountains. Those fighting to the bitter end against the victorious and determined warriors from Hawaii, were finally pushed over the Pali to their death. Those seeking a quick finish, in preference to the torture and sacrifice of capture, deliberately leaped into the awesome chasm below.

It took months of search before Kalanikupule was found. When the fugitive monarch was finally sacrificed to Ku, at the *heiau* of Moanalua, Kamehameha was proclaimed king of every island from Hawaii to Oahu. Only Kauai and Niihau remained to be added to his empirical crown. They were outland, relatively insignificant, and could be taken at his leisure.

Kamehameha had finally become master of his great dream. If the Kohala legend of his birth be true, he had, probably without realizing it, killed his own father, and sacrificed to Ku his own half-brother. On Oahu he forbade the usual wanton slaughter of captives, but he could not wholly prevent the excesses of retribution practiced by his own victorious warriors. Kamehameha's vassals were rewarded with posts as chieftains and governors over the great island kingdom. He returned to Hawaii as Kamehameha the Great.

But, while engrossed in the subjection of Oahu, the usual trouble had broken out at home. Namakeha, brother of Kaiana, and still loyal to the dead King Keoua, had led a rebellion. The seasoned and experienced Kamehameha landed his forces at Hilo. In utterly crushing this revolt, he fought his last war to unite the islands.

But Kamehameha was not at all certain the battling was over. Kauai still was not his. Its king remained defiant. One year following his subjection of Maui, Molokai and Oahu, Kamehameha and his fighters sailed from Waianae, with the full intent of invading Kauai. In the move, Kamehameha had again defied the advice of his kahunas and priests as to spiritual timing for the venture. He hadn't gotten half way to Kauai before his fleet was engulfed in a shrieking and destructive tropical storm. The courage and navigational skills of his ancestors were not enough. The big double-hulled war canoes that were not torn apart by the hurricane, were forced to beach at Oahu. Ku was not yet ready to deliver Kauai.

The conqueror returned to the big island of Hawaii somewhat humbled. Into the hills above Hilo he sent his kahunas and his workers. It took years for them to fashion the eight hundred peleleu canoes which Ku, through the sorcerers, indicated would be necessary for the proper and successful invasion of Kauai. The new craft were wide and deep, for the vicissitudes of storms and high seas. Their hulls were

KAMEHAMEHA THE GREAT (1758-1819)
A sketch, from life, made in his late years.

—Bernice P. Bishop Museum, Honolulu.

lashed together in pairs, decked at the stern, and equipped with masts and sails patterned after the visiting ships. They would carry many warriors, and plenty of muskets and cannon for this most urgent task.

But the new fleet was never destined for war. In 1810 both Kauai and Niihau entered voluntarily and peacefully into the nation. King Kaumualii, son of Kaeo, humbly surrendered himself and his islands to Kamehameha the Great. Kamehameha, in turn, sensibly responded to this trust by allowing Kaumualii to remain tributary king of the two outer islands. The great archipelago in mid-Pacific was at last united under one leader.

In consolidating his gains, and perfecting the government of his far-flung kingdom, the royal court traveled with Kamehameha as he moved from island to island. The first six years of his reign had been spent on his home island, in the provinces of Kohala, Kona and Hilo. He remained a year on Maui, in the red brick palace at Lahaina, which he had paid foreigners to build for Kaahumanu, his choice and favorite queen. Then the capital was moved to Waikiki, at Oahu—where Kaahumanu, Keopuolani, and others of his wives, were set up in lavish residence. Kamehameha continued to cling, for his court, to the great long-houses thatched with fragrant pili grass.

But finally, in the latter years of his life, Kamehameha returned once more to his home island of Hawaii. To the dismay of his luxury-loving chiefs, and the astonishment of his many foreign visitors, he established royal residence at his earlier home and favorite fishing resort—the once ravaged village of Kailua, on the Kona coast.

Here, from the friendly little bay, the coastline climbed swiftly from beach sand up to the high reaches of majestic Mount Hualalai. Here, for a price, visiting Anglo artisans erected European-style buildings out of coral. These were ample for his women, or for storage—but the king followed his own preference in structures built of native grass.

From Kailua it was paddle distance to the green sea waters abounding in the big and beautiful fish, such as *kahala, manini,* and *ahi.* From Kailua it was only a short canoe trip, or a day's journey by land, to Kawaihae, and the great *heiau* he had raised at Puukohola to his custodial god Ku.

VI

KAMEHAMEHA's hold over the island kingdom was autocratic and supreme. In his conviction that all the land under king's domain was his, he was acting within the frame of the feudal custom that had prevailed for centuries. But such identical concept among the sub-chiefs of the many island provinces was quickly broken up.

Kamehameha insisted that Alii rulers be a part of his court—far removed from their individual fiefs—out of immediate reach of their warriors, or the temptation to stage rebellion against supreme authority. Governors were appointed for the provinces, not always Alii, but proven in loyalty, and true to Kamehameha. Keeaumoku, father of Kaahumanu, became governor of Maui; John Young took over the direct management of Hawaii. Kaumualii was allowed the privilege of reigning out his life over Kauai and Niihau.

Kalanimoku,* nephew of Keeaumoku,* became the king's *kuhina-nui,* or prime minister. He was also royal treasurer, trusted confidant, and adviser. Kalanimoku was a good choice. He proved wise, just, and honorable. He was liked and respected by the foreigners, who had learned, through the years that his word was a true bond of performance. Ship captains, naval officers of many nations, and the foreigners who had started to settle on Oahu, Maui, and Hawaii, came to know Kalanimoku as "William Pitt," jovially comparing him to the contemporary prime minister of Great Britain. To the foreigners, who sought trade with Kamehameha through him, he was known as "Mr. Pitt," or "Billy Pitt." Glib, sharp, intelligent, and honest, he effected European dress, and ably transacted the economic affairs of the Hawaiian oligarchy.

The populace, who furnished the workers and the warriors, were, according to custom, still considered as Kamehameha's vassals and possessions. His also were the land, the food, and the forests of sandalwood now being coveted by foreign traders. Subjects paid tribute to the king. They raised the food. They cut, hauled and loaded the fragrant sandalwood for the ship captains who had purchased to the king's account, and to fill an eager market in China, where the wood was prized for carved chests, furniture, and incense char.

Over his people, Kamehameha held the power of life and death. They lived in their villages through his consent. Their efforts were paid for by their right to retain only that above and beyond what the king levied. Actually, Kamehameha's domain existed as a vast police state. But its peculiar form of servitude appeared to be perfectly acceptable to his subjects. They conformed willingly. They remained intensely loyal to their Alii masters—providing the foreigners did not meddle, or bring discord, into their lives and customs.

In the long period of peace and prosperity which followed the uniting of the kingdom, the once harsh and fierce Kamehameha mellowed under the influence of such men as Vancouver and the wise and

*Ka-la-ni-mo-ku: *Kah*-lah-nee-*moh*-koo.
*Ke-e-a-u-mo-ku: *Kay*-eh-ah-oo-*moh*-koo.

valuable counsel of the foreigners he was luring by favor into his court. He listened well. He could be reasoned with. He ruled with justice and understanding, unmarred by the capriciousness of autocracy—something completely new to the people. The hot temper and personal debauchery of his youth, the hunger for personal possessions and aggrandizement, were gradually sloughed off as vices, and in their place came a dignity and a mellowness that was impressive not only to his subjects, but to every visitor with whom he came in contact. To his people he was Kamehameha the Great. Mightiest of all the Polynesian kings.

As was the custom, and strictly his right, Kamehameha amply supplied himself with wives. Of the twenty-one females in his harem, seven had preferential status. These special queens bore him many strapping sons and marriageable daughters. In order to stoke his polygamous union with plenty of the awesome mana so necessary to keep atop the Alii, and to make certain this mana was passed on to the offspring, most of the wives were chosen from the high ranking chiefesses. The concubines were, of course, pure pleasure, and need not be highborn. Their issue, in order to avoid later complications, could be strangled and secretly buried by the kahunas and priests. But of the seven mana-radiating queens, came twelve unassailably royal children.

Keopuolani, daughter of Kiwalao, was Kamehameha's blood relative. Inter-family marriage, and even incest, was perfectly acceptable in closely preserving the Alii pattern. Keopuolani was mated to Kamehameha simply because she was sound in body, beautiful in face, and held the highest spiritual rank of any woman in the islands. She was issue from the greatest families of Maui and Hawaii. So awesome was her kapu that Kamehameha himself could enter her presence only when naked, and must always keep his handsome head lower than hers. In spite of these handicaps to intercourse, she bore Kamehameha two royal sons—Liholiho* and Kauikeaouli*—both destined to become kings of all Hawaii. It was said that, so sacred was their mana, when Kamehameha visited his prince sons, he was forced to lie on the ground, while the princes sat on his chest.

But the great love of Kamehameha—the first love—was Kaahumanu. She was high spirited, unmanageable, and guilty of infidelity with Kaiana, but in spite of her every fault, she remained the favorite queen. Her wild acts, and ungovernable passion, were always burdens to be borne. Yet to the equally impetuous Kamehameha she was worthy of a taming. Kaahumanu was the wife of his heart. She was contin-

*Li-ho-li-ho: *Lee*-hoh-*lee*-hoh.
*Ka-u-i-ke-a-o-u-li: *Kah*-oo-ee-kay-*ah*-oh-oo-lee.

QUEEN KAAHUMANU

Kamehameha's most treasured possession. From a watercolor by Choris.

—*Bernice P. Bishop Museum, Honolulu.*

uously at his side. But Kaahumanu bore him no children. Throughout Kamehameha's life, and long after, this brilliant and imperious woman was a mighty force in shaping the nation.

Two more of Kamehameha's wives were less precocious but equally beautiful sisters of his favorite queen. Kalakua and Namahana were younger than Kaahumanu. Kalakua bore him royal children, but Namahana, like her older sister, proved barren.

The kapu or tabu system was the unrelenting clutch Kamehameha held over his people—Alii and commoner. At his whim or compulsion it was engine for the cruelest sort of tyranny. He was ruler by birth, right, and conquest—but he reigned more like a benevolent autocrat. He accepted the kapu system, because its power was traditional to monarchs. He supported the ancient ways because they were the only law code the people had ever known, and the only form recognizable in holding the nation together.

There were few crimes, moral or physical, that were ordinarily punishable by death. But let any offender be cited for breaking an important kapu, and the king's vengeance was swift and sure. Here was death—and it was ingenious, and tendered without mercy. Usually the priests did the executions—clubbing, strangling, burying alive, *heiau* sacrifice, or driving the culprits into post holes in the erection of temples or Alii residences.

Kapu went to the very essence of living—fishing, hunting, diet, clothes, and even the time of the sex act. Women must not eat at the same table with men, or in the presence of their males. Certain foods were kapu to women. Certain women foods were kapu to men. During the menstrual periods the woman—kapu as unclean—must remove herself completely to the menstrual house. A dwelling could become kapu to human habitation or entrance through death, priestly edict, kahuna curse, or religious observance. Kapu could mean divine displeasure, if any man fail to properly respect or worship the grotesque wooden figures of the myriad gods, in the shrines, temples and *heiaus* of the kingdom.

For a commoner to stand in the shadow of an Alii, to fail to grovel before a king or chief, was certain death to the offender. Kapu hung over every human act. There were seasons when certain fish could be caught and eaten; there were times when they could not. There were days when fruits and nuts could be enjoyed. There were times when they must never be touched or possessed. When a king died, the failure to observe all the complexities of national mourning was open invitation to royal retribution.

KAMEHAMEHA I

From an early-day sketch.

—*Bernice P. Bishop Museum, Honolulu.*

VII

KAMEHAMEHA THE GREAT lived only until 1819, but to the end of his days there were no more wars. He held his widespread kingdom together by constant vigilance, and an internal strength that no dissenter dared assail. Up to his last breath he favored the British, and mistakenly believed his kingdom was under England's protectorate.

He was cordial and receptive to ships and visitors from other lands. He sought their presence; absorbed their culture and their ideas. He, through his *kuhina-nui,* and advisers, drove shrewd bargains with them in trade. In April 1810 Isaac Davis was murdered by some of Kamehameha's jealous and disgruntled sub-chiefs, but the king still was able to retain the capable advice and counsel of John Young. All through the final years, Kamehameha continued to build and strengthen his kingdom.

His native shipbuilders were kept constantly at work enlarging the Hawaiian navy. In addition to this prodding, Kamehameha purchased every foreign hull that their owners were willing to sell. An American trade ship, the *Lelia Bird,* became his flagship; with it the captured *Fair American.* On Oahu, at Waikiki, Kamehameha kept thirty small sloops and schooners, and a dozen more in Honolulu harbor. All of these ships were foreign built. All of them had come out of the profitable trade in sandalwood. But the formidable little navy was never forced to put to sea in war.

Compelled by the fact that even great men must die, Kamehameha called together his court, in 1816, to emphatically make known his wishes for the future. In the time he could no longer police or defend his kingdom, when the gods had fully and finally claimed him as their own, he wanted to be certain that the nation would remain unified and serene.

Amid pomp and ceremony, before his governors, chieftains and priests, Kamehameha proclaimed the line of royal succession. It must and would be through Queen Keopuolani, daughter of Kiwalao. The king had mated with her, not because she was Kamehameha's niece, but because her mother held highest female rank in the land, and possessed the highest possible mana. This fortuitous union had produced two princes with unquestioned right to rulership by birth and priority. The eldest son, Liholiho, was to be crowned king upon Kamehameha's

KAMEHAMEHA I IN 1818, ONE YEAR BEFORE HIS DEATH
Russian watercolor by N. Tikhanov.

—*Bernice P. Bishop Museum, Honolulu.*

death, and to exercise royal judgment and rulership even while the present king lived. The second son, Kauikeaouli, was next in line to the throne.

Kamehameha, as he faced death, was fully and unhappily aware of Liholiho's shortcomings. The heir-apparent was an hedonistic playboy, preoccupied with gambling and voluptuous women. The "holy prince" had developed an awesome capacity and endless craving for white man's whiskey. But Liholiho was a huge, handsome, rugged man—in the likeness of his father, and the stately Alii through whose favored lineage he had been born.

Recognizing the necessity for firm guidance of a nation laid in the hands of a capricious and pleasure-bent young king, Kamehameha publicly named his favorite queen—the iron-willed Kaahumanu—as *kuhina-nui*. This designation would actually make her joint-regent with Liholiho in managing the affairs of state. Kalanimoku would remain in favored position as high chief. But custodianship of the war god—the great Kukailimoku—was to pass to Kekuaokalani,* cousin of Liholiho.

When Kamehameha finally became gravely and incurably ill, and the kahunas and the priests no longer had power to pray him back to health, John Young sent to Honolulu for some foreign ship doctor to lend his *haole* skills to the healing. A noted Spaniard by the name of Don Francisco de Paula y Marin, with some medical knowledge, responded to the command. Marin reached Kailua in time to attend the dying monarch.

Not trusting fully the skill of the foreigner, the Hawaiians built a special house to the king's personal god, Ku, and proposed the last and most efficacious remedy—human sacrifice. The dying king forbade it. He pointed to Liholiho—"the men are kapu for the king." This grisly rite, always practiced at death of a great leader, was to be abandoned even at the mourning.

Kamehameha the Great died at Kailua on May 8, 1819, attended by John Young, the Spanish medical man, and the named heirs to power. All the traditional Hawaiian mourning customs were followed—with one exception—there would be no human sacrifice. The Kona area, however, was considered as defiled in death, and drastic mourning kapus were placed upon the people until the corpse could be desiccated, and the priests could strip Kamehameha's flesh from his bones. The great man's meat was carefully burned at the temple fire. The bones were tied into the *whinipili* bundle, wrapped in large leaves, and gently placed in a woven basket, fashioned from a sennit of ieie vines.

*Ke-ku-a-o-ka-lani: *Kay*-koo-ah-oh-*kah*-lah-nee.

After the rites were performed which changed the deceased king into an *aumakua*, or deified ancestor, trusted chiefs were given the charge of hiding the bones of Kamehameha the Great forever from the world and its people. These were secreted in a cave where "only the stars of the heavens know the resting place."

The entire kingdom was ordered into mourning. For two weeks the island of Hawaii was under complete kapu. People were forbidden to leave their homes. Anyone caught outside their dwellings, even to fish or gather coconuts, were put to death. And the Alii dutifully knocked out their teeth, or mutilated their flesh.

Haole historians make no note of Kamehameha the Great having died the bastard king—the son of Kahekili, out of the womb of Kekuiapoiwa. But there are Hawaiians—kahunas and verbal genealogists who insist that this is so—and that Kamehameha died knowing it was so. Whatever the verdict, the great king was an Alii of highest rank. He was the man who truly built the kingdom.

*   *   *   *   *

In accordance with rigid custom, Liholiho, the prince's four wives, retainers and retinue, took leave of Kailua, while the royal community was purified from its death defilement. Until this kapu could be lifted, and the bones of Kamehameha the Great properly secreted, the heir-apparent lived in seclusion in native Kohala. Then, with the last rite completed, the kapu was temporarily lifted by the priests. This phase of Polynesian mourning made a strange picture. All restraints were laid aside. Sexual license transcended family lines. Frightful and wild were the scenes of debauchery. And then, for the coronation, the kapu again was clamped down—but with modifications geared to the new event.

When Liholiho returned to Kailua to publicly receive the crown of the kingdom, he would face a rite of investiture unparalleled in pomp, ceremony, and gorgeous spectacle. When he stepped ashore from the royal canoe he would confront a mass of humanity never before known to Kailua. Streets and groves were packed with visitors from every part of the island. Tributes and gifts, brought to honor the occasion, had been stacked in huge piles, to be blessed by the priests, and later accepted by the new king. Crowds were martialed into tasks and positions by Kaahumanu, favored queen and widow of Kamehameha. So as not to unduly expose commoners to her mana, she performed this function from safe distance. Assistants transmitted the orders. They policed the throng. But the queen was boss, and everyone knew it.

With the first news from mountain lookout points, that the royal flotilla had been sighted, Kailua boiled with excitement. But, under the regal vigilance of Kaahumanu, the rush to the bay was orderly. Now so many people were assembled that the beach sands were covered, and the lines of humanity curved down even into the waters of the sea.

The open *halau*, erected especially for the public portion of the investiture, had been built up on the beach by a thousand willing hands. Its lengthy platform had been paved with smooth pebbles from the sea. On three sides it was enclosed by high screens fashioned of braided palm leaves, and decorated by red flowering hibiscus. Above the screens hung festoons of maile from the mountains. The fragrance of flowers and greenery hung cloyingly upon the air.

Banana trees, still bearing fruit, and the ti plants, had all been laboriously transplanted whole, until the *halau* entrance and its surroundings reminded of a tropical and fragrant garden. Now, as the boats, under the rhythmic shove of the paddlemen, swung the bend and drew closely to Kailua Bay, the *halau* platform was hastily crowded with Alii, waiting to welcome their new king.

The high chiefs and high priests, in their feathered cloaks and helmets, stood out bright and striking, as they moved, according to rank, in semicircle above the crowds and facing the sea. Each cloak had been woven of rare and beautiful bird feathers in the pattern dictated by Alii family heraldry.

The high chiefesses wore the *pa'u*—in the traditional weave of kapa cloth, or newer ones bearing ship trade influence, fashioned of bright silks and satins from China. Upon their wavy brown or black hair were coronets of red and yellow feathers, many further decorated with mountain orchids. But about each of their necks, indicative of their right to be present, hung the *lei-palaoa*, necklace of ancestral hair, with sea-ivory pendants. Here was their badge of nobility.

A more unmistakable badge of Alii lineage, and their link to the founding gods, was the fact that all of them—men and women—were heroically built to six feet tall or better.

When Queen Kaahumanu and her retinue regally strode to center position at the *halau*, there was a buzz of excitement. Over her *pa'u* of yellow satin from China she had donned Kamehameha's royal feather coat, and in her right hand she carried the king's ceremonial spear. Here was symbol of authority. And there she stood, imperious and commanding, awaiting the arrival of Liholiho.

For a woman to wear a king's royal feather cloak, to carry his kapu spear, was an assumption without precedence. The court, and presumably the people, knew of her appointment to Kamehameha's created position of *kuhina-nui*. That, in effect had made her, upon his death, prime minister of the kingdom and co-ruler. But no one present could have anticipated this blatant show of authority. Today, calm, confident, regardless of buzzing tongues, she wore her power for all to see.

Three paces to Kaahumanu's right stood Queen Keopuolani, mother of the new king. Holding hands with this queen were two small children—Prince Kauikeaouli and the Princess Nahienaena*—brother and sister to Liholiho.

Keopuolani, beautiful, sensitive, had been the sacred wife to Kamehameha. She was so highborn, and radiated such mana, that her life as queen had been lived in virtual seclusion. Like the queen bee, her existence had been guarded by retainers and priests to the extent that she was seldom ever seen in public. Unlike the imperious Kaahumanu, who had traveled constantly with her king-lover, shared his meetings with foreign dignitaries and ship captains, and actually lent sharp tongue and influence in policy decisions, the sacred queen had been a woman of softness, kindness, and adored by the people even in her seclusion.

For the purpose of breeding throne heirs of highest mana, she had served her king and kingdom well. Today, overshadowed by the feminine *kuhina-nui* of the polygamous royal family, she faced even the coronation in unobtrusive sanctity.

The remainder of Kamehameha's many widows were arrayed rearward at the *halau*, according to family rank and Alii standing. The comely concubines were forced to stand with the commoners.

To the left of Kaahumanu stood Kalanimoku, head chief of the nation, and Hewahewa, high chief and head priest of the temples. Conspicuously absent this day was Kekuaokalani, cousin of Liholiho, and the man appointed by Kamehameha as custodian of the war god Ku. The cousin had never been happy about the proposed joint regency. He mistrusted and hated the power-hungry Kaahumanu.

As the canoes moved in to shore there came instant and hypnotic quiet to the multitude. Previously, by royal kapu, all dogs had been muzzled; all chickens locked in darkened pens. Now from the canoes could be heard the chant of the priests. Everyone watched intently the glistening rhythm of the paddles, as strong men, working to song, brought the brightly decorated craft ever closer to shore. The crowd stood in silent adoration as the boats paused momentarily beyond the surf, and in formation. Suddenly the voices of the priests rose in chant; increasing in strength and tempo, until it was echoed back by the mountains behind them.

Then, with new and abrupt silence came the priestly cry. "Kapu a moe-e-e, Ka Moi!" Make way for the King!

Na-hi-ena-ena: *Nah*-hee-*ay*-nah-*ay*-nah.

The royal canoes came to beach. The people dropped prostrate to the ground. The Alii stood tense and waiting.

Down the steps of the *halau,* to the waterfront, walked Hewahewa, high priest. His song was the *mele inoa,* the chanted genealogy of the new king. Another priest followed him, singing the urgent *kahea.* They stopped at water's edge.

First off the canoes was the *ihe* bearer, which officially marked the presence of the king. Behind him came a priest bearing the kapu stick, marking the bounds to which commoners could approach the royal presence. Following him were the retainers holding high the long-staffed feathered *kahilis,* indicating royalty. The king himself came ashore on the shoulders of his mighty *kahu,* who had carried him thus from boyhood.

As the *kahu* gently deposited Liholiho to the sand, those who were not spread too prostrate could see that he was regally dressed in red British uniform, bright with gold braid and spangles. Over the foreign garb was his father's yellow cloak of *mamo* feathers. This, with the yellow feather helmet, was the badge of supreme authority.

There was a moment while the *ihe* and *kahili* bearers took position, and the priests and Liholiho's four wives could fall into line. Then the royal procession moved slowly upward toward the *halau* — to the throaty and continuous chant of the priests.

Liholiho paused upon the platform—a huge and magnificent man. His royal *mamo* cloak fluttered in the breeze, his red uniform showing splendidly. He moved with superb and haughty regality. His head, massed with curly black hair, and molded long and shapely from birth by hand massage, radiated strength and character. Only his lips and chin indicated the inner weakness with which he coped.

While he paused, Kaahumanu stepped forward. The new king was suddenly faced by a determined woman, wearing his father's cloak, carrying his father's spear. "Hear me, O He Alii Moi!" she cried. "Hear me, O Divine One! For I make known to you the will of your father!" She swung the spear in wide arc. "There are your chiefs! The men of your father! These your guns! This your land! *But it is you and I who shall share the realm together!*"

Liholiho, apparently stunned, looked around the assembled chiefs for some challenge to Kaahumanu's declaration. Kekuaokalani would have shouted protest. But Kekuaokalani was absent. From the Alii assemblage came low murmur. But no man stepped forward; no voice was raised. Liholiho stared again at the determined woman. Slowly he bowed his head in assent. Other than another low murmur, not a voice spoke out.

The priests stepped forward to continue the ceremonies. Liholiho properly responded to each. They sang *meles* extolling the virtues of the king's ancestors, and praising the greatness of his father. The entire assemblage prayed aloud, for heaven's guidance to the new king. When Liholiho publicly promised "I shall not depart from the pathways of my sire, the mighty," he did so with a voice choked with emotion.

The royal party moved on to the temple. Amid the wood and stone effigies Liholiho was invested with a king's priestly powers as representative of the gods on earth. His now naked loins were encircled with the sacred red *malo* of sovereignship. And there he was dubbed with the title of Kamehameha II.

When the young monarch stepped forth to again greet his people, there was a roar of approval and adoration. He had shed his foreign garb. Instead of *haole* cloth and gilded buttons, they saw brown sinew, nobly fleshed. High Priest Hewahewa loudly called out, "The mourning kapu is lifted! The king is ours! Go freely!" And the people shouted themselves hoarse with joy.

There would be lavish feasts for everyone. Gifts of substance would be laid at the new king's feet. Dancers would pound the earth all night. Singing would never cease until dawn. There would be joy and pleasure unconfined—and uncluttered by any restraint or kapu.

But the new king faced his reign with uncertainty and trepidation. Sheltered all his life, adored and spoiled, he fully knew how ill he was prepared for it. He had accepted the kingdom—to forever bear the title of Kamehameha II. But the addition to kingship of Kaahumanu—as *kuhina-nui*—had established a system of dual government never realized until now. Perhaps his father had meant well. But it was a little unique, and a little strange, to be intimately and publicly saddled with his father's favorite bed partner.

PART TWO

Liholiho (Kamehameha II) — the King of Hearts

I

LIHOLIHO had been the sacred child. His hair at birth had been long, black, and wore the promised wave of the future. His skin was gold-brown like that of Keopuolani, rather than the dark lava color of his father. At his birth, because he was first and male child from the womb of the highest born of all female Alii, the temple and court ceremonies had been lavish, and the people had brought gifts. King and priests had given him the name of Kalaninui Liholiho— "Heaven's Great Glowing." Promise and future rode the spiritual canoe of this prince.

As befitting a sacred child so generously endowed with mana, his guidance had been under direction of the priests. They had schooled him well in his duties toward the altars, the great wood and stone effigies of the gods, and the intimate role that kapu and worship played on the lives of men. At Kamehameha's insistence Liholiho had also been coached in the sterner arts of war and statesmanship. Big and strong, he easily developed his father's skill with spear, knife, and physical tumbling. But, because he was the sacred prince, he was carried on the shoulders of his *kahu* from childhood. His precious feet touched earth only for war training, or by necessity.

They had prepared him well to take over the kingdom according to the rigid pattern and customs of the past. Unfortunately, on the day he inherited it, outside pressures had changed that kingdom beyond any hope of return to the island world that had existed prior to the traumatic visits of Cook and Vancouver.

Liholiho, exposed to the rigidity of this native past, and the glowing enticements of the less inhibited aliens who already were moving through his father's kingdom, grew, as the crown prince, into a spoiled, pampered, and dissolute youth. Instead of taking up the burden of kingship with courage and determination, he faced the future with fear and uncertainty.

Intimation of his huge and overwhelming burden had come with Kaahumanu's bruising assumption of power at the very ceremony of his investiture. Liholiho knew, from the start, that he faced trouble from this meddling matriarch.

As crown prince, the king and chiefs had made certain he married well. Being the sacred youth, he was entitled to carouse and fornicate wherever the urge might take him. But when it came to marriage, he had been well coached in the requirements of state. The ultimate advantage of polygamy was that it gave a man multiple chances. By the time of his coronation he had wedded four highborn maidens out of the Alii—all of them possessed of perquisites and mana adequate for the most favored of the peers.

Liholiho's third wife, Kamamalu,* happened to be his half sister— but in the permissive pattern of the Alii that was acceptable. This beautiful girl was a little short of the six-foot stature of the Alii, but her antecedents were impeccable. She was sloe eyed, gentle, poetic. Liholiho loved her wildly. She was also high station enough to overrule any flaw in stature, since she was the daughter of Kamehameha by his queen-wife Kalakua. And Queen Kalakua was also a younger sister to the powerful Kaahumanu. So gentle Kamamalu not only combined two blood lines of royalty, but had inherited the comeliness and desirability that went with it.

His fourth and fifth wives were further helpings to the same mana. Kinau and Kekauluohi were also daughters of Kamehameha the Great and Queen Kalakua, full sisters of Kamamalu, and half sisters to the marrying Liholiho. They too were radiant prizes, but the new king's favorite was still the graceful singing poetess Kamamalu.

Liholiho was not unaware that he might face the exigency of marrying the higher born of his father's wives—maybe including his Aunt Kaahumanu—but, up until the coronation, Kamamalu was his own and preferential choice. Out of her he expected to bring Hawaii's future kings.

More than anything Liholiho wanted, for his reign, to preserve the peace and solidarity his father had so ably established. The kapu system, rigidly enforced by a strong-armed autocrat, had served flawlessly, so long as the people were subservient, willing, and adored their king. Liholiho was temple-trained to the system. He intended and hoped to as ably administer the code as had his illustrious father. But he was also cognizant of the undercurrent of unrest, vocally rising during the very time Kamehameha's breath began feebling out.

There were ambitious chieftains awaiting chance to rebel at the least sign of weakness in the great man's youthful successor. Kaahu-

*Ka-ma-ma-lu: Kah-*mah-mah*-loo.

manu, a strong-willed problem even to her husband, had shown open defiance and challenge before Liholiho could make his own rightful assumption of power. By establishing her as *kuhina-nui*, the dead Kamehameha had not brightened prospects for the new king.

Liholiho had already been advised that Queen Kaahumanu intended breaking up the kapu system; to remove its strangling claws from the people. But not even the priests or restless chieftains could have imagined the crisis would come with such swiftness.

The day after his inauguration as Kamehameha II, Liholiho was summoned to Kaahumanu's house. He had scarcely seated himself before she declared against kapu, and her personal intention of destroying it. First move of the new reign, she insisted, must be the complete abolition of all tabus regarding the eating habits of men and women. No more must there be segregation of the sexes at mealtime.

To Liholiho this was heresy. Since the days of the gods men had eaten their meals together, and women had eaten by themselves. Many foods available to men, must never be eaten by women—under pain of death's vengeance, either by a strike from the gods, or a club from the king's regulators. Kaahumanu was now proposing that henceforth women would not only freely eat of the forbidden foods, but would do so in the company of men. To complete the blasphemy, she calmly ate a banana in his presence. The new king fully expected the wrath of gods to sweep this defiant female off the earth. Bananas and pork were absolutely kapu to women.

Shaken to silence, Liholiho arose. Angrily he strode out of the contaminated house.

But Kaahumanu had barely started her campaign for women's liberation. Always she had been on friendly terms with the Queen Mother, Keopuolani. As the highest born of Kamehameha's many wives, and mother of the crown heirs to the realm, Keopuolani had been forced to live under such irksome restraint and kapu that she had been virtually a royal prisoner. Kaahumanu's defiance of the system found in the spiritual queen an eager listener. Kaahumanu deliberately coached Keopuolani for the next move.

At a summons from his mother, Liholiho found her seated at a low table. Upon it was spread a meal for two—with pork and other foods held tabu for women. Unfluttered and unafraid, Keopuolani asked Liholiho to sit and eat with her. First he shook his head in horror. Then, angrily, he refused. She then called her younger son, the boy crown prince Kauikeauoli. There, in the presence of the king, mother and son dined together.

Liholiho retreated, paralyzed with shock. The two most respected women in the kingdom had openly and defiantly blasphemed the gods.

LIHOLIHO (KAMEHAMEHA II)
Lithograph drawing from life, by John Hayter.

—*Bernice P. Bishop Museum, Honolulu.*

Deliberately they had invited retribution. Outraged by the new behavior, he ordered his fleet of canoes in readiness. Liholiho departed
Kailua as though it were a doomed city. In his own Kawaihae there
would be none of this mockery. His five wives would never eat in the
presence of men.

Word that the two highest ranking women in the realm had broken
kapu and had defied the gods, spread wildly among the people. In every
island there was panic and confusion. Some there were who approved—
mostly women. Others predicted a time of dire trouble. The king was
besieged by the more conservative chieftains. Few of them had ever
trusted Kaahumanu. His cousin Kekuaokalani, in whom Kamehameha
had entrusted the war god Ku, hastened to Kawaihae, to advise and
stand beside the new king.

Liholiho responded to the pressure by promptly issuing an edict
restoring the tabus that had been relaxed following his coronation. He
dedicated a new temple. He went along with the worried priests in
issuing fresh restraints on personal conduct. The war chief Kekuaokalani, who now held the identical role once so capably handled by the
great Kamehameha, demanded that the two rebellious queens be publicly handled for their acts; publicly sacrificed to the gods for their
heresy. His angry insistence that the new king put to death two of his
father's queens—one of them the king's mother—the other the king's
aunt—added bitter measure to Liholiho's problems.

The tabus guiding Liholiho's life, inheritance from his mother,
were much more stringent than those which governed the conduct of
Kamehameha, who had been born in lower rank. The pattern forced
upon the people was usually the personal kapu under which the king
himself lived. For Liholiho to impose his own more complicated and
extensive system of personal conduct would mean the laying of restraints upon his subjects even more stringent than those they had
borne under Kamehameha the Great. The problem posed was beyond
Liholiho's ability to cope. One point of personal acceptance, already
finding favor among Hawaiians, was traders' rum and whiskey. Liholiho went on a prolonged drunk while he pondered the dilemma.

As prince of the realm Liholiho had been coached in the arts and
skills of war—but he had grown up in the ripe and peaceful years of
the kingdom. He had been trained and educated to rule in the traditional way; embracing all the arts and prerogatives of the royal house,
as established and refined by his brilliant and dramatic father. That
ambitious and ruthless people of the realm would rise to challenge a
new and supposedly weaker monarch was a problem he'd never been
taught to face. The possibility of civil uprising was simply untenable.

Kamehameha had abolished the old system of land division. Traditionally the land had always been confiscated at the death of a king, and reapportioned to chieftains favored by and friendly to the new heir-presumptive. Kamehameha had done away with this brutal system of spoils, by simply declaring that all lands within the kingdom were his own—ousting the petty rulers, and appointing governors to manage the crown lands. A sub-chief under the crown was simply a lieutenant or an overseer.

Surfacing now were pressures and demands for Liholiho to return to the old way; to reapportion the kingdom among the highborn. There was a fawning upon him for favor—not only by the priests and Alii, but by a constant stream of foreigners seeking the lands and concessions they had been denied under the less genial and uncompromising Kamehameha I. When sweet talk failed to move the new king, there came bare and ugly threats.

In spite of the edict out of Kawaihae, the women of the realm continued to throw off the traditional restraints. Two great queens had openly and deliberately partaken of the forbidden fruits, and in the very presence of men. The gods had not struck them down. Both Alii and common women, after a secret try at pork and bananas, and having survived the experiment, grew bold in support of their dowager queens. Everywhere now "open eating" had become the militant cry of suddenly aroused females throughout the islands. The gods somehow remained hesitant about striking them down. And, in spite of the demands of Kekuaokalani and the angry priests for immediate action, Liholiho was reluctant about making war against a most essential half of the population.

The king's restoration of all kapus had been answered by Kaahumanu proclaiming that her city of Kailua was released from the kapu restraint on free eating. Women of Kailua, she declared, were entitled to eat what they pleased. They could eat with whom they pleased. Eating tabus in the capital, Kaahumanu announced with finality, not only were abolished, but could never be restored.

When the new king, cowed and perplexed, refused to move against sedition and rebellion at the very source, War Chief Kekuaokalani was furious. The very air was poisoned by unrest, confusion and indecision. The power of Kamehameha II as an absolute monarch was evaporating before he'd had any chance to test it.

While the king procrastinated, his court at Kawaihae became a hubbub of confusion. Delegations demanding new rights constantly harassed him. Bearers of bad news broke his rests and his slumbers. Foreigners by the score brought him gifts from every corner of the world, and an endless supply of rum and whiskey to liven up the personal life of a sovereign while they sought land bounties, trading concessions, and a share of the king's exclusive right to trade in sandalwood.

The sub-chiefs and loyal Alii swarmed his court for precisely the same reason. They resented the new invasion of Americans, Englishmen, Frenchmen and Russians, intent on seducing, for profit and advantage, this handsome son of Kamehameha. They too wanted their share of lands, a slice of the king's sandalwood monopoly, and private vassaldoms of their own. While music, hula dancing, and drunken revelry kept things lively at Kawaihae, the king tried to rest and relax through this period of national ferment. It was John Young, able counselor to Kamehameha, who kept the kingdom together during these crucial months.

Alarmed by the way things were going, wise old Chief Kalanimoku, and level-headed John Young, finally persuaded Liholiho to emerge from his fun long enough to convene a grand council of chiefs and Alii, to deal basically with the problems that threatened to inundate the kingdom. Liholiho assented. In August, three months after he had been crowned king, the top level Alii gathered at Kawaihae.

For days on end the chiefs wrangled and disputed among themselves, with little headway in patching up their grievances, or gaining any major concessions for themselves. With the exception of War Chief Kekuaokalani, all hung on with superb patience and tenacity. At night, at the feasting, at the singing, and the dance, they buried their quarrels and differences in the festive *luaus*. At the nocturnal feasts, under the torches, the bitter words and acrimony were postponed for the day to follow. But over this prolonged council hung the ominous fact that the war chief—the keeper of Ku—refused to share in the deliberation.

By prodding away at the new king and his counselors, at John Young, and Kalanimoku, the chiefs forced the crown to share with them the lucrative sandalwood trade. But the premise of immediate redistribution of land was postponed to the indefinite future. The right of women to defy kapu was a matter considered too hot to handle. It too was tabled along with other undecided issues.

But not even a strategy conclave of the Hawaiian Alii could longer be free of outside influence. While the council was pressing the king for rights and privileges, the French corvette *L'Uranie*, captained by Louis de Freycinet, dropped anchor in the little harbor at Kawaihae. John Young wasted no time in petitioning Captain de Freycinet to offer French friendship and protection to the harassed and bedeviled Liholiho. The commander, sensing an augury of fate for his govern-

ment, not only accepted the invitation, but addressed the grand council in the king's behalf.

The French commander openly pledged the support and friendship of his nation to the Hawaiian king, and promised to defend him against enemies within and without. He tempered the pledge with the declaration that Mother France had no territorial designs on the islands. The *L'Uranie* had been the second French ship to visit Hawaii. The earlier La Perouse expedition had, in itself, gained friends for France. By eloquence and persuasion Freycinet charmed king and chiefs into an amicable conclusion to their council.

The restless and rebellious chieftains were cautioned by Freycinet against the danger and disaster of civil war. He urged them to stand behind their intelligent and handsome new ruler; to rally to his support; to help him cope with the nation's problems. More was gained through peace and goodwill, he told them, than could ever be achieved by violence and rebellion.

The grateful Liholiho made personal visit to the *L'Uranie*, where, over the wine cups, he heard again the vow of eternal friendship of France from the lips of Captain Louis de Freycinet. On this occasion Chief Kalanimoku humbly asked for Christian baptism. For "Billy Pitt," a man nurtured a lifetime on the mystery and power of the jealous and all-pervading gods of the islands, this was a strange step. It must have impressed the ship's chaplain as much as it impressed the French artist Jacques Arago who, as a passenger on the corvette, sketched the deck ceremony. "Furnished with his passport to paradise," wrote Arago, "he [Kalanimoku] went home to his seven wives, and to sacrifice to his idols."

In resisting the chiefs at the grand council Liholiho had thought he was dealing with the major threat to his reign. This was not so. Scarcely had the Alii departed the grand council for their homes than a message was received from Queen Kaahumanu not only urging, but virtually commanding Liholiho to come at once to Kailua and join efforts with her in totally abolishing the kapu on free eating.

This persistent woman had determined not only to press the explosive issue, but had chosen a time when the king was already mentally distraught from public pressures. It angered Liholiho. He ignored her urgings. He was not yet ready to return to Kailua and its hornet's nest of problems.

◁ *THE HOME OF CHIEF KALANIMOKU, ISLAND OF HAWAII*
The woman is beating out kapa cloth.

—Bernice P. Bishop Museum, Honolulu.

But the king's rebuff was only temporary setback for Kaahumanu. The people were coming around, and she knew it. Serenely, tenaciously, she planned the greater rebellion. To her, free eating was only the opening skirmish to the major revolution aimed at toppling the entire structure of kapu.

Informants told Liholiho of her subversion of High Priest Hewahewa—the kingdom's virtual keeper of the kapu. Kamehameha's bones were scarcely dry, and already these two were constantly together. Temple priests, equally cognizant of the rebellious queen's influence on the sacerdotal top man, were unified in their resolve to fight the dissension now rampant at Kailua. But with the king's own mother publicly pledged to Kaahumanu's bold plan, the problem was endlessly compounded. In desperation the priests declared new and more stringent kapus upon the people.

But now, instead of stolid and universal acceptance of priestly pronouncement, there came vocal and angry opposition. If Kaahumanu had planned this, she had planned it well. Arrogantly and deliberately she moved into the breach; fanning the resentment; pointing to the oppressive stance of the priests. Liholiho could sense the pressures, even in his home city of Kawaihae. Steadily, ruthlessly, his father's favorite wife was forcing him into a decision that might be disastrous to himself and to his kingdom. For the first time in memory the spiritual solidarity of the people had been broken.

In November of that fateful year of 1819 came another message from the persistent queen. The great feast of *makahiki* would be held, according to tradition, at Kailua. Liholiho's attendance was a virtual necessity. His own mother had joined Kaahumanu in insisting he be present. Word was out that the two queens would use the feast to openly establish full emancipation on eating.

No one knew better than Liholiho that the kapu system was the very source of power. Upon this ultimate authority rested the structure of government and religion. To capitulate before the destroyers was to abdicate his rights as king. Nevertheless, knowing full well the consequences, and against the advice of the priests, Liholiho agreed to return to Kailua. It took courage to attend a feast planned for his hurt as skillfully as an ambush. Yet to punish a nation of women in rebellion would be a choice equally difficult.

In the manner he invariably faced crisis, Liholiho ordered out a pair of double canoes, loaded them with personal companions—men and women. With plenty of food, and plenty of ardent spirits, they put to sea. For two days the problems of state were forgotten while they feasted and debauched. But when the king and his party landed back at Kawaihae it was to find a fleet of canoes, sent by Kaahumanu and Keopuolani, to take the hung-over monarch and his retinue to Kailua.

In Kailua's great thatched palace, built by Kamehameha I, Liholiho spent the first night in a drinking revel in which the lithe and beautiful women were neither restricted nor restrained. The next night, chastened and subdued, he walked into the feast—carefully staged and planned by Kaahumanu.

This was the night of *kukahi*—third night of the new moon—first of the three sacred nights to Ku. Word had spread through Kailua of the innovations so boldly and shockingly planned. The *imu* pits smoked with their savory load of broiling pigs, wrapped and packed with fish, yams, vegetables, and greens. Two immensely long tables had been spread, and heaped with foreign eating utensils, Alii food such as coconut halves, *awa*, and fruit. One of the tables was for the men of the court, including ship captains and foreign emissaries. But, in unprecedented surprise to guests and public, was the other identical table set up for the women. Not even a kapa screen shielded the females from view.

Tension was in the air. The men, as they were seated on the low mats and cushions, looked about them, wild-eyed and nervous. The women betrayed their own fright and near hysteria with cackling laughs, chatter, and fearful glances at the men trying to settle themselves to the weirdest feast in Hawaiian history. To make the point of their first public emancipation a few females were already trying to bolster their courage by peeling and eating their plateside bananas in the very presence of men.

The king, strikingly attired in another British uniform of red, took his place at the head of the men's table. The male guests ran the gamut from feathered *kiheis* over bronze and naked shoulders, to whatever uniforms and haole attire the visiting ships could provide for those fortunate enough to have been invited to a court affair.

The women's table was presided over by Kaahumanu, with Hawaii's queen mother, Keopuolani, beside her. Keopuolani had already acquired a new husband—Kaiaimoku—and planned to marry into polyandry soon with Hoapili. She gazed affectionately at the men's table. Both her loves were there. The dowager queens were lavishly attired in China silk of regal yellow color. Liholiho's own favorite queen, the beautiful Kamamalu, held her royal place of honor. Between Kamamalu and Kaahumanu was a vacant plate and seat.

When all were seated, High Priest Hewahewa stepped to center, and raised both arms. Under flicker and flare of the rowed pitch torches, the bones and muscles of the old man under-crawled his shrunken brown flesh in ridges and ripples. The feather *kihei* fell back from his naked chest and shoulders. Other than kapa cloth *malo* at his hips and his priestly cape and helmet of feathers, old Hewahewa was naked. The high priest's prayer, in chanted verse, was a long and fervent one. Nervous stirrings and coughings broke the silence. When Hewahewa retired, every guest sat with fright and expectancy.

Then it happened. And it was almost unbelievable when they saw it. The handsome young king arose—a bright figure in red. He swayed for a moment, uncertainly, as he looked out at his audience. With pounding hearts and breath subdued, the guests watched as Liholiho started his walk to the women's table.

Mid-center he paused, as though to turn back. Plainly the king was not doing his chore with alacrity. Then he raised his dark head. He looked out defiantly, but unseeing, at those who wondered and waited. In a few more steps he was beside Kaahumanu and his own queen. Deliberately he sat down at the vacant place. The joy of his eating was exaggerated and staged. But for the first time in history, a king was taking food in the company, and in full freedom, with women.

Not until now did the people sense the irrevocable nature of this act. Not until now did they realize the implication of what they were seeing. Astonishment, joy, and horror were mixed and mingled as the guests reacted to Liholiho's heresy. There was the awkward silence while the congregation waited for the gods to strike down the man who had deliberately invited destruction. As the king continued to eat, and live, and neither he, the rebellious queens of Kamehameha, nor any of the assembled guests fell dead, the people livened again to their own fate.

Suddenly there were hysterical screams from the women. "He has broken the eating kapu!" one of them howled. "The kapu has no meaning!" another shouted. "The gods are false!",

From the women came more shouts and the clapping of hands. Some were audibly praying for forgiveness for their own part in this night of betrayal. Others brazenly cackled with joy.

But there was no mirth, and less noise, from the men's table. The males looked questioningly at one another. They were astonished. Some were dismayed and angry. It had taken only this simple act to wipe away a prerogative and right that every man possessed. In front of his woman, every one of them had stood as a god who controlled the pattern, and executed the law. So long as the king had abdicated kingship in his own house, no other man could be king in a lesser dwelling. If a woman could flaunt her husband's right to enforce the eating tabu, she would oppose any other tabu that might irk her. In this moment every man knew he had lost a right and an authority. That they had been stripped so suddenly and so cleanly, left them bitter and perplexed.

Throughout the meal the women remained nervous and hysterical. The men were tense and sad. For Hawaiians it should have been an auspicious night, and a time to remember. But for those assembled, it turned out to be anything but an happy feast.

Kaahumanu had already dispatched messengers to the other islands, calling for all *makahiki* and *kukahi* feasts to be open to both men and women. Having so thoroughly smashed the eating restraints in one dramatic performance, she followed with even more drastic edicts. With almost diabolical fervor she locked battle with the entire religious structure of the nation.

Some said this mighty woman had kahuna-bewitched the high priest Hewahewa. In the days that followed it was plain that she so thoroughly dominated this head of the temples that her slightest wish became his command.

"Burn the temples," she demanded. "Throw down the images of the gods. All of them are false. They have no power. Wipe them out of our lives!"

Within a week of the feast of emancipation, Hewahewa was leading a crew of naked, drunken priests in the demolishment of Kailua's most sacred shrines. "The gods cannot survive without the kapu!" the old man wildly proclaimed. With his own hand he set torch to the wood-and-grass temples, and the great wooden effigies before which tens of thousands of people had groveled through the centuries. The heavier images of stone were cast into the sea.

While Kailua was systematically desecrated, and Kaahumanu's orders for complete destruction of temples and effigies went out to the farthest parts of the realm, Liholiho walked mute and dazed through the debacle that was destroying the religious fabric of the nation. Sky-gazers and kahunas had convinced him that resistance was hopeless and useless. To escape his own view of the smoke, destruction, and civil uproar, he put to sea—the canoes again loaded with convivial men, willing women, and plenty of grog from the trading ships. And while he hid forgetfully from sight, Kaahumanu, with imperious madness, ordered complete destruction in his name.

After the incidence of first shock, the people adjusted to the new order with cheerful adaptability. The fact that families could eat together, with the petty restrictions on separate foods now lifted, and all this without the conviction that the gods would strike one down, or the king's regulators club one to death, was like a breath of wild fresh air. At last free of the awful fears, the people happily and willingly accepted the new edict.

Abolishment of the god-idols and destruction of the shrines were quite another matter. The people were not half so eager for this. They could accept the abolishment of kapu, but to burn the gods, to wipe worship and rich mystery from their lives, was too much for them to digest in one lump. Their basic devotion was no recent thing. It was ancient, rich with tradition, and the very motivation and endowment of their lives. Many refused to follow the royal command.

Instead of purging their minds of the gods, and instead of burning the great wooden idols, many of them worshipped in secret, and hid the statues in caves and secret places. The remote fishing and mountain villages of the islands were still untouched by the foreign heresies that had come with the ships. Not all Hawaiians had been able to watch sailors consume vast amounts of kapu food, enjoy sex with no thought of restrictive days, live as they pleased, in defiance of edict or divine wrath, and still remain alive. The insular people had never come up against such a fundamental testing of their faith and belief. Still, free eating was good, and welcome relief from a stupid burden. Abolishment of religious worship, and willful destruction of the gods—of this the village people wanted no part.

Other men in the complex structure of the priesthood were not like Hewahewa. They who still tended the shrines, and recited the people's prayers, were not yet seduced from their obligations by this mad head priest, nor by the strident queen and bedmate of the great Kamehameha. They called out loudly against the new king and his matriarchal court. While they watched their shrines systematically destroyed by the king's men, and themselves turned out of power and office, they set their voices and will to arousal of the people against such consummate lunacy.

The opposition rapidly gathered around Kekuaokalani, the royal keeper of Ku, and the man most violently opposed to Kaahumanu and the women-dominated son of Kamehameha. The war chief, even though cousin to Liholiho, and had inherited great power by direct decree of Kamehameha, was convinced the nation was being misruled by a weak and vacillating monarch; that a great and tragic wrong had been perpetrated on its people. He needed but little urging from the realm's defrauded priests to accept leadership of the resistance.

Kekuaokalani was a young man, and a fiery orator. He voiced his cause as a religious crusade against heresy and wickedness in high places. Chiefs and commoners joined the priests in rallying a fighting force to save the nation from decadance and destruction.

When they armed themselves for war, and declared their intention of overthrowing the duped king and his wicked government, Liholiho rallied enough to prepare for the threat. In this final showdown, he at last began exhibiting some of the calm and deliberate courage of his revered father. Wisely he called in Kalanimoku and John Young for advice and counsel. They, with Kaahumanu, suggested immediate attack upon the rebels. Hit them before they could muster their full strength. Destroy them before they could polarize the discontent into military might.

But the king again lapsed into hesitancy. He sensed the devastating nature of the national heartbreak. His first move was to attempt reconciliation with his angry and rebellious cousin. He could not remain unmindful of what the advantage of custodianship of Ku had done for his warrior father.

The rebel army, under Kekuaokalani, were assembling at Kaawaloa. The king's emissaries, Hoapili and Naihe, were dispatched to that town. And, since Hoapili was now his mother's lover, and would soon share a polyandrous marriage with her other husband, Queen Keopuolani insisted on joining the peace mission. Her presence alone should be enough to influence even an angry and rebellious war chief.

But not even the queen mother was enough. Kekuaokalani was swayed none at all by the highborn ambassadors. He was ready for war. He intended war. Liholiho's emissaries returned empty handed.

When Liholiho realized that fighting was inevitable, he reluctantly ordered the royal armies to make themselves ready for battle. Kalanimoku, as king's adviser, issued a proclamation of intent. High Priest Hewahewa, who had started the whole thing, made himself scarce to the court. But there was nothing meek or docile about the militant Kaahumanu. She insisted that the royal forces attack without delay. Even as they hesitated, a bloody insurrection broke out at Hamakua.

But not even at Kaahumanu's insistence, and even though Kailua was menaced from two sides, would wise old Kalanimoku throw the king's warriors on the Hamakua rebels. "The source of the war is at Kaawaloa," Billy Pitt reasoned. "To that place let our forces be directed. The rebellion at Hamakua is a leaf of the tree. I would lay the axe to the root. That being destroyed, the leaves will wither."

Kekuaokalani, as the "source of the war," had no intention of waiting for the king's men to arrive. In the dark of the night he moved his warriors out of Kaawaloa in the direction of Kailua. His plan was to take the capital by surprise. He hoped for quick, decisive victory. But Kalanimoku, expertly deploying the king's forces, met the rebels headlong at Kuamoo.

It was a frightful battle. The army of Kekuaokalani, in the frenzied dedication of a religious war, fought recklessly and bravely. Death was small sacrifice in their frantic effort to purge the nation of its sin; to bring to judgment the wicked counselors who had so grossly mis-

HIGH CHIEF KALANIMOKU (BILLY PITT) (left)
AND JOHN YOUNG

—*Bernice P. Bishop Museum, Honolulu.*

82

guided a king in the first half year of his reign. But valor and dedication were not enough against modern weaponry, and the tactical training the foreign advisers had given Liholiho's forces.

The rebels fought with spears, knives, clubs and what antiquated
muskets they had been able to trade or steal from the ships. All the
courage and fanaticism in the world could not prevail against soldiery
who systematically cut down fighting Hawaiians with volleyed rifle
fire, and cannonades. Slowly, deliberately, Kekuaokalani and his men
were worried back toward the Kuamoo shoreline; death and blood the
price for every step of retreat. Offshore, in a line of double canoes,
mounted cannon on deck, trained riflemen in the hulls, the royal forces
began decimating an army who preferred death to surrender.

Kekuaokalani had led his forces valiantly, but not even Ku could prevail against gunfire that had them pinioned from two sides. Already wounded, the gallant young war chief rallied and encouraged his men, until another rifle shot cut him down. When loss of blood no longer allowed him to stand erect, he sat on a nub of lava, firing his musket at the advancing forces until death laid him out as useless. His wife Manono, as was Hawaiian custom, fighting like a tigress at his side, gently covered the face of her brave husband with his royal cloak of feathers. A moment later she too dropped upon the lifeless body of her husband—a bullet in her left temple.

Despite the loss of its heroic leader, and the merciless slaughter of dedicated men, the remnants of the rebel army fought ten more long hours. By then it was but a bleeding shadow of yesterday's glory. With final capitulation of the battle's few survivors, the royalists moved on Hamakua and Waipio. There the remaining insurgents were decisively routed. Another tragic civil war was ended.

II

THE WAR demolished any concerted effort to restore the national and traditional religion of Hawaii. But this victory to the king and his fanatic courtiers was much too harsh and summary for the people. Happiness and tranquility were gone from the land. Violence, bloodshed, the uprooting of cherished beliefs, had left the people shocked and silent. With no gods or priests to sustain them, they now lived in constant and nameless fear.

Liholiho realized he faced a greater crisis than when he had defied his cousin in civil conflict. This time he courageously and compassionately took up the reins of leadership. Now, at last, he truly acted like a king.

By pardoning and granting amnesty to all the rebels who had come out of the bloody struggle alive, he showed a magnanimity never before known in island warfare. Traditionally, war captives were sacrificed on the *heiaus*, that the gods might assure peace and tranquility to the people for the future. Or the losers in the struggle might be hammered alive into the cardinal point post-holes for new temples or new dwellings for the Alii. But god-worship had been taken from the people. There would be no more temples. The Alii would have to seek some less drastic way of securing good luck for their pole-and-grass houses.

Liholiho, himself troubled, went among the people. He shared their mourning. He listened to their heartbreak. Being a sensitive man, he quickly realized that the ethos of his people had been shattered and destroyed. The belief that had guided and controlled every act of their lives had been torn from them, and nothing had been provided to fill the spiritual vacuum. By traveling among the people, by the obvious sincerity he radiated, and the overwhelming love he actually felt, Liholiho saved his kingdom from sure and certain disintegration.

Hawaiians continued to look upon their king as the sole representative of diety on earth—whatever form that diety might evolve. Even now the people had no doubts but what lineage of the Alii rocketed back through generations to the very gods who had formed the Pacific islands—Wa-ke-a and Pa-pa. Gods might, in this present hour, be disavowed, the idols overturned, the temples burned, but nothing could erase the belief that the big-statured and godlike Alii were partly divine. The divinity they possessed could be accurately measured by the amount of mana they were born to and claimed to radiate. Never, in all the realm had there been a king endowed with genealogically-proven mana equal to Liholiho, the second Kamehameha.

The people asked of their highborn only understanding and love. In his every act now, Liholiho demonstrated he could love; he did understand. The islanders responded with worshipful affection. Relief, joy, spontaneous demonstrations of trust and adulation were his wherever he traveled.

Every human must of necessity abide in some form of spiritual belief. By degrees the personage of Liholiho took the place of the wooden and stone effigies, the hundreds of invisible creatures—godlike and demoniac—who once had filled the minds of all. Liholiho was alive and real. He did not spy into every mortal act. He was not spiteful or vengeful. He had abolished the chafing burden of kapu. Secure in their new worship, the people became trustful and happy again. In loyalty no ruler could ever have been more secure.

To Kaahumanu and Billy Pitt went the far greater task of rebuilding an operational government after the kapu system had been eliminated as its main strength. Because of the blind and indestructible faith the people had in their Alii, the Hawaiian monarchy emerged from chaos unscathed; stronger, more secure than ever.

In this single climactic year the nation had lost Kamehameha the Great, crowned a new king, fought out a civil war, destroyed its own national religion, and emerged prosperous, confident, and on the brink of a new destiny. The nation was united. The world was clamoring at its doors. The king had won complete trust and obedience from his people. Destiny would record that these were the golden years of the Hawaiian kingdom.

III

It was the latter part of March, in the new year of 1820, when the American brig *Thaddeus* was first sighted off the Kohala coast of the big island of Hawaii. Had Liholiho known the portents sailing in with this ship, he would have been far wiser to have sunk it with his polyglot navy, or to have driven it off the shores before it could search out an anchorage.

As usual with the sighting or arrival of any new ship in Hawaiian waters, and as soon as the long boat of the *Thaddeus* touched shore, runners were on their way to Kailua bearing all available news regarding it.

In the boat was James Hunnewell, first mate of the *Thaddeus*. With him were two of the four native Hawaiian boys aboard the brig, returning to their homeland after years of sojourn in the dim outer world of the white man. The news the runners brought to the king was sketchy. The *Thaddeus* was captained by Andrew Blanchard; had suffered an interminably long voyage from Boston; and was seeking news and information about the islands, their king, and where to proceed for safe anchorage. Revealment of its strange cargo had been excitedly made by the Hawaiian boys. By the time these fragmentary details reached Liholiho, he quickly considered the ship a threat. He ordered its every move watched and reported.

A most astonishing thing about this American brig was the presence aboard her of these four Hawaiians. Young Prince Humehume, son of Kaumualii, king of Kauai, had been sent by his royal father to America to be educated. He was now returned—George (Prince) Tamoree (as pronounced by the Americans). The other shipboard Hawaiians were not of the Alii, but all were equally glad at this first viewance of their homeland after stifling terms at the Foreign Mission School at Cornwall, Connecticut. These young men had sailed away from their beloved islands as cabin boys or deck hands on American merchantmen, and had been schooled into the strange thought and ways of New England Christianity. Hopu and Honolii were natives of Kohala. Kanui was out of Oahu.

When they touched shore at Kohala they not only built a bridge of special interest to the *Thaddeus* because of their very presence, but brought the first information about the other peculiar passengers riding in with the American brig.

The *Thaddeus* was a mission ship—first of its kind. Aboard were American zealots who had pledged themselves to evangelize and save from heathenism the benighted natives of the Sandwich Islands. The company was headed by Reverend and Mrs. Hiram Bingham; Reverend and Mrs. Asa Thurston; Mr. and Mrs. Daniel Chamberlain, and five children; Dr. Thomas Holman, physician; teachers Samuel Whitney and Samuel Ruggles; Elisha Loomis, printer; their respective wives, and tiny children.

Daniel Chamberlain's mission was to teach the natives the best and latest methods of American agriculture. Dr. Thomas Holman planned to save Hawaiian souls by curing their ailments; Loomis, the printer, had brought a press, type, and plentiful supply of paper. His job was to spread the faith by the printed word—just as quickly as the native oral language could be translated into written vowels and consonants— and the people could, in turn, be taught to read God's message of salvation. What all of them desperately sought was permission to land. They must get their families and possessions ashore. They were most anxious to set up operations.

The natives of the Kohala coast, in ecstatic glee for the return of the Hawaiian boys and their message of peace and goodwill, had laden canoes with gifts of food and flowers. The young men of the villages had decorated their loin cloths with baubles and greenery, and had hung *leis* of flowers about their necks. The maidens had quickly wrapped their best and newest *pa'us* of kapa cloth about their shapely and eager hips, hung bright and fragrant *leis* about thir necks, and had adorned their dark and wavy hair with flower clusters. They sang a chant of welcome as rhythmically they paddled their outriggers and double canoes toward the *Thaddeus*.

Slowly the parade of canoes circled the ship, while the people sang in barbaric choir, and held up their offerings to the ship-weary pilgrims crowding the deck. The white visitors looked down curiously at the heathens they had come to save. They could see nothing beautiful in the brown flesh of the half-naked men—even though the men were superbly muscled, and glistened with the rime of the sea. They were shocked to silence by the conical and pointed breasts of the darksome maidens as they smiled joyously and seductively up at the Puritans out of New England. A moment later the Hawaiians were swarming up the ladder to the deck of the *Thaddeus*. And the missionaries got their first true glimpse of Hawaii.

Happily the natives laid their gifts of coconuts, breadfruit and bananas upon the deck, and embellished their offerings with the exotic and sweet-smelling flowers of their bounteous land. Then, one by one, they embraced the returning Hawaiian boys, cried over them, and chattered with them. When that was over, the undemonstrative missionaries, their shocked wives, and frightened children, warily eyed the natives from across the deck. The islanders, surprised at this lethargic reception—so different from the wild and abandoned joy of other ships—gathered together, and looked questioningly at their hosts. The people they saw were oddly dressed. They acted differently from anything they had ever before seen. It was confusing.

Gracious by nature, openhanded and generous, the natives smilingly presented their gifts, and climbed back down to their canoes. For an hour they circled the *Thaddeus* while she weighed anchor, and set her sails for the safer and more protective anchorage in the Kawaihae roadstead.

In the hour it took for departure the natives had plenty time to contemplate and chatter about the strange people they had just met. Why had the men brought their women and children along? If those queer looking females were not on hand, perhaps their men would have acted more in the pattern of other ship's passengers and crews. What was wrong with these women? Their sober faces indicated some deep and tragic sorrow. Their suffering must be very great, for them to be so sad-eyed and solemn. Too, they looked skinny and half-starved. Their long black dresses were a sign of mourning. The visiting Hawaiians honestly and openly pitied them.

As the *Thaddeus* set herself to round Upolu Point, the Hawaiians, singing and gabbling, followed in their festive parade of canoes. Not until they reached seas heavy enough to threaten their light craft did they paddle back to their Kohala villages. It had been an exciting day.

Aboard ship there was equal discussion and comment. The Hawaiian boys were shocked and disturbed to know that Kamehameha the Great was dead, stripped of his bones, and that another king now ruled the islands. It worried them too that their missionary sponsors saw evil and disgust in the naked bodies of the people of this beloved and beautiful land. They must warn other visitors coming aboard ship. It was wiser to cover themselves before climbing the ladder.

The Reverend Hiram Bingham's worst fears had been confirmed. The people to whom they were dedicating their lives truly *were* savages, of low estate; a frivolous, shiftless lot; probably as cannibalistic now as the day they had killed and reputedly eaten Captain Cook. The women were impressed by the lush beauty of the islands, and worried about the equally lush beauty of the maidens. They faced a real task in putting civilized clothing on these poor benighted women, and teaching them to launder, cook, and be ever mindful of God's Eternal Word.

The tired and sea-battered *Thaddeus* came to harbor at Kawaihae after the long and turbulent voyage that had taken 164 days to complete. The wearisome journey had brought them from New England, around Cape Horn, and up the trackless Pacific to the planned site of their mission in the Sandwich Islands. The *Thaddeus* had dropped anchor at Kawaihae in the night, and next morning, the dawn of April 1, 1820, Americans—men, women and children, waited eagerly on deck for their first chance to set foot on one of the islands that were to be their future and their destiny.

With Puritanistic concept, they considered this mission as a form of martyrdom. They expected and anticipated hardships. They were not underestimating their problems. These naked people had not the least inkling of the one true God. They stripped their skin to the world. They were lewd. They were lascivious in almost every act. They were frivolous, empty-headed, and apparently incapable of thought on life's deeper meanings. They neither toiled nor spun. They took their food as nature provided it, and with no thought whatever of tomorrow. They could not read or write—and this slow process of instruction would be necessary before Heaven's Writ could properly wipe away gayety and chatter. The mission the Americans had chosen would take not only this shipload of pilgrims, but many many more dedicated volunteers from Connecticut and Massachusetts.

The compulsion motivating these white visitors would have been, of course, an unanswerable riddle to the Hawaiians, had they known of it at the time. That anyone, even these strangely garbed and austere strangers, could have considered sojourn on the beautiful islands as abnegation and exile, was simply untenable in their minds.

Their gods had fashioned them as one with earth, sea and sky. They had been blessed lavishly in their land. Food could be had for the taking; the seas teemed with fish; everything man could desire was here in abundance. The climate was soft, languorous, and full of sunshine. Earth and sky had mated for the birth of Hawaii. Every island was a paradise of joy and plenty. That anyone could consider any part of it as lost, denied, or evil, was totally incomprehensible.

The Hawaiian boys aboard the *Thaddeus*, remembering the stern attitude of Kamehameha toward foreigners, and knowing nothing of the thought or policy of his son Liholiho, cautioned the pilgrims to ask permission of the king, or his chief in authority, before attempting to land or take ashore their possessions. Clear in remembrance was the Russian attempt at fort and colony at Waimea, and the unceremonious manner Kamehameha had obliterated it and had expelled these unwanted visitors. It would be better to come in peace. It was wisdom to seek permission.

So it was decided that one of the Hawaiian young men be sent ashore and, as linguist, parley with whomever was in charge at Kawai-hae. In choice, Humehume was passed over since he was Kauai-born, and no one was quite sure of the new king's feelings toward the once defiant monarch of the leeward islands. It was Hopu who was chosen. As a native of this island, Hopu would be warmly received, and had working knowledge of how to petition the Alii. If possible, he was to bring the headmen back to the ship. And, should the headmen fetch along their retinue, to make certain that all—men and women—out of consideration for the tender feelings of the American ladies—wear sufficient clothing to cover their repulsive nakedness.

After Hopu had rowed the dinghy ashore, the missionaries waited anxious hours for his return. Even though Hopu was born on this very island, and had been warmly received on the Kohala coast, there was no assurance he had not been murdered and eaten by the heathens. The visitors watched the shoreline and thatched villages nervously, their eyes and spyglasses trained on and alert to any signs of life and activity.

At last they saw the villagers streaming down to the shore. Soon two big double-hulled canoes moved out toward the ship, their paddles flashing and glittering in the tropic sunshine.

As they drew closer it became a beautiful sight. Expressions of relief and hope fell from the lips of the ship-weary pilgrims, who ached to once more set foot on solid earth. Noting the gaily bedecked craft, and the *kahilis* shining front and stern of both boats, the Hawaiian young men went into ecstasy. "Important people," they declared. "Maybe the king!"

The red and yellow of the *kahilis* grew more vivid and eye-arresting as both the huge canoes came in swiftly and surely. Amidship of one was a wide Chinese parasol of red silk. Important passengers indeed.

But it was not the king who rode the boat. He was at Kailua, worried and alert. The dignitary who stepped from the lead canoe was the king's counselor, High Chief Kalanimoku, known to every trader and diplomat as William Pitt of the Islands. Billy Pitt was the man who talked for the king. To Reverend Bingham, Captain Blanchard, and the Americans peering over the rail, Hopu loudly and obsequiously announced the high personage he had brought from shore.

When the huge man swung up the ladder to the deck, with Hopu respectfully distanced behind him, the ladies were relieved to see that Billy Pitt had properly dressed himself for the occasion. He swept aboard—graceful and imposing in beaver fur hat, white dimity coat, black silk vest, yellow trousers, and plaid cravat. And he actually wore shoes.

Kalanimoku was important all right. This man had just liberated his nation from civil war, and, as a French-baptized Christian, had led the fight to wipe out the Hawaiian national religion. Imperiously, with easy assurance, he bossed the welcoming ceremony.

In the best European manner the mighty man shook hands all around—men and women. He knew enough English to gain instant approval.

Then Kalanimoku ordered his retinue aboard. That done, he commanded his attendants to heap the deck with fresh fruit, vegetables, and flowers. American ladies made quick note that those in attendance were not clad as was Billy Pitt. Again their sensitive eyes were forced to stare on male nakedness, relieved only by *malos* strung precariously at the hips.

Now, out from under the huge parasol, and slowly and laboriously boosted aboard, came the mighty figures of two queens of the realm— two widows of Kamehameha the Great—Kalakua, and her sister Namahana. They were both properly and regally attired—Kalakua, because she was mother of three of Liholiho's queens, wore a dress of black velvet with gold brocade. Namahana, less favored, was attired in a long garment of yellow striped cotton. But as queens, each of them flaunted coronets of royal yellow feathers atop their dark heads. Like Billy Pitt, they seemed sure of themselves. Their manner toward the missionaries was most gracious and cordial.

Next aboard came two wives of High Chief Kalanimoku. As Alii, they too were big women. Their highborn husband soberly introduced this part of his harem to the Americans. But it was a bit disconcerting to note that they had come aboard more comfortably attired in the native *pa'u*. Their mighty teats, flowers on the nipples, were allowed to swing clear and free in the air. The thirty retainers who followed, all necessary to the comfort and wellbeing of the Alii, taxed the deck capacity of the little brig. Stiffly, to the distinguished visitors, Reverend Bingham presented the ship's captain, the mates, and the members of the missionary party.

Excluding the king himself, the *Thaddeus* had been honored by visit of the monarchy's highest dignitaries. It is possible that this boarding could actually have been authorized and directed by Liholiho, from Kailua. Certain it was that the royal visitors were fully accustomed to meeting people from other lands. They seemed relaxed and at ease with these sober-faced strangers from America. With the interpretive aid of the island boys of the missionary party, the queens and chiefesses chatted amiably with the somberly clad American women. Billy Pitt earnestly conversed with the men.

Chairs were lined up on the crowded deck—at least enough of them to properly seat the mighty women of the boarding party. Their retinue, hovering close, had to be content with perches on capstan, main chains and deck. Uneasy in the chairs, Kalakua ordered the attendants to roll out grass mats on the deck. When the mats were properly laid and aligned, the two queens gave up their unnatural chair bottoms and more languorously reclined upon the mats. Then, after the royal attendants had settled their queens, had wiped their mouths for them, had straightened their long black hair, the missionaries watched in fascinated horror while the two queens sought comfort in the heat by divesting themselves of their dresses.

In royal aplomb and serenity the two women spread out on the deck, their vast brown bodies naked except for their coronets of feathers, and the kapa *pa'u* covering their ample crotches. The missionaries tried not to allow four naked women to drive them into speechlessness. Frantically, nervously, they labored to explain to the fully relaxed visitors their reason for coming to Hawaii, and the message of peace and salvation they were bringing to this unsaved portion of the world. Just as earnestly was Hiram Bingham and the male contingent begging Billy Pitt for permission to go ashore and begin their ministry. The ship's crew, from quarterdeck and ratlines, were looking down on the strange parley with amused interest.

It never dawned on the missionaries that the amiable and good-natured Queen Kalakua was mother to three wives of the present reigning monarch—one of them his total favorite. Because Billy Pitt wore trousers and beaver hat, the pleadings and petitions for a landing went solely to him.

Probably forewarned, Kalanimoku's answer was polite and simple. "The permission is not mine to give. Your right to land and live on the islands must be decided by the king."

"Then we cannot go ashore here at Kawaihae?" begged Reverend Bingham. "Sir, we have been months aboard this ship!"

"I understand. I know about your God. But you and your people must remain aboard. The king alone can permit you to land. And the king is at Kailua."

So it was decided that the *Thaddeus* must sail on to Kailua. It was decided also that the royal party, with all its retinue, would travel with her.

As evidence of goodwill and good intent, however, high chief Kalanimoku agreed to take one member of the missionary party ashore and show him Kawaihae—the town once holy to Kamehameha the Great. It was Hiram Bingham who rode the royal canoe to the beach.

In spite of the enthusiastic tour conducted by Billy Pitt, the Reverend Bingham returned to the ship disturbed and unimpressed. The natives, content to live in grass huts, unclad and unmindful of the necessity for piety and toil, reminded him of how great was the task ahead. They were much too frivolous and happy. And the sites of the abandoned heathen temples, and the immense Puukohola *heiau*, which Kamehameha had erected for human sacrifice, filled him with loathing and disgust. When the *Thaddeus* finally lifted anchor for her sail down the Kona coast to Kailua, the Reverend Bingham had re-dedicated himself to the task of fashioning this irreverent land into a pattern more acceptable to Christ.

The voyage of the *Thaddeus* to Kailua proved a strange one. Mattresses were brought up on deck for the royal party, and a deck full of bronze nakedness was most offensive to the ladies out of Boston. Billy Pitt, as the properly attired linguist, accepted the invitation to share meals with the missionaries at their civilized table. The royal ladies, however, would have none of this.

Reclining in comfort, their fish and poi were brought to them by their retainers—frequently, and without the least heed as to proper and scheduled times for dining. When they were hungry, which seemed most of the time, they ate. The missionaries, who spied on them with secret fascination, stared in wonder and disgust as they slurped and fingered their pasty gruel, and belched and chattered happily over food that had little appeal to the Anglos.

It bothered the missionaries to surreptitiously watch the fawning attendants wait on the royal ladies in everything from keeping their poi bowls filled, to lighting their pipes, wiping their faces, and tending to their natural functions. Apparently there were many things in Polynesia which needed correction.

Especially annoying was the suddenly changed attitudes of the converted Hawaiian young men, whom Bingham and the missionaries had expected would lead them triumphantly into the land of their unsaved fathers. Now the lads cackled and laughed like blackbirds as they mixed with their kind. Christian restraint and Puritan soberness had vanished. They howled in glee. They gabbled in joyous abandon with their heathen friends. They had instantly shed the studious discipline that had guided them through the preparatory classes back in Connecticut.

Had the missionaries been half as facile with the Hawaiian tongue as were the native boys with English, they would have been considerably more amazed. Much of the conversation pivoted around the mental yardstick the natives were laying on the missionaries.

The black-clad disciples of Christ, to them, were queer, sad men. But it was their women who were strangest of all. Thin as splinters; they looked half-starved and ill. Their wasplike waists were unfit for childbearing. Their melancholy attitude probably stemmed from the fact that they were sick. Poi and fish, amply and frequently served, might yet save them from the wasting death. And, if they willingly accepted it, might eventually fatten them out to some semblance of desirability. The sight of these poor, deprived people was half comic, half pathetic.

But it was the necks of the women—sticking up out of frail shoulders like white candlewicks—that brought the laughter and the comments. The term "longnecks" was first applied aboard the *Thaddeus*. And this appellation to American missionaries became a continuing part of Hawaiian talk.

The *Thaddeus* had set sail from Kawaihae on a Saturday night. Next morning, after the missionaries had eaten their prim and prayerful breakfast, and the natives had slopped, chattered and laughed through their own first feeding, the Reverend Bingham led his black-coats and longnecks out on deck for the usual Sabbath observance. It was a weird congregation he faced; a capsuled sample of what lay ahead.

Bingham started out with a hymn, quaveringly and thinly sung by the Americans—men, women and children. He finished a mighty prayer of gratitude to God for their safe arrival in the Sandwich Islands, and for their almost miraculous deliverance from the hazards of storms and seas. He prayed especially for help in saving the deprived heathens among whom they had come to labor. But the deprived heathens on the deck of the *Thaddeus* scarcely looked up from their card playing and pipe smoking as the Christians went through their sacred act.

Irked at this crass disregard for the Lord's work, Bingham, through Chief Kalanimoku, reprimanded his naked and preoccupied audience. Queens Kalakua and Namahana roared their answers back to Billy Pitt, for translation, and in no uncertain manner. Hawaiians, they said, were not bound by the religious tabus of the white men. But they had no objections to the white men's worship. If the white folks wanted to continue, it was all right for them to proceed. The affront to Bingham was made doubly obvious when the Hawaiian boys, whom they had brought back from America, definitely were in agreement with their queens.

So, while the natives played cards and smoked — vices already adopted from previous white visitors—Bingham delivered his impassioned sermon. Little of it was interpreted, even by the young men they had trained as linguists. Bingham was forced to close his first meeting with the heathens on a note of failure. He had been told that the natives of the Sandwich Islands had only last year disencumbered themselves of all godlike belief. It was frightening to realize that they intended to keep it so.

But worse, at the finish of the service, Queen Kalakua started bellowing commands. One of the big woman's retainers brought out a roll of white cambric. It took busy translation by Billy Pitt and the Hawaiian boys to make plain that Kalakua was demanding that white women cease their stupid singing and praying, and get immediately to work at sewing her a dress. She wanted to appear especially attractive when she stepped ashore at Kailua.

This chore the longnecks utterly refused to do. Today was the Sabbath Day. Christians and missionaries performed no labors—not even sewing—on Sunday. Imperiously the queen insisted the longnecks get busy on her dress.

Unaccustomed to having her commands ignored or disobeyed, Kalakua flew into monumental rage. But the longnecks remained adamant. The Sabbath could not be defiled, they insisted. Only when they promised they would indeed fashion the queen's cambric into a gown—in time for her to meet the king and people at Kailua—did the mighty woman subside. Once assured that this would be so, she again became the amiable and laughing center of conversation aboard the *Thaddeus*.

Early Monday morning Kalakua sent messengers to the missionaries that she was waiting on deck for the longnecks to get on with the sewing. She had accepted the strange Christian kapu on Sabbath needlework. Now that it was a new day, and the kapu was lifted, Kalakua was anxious and insistent they proceed with the task.

The white women, just as anxious, took their assigned places on the deck mats—bringing with them their scissors and sewing kits. While Kalakua stood center, in majestic nakedness, Mrs. Holman measured for fit. Mrs. Ruggles scissored the cambric to queen-sized segments. Mrs. Thurston and Mrs. Chamberlain busied themselves with the stitching. While sister-queen Namahana enviously looked on, smilingly alert, the yards of cambric were skillfully fashioned into a robe of white. Considering the height and the girth, it was the nearest approach the longnecks could make to the mode of 1820.

The deck boiled with anticipation and pleasure. Chatter was endless. The seamstresses were offered bowls of poi, and even pipes packed with tobacco, to make their task easier and happier. Dark eyes, out of dark faces, stared on in joyful anticipation and fascination. When

Queen Kalakua stood before them in white magnificence it was a festive and happy moment. And it was a triumphant one for the longnecks.

They hadn't been able to do much about a slender waistline, but
the gown had been given flowing sleeves. They had done their job most
skillfully. The queen, proud and happy in her airy elegance, was presented with a lace cap, decorated with artificial roses, and a "worked"
colored neckerchief. The longnecks appeared as proud of their job as was
this widow of the great Kamehameha. They had accomplished more in
gaining heathen respect and friendship than all of yesterday's prayers
and preaching.

IV

BINGHAM and his missionaries had reason enough to worry as to their
reception by Liholiho the king. Certainly by the time the *Thaddeus*
dropped her rusty anchor in Kailua bay, Tuesday morning, the royal
community was waiting for the ship, and alive with excitement. Fully
apprised of the pilgrim vessel's slow southing of the island, the people,
sensing something new and dramatic, had converged on Kailua. They
were just as anxious as the king to view these new foreigners, and hear
firsthand their intent. Any ship, from any land, invariably brought
crowds. In the *Thaddeus*, and its mystery, this was especially so.

Officially, besides housing the king and his court, Kailua was home
to more than three thousand people. But today it had doubled in population. Probably the least like paradise of any of Kailua's coastal towns,
Kailua had been chosen by Kamehameha as his preferential capital
because of its unexcelled fishing and excellent surf, and because it had
been central in dealing with the internecine wars that had been the
constant preoccupation of the last great king. Liholiho continued to
maintain his court at Kailua because of the royal compound already
established. He, like Kaahumanu, placed great value on Kailua's exceptional fishing. And the machinery of Hawaiian government was
already in operation at this port.

There were rumors, however, that a change was imminent. The
talk was that Liholiho, now that the rebellion was settled, planned to
move his capital to Lahaina, on Maui; or to Waikiki, on Oahu. But
this day, at Kailua, he and his court were very much in residence.

The Kona coast is the barren side of Hawaii. Great lava spreads are
relieved only by occasional patches of cocopalms and hau trees. In
1820 Kailua's grass houses extended splotchily upward from the beach-
front, far up the slopes toward the more green and timbered base of

ancient Mount Hualalai—dominant backdrop to the town. Kailua had none of the lush green softness of Lahaina or Waikiki. Its sparse pattern was dominated by two huge buildings of masoned coral, built by Kamehameha, but never used by him as residences. He, like Liholiho and the dowager queens, had always preferred their houses of the more native and better ventilated thatch. The royal compound, multiple housed, was still native-style in woven grass—but the largest and most lavishly furnished in all the islands

Today, being a "boat day" of especial interest, the whole town kept lively watch for the *Thaddeus*. The green waters of the sandy cove were hosting hundreds of swimmers, racing canoes, and surf boards. Under the palm fringe of the beach there was card playing, chanting, and groups preoccupied with dancing the graceful hula. Under the shadier hau trees, farther up the beach, others sat out the time stringing flower leis for the welcoming, or plaiting the green fronds into lauhala mats. The older folks were content to sun themselves on sand or rock. But everywhere was joy and the primordial happiness with which these people were so innately endowed.

Liholiho, who had mentally chewed out the sketchy reports about this American ship and its purpose, waited for its arrival with apprehension and with anger. He knew now that Kalanimoku, and the widowed queens of Kamehameha—his mother-in-law Kalakua, and her sister Namahana—all had boarded the ship at Kawaihae. He would get the full and true report when they arrived. Queen Kaahumanu, who still maintained her own lavish court at Kailua, was on a fishing trip; absent from today's problems. And, for this lack of imperious meddling, the king was glad. Whatever these Americans were after, he would hear it out in his own way.

When the *Thaddeus* hove into view, it was cue to the pageantry to which Hawaiians were born. Here at last, with hopeful finality, the ship dropped anchor—eighteen thousand miles from her home port of Boston. The missionaries, watching eagerly over the rail, saw the ˌmassing of humanity at water's edge, and the huge double-hulled royal canoe being swiftly and rhythmically swept by the paddle crews outward toward the ship. The canoe, gaily decorated with Cantonese silk streamers, and royal heraldry, pulled alongside. But it was quickly obvious this was no shore boat for the Americans or the ship's crew. Only the royal party and their retinue were allowed to board the craft.

When the royal canoe touched shore there was a blaring of conch shells, and a chanting of the *mele inoa* to Kamehameha's queens. Kalakua, strikingly celestial in her white cambric dress and embroidered cap, headed the procession through the bowing and groveling lines of people. It pleased her immensely that they took chattering notice of her new garb. In fashioning it, the longnecks had performed well.

Close behind her was Namahana, less theatrically regal. Though she also had been a queen to Kamehameha, and sister to Kalakua, her mana was not nearly so great. None of her daughters were wives to the new king—Liholiho—Kamehameha II—as were the daughters of Kalakua. Immediately behind the dowager queens walked High Chief Kalanimoku, anxious to rid himself of the chafing and pinching white man's clothes and shoes. He was followed by his wives, and the droves of royal attendants. To the sound of chanting and cheering, the party headed up the northerly rise toward the grass palace—once home to Kamehameha, now the royal abode of Liholiho.

The missionaries, still prisoners on the brig's deck, watched the shore pageantry with sour envy. They could hear the drum beats, the chants, and the mighty chorus of voices as the heathens rendered homage to their Alii. The Americans were now most keenly aware of the almost insuperable task of civilizing and evangelizing Hawaiians. But they could not help but be impressed by the savage and exciting beauty of the sounds and sights to which they were witness.

It was hours later before a less ornate canoe put out from shore to bring some of the Americans in for scrutiny. The people, aware of the protocol and anxious to see their new visitors, had patiently remained on the beach and in the streets. Only the Reverends Bingham and Thurston, with Hopu as interpreter, and Captain Blanchard of the *Thaddeus*, were allowed to board the canoe. Dr. Holman was also privileged to come ashore, but with the admonition to proceed directly to the house of John Young. The other men were to go to the palace.

Their welcome ashore was ebullient and noisy. During the pause, Dr. Holman was immediately and mysteriously led away. Reverend Bingham stared down his nose at the chanting, dancing people. To him, their gayety and abandon were painful irritations. Slowly the Americans were moved through the lines, but when stopped by a man, whose vast bulk plainly marked him as Alii, Hiram Bingham vocally protested the delay and the interference.

The creature was naked except for the *malo*, and the feathered cloak hanging casually backward from his immense and hairy chest and shoulders. This was more than offensive to the securely clothed Bingham. But Hopu instantly groveled before the man. Obsequiously he introduced the huge brown native as High Chief Kuakini, brother to Queen Kaahumanu.

Bingham, not at all impressed by the polygamous and incestually interrelated Alii, quickly turned down Kuakini's proffered invitation to his big house. Hopu, appalled by the discourtesy of the Americans, frantically urged them to accept the hospitality. Without ever realizing that Kaahumanu possessed life-and-death power over any Christianizing effort, the missionaries grudgingly took time out to enter the thatched dwelling of the absent queen's brother.

Kuakini, noted for lavish living, offered them an impressive array of native foods, prepared especially for the visitors. They partook of the strange offerings sparingly, almost with fright. Austerely and abruptly they rejected the rum and wine Big Kuakini eagerly tendered. However, the fresh milk of the coconut was accepted, tried, and relished by the ship-starved travelers. They were forced to suffer through a round of hula dancing, which their host insisted they view as special honor. Finally Reverend Bingham, using the urgency of the royal visit as excuse, got them free of Kuakini and his house.

It was Hopu who insisted they make yet another stop—at the dwelling of John Young. By thatched grass standards, Young's home, too, was lavishly furnished and remarkably livable. Bingham was more appreciative of this visit with a fellow white man who could converse freely and willingly in English. But, even though John Young had been confidant and adviser to Kamehameha the Great, and held a like post with King Liholiho, the evangelists were appalled by the fact that this Englishman was contentedly mated to native women. But John Young proved polite and cordial. He had already dispatched the American physician, Holman, in the direction of Alii sickness. And he allowed the other American men to proceed on their way without further interruption.

The king's half-naked guards ushered the Americans into the great thatched palace, directly into the big room where, at one end, the king and his wives were eating at a long, low, leaf-covered table. His Majesty did not rise from his dinner, but acknowledged his visitors with half smile and slight nod of his handsome head. After pointing to a corner of the room where they might sit and wait, the Americans squatted on the lauhala mats to bide his pleasure.

It was long in coming, and the preachers and sea captain squirmed with impatience and discomfort while the eating went on with noisy merriment. The royal family seemed completely oblivious to their presence. They acted as though their American visitors did not exist.

After what seemed hours of waiting, and the day had gone into afternoon, the king arose. Four of his wives hovered over a delayed and animated discussion, apparently centered on the foreigners. At long last they retreated to the room's other corner and, after spreading themselves out on the mats, they began dealing out the playing cards with which the Alii seemed compulsively obsessed.

At the opposite end of the room was a pair of massive, richly carved Chinese chairs. These apparently served as thrones. Liholiho, dressed for today in British uniform of blue and gold, and his favorite wife and half-sister Kamamalu, brightly garbed in *pa'u* and shawl of yellow Cantonese satin, sat stiffly and regally down in the chairs. Not until they were seated, and their swarthily handsome faces wiped of all traces of food, did their attendant indicate to the floor-cramped men that they might have royal audience.

Hopu led them to his king—throwing himself prostrate before the monarch. After this courtly recognition of Alii and mana, the awed and frightened young man presented Reverends Bingham and Thurston, and Captain Blanchard. In the language of his ancestors, Hopu described the missionaries as disciples and servants to the Great God who had made heaven and earth. Hiram Bingham wasted no time in stating his case, and making his plea. Hopu had to work furiously to translate the message to the now courteously attentive Liholiho.

Bingham, representing the King of Heaven, offered salvation and eternal life to the king of the Hawaiian nation. More humbly did he beg permission for the missionaries and teachers to settle on the islands; to preach the word of God; to instruct the king, his wives, his children, and all his people in the wonderful gift of reading and writing—as used by the haoles. The Great God was desirous that Hawaiian people read for themselves the life-giving message the American missionaries and teachers had brought from the outer world.

Liholiho was not discourteous, but he was puzzled. More apparently, he seemed totally unimpressed. Frantically Bingham reiterated the plea for their party to come ashore. To this the king would give no definite answer. They could not come ashore, he insisted, until he had made up his mind. And, should he consider it unwise, they could not land at all.

Captain Blanchard worriedly shook his head. Face to face with the possibility of failure, Bingham redoubled his efforts. But the king was adamant. He grew quickly weary of their importuning. He insisted they return to their ship. As to their request, he wanted time to ponder the matter.

When the Americans finally turned to leave, Liholiho explained that Queen Kaahumanu, the *kuhina-nui*, would help him decide the issue—quickly as she returned to Kailua. Bingham, not realizing the powers vested in this woman as to the spiritual interests of the people, considered the reference as only one more encumbrance to their destiny and their hopes. Sadly, discouraged, the men retreated to the *Thaddeus*. Only Hopu was allowed to remain ashore.

Next morning the missionaries were again back at the palace, importuning the king. This time they bore gifts—a leatherbound Bible, and an ornate magnifying glass for His Majesty's amusement. After explaining the word of God housed in the yet unreadable book, and after showing the king how to double the size of anything by looking through the amazing glass, Liholiho received the gifts most graciously. But about the Americans coming ashore, let alone establishing residence, he remained obdurate.

In Kailua there was much talk about the missionaries and the impasse they faced with the king. The Hawaiian boys of the *Thaddeus*, now comfortably housed ashore with families and friends, suggested to the frustrated Hiram Bingham that perhaps, because they were Americans, and the fact that Kamehameha II believed his nation to be under British protectorate, might be prime reason for royal hesitance. America was only now emerging from war with Britain. The king would not want to offend Captain Vancouver, or the nation from which Hawaiians had copied their flag.

Back came Bingham to nag the king. He read the bored and surfeited Liholiho the instructions from the American Congregational Board of Missions as to their policy of absolute non-interference in matters of state. He frantically pledged to the monarch and his chiefs that sole interest of the movement was to preach the word of God; teach the people to read; to instruct them in a better and happier life. Liholiho proceeded to compound the frustration by ordering John Young to write King George, in England, as to how might the British monarch feel about American missionaries living and working in the islands.

Reverend Bingham, utterly crushed and discouraged at the possibility of living months aboard the *Thaddeus* while English King George pondered issues in an island nation on the other side of the world, tried every device possible to win friendship and support. As last resort he invited Liholiho and his wives to come aboard the *Thaddeus*, to dine with the missionaries and their women, to learn firsthand the type of people who so frantically and persistently begged permission to live and work in his beautiful land. Liholiho, surprisingly and willingly, accepted the invitation.

So, late afternoon of April 6, the great royal canoe put off from shore, bearing the king, five wives, high chief Kalanimoku, and the retinue of servants so continuously necessary to the wellbeing of Alii. Again, among the sanctimonious Christians, came that worrisome matter of clothing. It seemed, to the missionaries, that even among noble Hawaiians, instead of dressing for dinner, they undressed.

When the mighty king stepped on deck, he came—as Mrs. Thurston, wife of one of the reverends recorded it—"entirely destitute of hat, shoes, stockings, pants and gloves." But the yellow *malo*, the girdle of green silk passing under his left arm and knotted over the right shoulder, the sea ivory *lei niho palaloa* hung about his corded neck by a solid gold chain, and the wreath of yellow feathers, needed no regal additions to mark him the highest and most revered man in the land.

High Chief Kalanimoku had again pinched himself into European garb, much to the relief of the pious Americans. And this time the island's royal and highborn wives respected the unbelievably harsh tabus of the white visitors by showing up in vividly hued costumes of Chinese silk, modeled vaguely after the creation worn off the ship by Queen Kalakua.

It was painfully evident the king had over-indulged in ardent spirits before leaving his palace. But his tippling had mellowed his austerity; had rendered him a graciousness and tolerance new to Hiram Bingham and the brethren. The dinner, served on deck, through the combined efforts of the ship's galley and the mission wives, passed off most agreeably. The huge Hawaiian women stared and smiled incessantly at the skinny and sad-faced wives who were striving so desperately to serve them in the lavish manner of the Alii. The talk, cordially and happily toned, took constant effort of Billy Pitt to bridge the conversational gap between the races. After the dinner the royal guests were entertained by Protestant hymns sung with strength and feeling by the New Englanders.

Having learned the hazards of discussing business with Hawaiians during the festive times—eating, dancing or singing—Hiram Bingham forced himself to remain silent on the desperate and compulsive issues. The king rewarded this thoughtfulness by taking leave of the ship with the most gracious and polite of alohas, and an invitation for the missionaries and their wives to dine with the royal family at the palace on the morrow.

Bingham knew, as he retired, that silence had been his best ally.

*   *   *   *   *

When the missionaries, and especially the American women, went ashore next day, they were greeted most curiously by the natives who had assembled on the beach to view the longnecks and their black-garbed husbands being escorted to the royal dwelling. Native fingers touched, pinched and rubbed the strange dresses that covered most of the missionary women's bodies. What little of pale American flesh that stood exposed was fingered to ascertain if indeed it were real.

The pinched waists, and sedulous hiding of the human anatomy, prompted many Hawaiian women to explore, and to ask if the long-necks actually possessed mammary appurtenances and generative organs. Certainly these were the strangest creatures ever to set foot on the island. But it was the friendliest sort of search and scrutiny. The American women realized they were being welcomed. And the missionary party reached the palace without being driven to hysterics by the curiosity of their audience.

The dinner was lavish—fish, pork, poi, yams. There were coconuts, fresh sliced, and in delicate and tasty pudding. The king and his family were most cordial and gracious. And the American women got their first view of the lewd and hip-waving movements of the hula, as it was danced to drums and chant by both women and men. Evil as the hula appeared to be, it was accepted in the spirit and frame of what it was intended, a touch of joyful hospitality by their host.

But Hiram Bingham, by now grown desperate, grasped any moment possible to reaffirm his request for permission to land his people. "If we are allowed in your country," he promised, "we will teach you and your people to read and write. You shall have this skill—as do people from other lands."

"Let me see you write my name," Liholiho demanded.

This Bingham proceeded to do. He handed the piece of paper, upon which he had penciled "Liholiho—Kamehameha II," to the king.

Liholiho studied the writing. He turned it in every direction for scrutiny. Finally he handed it back to Bingham.

"It looks not like myself," he said. "Nor does it look like any other man."

With that he dismissed the matter. A moment later, he dismissed his guests.

Sad faced, utterly discouraged, the missionary party returned to the ship. Every effort had been rebuffed. No progress had been made.

They no longer could endure living in the cramped quarters of the *Thaddeus*. Neither could they, in honor, return to America in complete defeat. And as the days lay upon them in heat and despair, Captain Blanchard commenced pressing for a termination of the maritime contract. He wanted to get on to Honolulu, to dump his passengers, to reload with more profitable cargo. He was insistent the missionaries disembark—with or without royal approval.

Fortunately, on April 10, Queen Kaahumanu suddenly arrived in Kailua after her prolonged sea excursion. The welcoming celebration tendered the great woman was especially lavish and colorful. The queen's feast was spread in the grove. The fish was contributed from the queen's catch; the poi from her own taro patches. But the pork, the coconuts, the fruits and vegetables, were tax gifts from the people.

Reverends Bingham and Thurston boldly crashed the party. But their arrival was after the gorging, and the *awa* drinking. It was just as well. By now they were convinced this dowager queen wielded enormous power. They had been told that a decision from her could still drastically affect their destiny in Hawaii. They had prayed before leaving the ship. In faith and hope they brought Hopu along to interpret.

There was no difficulty in locating Kaahumanu. The feast had been cleared away. Mid-center of the grove, at a place of honor alongside the still savory-smelling fire pits, and illuminated by an hundred kukui torches, reclined the most regal and distinguished woman of them all. Smoking an English pipe, indolently reclining on her enormous lauhala mat, was Kaahumanu, favorite bedmate of Kamehameha. More important, as *kuhina-nui*, she was the confirmed and acknowledged prime minister of the empire which Kamehameha, greatest warrior king in Polynesian history, had spent a lifetime putting together.

Her ample hips were wrapped in a *pa'u* of royal yellow satin. Her silken *kihei* of purple was flung casually enough over her shoulders so as to reveal the enormous and symmetrical breasts that were the envy of Hawaii's women. From her neck, and between the nippled mounds, hung the royal *lei niho palaoa*. Her black hair and pleasantly appealing face were crowned with a coronet of yellow feathers. Her features were imperious, even at rest.

Around her swarmed the personal servants—wiping her brow, scratching her back, bringing food to match her every whim that might have followed an already enormous meal. The missionaries were quick to note that the people fawned over Kamehameha's queen with as much devotion as they tendered Kamehameha's son. There was no question but what this royal and favored matriarch could help them—if only she could be persuaded. A good look at Kaahumanu, and they took new heart.

Her attendants announced their presence. But Kaahumanu was not yet in the mood for talk. For hours they had to sit through the greatest display of chanting and hula dancing they had ever witnessed. The performers came on like a disciplined army. Row upon row of beautiful white-teethed, flower-haired maidens, conically breasted, their swaying hips draped in the wide leaves of the ti plant. The male dancers wore nothing but scanty *malos* to hide their nakedness. The only other piece of male attire were anklets of dog teeth which clicked and clattered with the clapping hands, as the chants and earth-pounding went on in increasing frenzy.

More and more dancers appeared, the chanting increased in volume, until it seemed that everyone in Kailua had share in the orgy. Occasional bursts of music, nose flutes and in high male falsetto, added a barbaric and hypnotic effect. None of this was lost on the two missionaries as they waited on the pleasure of this spoiled and autocratic woman. Hopu alone seemed to enjoy it.

The Americans were exhausted and disturbed by the time Kaahumanu finally beckoned them to her. The lip-scourging that followed taxed the frightened Hopu's linguistic abilities, and drove out the last desperate hope. "Hawaiians are finished with gods and god worship," the queen declared. "Their temples have been destroyed. No longer do our people bow and grovel before the gods. Because the gods oppress, enslave, and sadden, Hawaiians want no more of them. Americans must not bring this sort of thing back to the islands."

Bingham frantically tried another tack with the imperious woman. Patiently, and calmly as possible, he explained the learning they intended to give the people; that they were qualified and most anxious to teach Hawaiians to read and write. On this point alone was Kaahumanu vulnerable. From the beginning she had envied the foreigners in these skills. She was quick to concede that learning was a good thing. But no more worship, and no more religious tabus must come to Hawaii. With that decree, she abruptly dismissed the missionaries.

In final despair the two men sought out John Young. This wise and seasoned Englishman, noting their crestfallen mien, suggested that they cease striving for permanent residence. "The British, whom the king respects, and looks for guidance, might not allow your mission. Neither Liholiho nor Kaahumanu, after last year's war against the gods, are prepared or anxious to allow another religion. Your learning, they respect. Book learning, they deeply desire. Your Dr. Holman is already doing much good. He has been treating the sick here in Kailua in a manner different and superior to the kahunas. My suggestion is that, instead of pleading for permanent residence, that you ask only for a year's trial."

Next day the two Americans were back at the palace. John Young, as interpreter and advocate, appeared with them. From royal spies Liholiho already had learned of Bingham's and Thurston's visit to Kaahumanu. Young told the king about Dr. Holman's unselfish efforts as a physician. And it was Young who made the suggestion for a year's trial.

With graciousness and good humor, apparently anxious for any reasonable solution to the impasse brought on by the nagging foreigners, Liholiho readily and unhesitatingly agreed to a year of probation. He warned the missionaries, however, against seeking power by establishment of religious kapus; that any meddling with the king's rights and prerogatives would earn them instant eviction from the kingdom. And, under no circumstances, were other shiploads of missionaries to join them.

But, when Bingham made the suggestion that their Christian colony might better be planted at the growing city of Honolulu, instead of Kailua—and it was translated by John Young—His Majesty's temper flared.

"How is it that all foreigners want to live at Honolulu? I think you foreigners want to *take* Oahu! You will stay at Kailua. You will remain here—where I can watch."

Young next asked for assignment of grass houses for the missionaries. Grudgingly the king offered one large house. After Young explained that even a large house was much too small for a shipload of visitors, the king finally agreed that *some* of the Americans might go to Oahu on the *Thaddeus*. But Dr. Holman, especially, must remain at Kailua. The doctor must keep his medicines and instruments at Kailua. It was decided that Reverend Thurston and his family would remain with the Holmans.

Hiram Bingham, by persistence, had won for the Lord.

At last the *Thaddeus*, with the remaining missionaries, and all the printing equipment, set sail for Honolulu. They had gained the king's permission to open up the first Christian penetration of the Hawaiian Islands.

Had Liholiho possessed the hardness of his father, the prescience of his star-gazers and kahunas, or had he conferred more closely with Kaahumanu, he would have sent the *Thaddeus* back to Boston with its missionaries still aboard. At the very least he would have done better to have kept them under his thumb at Kailua.

It would later be said that the missionaries brought the word of God to the islands of Hawaii. And in the end, the Hawaiians would have the word of God—but the missionaries would have the islands.

V

LIHOLIHO had no opportunity to deal with the other foreign incursions into his domain as thoroughly as he had dealt with the missionaries aboard the *Thaddeus*. It wouldn't have mattered—the results were to be the same. And eventually just as tragic.

To seafarers the Sandwich Islands were strategic—the most important landfall in the wide Pacific. Within three years after the young king came to power, ships by the hundreds were porting in at Hono-

MISSIONARY, AT KAILUA, PREACHING UNDER SCREEN OF PLAITED COCONUT LEAVES

lulu, Lahaina, and Hilo. All of them had trade goods. All of them needed supplies and water. All of them had crews grown horny by months at sea, and anxious for all that Hawaii could offer in exchange for their silver. Liholiho's kingdom was both enriched and debauched.

Kailua, on the Kona coast, dear to Hawaiians because the sea around it yielded wondrously in fish and shellfood, had little to offer visiting ships, either in water, trade advantages, or ready-yielding cargoes. As had been rumored, Liholiho soon found it necessary, because of foreign pressures, to move his capital to the busier port of Lahaina, on the island of Maui. More and more, because of the insatiable hunger for foreign luxuries, did the Alii court these visitors from other lands.

When the ship captains had first begun coveting sandalwood as China-bound cargo, Kamehameha the Great had put royal kapu on every tree. Sandalwood was acknowledged as the king's possession. It was his alone to sell. When, at the Kawaihae council, Liholiho granted permission to the high chiefs to share this royal monopoly, he had made as grave a mistake as he'd later done in listening to the persuasion of Hiram Bingham.

Now the chiefs were enriching themselves—but at the cost of virtual slavery of their vassals in cutting and hauling the fragrant wood to fill the visiting ships at Lahaina, Honolulu and Hilo. Unused to physical abuse and hard labor, the natives were dying by the thousands. The strength of the nation was perishing, that chiefs and their harems might wear the silks out of China, and furnish their grass dwellings with the luxuries from other lands. Syphilis, measles, smallpox and tuberculosis—never before known to the islands, and to which the people had no natural immunity—had come with the ships and their sailors. Sickness and death already were ravaging the villages.

For the Alii these were the greatest of times. For the common souls, no longer even permitted to worship their gods, it was a decade of heartbreak and trouble.

Liholiho's new court at Lahaina became a lavish one. His feasts and debaucheries were on a scale never before known. Enterprising Yankee traders had built a ship in New England, gaudy and luxurious enough to satisfy even the critical eyes of this profligate king. They had named her, at launching, *Cleopatra's Barge*. The lovely brig was sailed around the Horn to Lahaina. Heeding the compulsion in his blood, seeded there by an ancestry of the world's boldest navigators, Liholiho promptly bought the vessel for ninety thousand dollars, payable in sandalwood. He named his ship the *Ha'aho o Hawaii* (Pride of Hawaii). But to the knowledgable haoles she was forever known as *Cleopatra's Barge*.

This ship became the scene of Liholiho's diversions; the royal quarters for feasting, for drinking, for debauchery. She was his traveling headquarters from port to port. When Liholiho moved his capital from Lahaina to Honolulu in 1821, *Cleopatra's Barge* transported the royal household to Oahu. He had traded his grass palace for a mansion afloat.

The young king had .abundant reasons to flee from land. Constant harassment by favor-seeking haoles, endless squabbles of grafting chiefs and governors, the usurpation of his rights by the haughty and imperious Kaahumanu, all conspired to make his court a nightmare of pressure and intrigue. His domestic household, which included five wives, numerous relatives and friends, children, foster children, concubines, and the army of servants and retainers necessary to wait on them, had grown into a problem that took a lot of sandalwood and ship cargoes to maintain.

When Keopuolani, his majestic mother, or his polygamous stepmother Kaahumanu, paid state visit, each brought along their new polyandric husbands, scores of retainers, and their own hangers-on. Liholiho often had to daily feed a household numbering as high as half a thousand mouths. Alii, as part of their prerogatives, were chronic visitors. The only peace for the king was to escape from the tumult.

Cleopatra's Barge, the floating palace, became Liholiho's haven away from home. Aboard it he staged his monumental carousals with chosen and convivial companions. Since, like the great Kamehameha, he had only one chosen and endless love, he often included the favored wife—beautiful Kamamalu. That she was also his half-sister was no onus among the Alii. She was his favorite. He loved her. In his household and affairs of state, Kamamalu occupied the same exalted place as had Kaahumanu in the affairs of Kamehameha the Great.

But while the Alii prospered, the kingdom rotted. And Liholiho knew it. To cope with the haole incursions, he hired haoles. The Christian missionaries, now firmly established at Kailua, and with schools and printing plant operating at Honolulu, had offered constantly to teach the king to read and write. Liholiho would have liked that, but he had no time. Instead he hired secretaries, such as the Frenchman John Rives. John Rives [known to the Hawaiians as Ioane Luwahine] handled the king's letters. And, more especially, he wrote and published the king's proclamations.

The whaling ships had discovered Honolulu and Lahaina. These, with the trans-Pacific merchantmen, had turned Hawaiian ports into brothels and hubs of lawlessness. When their hundreds of crewmen were turned upon the once green and lovely towns, the communities became bedlams of licentiousness and drunkenness. Liholiho ordered Rives to post the seaports with warnings of imprisonment to law-breaking haoles, and up to death for native Hawaiians who aided and abetted the corruption. It was a brave attempt, but it had little or no effect upon a condition that already was eating like a cancer at the nation.

Discovery of sperm whales off the coast of Chile in 1791, by a six-ship American fleet abandoning the over-hunted Atlantic, opened the vast Pacific to the long ranging predators upon these prized mammals of the sea. When Chilean waters became overcrowded by New England whalers, the fleets, in 1819, moved on to the equatorial waters bordering Peru. In 1820 American whalers were combing the waters off Japan, and a little later the seabanks of the Pacific Northwest. When the really lush hunting grounds of the Arctic were opened up, the entire Pacific became the whalers' sea—south to Australia, west from North America to the waters of the Orient—with the Hawaiian Islands mid-center hub of the wheel—the one imperative port of call to rest, un-limber, and provision ships that spent years on single voyages out of New England.

In 1819, the year that Liholiho gained his crown, only an occasional British whaleship, up from Australian waters, touched at Hono-lulu. In that climactic year the American whalers *Balena* and *Equator*, out of New Bedford, put into Kealakekua Bay, and took the first whale out of Hawaiian waters. When whales were discovered peacefully swimming the Lahaina roadstead, the American whaleships swarmed upon Liholiho's kingdom in ever-increasing numbers.

Twice a year the whalers hit Hawaii. The effect was staggering. In March and April these lonely prowlers of the deep crowded Hono-lulu harbor, and the quieter and more protected waters of Lahaina roadstead—prior to their long sailings to the northern and Arctic hunting grounds. In October and November they were back, to pause before pursuing the whales south into equatorial waters.

Four-fifths of these ships were out of New England. They courted royal favors, and they corrupted chiefs and the people. But the breed of men they ejected to the towns and beaches of Hawaii were a lot different from the black-garbed missionaries of New England's *Thaddeus*. Bringing no women with them—long-necked or otherwise—they preyed upon island females with the same eagerness and tenacity they hunted their whales.

The hundreds of trade ships now leeched the kingdom of its fragrant sandalwood, its vital food supplies, and everything they could exchange in cargo for sustenance, Alii aggrandizement, human virtue, and whiskey. Surreptitious purveyance of the king's land had become a major problem, and Liholiho's concern. Enslavement of a once free people to supply the endless demands for sandalwood and foodstuffs was another fearsome specter. Epidemics of new diseases, never before known, and for which Hawaiians had no immunity, were destroying the people just as surely and viciously as were the avaricious petty chiefs for their own enrichment.

Now the Christians, without heed to probation or royal decree, were spreading their strange doctrine among the oppressed, sick, and unhappy natives on Oahu, Maui, and the king's own island of Hawaii. In spite of Hiram Bingham's pledge, other missionaries out of New England were joining the original flock, and adding strength and voice to their teachings and preachings among the populace.

Liholiho, sensitive to the awesome storm now blowing across his islands, blamed himself when reprisals against the seduced lesser chiefs, and the Christians, had no effect upon the catastrophic forces now loosed upon the nation.

In their efforts to educate the Hawaiians, the missionaries and their longnecks were consistent to their promise—even though the learning was purveyed with Christian bias. In the *palapala*, or the training to read and write, these patient and persistent Americans proved immune to opposition, and truly dedicated. Bingham, his assistant pastors, and Elisha Loomis and his printing plant at Honolulu, were studiously and doggedly at work in the enormous task of reducing the vocal chaos of the Hawaiian language into a twelve-letter alphabet of five vowels and seven consonants. In the assemblage of Polynesian talk into words and phrases the characteristic glottal stops had to be acknowledged, without any visible delineation. The work was slow. It was years before the first Hawaiian primers and spellers finally came from Honolulu's Christian press.

But the English language the persistent missionaries already had. Their ability to teach it to the intelligent and quick-witted natives made the same phenomenal progress as did their evangelization of the islands. The Alii, anxious for the *palapala*, quickly enrolled themselves in the special classes of the Christian teachers. As bereft of god-worship as the most humble of their charges, they ignored the ban Liholiho had hoped to enforce, learned English, read the Scriptures, and joined the Congregational Church. They talked now in the name of Jesus, and to the glory of the new God.

High Chief Kalanimoku had already given Christianization an early start when, aboard the French warship *L'Uranie*, captained by Louis de Freycinet, he had taken baptism from its chaplain. It was natural that Billy Pitt, already at least partly Christian, would throw his influence at court on the side of Hiram Bingham and the missionaries during the protracted negotiations for right to land. And certainly, once the missions were established, he slowed the royal hand against their removal.

Queen Keopuolani, mother of Liholiho, and the highest born wife of Kamehameha the Great, was first of the royal household to embrace the new faith. Loyally the great woman studied the *palapala* under direction of Mrs. Thurston. She learned of the one true God, the Savior Jesus, and was baptized by the Thurstons into Christianity. That the queen prided herself in the two new husbands she had acquired since Kamehameha's death did not stay her acceptance as a Congregational-ist. Polyandry, of course, was frowned upon by the strait-laced Americans, but since Keopuolani was so universally loved by the populace, and her example would have profound effect upon the Christian cause, the Lord generously allowed her plenty of time to shed her excess mates. And Keopuolani took plenty of time in doing it.

Liholiho's own queen, the beautiful and talented Kamamalu, had become enamored of the sect. Though she submitted herself to the rigors of the *palapala*, she respected His Majesty enough not to go all the way to conversion. As to Kaahumanu, co-ruler of the kingdom, it would be a long time before she allowed herself to be counted for the cause of Christ. But the Bible classes became so popular with the Alii that there was little time or opportunity left for the commoners. Christians truly had become a force within the islands.

Compared to the avaricious onslaughts of the other visitors, the missionaries seemed the least of the threats. In turn, the missionaries were appalled by the irresponsibility of the high chiefs, including the king, toward the increasing oppression of the common people. Alii were living in material glory. But their once happy and contented serfs were suddenly existing in squalid misery. Overtaxed, overworked, and ill with strange diseases, they were ripe for the divine harvest.

But the king and his higher counselors were sadly aware that the nation was being badly served. Haole influence was worse than any storm or trouble ever before known. Honey-tongued when seeking advantage, the haoles were hard and avaricious once they acquired influence and power. The Hawaiians—trusting, open-handed, and generous—were falling fast prey before a smart and educated estab-lishment against which even the cautious and sensitive Liholiho seemed powerless to cope. He tried his best to govern his seething and ferment-ing land—first from Maui, and then from Oahu. In frustration he would put to sea in *Cleopatra's Barge*, to court wisdom in vast silence, or to drink himself to the stupors with haole spirits.

Always he remembered the great Englishmen. They had handled problems with ease. Their advice was always helpful; always right.

They had materially aided in awakening his nation. They had offered to protect it in times of stress.

Liholiho was too young to remember the great Captain Cook, who, first thought to be a god, had perished in a fluke of misunderstanding. But his father remembered him. His father had been deeply and personally involved with that other great Englishman, Captain Vancouver, in his numerous visits. Vancouver had taught things to Kamehameha that had made him immortally great. Vancouver had brought animals, plants, and new and superior ways of doing things. The flag of Kamehameha's nation was copy of the British union jack. Liholiho had always been convinced his nation was a military protectorate of Great Britain.

His great need was to study the haoles in their own lands—the better to equate and cope with them in his own kingdom. The mighty empire of Britain was accepted as the kindly protector of his own troubled nation. It was the one source that could steady, guide and teach a groping young monarch.

In 1823, the fourth year of Liholiho's reign, he made the decision.

*   *   *   *   *

It was November 27, 1823 when King Liholiho and his royal party boarded the English whaleship *L'Aigle* at Honolulu. Its captain, Valentine Starbuck, was not unaware of the distinguished passengers he was carrying back to England. It was choice of his vessel that had come as Starbuck's surprise. He could only hope that a ship whose holds were filled with sperm oil would not prove too offensive to a king of all the islands.

Starbuck, in deference to distinguished passengers, made his deckhands clean and tidy up ship; to scrub her down from stem to stern. The fastidious Liholiho would have much preferred a trim warship of British registry, but the *L'Aigle* was the only craft England-bound at this crucial time. Most of the vessels in port were American. It was London he wanted and needed—not New York or Boston. Liholiho was adamant—his conference must be with none other than King George IV. Noisy, crafty Americans had no king. The *L'Aigle,* unlike American whalers, had cabins spacious enough for the royal party. Though headed around Cape Horn, by way of Valparaiso, it would not touch

 CHRISTIAN SERMON BENEATH THE KUKUI TREES, KAUAI
From a drawing by A. T. Agate.

—Bernice P. Bishop Museum, Honolulu.

at the ports from whence came the Americans. Its voyage, answering a fundamental and ancestral sea-call to Liholiho, was to England.

The missionaries, joined by an Englishman—Reverend William Ellis, who had been laboring with the Tahitian Polynesians, and had briefly joined forces with the American evangelists in Hawaii—had written letters of introduction and approbation to ease Liholiho's problems in the little known lands of the haoles. Graciously Bingham had also explained in writing that Liholiho's state visit was culmination of the young king's desire "to gain information, political and commercial, to gratify curiosity, to achieve by the tour something great in his own estimation, & eventually to increase his wealth & power . . . He desires to have an interview with the king & court of England, to obtain some advice, & perhaps assistance, to enable him the better to govern his own people & to maintain a better regulated intercourse with foreigners who visit or reside in his islands."

The trip, however, scheduled earlier and by better ship, had been forced into postponement by the unexpected death, in September, of queen mother Keopuolani. The great woman had died on the island of Maui. The royal funeral at Lahaina had been one of wailing and Polynesian excess, but, since Her Majesty had expired in the Christian faith, the mission there had somehow held the national mourning down to the bounds of decorum. Even though Keopuolani was a woman much beloved, and her mana exceeded anything known by the Alii, there had been no human sacrifice, no teeth-knocking, no fleshly disfigurement to prove one's grief. American missionaries had walked in the procession. Liholiho had allowed them to say their prayers. They had been free to preach their eulogies in the haole way.

But national and personal mourning had prevented Liholiho's departure until the barren month of November. In matters of state, the king had appointed his ten-year-old brother Kauikeaouli to succeed him in the event of his death abroad. Dowager Queen Kaahumanu was named as regent in his absence—in addition to her rights and duties as *kuhina-nui*. If anyone could keep the haoles and sub-chiefs in line, it would be Her Imperious Majesty.

When the *L'Aigle* sailed out of Honolulu harbor on November 27, 1823, the royal party included Liholiho; his most favored wife Kamamalu; Chief Boki, governor of Oahu and his favorite wife Liliha; Chiefs Kekuanoa, Kapihe, Manuia, and John Young Kanehoa, son of John Young. Included were a few personal servants, Liholiho's trusted secretary and interpreter, the facile and clever Frenchman John Rives, and a chest filled with haole gold coins. The *L'Aigle*, with its limited quarters could not accommodate royalty on the scale of anything comparable to that of *Cleopatra's Barge*, but the farewell was lavish enough to satisfy even Liholiho's obsession with theatrics and opulence.

From everywhere in the islands came the chiefs and the Alii to say aloha to their young king, and to sing the praises of one who dared voyage into the unknown. They were joined by everyone in Honolulu—native and foreign, godless and missionaries—and half the population of Oahu.

Queen Kamamalu who, besides beauty, had inherited the royal family's extraordinary gift for poetic expression, cried out to the assembled multitude, before she stepped from shore. The cadent verse was her own:

"Ye skies, ye plains, ye mountains and great sea,
　Ye toilers, ye people of the soil, my love embraces you,
　To this soil, farewell!
　Yea, land for whose sake my father was eaten by deep
　　　deep sorrow—farewell! alas! farewell!"

The crowd, already emotion charged, were quick to catch the deathly significance of this valediction. There were cries of grief when their beautiful queen touched on Kamehameha—her father—and the king's father:

"We both forsake the object of thy toil.
　I go according to thy command:
　Never will I disregard thy voice.
　I travel with thy dying charge,
　Which thou didst address to me."

When the young king and his comely and talented mate stepped aboard the British ship, it was the last their people ever saw of them.

VI

It was May 18, 1824 before the *L'Aigle* had wallowed her way through Pacific waters, rounded Cape Horn, crossed the Atlantic, and had discharged her weary travelers, along with the cargo of whale oil, at the safe harbor of Portsmouth, England. Captain Valentine Starbuck personally conducted the royal party to London.

The British government was caught by surprise. But quickly as the master of the *L'Aigle* announced the presence of the distinguished visitors from Polynesia, it responded with the traditional high tact and courtesy reserved for royal visitors from other parts of the world. The Hawaiians were lodged at the fashionable Osborne Hotel. The Honorable Frederick Byng, of the foreign office, was appointed to extend them all courtesy; to attend their every want.

When Liholiho dug into his chest of gold coins, to outfit his Hawaiian delegation with London's more fashionable apparel, it was discovered that his treasure had mysteriously shrunken to less than half the twenty-five-thousand dollars worth of gold he'd carried out of Honolulu. Suspecting both Rives and Starbuck for the chicanery, he did the best he could with what he had. Certainly no more stately and distinguished king had ever visited England's shores; no more beautiful queen than the almond-skinned and black-haired Kamamalu, and no more lovely consort than Liliha, Boki's dusky, vivacious, teen-age child-wife.

Liholiho and Kamamalu were excited and entranced with London's theaters. In every visit, including the one to Drury Lane's Theatre Royale, they occupied the royal boxes as special courtesy of His Majesty's government. Britishers ogled the dark and stately visitors. Distinguished painters did their portraits. Newspapers took special heed of their presence in London. Popularity rose with their every public appearance.

The Honorable Mr. Canning, Secretary of State for Foreign Affairs, fully aware of the strategic importance of the Sandwich Islands to the affairs of empire, held a state reception in their honor. He and Mr. Byng, cognizant of the hopes and wishes of Liholiho, made arrangements at Windsor Palace for the all-important audience with King George. In preparation for the event the two diplomats patiently coached the exotic novitiates in the manners and protocol necessary for an effective presentation.

But before this most essential audience with King George could be consummated, measles struck the Hawaiian party. Among the first victims were Liholiho and Kamamalu. The lovely Hawaiian queen was helpless before the haole disease. She, like any and all of her people, had no generations-old resistance to the white man's malady. The fever blazed rapidly into pneumonia. In gracious response to the plight of the visitors, King George sent his personal physician to minister to the stricken Hawaiians.

As to Queen Kamamalu, the case, from the start, was hopeless. On July 8, 1824 she was dead. The bedridden Liholiho, wild with grief from this sudden loss, grew weaker and less voluble by the hour. With constant murmur of his beloved queen's name, he lapsed into coma. Liholiho died on July 14. He was never able to present his case, nor plead his cause, before the British government.

QUEEN KAMAMALU IN LONDON, 1824
British lithograph by John Hayter.

HIGH CHIEF BOKI, GOVERNOR OF OAHU,
AND HIS YOUNG WIFE, LILIHA
Lithograph by John Hayter during their London visit.
—*Bernice P. Bishop Museum, Honolulu.*

118

With the death of Liholiho, Chief Boki, as governor of Oahu, took over leadership of the ailing delegation. The Osborne Hotel rang strangely with the wailing cries of Hawaiian mourning, and Boki and a couple of the chiefs each knocked out a tooth. The bodies of the king and queen of Hawaii, instead of the traditional severing of bones from the flesh, were sealed into sturdy British caskets, and placed in the holding vaults at St. Martin's Church. Mourning howls eventually ceased from sheer exhaustion, but the summer was gone, and it was September 11 before the remaining weak and sickly Hawaiians could be presented before England's king.

By then most of the royal gold had either been spent or had surreptitiously disappeared. There had been a lot of fighting along with the mourning—between Boki and the confidants and retainers of Liholiho and his family. One casualty was John Rives, the Frenchman secretary and interpreter. There was no other choice than to "expel" Rives from the delegation. John Young just as adequately and effectively substituted in the role of linguist.

In the brilliant and sympathetic manner England's foreign secretary Canning presented the Hawaiian case before his office and the king, there was really little need for the services of Rives. King George asked Boki to explain to his court and government the reason for the royal Hawaiian visit. "We have come to confirm the words which Kamehameha I gave in charge to Vancouver," Boki declared, with Young's interpretation. "Our great king told Vancouver, 'Go back and tell King George to watch over me and my whole kingdom. I acknowledge him as my landlord and myself as tenant . . . Should the foreigners of any other nation come to take possession of my lands, then let them help me.'"

King George, listening attentively, gave his own answer to Boki's appeal. "I will attend to the evils from without," he promised. "The evils within your kingdom are not for me to regard: they are with yourselves. Return and say to your new King Kauikeaouli—to Kaahumanu, and to Kalanimoku—that I will watch over your country. I will not take possession of it . . . but I will watch over it, lest evils should come from others to the kingdom. I am agreeable to those ancient words."

Subsequent events proved that the British sovereign's comforting and high-sounding talk to the saddened and shattered Hawaiian delegation was not just diplomatic rhetoric. Within two weeks Captain Richard Charlton, who had cruised the Pacific islands in the continuing British naval penetration which had begun with Cook's and Vancouver's voyages, was appointed British consul for "the Sandwich, Society, and Friendly Islands." Charlton's acquaintance with Liholiho

HAWAIIAN ROYALTY VISITS A LONDON THEATER
A "done from life" drawing by J. W. Gear depicts Liholiho,
Kamamalu, Liliha, and other members of the royal party at
Drury Lane's Theatre Royale.

—Bernice P. Bishop Museum, Honolulu.

had been renewed in London only weeks before the king's death. At that visit Liholiho had made promise to the friendly Britisher of land upon which to reside, should Charlton decide to return to the islands either as private citizen or in governmental capacity. The British foreign office, with Charlton's appointment, moved quickly into the advantage.

It was the fate of Liholiho to have visited England at a time when British commercial interests were looking to the Pacific islands for expansion of their worldwide trade. The voyages of Cook and Vancouver had been published and widely read. England, ever alert to every possibility for trade, had been intrigued and impressed by the glowing praise these discoverers had centered upon the beauty and untapped resources of the Pacific archipelago they arbitrarily had named as the Sandwich Islands.

Nor had the British government been blind to the fact that France, Russia, and the United States were equally impressed, and similarly disposed. These nations had all made official and unofficial penetration of the islands. Their lust and push had been one of Liholiho's greatest concerns; one of the prime causes for his London visit. The posthumous appeal to King George IV proved as effective as though Liholiho had been alive to deliver it.

At Secretary Canning's suggestion the king ordered that the Hawaiians be returned to their native land with honor worthy of a great sovereign. The *Blonde,* a forty-six gun naval frigate, was to voyage to the Sandwich Islands. The ship was to be captained by Lord Byron (the Right Honorable George Anson, Lord Byron, R.N.). The poet Byron had died only a few months previous to Liholiho's tragic demise, and the title had passed to his cousin, now in service to His Majesty. Lord Byron, and the *Blonde,* were to convey the Hawaiians and their dead rulers back home.

The royal coffins, rich and splendid boxes, were removed from the vaults of St. Martin's. They were conveyed with military escort to Portsmouth, where they were ceremoniously placed aboard the British man-of-war. The Hawaiian delegation, including Boki and Liliha, but minus the Frenchman Rives, were escorted with regal pomp to the ship that would be their sea home for the long voyage.

The *Blonde* was a step above Starbuck's *L'Aigle.* Liholiho, who had possessed a compulsive love for ostentation, would have approved of this method of conveyance. The ship's quarters were as beautifully appointed and as comfortable as those on *Cleopatra's Barge.* Had he lived, Kamehameha II would have enjoyed the naval honors rendered by the most powerful nation on earth to a monarch on visit to the realm. Unfortunately he and his lovely Kamamalu were below deck in the dark boxes.

Liholiho's ten-year-old brother Kauikeaouli was now king of all Hawaii. The dead monarch would never know of the secret instructions Lord Byron was carrying to the homeland. "You will be apprized of the position in which these Islands stand with regard to the Crown of Great Britain, and that His Majesty [King George IV] might claim over them a right of sovereignty not only by discovery, but by a direct and formal Cession by the Natives, and by the virtual acknowledgment of the Officers of Foreign Powers.

"This right His Majesty does not think it necessary to advance directly in opposition to, or in control of, any native Authority;—with such the question should not be raised, and, if proposed, had better be evaded, . . . but if any Foreign Power or its Agents should attempt, or have attempted, to establish any Sovereignty or possession . . . you are then to assert the prior rights of His Majesty, but in such a manner as may leave untouched the actual relations between His Majesty and the Government of the Sandwich Islands; and if by circumstances you should be obliged to come to a specific declaration, you are to take the Islands under His Majesty's protection, and to deny the rights of any other Power to assume any Sovereignty, or to make any exclusive settlement in any of that group."

The dead Liholiho had gotten from Britain all he had traveled so far to obtain. He was never to know that Lord Byron, commanding the stately ship winging him homeward, carried the secret right to a lot more than he had bargained for.

PART THREE

Kamehameha III and the Meddlesome Matriarch

I

ROVISION of an extra husband or two for the plural wives of a king was called the *punalua*, and was an institution understood and accepted by all loyal subjects under the Hawaiian monarchy. Kamehameha the Great had never been fussy or concerned about the *punalua* in his own harem—providing the custom was kept imperiously out of reach of the two queens who ranked vitally important to his life. Out of twenty-one wives, nineteen of them could dawdle sexually with other men free of the wrath of a jealous king. Keopuolani, the flowered embodiment of spiritual mana, the mother of royal heirs, had been kept sacrosanct. She was Hawaii's queen bee, hived in worshipful, luxurious seclusion. Not until the bones of Kamehameha were sacked, did Keopuolani recoup her loss to male redundancy—by immediately embracing polyandry.

Kaahumanu, the conqueror's one great love life, enjoyed men. She wanted men—to the point of being a royal problem. This queen was a regal, handsome woman, in the magnificent pattern accepted and appreciated by Hawaiians. Samuel Kamakau, Alii scholar and historian, described her as "Six feet tall, straight and well formed without blemish, and comely. Her arms were like the inside of a banana stalk, her fingers tapering, her palms pliable like the *kukunena* grass, graceful in repose. Her cheeks, long in shape and pink as the bud of a banana stem; her eyes like that of a dove; her nose narrow and straight, in admirable proportion to her cheeks; her arched eyebrows shaped to the breadth of her forehead; her hair dark, wavy and fine; her skin very light." Vancouver described her as "one of the finest women we had yet seen on any of the islands."

This was the great Kamehameha's bundle of passion. But never once did he extend the *punalua* to her. To curb Kaahumanu's romantic escapades with lesser chiefs, he placed a royal kapu upon her. Her body was not to be touched by other men. Punishment for trespass was death.

Important and handsome men, like high chief Kaiana, had found her infinitely worth this lethal risk. Some paid the supreme forfeit for flaunting the royal edict. Always and ever she stood an inviting temptation to anyone bold and reckless enough to risk it. In 1809, when Kamehameha put to death his own nephew, Kanihonui, for committing adultery with Kaahumanu, the queen threw such a monumental rage over her suddenly aborted love affair that she threatened to seize the kingdom from her husband—to give it, by civil war, to young Liholiho, long ahead of his appointed time.

The people knew this queen for what she was. They loved her for it. Her temper, easily aroused, could turn her into a wild animal. She was single-minded in purpose. She was ambitious and intelligent. To her subjects, unless she felt they needed chastisement, she was kind and understanding. She visited their grass dwellings. She romped with their children. She listened to their talk. Faults and virtues—they worshipped her for both.

But after Kamehameha expired, and the priests had hidden his sack of bones, the irksome kapu on Kaahumanu was lifted. By now she was middle-aged, but still a prize. And as *kuhina-nui* to Liholiho, she possessed and wielded awesome power. With the death of the Conqueror, her dark eyes grew hungry once more.

Her most ambitious conquest was that of Kaumualii,* king of the rich and beautiful island of Kauai. In this she accomplished something the great Kamehameha had never been able to do.

Kauai was the only island never put to bloody subjection of the Conqueror, and the only island in the Hawaiian union allowed to retain its autonomy under Kamehameha the Great. It had ridden out Kamehameha's wrath and the certainty of invasion because its handsome and intelligent king considered it wiser to 'join than to fight. At the very time Kamehameha had assembled his mightiest force at Oahu for reduction of this smug little island, King Kaumualii landed at Waikiki with his own lavish and impressive court. Here he had won amnesty and security by diplomatically offering his kingdom to Kamehameha.

The sandalwood trade had begun to enrich both Kamehameha and Kaumualii, and the foreign shippers, knowing that another inter-island war would paralyze their traffic in this lucrative export, were pressuring the holdout king to come to terms before hostilities could commence. They knew, as did Kaumualii, that Kamehameha had assembled an invasion fleet of thirty foreign-built sloops and schooners at Waikiki, and a dozen more, headed by the flagship *Lelia Byrd*, a former American brig of 175 tons. It was Nathan Winship, a shrewd and wise Yankee sea captain, who convinced the king of Kauai that tribute was

*Ka-u-mu-a-li-i: *Kah*-oo-*moo*-ah-lee-ee.

not enough. In 1810, with Winship in the role of mediator, the king and court presented themselves in dignified surrender at Kamehameha's Waikiki palace.

Remembering the fate of Keoua the Younger, Kaumualii had been understandably reluctant at making himself a ready subject for reprisal and death. Without the guidance of Winship, and his promise that American sea captains and crews would stand protectively in his behalf, it is doubtful that the king would ever have set foot on Oahu. But Winship was right in his appraisal of Kamehameha. Pleased at this fortuitous turn in the final and complete union of all the islands, the Conqueror magnanimously rewarded this acknowledgment of his supremacy by allowing Kaumualii to retain his monarchy and island as a fief, subject only to continued loyalty and tribute.

Kaahumanu, who alone of all Kamehameha's queens, shared state functions and was allowed to voice opinions and take part in the king's decisions, was impressed by the opulence, dignity and finesse of the Kauai court. More than anything, it showed the English and American influence. One of the king's sons, Humehume,* was actually being educated in America. But, more than anything, Kaahumanu was fascinated by the handsome and gracious King Kaumualii.

As an Alii, she knew him to be of the highest possible lineage. She knew that the people of Kauai believed their king to be so masculinely beautiful that his very life had been infused by the gods. Fawned upon alike by natives and foreigners, his every move was impressive and sensually exciting. Like all the *Alii-moku*, he possessed a harem, but accompanying him at Oahu was the counterpart to Kaahumanu—a favorite, young, and lately acquired wife. This was the lovely Kapule.* Like her Oahu image she was intelligent, ambitious, and possessed a voice that was heeded by her king. While the men joined in the amenities, these two women haughtily took one another's measure. Even as Kamehameha graciously pledged amnesty and respect to this beautiful royal couple, his favorite queen was subtly making plans for the future.

Up to the death of Kamehameha there was nothing but peace and tribute out of Kauai. Like all other islands in the union, it prospered under the burgeoning ship trade. In face of all the pressures of foreign influence, the king's court at Kauai continued with the gracious pageantry of the old days. Everywhere the name of Kaumualii was praised. Everywhere Kapule was acknowledged with awe and reverence. Kaahumanu had already rated Kapule as political enemy.

After the Conqueror's demise, and for the coronation of Liholiho, King Kaumualii, and his Kauai, sent lavish tribute. But Kaumualii did

*Hu-me-hu-me: *Hoo*-may-*hoo*-may.
*Ka-pu-le: *Kah*-poo-lay.

not journey to the island of Hawaii to share in the ceremonies, nor did he surrender his kingship to the son of Kamehameha the Great.

Worse, after Liholiho had established his capital at Honolulu, there came a letter from the king of Kauai addressed to Kamehameha II as "The King of the Windward Islands." The offensive implications of this salutation were not lost on the new monarch. There was speculation that Humehume [Tamoree], who had returned to the islands on the *Thaddeus,* was resentful of the inferior status of his father as ruler, and had influenced him against Liholiho. Kaahumanu, as *kuhina-nui,* chose to believe that it was the work of Queen Kapule.

The letter had merely annoyed the easy-going Liholiho, but in Kaahumanu it had aroused fierce resentment. She demanded immediate reprisal against Kauai. There must be chastisement for its arrogant rulers. And she never ceased pressuring for the vengeance.

The affair of July 21, 1821 was ostensibly to have been an all-day fishing excursion in the royal twin-hulled canoe. To share the holiday Liholiho had invited Boki, governor of Oahu, the high chief Naihe, and high chiefess Kapiolani. Aboard were thirty others, including attendants and the crew, experienced with sails and paddles. It was a festive, joyous outing—until the craft reached Ewa point. Suddenly the king ordered the crew to head the boat for Kauai. The convivial guests were instantly sobered and shocked at Liholiho's sudden decision to chance sixty miles of open water, and the treacherous Kailiewaho channel, with only a racing craft, and without water, provisions, or navigational instruments.

Voluble and noisy protests were silenced when the headstrong Liholiho threatened to swim for Kauai should the crewmen heed the worries of the guests, and turn back. Since he was king of all the islands, there was nothing to do but accept the theatrics, and continue on. It proved a wet and perilous night, with Liholiho himself chanting the ancient songs to the wide and threatening sea. Twice the sleek, frail craft almost capsized in the violent tide of the channel, and guests and crew were kept eternally busy with the gourd bailing-dippers. At dawn the royal canoe was beached at Waimea Bay, on Kauai, and the weary king and his exhausted crew and passengers tumbled to the sand.

King Kaumualii was caught completely off guard by this unannounced and unorthodox state visit. As quickly as identity of the notables was established, Liholiho and his friends were escorted to the Waimea palace, where every comfort in food, clothes and drink was provided by the nervous and surprised Kaumualii.

A cutter was immediately dispatched to Oahu with the news that the king had arrived safely at Kauai. Liholiho sent explicit instructions with the messenger that he wanted *Cleopatra's Barge* at Waimea.

Queen Kamamalu, and another wife or two, along with plenty of retinue, were ordered to make the voyage with it. What was lacking in pomp in this limp opening visit would be made up on arrival of the luxurious and ornate state ship.

But while Liholiho awaited arrival of his floating palace the gracious King Kaumualii and his majestic Queen Kapule made every effort to please and entertain their royal visitors. It is probable that the monarch of Kauai sensed there was more to Liholiho's presence than just an improvident canoe trip. On hand also, at Waimea, was the familiar face of that persistent missionary, Hiram Bingham. The indefatigable American was at Kauai coaching the royal family on the matter of Jesus, the *pule* [religion], and the reading and writing proficiency of the *palapala*.

Sensing that Liholiho's visit, however informal, had deeper significance than mere card playing or carousing, Kaumualii sped orders out to his tax collectors to gather tribute. At the first of the state feasts, and as quickly as the guests were rested, the island king made a most proper and gracious obeisance to Liholiho. In the presence of all, including his visitors and advisers, he declared:

"King Reho-Reho [Liholiho], hear! When your father was alive, I acknowledged him as my superior. Since his death, I have considered you as his rightful successor, and, according to his appointment, as king. I have plenty of muskets and powder, and a plenty of men at command—these, with the vessels I have brought, the fort, the guns, and the island, all are yours. Do with them as you please. Send me where you please."

For an uncomfortable interval Liholiho pondered the matter. "I did not come to take away your island," he said at last. "I do not wish to place anyone over it. Keep your island. Take care of it just as you have done."

The Reverend Hiram Bingham wrote of this epochal event: "Thus, without noise or bloodshed, the treaty, made with the late king, is recognized and ratified with his son and successor—a treaty, which allowing [Kaumualii] the peaceful possession of the leeward islands, as tributary king. In this transaction it is difficult to say to which of the two has shown the most sagacity or magnanimity."

Plainly Bingham had once more failed to recognize the subtle hand of Queen Kaahumanu in the affairs of state, or of her canny ability to manipulate kings in fulfillment of her own wants and ambitions.

Next day, far ahead of *Cleopatra's Barge*, another sleek canoe put into Waimea. With the crew was Liliha, beautiful young wife of Boki. Liliha joined her husband in the round of feasts and dances now heralding the distinguished visitors. But when Liholiho's floating palace arrived at Waimea Bay, with its royal passengers, the big village became a scene of color. The festivities went on for days.

Tribute was piled up. The island's finest foods were hauled in for the royal feasts. Beneath the shading branches of the enormous breadfruit and kukui trees were spread the makoloa mats, greened out by the wide and fragrant strips of ti fronds. Upon these ribbons of green were piled the island's choicest foods—Kauai's own royal pink poi, and a lavish spread of every conceivable fruit and comestible the island afforded. From the smoking *imu* pits came the hot pork, roast dog, baked seafood, yams, and root vegetables. At night the chanting, dancing, joyous party was lit by scores of kukui-nut torches. Never was the island to witness a more joyous event.

Presiding over all was the cultured, gracious Kaumualii. With him was his equally handsome son and heir-apparent, Prince Kealiiahonui*—a young man in his twenties—and Kauai's buoyant and attentive Queen Kapule. In the elaborate gift-giving ceremony of *hookupu*, the royal family of Kauai honored Liholiho and his wives with leis of fragrant ginger blossoms, their personal gifts, and the generous tokens of hundreds of subjects as they piled their offerings at the feet of the most distinguished Alii ever to visit the leeward islands. The feasting, the chants, the hula, were carried on day and night, to final and utter exhaustion.

While the tribute was being loaded aboard *Cleopatra's Barge*, Kaumualii and Kapule escorted King Liholiho and his consorts, Boki, Liliha, and the other high dignitaries from Oahu, on a leisurely sightseeing tour of Kauai. Liholiho, who had never before visited the island, was entranced by its waterways and verdant beauty. With feasts and festivities at each night's stop, the state visit extended into summer's finish. That Kaahumanu, as *kuhina-nui*, had failed to present herself at this leeward court was a nagging question to Kaumualii. It became a matter of deep suspicion to Kapule.

Early in September Liholiho at last announced his departure. On the night of September 18 he staged a farewell party aboard *Cleopatra's Barge*. But the royal invitations included only King Kaumualii, and the playboy heir-apparent, Prince Kealiiahonui. The slighting of Queen Kapule at this aloha affair was intentional. Assumption was that the two monarchs were merely closing ranks for convivial company, and that in the profligate crown prince, Liholiho was seeing and appreciating an image of his own earlier self.

The party was in full and festive swing, and the prince had drank himself into paralysis, before King Kaumualii noticed that the

*Ke-a-li-i-a-ho-nui: *Kay*-ah-lee-ee-ah-hoh-*noo*-ee.

ship was already underway. At his questioning, Liholiho assured that it was merely a joyful moonlight cruise. But when the wise and suspicious Kaumualii saw by the stars that the course was set directly for Honolulu, he realized that he and his son were being kidnapped. As his beloved Kauai faded into the black and distant west, he knew he would be lucky if ever again he was to see the island of his kingship.

* * * * *

It was no accident that Kaahumanu and her retinue were on hand to meet the ship at Honolulu. Immediately she took in tow the handsome and urbane captive king and his attractive son. In spite of the elaborate and festive welcome, equalling the splendor the royal visitors had enjoyed at Kauai, Kaumualii realized he had been mortally betrayed. In viewing the bright-eyed and eager Kaahumanu, so constantly at his side, he began to sense purpose in the coup.

Everywhere in Honolulu, at the royal palace, at the village at Waikiki, they were rendered full homage as rulers of Kauai. At a lavish state feast, Kaumualii was publicly acknowledged as such by Liholiho himself. The only painful reminder was that, in spite of the fact he would always and forever be king of Kauai, he must henceforth reside on Oahu. The monarch, so obliquely honored, could only meekly bow to the inevitable. Men and chiefs courted his wise and gentle presence. Women adored him. But the custodial and attentive creature most constantly at his side was the passionate and possessive Kaahumanu.

The crown prince entered into Honolulu's wild and earthy circle with alacrity. He had only moved from Kauai's court into a brighter and happier one. Kaahumanu was as pleased with the son as she was with his father. The crown prince wenched and tippled with joyous abandon, but King Kaumualii moved with more thoughtful and civilized detachment. He requested a resumption of the *pule* and the *palapala*, with which he had been engrossed on Kauai under direction of Whitney and Bingham. Kaahumanu, herself anti-Jesus, but not opposed to learning when unaccompanied by God worship, acceded to her consort's whim. She personally escorted him to Honolulu's mission house. She enrolled her royal pupil with Rev. and Mrs. Asa Thurston.

Either King Kaumualii was captivated by the sensuous charm of Kamehameha's dowager queen, or he passively surrendered to the inevitable—for, after a lavish feast at Kaahumanu's house, and after the guests and dancers had departed, the two laid themselves down on the wedding couch. It had been carefully prepared with China silk and kapa mats, copiously dusted with the fragrant aphrodisiac *hinalo*. In ancient ceremony, the attendants covered the bridal pair with wedding kapa. Henceforth the King of Kauai and the Queen of Hawaii were man and wife.

But Kaahumanu's conquest was not entirely glandular. As *kuhina-nui* of all the islands, she immediately set up a new government at Kauai—to completely divest the hated Kapule of all power. While the true king engrossed himself in the *pule* and *palapala* by day, and the eager loins of Kaahumanu by night, the ambitious and crafty queen appointed and installed the loyal and distinguished high chief Kaikioewa as governor of Kaumualii's kingdom.

Only one thing was left that might threaten Kaahumanu's intrigue. The heir-apparent, Kealiiahonui, had been as popular at Kauai as he was beginning to be in Honolulu. There was always the possibility that Kauai resentment against the abduction of its king might boil up into revolt under a rallying cry for the crown prince. This was the one real danger to unity of the all-island empire.

Kaahumanu's sexual conquest of Kealiiahonui was probably her highest achievement. With the simple directness which was so characteristic of her she announced she was marrying the heir-designate of Kauai. That he was the son of her new husband had little meaning or consequence among the Alii. In the impulsive and devastating candor with which she took anything and everything she wanted, Kaahumanu made fast and furious love to the young man. When the older woman went under the marriage kapa with junior, she not only had two husbands—father and son—but with her coitive prowess alone, she had conquered the only island her sainted Kamehameha had failed to take.

II

FROM 1821 TO 1825—the three-year span from the time Kaahumanu acquired her two new husbands, to the time of Liholiho's and Kamamalu's tragic death in London—this despotic and ambitious queen underwent curious transformation. First of all she was *kuhina-nui*, and during Liholiho's short reign, Kaahumanu not only indirectly ruled the islands, but managed the vacillating son of Kamehameha like a puppet on a string.

Not content with seducing the king and crown prince of Kauai, she further humiliated its queen Kapule by a triumphal tour of the leeward island. Though Kauai had never failed to pay full tax and tribute to Kamehameha and Liholiho, its new queen served notice that this strange royal visit would include the island-wide collection of all levies allegedly due the central government—which then had its capital wherever Liholiho allowed *Cleopatra's Barge* to drop its anchor.

In pomp and style, in the shiny carriage and immaculate horses brought by ship from Honolulu, the mighty Kaahumanu traveled Kauai with her famous retinue. On the carriage's padded seat, sitting between her two husbands—the king of Kauai, and the crown prince—the regal queen nodded triumphantly to the cheering people, and accepted their homage. It had taken four ships to convey the royal party and equipage from Oahu. The traveling pageant was quickly swelled to nearly two thousand people—including high chiefs and chiefesses from both Oahu and Kauai, and singers, dancers, and acrobats brought in with the visitors. The only person of importance not included was Liholiho himself. This was Kaahumanu's affair and, from it, he had kept himself aloof.

King Kaumualii had returned to his beloved Kauai dressed in high European fashion—broadcloth pantaloons, richly topped with buff satin waistcoat, cuffed out at the bottom with white silk stockings, all overwrapped with a dress coat of black velvet. The ornate chain of his gold watch flashed modishly across his front. He handled his gold-topped walking stick with the same easy assurance his ancestors once had swung their spears.

Prince Kealiiahonui, from native view, had always been an elegant sight. He now moved through the pageant with arrogant charm. Over his *malo* of yellow satin, his purple satin *kihei* was draped with the classic confidence of a Roman centurion. A thousand female eyes doted on him. A thousand males were envious.

But Kaahumanu, her junoesque figure wrapped in satin *pa'u* of royal yellow, and an exquisitely fashioned feather cloak, was the picture of a queen in the Alii tradition. She allowed her regal self to bow and smile in return for the bows and smiles of the throngs who greeted the royal party. Plainly she savored the sweet fruits of victory.

The tour of Kauai was a triumph in every conceivable way. Queen Kapule, through the state banquets at the big palace on Waimea Bay, conducted herself with flawless dignity. Without outward sign of the humiliation with which she was inwardly torn, she confronted the imperious woman who had supplanted her. Kaumualii directed court and social functions with the same impeccable casualness and charm with which he had presided over Kauai's affairs before the abduction.

He met and discussed island affairs with the Oahu-appointed governor Kaikioewa. With Kaahumanu he made special call on missionary Samuel Whitney, and encouraged him to spread the *pule* and *palapala* more deeply through the villages of Kauai. Kaahumanu, accepting the fact that both her new husbands were practicing Christians, ceased fighting the sect. During the sojourn she actually sped a command to

Honolulu for the longneck mission to hurry additional books to the leeward island.

Her new and generous approval of the missionary efforts were not matched by her confidence in the internal affairs of government. The charming Kapule was still a woman, and as ambitious a queen as herself. Nor was she one to take public humiliation with complete docility. In some way she would fight back. Kaahumanu, with female prescience, was sure of it. Court gossip was that Kapule planned to take the half brother of Kaumualii—Prince Kaiu—as her husband. Prince Humehume, American educated and Christianized, and a part of the *Thaddeus* congregation, was preaching insurgency along with his religion. Kaahumanu, thoroughly worried, wanted victory to be sure and permanent.

Before leaving Kauai, December 1822, Kaahumanu named her own brother, High Chief Keeaumoku, as governor—to replace the aged Kaikioewa. Previous to this she had appointed her other brothers to equally high positions—Kuakini as governor of Hawaii, and Kahekili as governor of Maui. She now had three islands under her personal suzerainty. She charged Keeaumoku to keep close watch on any revolutionaries on Kauai; and continual scrutiny of Queen Kapule.

When the ships returned to Honolulu, heavy laden with tribute and bearing one of history's strangest royal parties, it ended the last visit King Kaumualii would ever make to his island.

III

UP TO THE DAY Liholiho had sailed for England he had been plagued by the ambition and intrigue of his *kuhina-nui*. Wherever he could, as in the matter of the Kauai monarchy, he had placated Kaahumanu. But as king of all Hawaii, he was wearied of her meddling in affairs of state. While he retreated to *Cleopatra's Barge* to rest and meditate, Kaahumanu mouthed decrees and dictated policy. Worse, the people loved her for her monumental aggressiveness, her monumental rages, and her physical conquests as a woman. It was well that no son ever was born to her, by any of the kings, princes, and high chiefs with whom she was known to have bedded down. By fair means or foul, Kaahumanu would have made him monarch over all the islands.

The canny haoles sensing the divisive situation between Liholiho and Kaahumanu had used every effort to widen the breach. They resented the Hawaiian king's monopoly on trade, and his persistent effort to keep them from acquiring property and power in the islands. They employed every stratagem to split the kingdom and foment revolution.

Haole trader J. C. Jones, in a letter written shortly after Kaahumanu's triumphal tour of Kauai, stated: "There appears to be some fear that Kaahumanu and Kaumualii intend to take possession of the Islands. I am endeavoring to make them [King Liholiho and Boki, governor of Oahu] believe that this will be the case in order that we may sell them powder and muskets."

A lot of the problems Liholiho carried to England with him had been prompted by the internal discord arising from the power usurped and exploited by his father's widow, and the constant pressure of haoles to use the breach and tension for their own personal gain.

The puissance of the foreigners to break the ancient system by which all land was owned by the king had already reached intolerable proportions. Liholiho's people, and those of the loyal Alii, beseeched him up to the time he departed for London, to drive the avaricious and seditious haoles from the islands. Foreign interference with the nation's internal security, the pious meddling of the American missionaries in his personal affairs, and Kaahumanu's heartbreaking and hurtful assumption of power, were the burdens that sent the second Kamehameha on the long voyage.

Reverend Charles S. Stewart, member of the second shipload of American missionaries, interspersed his written comments on the state of the heathen Hawaiians among whom he labored, with open admiration for their personal beauty, dress and pageantry. "Gross darkness covers the people, and thousands are perishing in the depths of sin and ignorance," he sadly deplored. His fellow missionaries, coaching a people who considered happiness and laughter as virtues higher than austerity, long faces, and long necks, would "doubtless receive such rewards in heaven as to make the angels weep with envy."

In describing a confrontation with stately Kaahumanu he said, half disdain and half admiration: "She was dressed in the native *pa'u* consisting of about twenty yards of rich yellow satin, arranged in loose and graceful folds with a full end hanging negligently in front; the upper robe was of purple satin. It was cast over one arm and shoulder only, leaving the other exposed, and flowed in its richness far on the ground behind her. Her hair was neatly put up with combs and ornamented by a double coronet of exquisite feathers in colors bright yellow, crimson, and bluish green. She appears to be between forty and fifty years of age; is large and portly, still bears marks of the beauty for which she had been celebrated, but has an expression of greater hauteur than any other islander I have yet seen."

*Ha-o-le: *How*-lay. Any foreigner—especially Americans.

Stewart considered Kaumualii "the captive king." He described him as "a fine figure with a noble Roman countenance . . . manner pensive . . . The chains with which Kaahumanu binds him are far from being silken."

With the departure of Liholiho and Kamamalu for England, and under the regency conferred on her as *kuhina-nui*, Queen Kaahumanu had stepped forth in unassailable glory. By now, sensitive to the gentle influence of Kaumualii, she had softened enough toward the longnecks to attend church, and even to study the *pule* and *palapala*. Other foreigners found her a ruler both harsh and tough.

With Liholiho's absence she had assumed the regency with verve and enthusiasm. And, as with the death of her beloved Kamehameha, she could not resist her penchant for governmental change. Foreigners, from merchants to sea captains, quickly came to realization that this old lady was wise to their tricks. She was shrewd, and, unlike Liholiho, could neither be coerced or out-talked. They soon found it safer to walk the narrow path of honesty than to risk one of her tempestuous public denunciations. Missionaries were more than eager to keep in her favor. They courted her as assiduously as did the sandalwood traders. The natives, who adored this sexy and volatile old queen, followed her advice and decrees happily, willingly.

Her frequent visits to Honolulu from her Waikiki palace were always impressive sights. Captain Dixey Wildes, an American shipper, had presented Kaahumanu with a magnificent carriage out of Boston. To draw the shiny vehicle she used a dozen *malo* clad retainers, happily proud of the honor to trot the queen to town. At the carriage front was a high coachman's seat. At its rear, and equally high, was the footman's perch. On the driver's seat, vividly swathed in China silk, sat the great Kaahumanu. Astern, on the footman's box, always smiling and amused, sat the youngest of her husbands, Kealiiahonui—joyously sure of himself, in satin version of the native garb. The padded passenger compartment housed the queen's "treasure," Kaumualii, King of Kauai. His Majesty, in solitary grandeur, was always immaculately styled in clothes of foreign cut, of rich and splendid texture, and usually of light gray or fawn. Handsome as he was, the "captive king" wore a look of sad resignation.

The new haole style house which Kaahumanu was having built at Waikiki for her "treasures" was far enough completed for the missionaries to conduct both *pule* and *palapala* on the premises. The Reverend Mr. Bingham, however, never too deeply impressed by the depth of Kaumualii's conversion, was frankly dubious about any Christlike change and influence on the imperious old queen. Kaahumanu loved pomp and pageantry. There was no stuffing of this big woman into the Mother Hubbard type garb of missionary gingham and calico. She continued to live in open polyandry, and never ceased to proudly exhibit her two husbands. As to the pleasure-loving and contemptuous Prince Kealiiahonui, the longnecks could only shake heads in despair.

By early May of 1824 Kaahumanu had—by ruthlessly driving the carpenters and painters—put finishing touches on the royal mansion, and had luxuriously installed her beloved Kaumualii therein. But it came too late for any normal enjoyment of the sumptuous dwelling. Kaumualii had been carried into the house a sick man. On his bed, kept festooned with ropes of fresh maile, and surrounded with fragrant and beautiful flowers, Kaahumanu's "treasure" grew ever weaker. The gentle king, knowing that death was near, dictated his will. The kingdom of Kauai was bequeathed to Liholiho, irrespective of the presence of a crown prince in the house. Kaumualii's personal possessions would be divided between Kaahumanu, his children, and loyal retainers. His lost queen—Kapule—received nothing.

By May 20 Kaumualii had slipped into coma, and the missionaries were summoned. Prayers were said, hymns were sung, but Christian magic failed to revive the king. Next day the desperate Kaahumanu called in the kahunas and sorcerers. Incantations, incense, and wailing *meles* proved even less efficacious. The king dropped ever deeper into the sleep of death. By May 25 the new mansion was kept constantly surrounded by Honolulu's natives, and others from every portion of Oahu. They sobbed, chanted softly, and asked for return of the priests which the queen had so imperiously banished. So as not to disturb her sick man, Kaahumanu closed and barred the doors to intrusion, and shuttered the windows. Wild with grief, she kept a lonely vigil.

Next morning, May 26, 1824, Kaumualii breathed his last. When it was starkly apparent that the king was dead, she herself prepared the funeral couch upon which he would lie in state. The beautiful new Chinese divan was covered with green velvet and trimmed with pink satin. Upon it she gently laid the frail and wasted man. At his head was spread his royal feathered war cloak. At his feet the smaller Alii cloak of state. Maile ropes were festooned above. At the couch corners stood the royal *kahilis* of sacred feathers. Kaahumanu covered her dead man with a shroud of yellow satin, and around his handsome head she arranged the coronet of yellow feathers. Unlike the great Kamehameha, whose death grief was shared by twenty-one wives and many concubines, Kaahumanu had this king's bier to herself. This time she could sit alone with her dead.

When finally Kaahumanu opened the doors to outside mourners, it was apparent to all that something vital had gone out of this queen of two dynasties.

After the natives had expended their excesses in mourning, she turned her king over to the longnecks for their best in Christian services. The body of Kaumualii was dressed in the uniform of a British hussar; the foreign medals he had received, pinned to his chest; the whale-tooth *lei niho palaoa*, Alii badge of rank, hung around his neck. The Reverend Mr. Ellis, a proficient linguist, conducted the service. A native choir sang Christian music. After the impressive funeral, Kaahumanu ordered the expensive coffin closed and sealed. Briefly and decisively she announced that her beloved would be transported to the island of Maui—to be buried in hallowed Christian ground—side by side in the mausoleum with the Christian queen-mother Keopuolani. It took twenty brigs and schooners to transport the funeral party to Lahaina.

This second funeral was met by thousands of mourning Hawaiians —many of them coming from the king's own island of Kauai. Among the mourners was the king's former wife Kapule, and his American educated son, Humehume. Throughout this Christian rite, both of them remained tight-lipped and sullen.

Kaahumanu and her younger husband remained at Lahaina to be near the mausoleum housing the man so close to both of them. Subdued and silent, the queen continued to mourn. But even death of his father was not enough to sustain Kealiiahonui in grief. His roving eye spied a new sweetheart—the young and vivacious Kekauonohi. With a fresh clutch in love, Kaahumanu's second husband calmly deserted her by leaving Maui with the younger and more beautiful conquest. Again Kaahumanu was left a dowager queen.

This second catastrophe was too much for her. She was never again the same. What she did not know was that further blows of shattering import were in the offing. Only a month from the time of Kaumualii's interment at Maui, Liholiho himself would be dead, in far away London.

*   *   *   *   *

George Tamoree, who had come back to the islands as a converted missionary on the *Thaddeus*, but known to his people as Prince Humehume, left the Maui grave of his father a disillusioned and bitter Christian. Both he and Queen Kapule harbored nothing but hate for Kaahumanu, no matter how grief-stricken she appeared to be. Humehume baldly declared that the "old woman" had poisoned his father. Although Humehume was not a prince by Kapule, both felt they had been grossly wronged.

Kapule, however, was willing to live with her sorrow and humiliation. But Humehume, on his return to Kauai, cast off all Christian piety and restraint. He organized the island's disgruntled high chiefs and dissidents into a revolutionary army to overthrow the grip held by the world-traveling Liholiho and his autocratic regent. He would take his dead father's place as king of Kauai.

On August 4, 1824, these rebels attacked the fort at Waimea. Long neglected, it was easily and quickly overwhelmed. Victory was celebrated by the rebels firing all the fort's ammunition exuberantly into the air.

At first signs of Kauai's unrest, Prime Minister Kalanimoku had hurried to the leeward island. He had hoped, by his presence, to head off trouble, but Humehume's insurgents had acted decisively in spite of it. Old Billy Pitt, however, was a veteran of other national crises, and he wasted no time. While he listened to the complaints of the chiefs, and viewed with alarm the people's rising antipathy toward longnecks and foreigners, he sped a request to Oahu for soldiers to deal realistically with revolution.

But, before help arrived, Kapule herself came out, brandishing her vanished husband's sword. With drawn blade the queen personally led her own loyal warriors in an assault that retook the fort from Humehume. Both she and Kalanimoku were certain that this was by no means the end of the war, and decisive battles were yet to be fought. But on August 18 the situation further changed with arrival of forces from Oahu and Maui, under command of Governor Hoapili. Another vicious battle was fought—in the foothills near Hanapepe. Here the untrained rebels were hopelessly outclassed by the seasoned veterans of Hawaiian militia, and one hundred and thirty of them died. Humehume, captured in the mountains, was hauled before Kalanimoku. One look at the pitifully discouraged and defeated young missionary, and Billy Pitt wrapped his own cloak around the youth's shoulders. "You shall live," he said.

A grand council of Kauai chiefs was called to deal with retribution and to hear out grievances. Kaahumanu, emerging from her vapors of grief, came over from Maui. At last the ancient and timeless independence of Kauai was abolished. The island was declared fully subject to the united kingdom, and its monarchy dissolved. All chiefs who had shared in the rebellion were banished to other islands, where they could sponsor no more mischief. Humehume, his wife and child, were forever exiled to Oahu. There, as George Tamoree, this former prince would be close enough to the longnecks and the *pule* to seek the Lord's forgiveness.

The people of Kauai had witnessed a strangely changed Kaahumanu. Her re-entry to the island was nothing like her former opulent and exuberant visit. Light of love was gone from her dark eyes. Her

animal-like passion had vanished. She was decently courteous to Kapule; she was subdued; she was silent. She stayed on at Kauai—up to
the time that news broke into the islands of the tragic loss of Liholiho.
All through her quiet sojourn she took a house alongside the Whitneys.
From the missionaries she asked for personal coaching in the "Christ
life."

Suddenly she was giving public endorsement of the new religion.
She went to church; she knelt at the altar. When she ordered a survey
of the big island of Hawaii, for the purpose of establishing churches
and schools in that reluctant field, everyone agreed that the old woman
had indeed changed. Reverends Thurston and Ellis were ordered to
report to Hawaii's governor, Kuakini—Kaahumanu's own high-living
brother. Full aid and cooperation was promised. Kaahumanu had at last
surrendered herself and her people to the faith.

IV

NEWS of the death of Liholiho and Kamamalu were brought to the
islands by arrival of the whaleships *Almira* and *Peru*, March 9, 1825.
The doleful tidings were confirmed to the people when Prime Minister
Kalanimoku announced, at a Protestant midweek prayer meeting in
Honolulu, that the king and queen were truly dead. He asked Hawaiians "to mourn the death of the king with sorrow of heart, and to
observe two weeks of prayer."

In the inexplicable Polynesian manner, news of the tragedy spread
across the islands with telepathic speed. The air was soon filled with
mourning wails of the people. But in complete variance of what might
have happened a generation earlier, there was almost total absence of
violence and disorder. Liholiho had been a popular monarch, and his
beautiful Kamamalu deeply loved, and yet public grief was expended
in tears and keening, with only a few of the unregenerate Alii mutilat-
ing themselves and knocking out their teeth. Christianity had by now
wiped away all urge to light fires on the *heiaus*. Gone forever was the
traditional orgy of human sacrifice.

Kaahumanu returned from Kauai, and immediately retreated to
her mountain home far up Moana Valley. Here, sad, and ill in health,
she waited for further news of the tragedy from London. Now, with
sudden and unprecedented cooperation, she worked with the aged
Kalanimoku, and the uncrowned child king, in coping with the affairs
of state—aggravated by a nation plunged suddenly into mourning.

She had named her green and rustic retreat Pukaomaomao,* the
"verdant portal." Here she had hoped to find peace, regroup the shat-

*Pu-ku-a-o-ma-o-ma-o: *Poo-kooh-ah-oh-mah-oh-mah-oh.*

tered parts of her life, and somehow regain the poise and fortitude
necessary to hold the nation together through its crisis. But the instant
the dowager queen took residence in Moana Valley, the attendants
labored to make it fit abode for the great one.

Here it was perpetually springtime. Below the lush growth hanging
down the mountainsides, great patches of taro, sweet potatoes and
bananas were set out by the workers. Beside the roadway that me-
andered up to the huge grass house were planted the perpetually flowering hibiscus. A grass lawn was seeded, foreign style, upon which were
moved ohi'a-lehua trees, for blossoms, and ohi'a-ai for the crimson fruit.
It was assumed that the pleasure-loving queen would resume her opulent court and social life as soon as she emerged from mc ning the personal and national tragedies.

As always, her presence acted like a magnet. Up Moana roadway
came the Alii—Kalanimoku in his bright yellow wagon, drawn by
curried horses; Liholiho's four bereaved and living queens, riding
horseback with their retinues behind them afoot; the heir-apparent,
Liholiho's eleven-year-old brother Kauikeaouli; and sometimes, from
Maui, his beautiful child sister, Princess Nahienaena,* always traveling the road by royal carriage. Then there was the endless parade of
worshipful commoners, bearing food and gifts for their beloved Kaahumanu. This mourning had little semblance to the time of Kamehameha
the Great. The queen, who once so boldly had abolished the kapus,
now found herself unexpectedly harassed and worried in the midst of
sorrow's contemplations.

On April 16 the British war sloop *Active* dropped anchor in Honolulu harbor. Aboard her was the new English consul-general Richard
Charlton, his wife, and his sister. His Majesty's government had made
certain this important man arrive first, to set the stage, and prepare
the people. Charlton not only brought full and intimate details of Liholiho's visit to England, but explained the deaths of the royal couple,
and the fact that their bodies were homeward-bound on the *Blonde*.
He brought with him letters of explanation and instructions from
Hawaii's own Boki, governor of Oahu.

The frigate *Blonde* was sighted May 4 as she breasted the coastline
of Maui. By the time the warship came to anchor at Lahaina, thousands
had gathered at the beach. The moaning and wailing Hawaiians were
headed by Maui's governor Hoapili, father of Liliha. A boat was lowered from the British ship. When the navy oarsmen brought it close
enough for scrutiny, a cry went up. "It is Boki!"

---

*Na-hi-e-na-e-na: *Nah-hee-ay-nah-ay-nah.*

KING'S PALACE, TOWARD WAIKIKI, OAHU, IN 1826
From an unsigned watercolor.

—Bernice P. Bishop Museum, Honolulu.

When Boki and Liliha were helped ashore, Hoapili laid back his head and gave vent to the ancient and long-drawn Alii grief cry. Then, when the old man threw himself prostrate at their feet, and lowered his face to the sand, every other chief and Alii did likewise. The cry of lament that burst from a thousand throats of the multitude drowned out the roar of Lahaina's surf.

Not until minutes later did the chiefs arise. Hoapili rushed into the arms of the weeping Boki. Liliha tightly hugged the little Princess Nahienaena, Liholiho's sister, while they wept together. When the people were calm enough, Boki spoke to them. Lord Byron would come ashore tomorrow. The great commander himself would talk to them. When the Alii departed for Hoapili's house, the crowd bedded down on the beach, to watch the big ship bearing the bodies of the king and queen bob at anchor offshore, and to patiently await another dawning.

Next morning, as promised, Lord Byron stepped ashore at Lahaina. Under the cockade, and braid and spangles of his naval uniform, was a man of sympathy and understanding. He genuinely sensed the grief of these people, and reacted sensibly to it. Before delivering his message he talked individually to the grieving Alii, and then spoke to all who had patiently waited at the beach. Though it was the formal written message of King George he read, he added his own thoughts to it. And the people were impressed by this kindly man who had traveled so far in bringing back their own monarch.

At five that evening the *Blonde* set sail for Oahu. Aboard were Hoapili, Nahienaena, and all of Maui's Alii. Next morning the ship stood in Honolulu. The people, alerted by the sentinels, already were massed to meet her.

At the head of the thousands of mourners was Kaahumanu. This time she was not flamboyantly dressed in her bright silks. This time her *pa'u* was of native kapa cloth, of subdued color, and gone was the animal-like vivacity of other years. She stood there, an old woman, groaning and wailing along with the least of her people. The crown prince was not with the high Alii awaiting the boats from the naval frigate. He remained at the Waikiki grass palace, grieving in private, and waiting officially to receive those representing his dead brother, and the high emissaries from King George.

First ashore were Boki, Liliha, the princess, and Hoapili. The next tender brought those Alii who had visited England with the deceased king and queen, and those who had joined the ship at Lahaina. The British dignitaries, skilled in manners and protocol, did not intrude or come ashore with these parties in sorrow. And for an hour the Hawaiians groveled through an orgy of wailing on the beach.

From there the royal party, and high Alii, moved to the church of the longnecks, where Reverend Bingham conducted a prayer service in the Hawaiian language he had mastered. Tearfully Boki took the rostrum and told all the happenings in London; the sudden sickness which had assailed the royal party and their delegates; the loss in death of Liholiho and Kamamalu. He told of the meetings with the highest British officials, and with King George. He answered the grave question in their minds—"what did England's king say about the Christian religion?"—by revealing that the king's answer was exemplary only. The English people, he told them, including their king, were universal in acceptance and devotion to Christ. And now he, Boki, was convinced from all this that the Christian God was the true God. He had returned to Hawaii fully as ardent as Mr. Bingham in urging the people to study the *pule* and the *palapala*. Without Christianity, Boki was certain, the nation would die or be destroyed.

On Boki's words, in that hour, hinged the fate of Christianity in the islands.

Next day the British officials joined the natives in an official reception to Lord Byron, staged by Prime Minister Kalanimoku in his grass palace at Pokuhaina, on the harbor's southeast shore. Kaahumanu was stunned by the lavish preparation old Billy Pitt had made for the affair, and was a little jealous. Now, with both her own royal husbands vanished, and Kaumualii's big new house dark and kapu because of death, it no longer was mete for her to host anything on this Alii scale.

Kalanimoku's palace had been festooned with maile and, for the occasion, was exotically fragrant with freshly gathered leaves and flowers. Upon the dais, flanked by royal *kahilis*, an elaborate Chinese sofa had been transformed into a double throne of royal yellow for the eleven-year-old heir-apparent, and the nine-year-old princess. Governor Boki, and an honor guard of Alii, escorted Lord Byron and the British ship party to the palace. Included was the new British consul, Richard Charlton, the scientists sent by Great Britain to map and study the resources of the Sandwich Islands, and Robert Dampier, an artist, London commissioned, to paint the portraits of Hawaiian royalty.

Their arrival at the palace was heralded by a long and echoing blast by the royal trumpeter from his conch shell. The Britishers were astonished, upon entering the big hall, at the assemblage waiting to greet them. On either side of the throne were the highest Alii in Hawaii's united kingdom. Lesser dignitaries, including many invited haoles, were double lined to the kapa cloth of the seating and dining areas. Everyone arose at entrance of the Britishers—except the prince and princess on their thrones. Boki personally presented Lord Byron to the royal children, and then to each of the high Alii present.

To the assemblage Lord Byron rendered formal salutations from King George and His Majesty's government, and expressed the king's personal sympathy to the Hawaiian people in their loss. After Kalanimoku's amazingly facile response to the greeting, Lord Byron presented the gifts send by his Britannic Majesty to the Hawaiian royal family. The young prince received a Windsor uniform, complete with cockade and sword. The buttons were marked, with the royal G.R. Fatherly and kind; Lord Byron held the uniform up to the delighted youngster. When he saw that it was perfect fit, he put his hands upon the boy's head and expressed the wish and hope that Kauikeaouli would make his people a great and wise king. The act instantly endeared His Lordship to every Hawaiian present.

For the princess there was a lovely gown of latest London fashion. To Prime Minister Kalanimoku went a small wax sculpture of the deceased Liholiho, and a gold watch, its case engraved on one side with the British royal arms, and on the back with the name and seal of Kalanimoku. For Kaahumanu there was a beautiful silver teapot bearing the British royal crest, and engraved with her name. Each of the high chiefs and chiefesses were tendered a gift from Britain.

Kalanimoku responded on behalf of the Hawaiian royal family and nation. He expressed gratitude for the gifts, but more importantly for the friendship of the British people toward Hawaiians, and for the kindness and consideration shown the Hawaiian royalty and official party during its tragic visit to His Lordship's nation. Lord Byron responded most graciously. Hawaiian foods were served. The British commander returned to the *Blonde* in full knowledge he had wisely and discreetly handled his assignment.

On May 11, 1825, at 12 noon, the English caskets of Liholiho and Kamamalu were brought to shore by the pinnace from the *Blonde*, its eight naval oarsmen rowing in matched time. From Honolulu waterfront, along a roadway aligned either side by Hawaiian warriors, the cortege bearing the bodies of their king and queen moved slowly toward the mission church. Heading the solemn procession were twenty brown and muscular Hawaiians carrying the royal feather *kahilis* high and proud. Behind them marched a detachment of marines from the *Blonde*, their British muskets in reverse position. The ship's band, in slow step, and playing a funeral dirge, was followed by the ship's chaplain and the American missionaries.

The wheeled catafalques, each draped in black, and each drawn by forty chiefs of the Alii was followed by the young prince in his new Windsor uniform; consul Charlton walking at his side. The little princess Nahienaena, in her new London frock, was escorted by Lord Byron in full blue dress of a British naval commander. Next in line was Kaahumanu, as *kuhina-nui*, garbed in black, and behind her Prime Minister Kalanimoku and Liholiho's four remaining polygamous queens. Marching sailors from the *Blonde*, Honolulu's more illustrious haoles, and the solemn-faced commoners finished out the procession.

The cortege halted at the doors of the American church. There the *Blonde's* chaplain, Mr. Bloxam, read the Church of England burial service. Rev. Hiram Bingham, in the facile Hawaiian he had acquired, rendered a fervent prayer. He spoke briefly of the great king who had opened his islands to Christ and Christianity. And these words, too, were in the language of the people.

Final halt of the funeral procession was at the big house of Kalanimoku. This time the great hall of the prime minister's dwelling wore the black of mourning. The dais, where a few days previous the young prince and princess had sat enthroned, had been draped with black cloth in place of its fragrant flowers and greenery. Upon it were laid the royal caskets—there to remain in state until the mausoleum was made ready.

The funeral procession in itself had all the allegorical ingredients of the state of the Hawaiian monarchy in this hour of its crisis. The interplay of British and American interests were significant even in the death march of its king. Not until after the final prayers were said, and all foreigners had departed, did the Hawaiians at last feel at home and as one with their noble dead. Once free of the haoles, and their repressive pall, the natives took over in their own way. At last, within the great hall, and out across Oahu, came the chanted *meles* and uninhibited wailing of the island people.

V

THE grand council of chiefs, June 6, 1825, proclaimed the young brother of Liholiho, Prince Kauikeaouli, as king of the united islands. He was given the title of Kamehameha III. Dowager Queen Kaahumanu and Prime Minister Kalanimoku were named as joint regents until the youthful sovereign gained the necessary years and experience. Boki, governor of Oahu, and confidant of the dead Liholiho, was appointed as privy counselor to the boy king. Mr. Bingham would continue to coach the lad in the *pule* and the *palapala*.

Hawaii's grand council did not reach accord without rhetoric and argument. Boki spoke at great length about the things he had learned and observed from his journey. Eloquently and persistently he declared that the British empire was the governing pattern his people should study and adopt. Like the Hawaiians, Britishers put high value on tradition and their ancient culture, Boki maintained. Britains too had kapus pertaining to personal conduct, manners, and individual behavior. Religion, moral values, and respect for law had welded Englishmen into a mighty nation. He hoped Hawaiians would heed the things he had learned about this people.

In comparison, he argued, the civilization as presented by American missionaries differed greatly from that of England. In England, citizens were not burdened with the onerous restrictions asked by the longnecks. Sunday tabus, which forbade Christians building fires on the Sabbath, going swimming, and canoe racing, should be immediately abolished. Englishmen had no such stupid rules. In conclusion Boki recommended that the Hawaiian kingdom mold its government—religiously and politically—in the manner of the empire of King George.

Mr. Charlton, the British attaches from the *Blonde*, and a few resident Americans, were allowed voice in the assembly. Each spoke according to his convictions, and along the pathway of his interests. The land policy, established by Kamehameha the Great, was again hammered out as reaffirmation. Chiefs could still hold their possessions—subject only to forfeiture by treason. The learning program, instituted throughout the islands by the missionaries, was given official endorsement. Even their kapus were acceptable as policy, in spite of Boki's negative affirmation.

When Lord Byron's turn came to speak, he was greeted enthusiastically by Alii and commoners. His impeccable conduct and deep concern had won him many friends. Already he was known as "The Great Chief of Beretania [Britannia]," and he was greeted in their council with an aloha both heartwarming and convincing. To the chiefs he read his list of prepared suggestions from the Crown. He defined personal liberties according to English law, and advocated uniform and fair taxation. Few of his admonitions varied greatly from Hawaiian practice—other than that of trial by jury. His valuable suggestions as to port regulations found later adoption by the council.

But to Mr. Bingham he leveled pointed questions as to the real purposes of American missionaries in the islands. He openly objected to the rumors he had heard that Americans were at work drawing up a code of laws for Hawaiians. The American educational program he could accept and endorse. Their evangelization of the natives, so long as repressiveness did not destroy the joy and spirit of the people, was probably a good thing. But there must be no internal meddling with the government of the Hawaiian kingdom.

Bingham, in turn, and without hesitancy, defended his mission and the American efforts. He made plain that the American Board of Mis-

sions forbade all interference with the native government. Furthermore, he stated, there had been no tampering with the politics or commercial interests of the nation. Missionaries were present solely for the
purpose of spreading the word of God, and teaching the people to read
and write the English and Hawaiian language.

Satisfied and relieved, Lord Byron thanked Mr. Bingham, and concluded his remarks by commending the American missionaries on their
humanitarian efforts, and their amazing accomplishments in trans-
forming the oral Hawaiian vernacular into a written and printable
language. He even urged Hawaiians to avail themselves of the good
things being offered by these selfless souls.

Kaahumanu, feeling deprived and overshadowed at this high council, did not arise to lend her fiery spirit and affirmative voice. She
seemed to be an entirely different woman from the mighty queen who
had destroyed the priests and wiped away the ancient religion.

But Lord Byron, accepted everywhere now as "High Chief of Beretania," was wisdom's choice for this mission. With astuteness and an
innate sense of the correctness of things, he respected the Alii and all
the complexities of their culture, ceremonials and tradition. He knew
when to move Britain into the royal circles, and when to retreat into
unobtrusiveness. A lesser man, with authoritative trappings of the
British empire behind him, would have bullied himself through the
Honolulu scene; dominated the sorrowful deliberations of Hawaii in
one of its most difficult hours. Because he and his men kept to the ship
when not needed, and graciously joined the Alii for advice and encouragement when asked, the islanders quickly placed him in the pan-
theon with the other great Englishmen who had visited them in the
past.

His Lordship, shrewdly aware of the power and importance of
Kaahumanu, and perceiving her withdrawal and neglect at the Honolulu high council, paid gracious homage to the lonely queen of Ka-
mehamcha the Great. On June 9, when the *Blonde* made preparation
for a voyage to the island of Hawaii, Lord Byron invited Queen Kaahumanu to accompany him to the isle that once had been seat of the
kingdom.

This courtesy and notice quickly brought the old lady out of her
despond. With alacrity and gratitude she accepted the invitation. She
boarded the British ship with thirty attendants, and a lot of the ancient
pomp and ceremony. Byron rendered a salute of nine guns to the
mighty queen. In choosing her, Byron had chosen well. Quickly as the
Blonde dropped anchor at Hilo Bay, on Kaahumanu's home island, she
ordered and received a lavish welcome for the man from "Beretania."

At Kaahumanu's command a beautiful new grass house was quickly erected for the distinguished visitor, complete with fragrantly fresh mats, and furnished with the best and latest in Chinese and American beds, tables, chairs and dishes. Servants were assigned for constant attendance on the wants and feeding of the British commander and his staff of geographers and scientists. Supplies of food and native gifts were repeatedly delivered to Byron's grass palace, and the highest chiefs on the island called daily to pay their respects.

When Lord Byron hinted that he and his scientists would like a close view of Mauna Loa, Hawaii's great volcano, Kaahumanu made swift and efficient arrangement for their forty mile mountain journey. With no horses available at Hilo, the trip, by necessity, must be made afoot. To make the excursion as easy as possible for the distinguished visitors, houses were erected, and rest stops provided, every twelve miles. Kaahumanu made available not only a small army of servants to assist and carry the provisions of the expedition, but she saw to it that a *manele* and husky native bearers were constantly on hand so that His Lordship could be carried when he preferred not to walk.

At every rest station the expedition was joined by friendly but strange natives who still spent much of their lives worshipping and placating Hawaii's most erratic and beautiful goddess, Pele. By the time the party reached the brink of the roaring mountain, two hundred respectful natives had joined the Englishmen.

The timing was fortuitous and right. Pele put on an awesome show for the visitors. Looking down the crater, they stood transfixed until deep into the night-time. For the Englishmen it was like a view into the eternal fires of hell. Shafts of flame, earth-shaking belches of smoke and odorous vapors, poured out of the bowels of the earth. While the ground under them shook and shuddered, fiery rivers of molten lava flowed through the fissures, with a roar both thunder and moan. When Lord Byron retreated to Hilo he had full understanding of why Pele was still the awesome goddess of Hawaii.

On July 8 the *Blonde* set sail for Honolulu—laden with such a cargo of tribute and gifts to Queen Kaahumanu that it had taken two days for Byron's sailors to load. The bay where the ship had stood at anchor was now named Byron's Bay, in his honor. At Honolulu, where Kaahumanu's tribute was unloaded, and supplies for the home voyage put aboard, Byron and his men talked much of their exciting trip to the big island and its wonders.

The time had come for leaving, and Lord Byron made his aloha calls upon the gracious friends he had gained in the exotic and beautiful island kingdom. Convinced that the nation was perfectly capable of governing itself without outside interference, and sensing no immediate threat to its sovereignty by other nations, he decided to heed the more temperate and diplomatic parts of his instructions. He had grown to love and trust these people. They were bridging courageously and nicely the crisis of Liholiho's sudden death. In Kaahumanu, Kalanimoku and Boki, the young king had seasoned and dedicated counselors. King George, and His Majesty's government, would be well advised to leave the Hawaiian nation to its people. Byron made his farewell amenities—with the promise that England was Hawaii's closest ally. That help would come whenever their new king needed or desired it.

On July 12, 1825, the day of sailing, Kalanimoku, Kaahumanu, Boki, and other high Alii, made final visit to the *Blonde*—an affectionate and touching aloha to a man who had earned both respect and love. Lord Byron acknowledged the presence of his distinguished visitors with a salute from the *Blonde* of fifteen guns. And, when his guests were safely returned to shore, the British warship slowly glided out to sea.

On the way out, she returned once more to the big island of Hawaii — this time to the leeward side, and Kealakekua Bay. There, on the bluff above, and with the help of friendly Hawaiians, they found the grave of Captain Cook. A capstan bar from the *Blonde* was cemented into a small pyramid of lava rock. On this monument, over the mortal remains of the great British explorer, an engraved brass plate was fastened to the bar.

"To the memory of Captain James Cook, R.N., who discovered these islands in the year of our Lord 1778. This humble monument was erected by his fellow countrymen in the year of our Lord 1825."

After that was finished, the *Blonde* sailed out of the bay where Cook had died. It was a long and memory-filled voyage back to England.

VI

HAD Lord Byron exercised all the options and prerogatives invested by King George and His Majesty's government he could have departed Honolulu leaving the Sandwich Islands wholly under British control. His faultless diplomacy had won the hearts of Alii and people alike. Kamehameha I, and his son Liholiho, both had offered their nation to the protectorate of Great Britain. In graciously handling the London deaths of the monarchs, King George and Lord Byron had won the nation's total gratitude. Boki, Liliha, and the entire royal delegation, had returned from England thoroughly pro-British in thought and sentiment. But in spite of the power in him vested, and irrespective of his affectionate reception in the islands, His Lordship was satisfied that the people of the Sandwich Islands were fully capable of directing their own affairs, of defending themselves, and that their government would be honestly and wisely conducted under the regency.

Lord Byron's notice and attention had brought Kaahumanu back to strident leadership. Her brothers were governors of the outer islands. Now, with the blind loyalty the people gave her—the voice of Kamehameha's queen being accepted as the voice of the great Kamehameha himself—the aging woman emerged again as a creature of formidable power. Boki and Liliha, completely under the spell of British pomp and grandeur, likewise would never again be silent voices in Hawaiian governmnt. The young king, who adored them both, emerged closely and affectionately pro-British. Kalanimoku, even though he was Boki's older brother, prime minister and regent, insisted on remaining independent of the emerging power struggle between Kaahumanu and the London-slanted governor of Oahu. It was Billy Pitt who truly acted the elder statesman through these years of crisis.

Kaahumanu hammered on the necessity for a complete new code of laws for the kingdom. Boki was just as insistent on the same theme, though the laws he suggested were more British than they were island. Both factions wooed the support of young King Kauikeaouli. Though unversally accepted as Kamehameha III, he still was too young to cope with the imponderables.

Left to their own wits and wisdom, the native leaders probably would have solved their problems in government justly, and in their own best interests, but now the foreigners—British, French and American—moved into the circles of debate. Though they were citizens of other nations, they made their growing power felt by wooing whatever faction they believed would render greatest return for haole support. The prize to them—economic supremacy.

The series of high chief meetings which followed Lord Byron's departure took on rough and crude form of a debating legislature. But in these gatherings, and under the pressures, the schism of the Alii factions only deepened and grew more bitter. The one reform upon which all Alii leaders found instant agreement, was the bitter necessity of controlling the cesspools of vice and debauchery reigning unchecked in the harbors of Lahaina and Honolulu. Seamen, coming ashore after months aboard whalers and merchantmen, sought drink and women at any cost and by any means. Hawaiian girls were lured aboard ships; the ships often putting to sea with the pretty youngsters as sexual captives. Lahaina and Honolulu waterfronts were lined with brothels and grog shops. Against haole protest, a kapu forbidding traffic in flesh and drink was unanimously passed by the usually quarrelsome grand council.

The new law, fully backed by the crown regency, and governors Boki and Hoapili, was bitterly and hysterically resented by the sailors who found themselves in the prison stockades of Lahaina and Honolulu. In October 1825 the British whaleship *Daniel* discovered that all the young women of Lahaina were under governmental kapu. Frustrated and angry seamen, blaming the missionaries on Maui for this unaccustomed outrage, made open assault on the home of Reverend William Richards. The missionary and his wife were threatened with death unless the ban on women was immediately lifted. Calmly and deliberately the Richards' stood up to the rough men who invaded their home. Next day governor Hoapili surrounded the Richards house with a guard of equally tough Hawaiians.

In Honolulu Reverend Bingham was threatened with a horsewhipping for his writings against the foreign residents who were enriching themselves by systematically robbing the natives of their economic wealth, and destroying their morals and health by selling them into sin. In every open or overt haole attack on the missionaries, Hawaiians rallied to their defense.

More than that, Queen Kaahumanu, now once again in forefront of government, made public announcement that at last she was accepting Christianity—without reservation. She and seven members of the high Alii would publicly join the American church. On December 5, 1825, they were baptized. Kaahumanu was given the Christian name of Elizabeth. It was an epochal day for the longnecks—and their greatest triumph since the conversion of Queen Keopuolani. But unlike Keopuolani, who had accepted Christ while living with two husbands, Kaahumanu had been fortuitously lifted out of polyandry by death and desertion.

The opposing faction immediately accused the big woman of turning religion into politics. Already alarmed by the growing power of the missionaries, they saw in Kaahumanu's dramatics a blatant attempt to gain mass control of the people by pandering to their religious natures.

Their fears appeared justified when, two days later, Kaahumanu called a meeting of the grand council for the purpose of finalizing a new set of laws for the nation. It was held in the back garden of Kalanimoku's big house, and, for the first time, the missionaries attended in full force. The chief's dwelling and yard were half filled with worried foreigners. Tension, anger and animosity poisoned the air.

With characteristic boldness Kaahumanu proposed that the biblical Ten Commandments serve as basis for the proposed Hawaiian code of law. Instantly Governor Boki sprang to his feet in opposition. The entire foreign colony, led by British consul Charlton, and American consul Jones, vociferously backed the governor. Boki, encouraged by this support, lashed out at the old queen. Her proposal, he charged, was the work and connivance of the missionaries. Openly denouncing their meddling into Hawaiian affairs, he reminded them they had publicly repudiated any right to formulate the nation's laws. "It is not for them to do," he insisted. "It is for the king, and for him only."

Boki, unequivocally pro-British since his return from London, was of the opinion that no laws should be adopted by the council until they had met with full approval by the British government. Mr. Charlton, of course, promptly endorsed Boki's suggestion.

Kaahumanu arose majestically, defiantly. Let the council then draw up the best code of laws possible, based on the highest and noblest premise known to the Alii, and send them back to England. Let this King George "strike out such as he pleases—and such as he approves let him send back." She further proposed that her brother, Kuakini,* governor of Hawaii, take the proposed code to England.

Boki, set aback by Kaahumanu's skill and temper, suggested: "Let Mr. Charlton, the consul, *write* to England."

The mighty woman snarled back. "Do you not know that Consul Charlton is a liar? That no confidence is to be placed in anything he says?"

Since the brusque exchanges were conducted in the Hawaiian language, and Mr. Charlton had not yet had time to master the staccato-like vernacular, he sat down smiling and amiable through the uncomplimentary charges the dowager queen was leveling.

Kuakini, who had remained quiet and silent until now, arose and stood with his sister. "I wish you all to listen," he demanded. "I am about to say something of importance."

"The Ten Commandments?" Boki growled.

But Kuakini would not be put down. "If England gives us laws— she will send men to see that they are executed. Our harbors will be filled with ships of war, and our vessels cannot go out or come in without their permission. We shall not be visited by American ships, without leave from Great Britain. We shall forever be their servants. We shall no more be able to do as we please." Many high chiefs were vociferous in their approval of what big Kuakini had said.

Cornered and nervous, Boki desperately turned to the young King Kauikeaouli, who, in his new Windsor uniform, sat silent and bored with the wrangling going on in Kalanimoku's house. "Let our king make a statement," Boki insisted. The boy arose, shy and diffident.

After Kauikeaouli had stood for an embarrassing moment, with no statement forthcoming, Kaahumanu asked what his opinion might be

*Ku-a-ki-ni: *Koo*-ah-*kee*-nee.

in regard to the council adopting the Ten Commandments as law of the land.

The king looked straight and defiant at the plural wife of his father. At last his voice came clear and direct. "It would be well to defer the laws," he said.

Boki smiled triumphantly. The matter was dropped. The young king left the circle, followed by his armed guards.

With the proposed code of laws for the Hawaiian kingdom tabled for another council's consideration, Kaahumanu knew she had lost this round of her power struggle to Boki and the king. But the monarchy, by trial and error, was groping its way toward constitutional government. The councils of chiefs were the beginnings of a legislature. The marring and jarring note was that foreigners were already speaking out as though it were their vested right.

These haole external pressures and persuasions were being felt on the entire Alii ruling structure. In spite of all the high sounding diplomatic gabble of envoys, missionaries, and shipping offices, there was unquestionable meddling in internal affairs. In a nation painfully groping toward modernity, these pressures were more divisive and hurtful than helpful.

Boki and the young king were so pro-British in attitude that their every move must square with the thoughts of King George, Charlton, and the protectorate they assumed that Britain had thrown over the islands. Kaahumanu, now that she had become a rock-ribbed Christian, was openly accused of being under the spell and control of Hiram Bingham—or "Binamu" as the natives called him. She remained adamant about incorporating the Ten Commandments into the national code of laws. She tyranically enforced the kapu on native girls swimming out to ships, and offering themselves to the crews. She fought against the waterfront bawdy houses where they were sold in whoredom, and the grog shops that kept Honolulu and Lahaina in continuous debauchery. She made no pretense about openly favoring the missionaries. She endorsed the *palapala*, and its sale of Hawaiian grammars and spellers; the *pule*, with its tracts and Protestant Bibles.

Kalanimoku, as prime minister, endeavored to steer middle course between these bitter and vocal factions. He, and sometimes Boki, received the complaints of the foreigners against the royal family and the chiefs, not only for meddling in their shipping and trading affairs, but for the unpaid bills owed haoles for the clothes, furniture and luxuries they had hauled to the islands for the enrichment of the Alii. Hundreds of shiploads of sandalwood had been promised as payment for the goods already delivered. American traders were especially vociferous about their unpaid claims. Not only were they not receiving their promised sandalwood, but the Hawaiian nation was deeply in debt for those fine American ships furnished to Liholiho for his inter-island traffic and royal navy.

Traders had other gripes, too. First of all, they hated the mission-aries for their blue-nosed tabus. They loathed the big queen who, as regent to the king, worked hand-in-glove with Bingham in kapu en-forcement. Then there was the matter of ship desertions. Enjoying the islands, as beachcombers, thieves, business proprietors and farmers, were a thousand escapees from the hellships of America. Their premise was direct and simple. Why should one suffer through the misery of whaling, the interminably long voyages around the Horn and across Pacific to China, when paradise, with a willing native girl or two, was here for the taking? Food meant only the effort of gathering it. If one still possessed ambition, there were business opportunities aplenty at Lahaina and Honolulu. But the shipping companies, crippled by the loss of men, raged at and blamed the struggling government of Hawaii.

Americans went much farther with their protests. They petitioned President John Quincy Adams of the United States for armed reprisal and protection against the non-paying and non-caring Hawaiian monarchy. They demanded warships for Honolulu and Lahaina—to enforce their just dues in sandalwood—to round up deserters at gun-point. American commercial interests, they claimed, desperately needed governmental backing.

America answered its countrymen's grievances by sending the eighty-eight-foot, twelve-gun schooner *Dolphin* to Honolulu. The stars and stripes fluttered from her masthead, but to the haoles in Hawaii, who had been expecting Commodore Hull's flagship of the Pacific squadron, she looked much too puny to intimidate Hawaiians into proper respect. The *Dolphin* was smaller even than *Cleopatra's Barge*. The beds of assignation on the king's ship held more awe for Ha-waiians than the twelve tiny guns of this war toy.

But the *Dolphin's* forty-seven-year-old skipper, Lieutenant John Percival, possessed in brusque toughness more than enough to compen-sate for the tiny craft he commanded. His ship already had swung by the Mulgrave Islands to pick up mutineers from the American *Globe*, and, small as she was, Percival intended the same lively service to his countrymen in Honolulu.

He got off to a bad start by sailing in on a Saturday. The *Dolphin* was neither challenged nor saluted. Percival sent word, by the pilot, that his ship would exchange salutes with the Honolulu fort next morning, Sunday. Governor Boki examined the request, consulted Kalanimoku, and finally Kaahumanu. The mark of the Christian queen was apparent in the message Boki sent back to Percival. "Our gunners do not work on the Lord's day. Let the salute be fired on Monday." Percival was infuriated by the lack of respect, and apparent stupidity of the Hawaiian government. Regardless of the note, the *Dolphin's* guns boomed out on Sunday morning. For answer, the mission church bell rang across the harbor.

Not until Monday morning was the *Dolphin's* second salute properly answered by the fort's guns. But by that time Lieutenant Percival was in black mood. If this were international diplomacy, the American government had chosen the wrong man.

Percival had gone to sea as a boy, and had risen to first mate of an American merchantman. During the War of 1812 he had been seized by a British press gang in Lisbon and had been forced into navy service aboard the *H.M.S. Victory.* He, with other American prisoners, had escaped this unwilling servitude by overpowering their officers. Since then, as a hard driving American naval man, he had hated Britain with a passion.

For years he chased pirates in the Atlantic and Mediterranean. Now he, and his tiny ship, were attached to the Pacific Exploring Squadron. After gathering up the *Globe's* mutineers in the Mulgraves, "Mad Jack" Percival was in Honolulu harbor to look into the matter of American ship desertions; to see that the Hawaiian chiefs settled their just debts. His vow was to give them their come-uppance for every slight.

Mad Jack and his *Dolphin* came in belligerent—but the ship was a weak hull for his anger, and housed a horny crew. It put a strain on her to even fire the salvo that announced this presence of American naval might. And it required all her crew and a lot of native help to beach the *Dolphin's* barnacled hull for much needed repairs. Still the gracious Hawaiians offered housing for Percival and his men. But Mad Jack wanted none of it. His seamen were quartered in "The Hulk," a broken-down vessel moored near the shipyard. Percival and the deck officers took lodging at the notorious Wooden House Tavern, run by Marshall & Wildes. A little astute hunting, however, and the commander found himself a grass house and a soft, warm housekeeper.

Long years after the "Mad Jack" episode was over, Queen Kaahumanu remembered. "When the chief Lord Byron came from Great Britain as a friend, we offered him a house, which he occupied as our guest. When this man Percival came we offered him a house, but he refused it, and joined himself to our enemies." Percival enjoyed the grass hut and its sensual offerings, but, unable to stomach its fish and poi, he took drink and meals at the haole tavern.

Kaahumanu, Kalanimoku and Boki were perplexed by this American's unfriendly attitude. Boki agreed to visit Percival. He would sound out the reason for this visit to the Hawaiian nation.

He found Percival drinking at the tavern, storming and pounding table over the calamity that had befallen Hawaii. American missionaries had clothed island nakedness. They had saddled a beautiful people with Christ talk. They had moved every viable woman from the waterfront.

Still there were portions of Mad Jack's tirade to which Boki, like the Honolulu's haole business entrepreneurs, was in agreement. "As to the missionaries?" Boki asked. "Do they have authority from the American government to make laws for Hawaii?"

"I know of no authority," Percival answered. "My country does not interfere with the internal concerns of *any* government."

In the next question Boki was less timid. "In America is there a law that forbids women to go to the ships?"

"Hell no! Only when the women are riotous!"

The burly commander leered across the table at the big, brown native governor. "Have these damn missionaries interfered in the affairs of *your* government?" he demanded.

"Well, yes," Boki hesitantly admitted. "They want our chiefs, and our old Kaahumanu, to turn the Ten Commandments into law."

"Who's responsible for keeping the women away from the ships?"

"Kaahumanu and Binamu."

"Who is Kaahumanu?"

"She is our queen regent. Widow of the great Kamehameha."

"What about your king?"

"He is not yet a man. His name is Kauikeaouli. For now, Kaahumanu and Kalanimoku rule for him."

"And this Binamu?"

"That is Hiram Bingham—head of the missionaries. He too is American. He has much influence—especially with Kaahumanu."

Percival whopped the table with his big hand. "I got here none too soon."

Boki's visit, when reported to the regency, added nothing to their peace of mind. Unlike Lord Byron, the American commander made no attempt to present himself or his credentials. The astute and vigilant Kaahumanu ordered her spies to watch and shadow this haole and his lechers; to allow no women for their use, under pain of death.

But Mad Jack's crew, after months at sea in the leaky *Dolphin*, were howling for sexual release. To break the doldrums of their first Sabbath ashore, they joined with other knowledgeable foreigners for an excursion up Pearl River. There maidens, tending their fish traps and taro patches, could more easily be caught and seduced.

But Kaahumanu's emissaries were ahead of the men. Her kapu was on every female encountered. Women were to keep totally out of sight. No fish were to be drawn on the Lord's Day. No patches were to be worked on the Sabbath. If the men asked for food, it must be served cold, from Saturday's baking. Under no circumstances were the foreigners to be accommodated. The *Dolphin* commander and crew returned to Honolulu harbor dissatisfied and furious.

Not until two weeks from his arrival did John Percival visit the mission, and present himself before the hated Bingham. As usual, with visiting sea captains, he was fed at the Bingham table. After the missionaries were regaled with Percival's news from home, and the high points of his fantastic career in the United States Navy as a willing hand, and in the British Navy as an impressed seaman, his hatred of England spilled over in rough and dramatic talk. He had even less good to say about Hawaiian natives. He hadn't been impressed by the pussyfooting governor, Boki. When Kaahumanu herself appeared at the mission, and sat down as welcome guest at the very table with the voluble American, he leaned to the Binghams and openly declared "I hate the sight of that woman!" Thinking that the big queen had no understanding of the English language, Percival lashed out at the spying and meddling she had effected at Pearl River. The wise old lady knew when to keep her silence. She now knew exactly where to target her own implacable hate.

The missionaries next came under Mad Jack's personal rebuke. They were foolish to imagine there could be any true converts among the natives, even if they flocked to Christian meetings. The whole attitude was wrong. The system was wrong. Instead of regulating lives and morals of the adult population, missionaries should teach only the children. If they would concentrate their efforts on the young ones, cease meddling in the affairs of another nation, and allow grown Hawaiian girls to return to their old ways, he would commend the mission, and support their efforts. But if they persisted in the errors of their ways, he would report them to the American government. He was certain that steps would be taken to stop the nonsense.

As to the king, the regents, and the Hawaiian chiefs, John Percival would call for a meeting with them. Since he had "something unpleasant to say," he wanted no American missionaries on hand for the talk. "I do not want them to think that you missionaries have anything to do with the government I represent."

The council of chiefs, as usual, was held in the green and fragrant yard of the prime minister's house. As host to the long awaited confrontation with the representative from America, Kalanimoku made special effort to effect the role of William Pitt this day. He put on his hated shoes; he wore the best of his English cut clothes. Governor Boki, who had actually been to England, and had previously faced the mercurial Percival, wore the clothes Liholiho had bought for him in London. The young king came in his Windsor uniform. But Kaahumanu, who now was on the side of Jesus, wore the loose-fitting Mother Hubbard of gingham which Hiram Bingham and the missionaries insisted native women should garb themselves. The gown, cut to queen size, seemed unbelievably severe in comparison to the flamboyant silks and satins the matriarch had once worn as favorite of two kings.

After weeks of convivial fraternization with the haoles of Honolulu, John Percival had reached the conclusion that the long-standing debts of the Hawaiian Alii to American shippers was a feeble matter compared to the kapu old Kaahumanu had placed on the women. He was convinced the missionaries were blue-nosed meddlers, the natives who allowed themselves to be so used were dupes, and he strode into the meeting boorish and belligerent.

His first question was, "Who is the king?" Kaahumanu pointed to the quiet and reserved youth in the British livery. "Who is his guardian?" Percival demanded. When Kaahumanu pointed to herself, Mad Jack caustically eyed the big figure in the house sack, and let out with an undignified laugh.

"Who runs this country?"

"Myself and Kalanimoku. Kalanimoku is prime minister—but the prime minister is in my charge."

"And Boki?" Percival pointed to the big man, ill at ease in his London clothes.

"Boki is governor only of Oahu," Kaahumanu promptly answered.

"Then I've been talking to the wrong chief. Since, in essence, *you* are the king—then, what I have to say is for you to hear."

"As chief from another land, why are you so angry?" Kaahumanu asked.

"Who put the kapu on the women?"

"It was by me."

"Who told you that women must be kapu to sailors?"

"It was God," Kaahumanu promptly replied.

Percival laughed. "That means Bingham."

"It was Binamu who made the word of God known to us."

That did it. Lieutenant John Percival, using the United States of America as his authority, launched into a fierce tirade. The strict kapu was foolish, impractical, and must end, he declared. Hawaii would do well to quit listening to the bad advice of people who had no understanding of life's necessities. In America, and in England, there was no punishment for prostitution. Women who served sailors were not threatened with their lives, or thrown into jail. These women might not be favored of God, but they were not kapu. It was not wrong of them to take money, or cloth, or trinkets from foreigners for providing something fundamentally necessary to lonely sailors.

Billy Pitt and Boki both broke into the angry lecture. They wanted only that their people turn from wickedness and disease, they tried to explain. If prostitution was allowed in America—then let American sailors seek their own women there—but not in Honolulu or Lahaina. If Lieutenant Percival had brought haole women with him, on his ship, the chiefs would have laid no kapu upon them.

Percival explained that it was not for himself that he wanted women. Whether it was wrong or right in the sight of God was no concern of his. He was thinking only of his crew. They needed girls. They were violent and restive. He feared what would happen if women continued to be withheld.

He reminded them of the days of their great Kamehameha. In those times the Hawaiian nation had "attended properly" to the ships of America and England. In those days there was no trouble. In those days the people were happy.

"In those days the Word of God had not arrived," Kaahumanu's great voice boomed angrily. "In those days we were dark minded. We were lewd. We thought nothing of killing, and of burning people alive. But God, through the missionaries, has shown the better way."

Percival then laid down the ultimatum. The kapu must be lifted at once. Women must be allowed to service the ships. Also he had come to Hawaii to see about the huge debts which Hawaiian chiefs owed American shippers. He would come back in a few days to receive an answer from the chiefs as to the freeing of women, and he would come back expecting either payment of the debts, or that the chiefs sign the papers he would bring. These papers would levy all unpaid debts of Kamehameha II, and all of the lesser chiefs' unpaid debts, as a financial responsibility upon the Hawaiian kingdom. The nation must realize its obligation to pay out every dollar owed to American shippers—either in money, or in sandalwood.

On that dour note, Percival took his leave of the council.

Instead of the promised meeting with the chiefs, Percival, before the week was out, summoned Queen Kaahumanu. But he had underestimated the big woman. She'd come to hate this vulgar and noisy American as much as he hated her. Boki and Kalanimoku had both been right. Englishmen were men of God, and gentlemen. This naval commander, alongside Lord Byron, was like comparing a pig to a sailfish. She could just as easily hate America, were it not for Hiram Bingham, the gentle missionaries, and the glorious word of God they had brought.

Before facing Mad Jack Percival, Kaahumanu first sought the advice of Hiram Bingham. Binamu urged her to trust in God; to stand true to her convictions. So, in spite of the furious tirade she received from Percival, she defiantly refused to release the women for sailors' pleasure, and she refused to sign the papers of indebtedness on behalf of her nation. But back to the worried chiefs she carried Percival's message. He demanded one more meeting, at Billy Pitt's house. On Sunday morning he would tell what America would do about the unpaid debts, the defiant old queen, and the uncooperative women.

On that Sabbath, at the prime minister's residence, the worried Hawaiians began arriving. Boki and Namahana came in first; other chiefs and chiefesses followed. This time, contrary to Percival's orders, Hiram Bingham made his appearance. Binamu had become greatly concerned with the evil pressures being laid upon his Christian Alii. This day he intended being counted on the Lord's side. It was expected too that Mr. Charlton would be on hand to stand up for Britain's interests. Neither Kaahumanu nor Kamehameha III had yet arrived.

It came suddenly, and without warning. Three burly seamen, brandishing clubs, charged across the veranda, and reached the front door of the house. Like madmen, they laid on with their clubs until the door was smashed open. To the startled Kalanimoku they howled, "Where are the women?"

They were only the vanguard of a mob of an hundred or more seamen—crewmen from the *Dolphin*—sailors from numerous whalers and merchant hellships that idled this Sunday in the port of Honolulu.

Billy Pitt's usually urbane smile toward foreigners froze at sight of the pugnacious intruders. "There are no women here," he said curtly, pushing shut what was left of the broken door.

Sensing the peril, he and Boki insisted that Hiram Bingham get clear of the premises; back to the mission house. The female high chiefess, Namahana, and her husband, pushed and pulled the man of God out through the side door to the yard. There they found themselves full center to a shouting, shoving mob of American sailors. It took heavy effort of the two big Hawaiians to fend off blows from the club-swinging madmen, when they saw that Old Binamu himself was their prize. Behind the slowly retreating missionary and his faithful natives could be heard the shouts, and the crash and tinkle of glass, as the mob smashed its way into the house.

On the outskirts of the surging crowd had gathered the Hawaiian natives, uncertain as to what they should do in the crisis. At mission schools they had been taught to avoid violence, to practice the Golden Rule, to have nothing more to do with the warring past. They had been coached to the understanding that officers and men of the visiting warships—especially English and American warships—were their friends; their protectors. Now they were witnessing the beloved preacher and teacher, Binamu, being jostled, threatened and profaned at by sailors from his own country. In one hesitant instant the native men shed their Christian gentility. It was that same sudden change their fathers had experienced — from God-worshipping children before Captain Cook, to the most savage kind of warriors. Unhesitatingly they swept in upon the sailors.

With flailing arms and hard fists, shouting the battle cries of their ancestors, they waded into the mob that was wrecking Kalanimoku's beautiful house. Not even the clubs of the sailors were match for strong brown arms skilled at cracking heads and threshing earth with their adversaries, kanaka style. Not until the howling, shouting Hawaiians had rescued their preacher, cleared the premises, and driven the surprised seamen back to the waterfront, did they cease their Sabbath war, and return once again to Christian docility.

This time it was Mad Jack Percival's turn to account for the damage and the outrageous acts of his men. When, an hour later, he entered the prime minister's residence, and personally witnessed the appalling mess for which he was directly responsible, he actually apologized on behalf of his nation, and more particularly for the acts of the *Dolphin's* crew. The sailors would be chastised. Cost of repairs to the house and yard would be taken out of crew pay. The commander was truly sorry for this breach of navy manners.

The angry Queen Kaahumanu was present to hear Mad Jack's apology. Unmoved by it, she scorched him with an unchristian volley of choice Hawaiian epithets. Unable to understand them in Hawaiian version, Percival could not mistake their import.

This big woman invariably stirred his ire. Percival shed all contriteness. Once more he lashed out at the Hawaiian chiefs for their stupidity and unconcern for debts and needs. Once again he placed full blame upon them for the action of his men. If the chiefs did not immediately lift the kapu on Honolulu women, such acts would happen again and again—so long as there was a ship's crew in port.

He bluntly reminded them that he was coming back with the paper they must sign. In name of the Hawaiian nation, they must guarantee full payment to American shippers for all debts owing them. If they failed in this obligation, they could expect more American warships in port—with guns trained on everything from Waikiki to the mission. And, if they didn't want equal measure from the *Dolphin* itself, they had damn well better release females to their functions.

The big queen and her fellow chiefs now were reluctantly forced to the realization of how difficult it could sometimes be to follow the Word in its purity—and still hang on to tranquility and common sense. In the days that followed Bingham was insistent that his converts remain steadfast in preserving the chastity of Honolulu's willing maidens. As to the debts of Liholiho and the chiefs for their ships and luxuries, he was less adamant. The *palapala* had not yet taught them enough to decipher the thick sheaf of documents which Percival presented for their signatures, but all the chiefs of the council, with the exception of the king, signed it in behalf of the Hawaiian nation. There could be no question but what Mad Jack Percival had brought hell and fright to Honolulu. The *Dolphin* was a small ship, but a frenzied genius commanded it.

Before the week was out, Kaahumanu had reluctantly lifted the kapu.

The stockade was opened. The frail sisters incarcerated therein joined scores of other willing *wahines* in the happy task of servicing the ships' crews. Boatloads of them went out to the tall masted vessels that dotted Honolulu harbor. There was dancing on the decks of the *Dolphin,* the merchantmen, and the whalers. It was even better this time. Girls could keep all the money they received—without having to divide any portion of it with agents of the Alii.

John Percival, to the haoles, was hero of the islands. Shippers took new heart. The old queen had been stopped short in her imperious tracks. The meddling missionaries had been hit where it hurt. And sailors were happy that once more Honolulu was the free and easy port of olden days.

One by one the whaleships departed for their long and lonely traverse of the seas. Except for the occasional porting of a merchantman, the *Dolphin* and her pugnacious crew were left alone to Honolulu.

Finally, on May 11, 1826, the tiny warship lifted sail and departed the islands forever. The chiefs sighed with relief and joy at sight of her fading exit. Mad Jack and his crazy crew were gone at last. The American scourge had sailed back to the place where it belonged. Jesus was still with the people. Honolulu's soiled doves were again rounded up and returned to the stockade.

VII

VISITATION of another American warship in that same climactic year was, at first, viewed by the chiefs as a national calamity. It was late fall when the *U.S.S. Peacock* dropped anchor in Honolulu harbor, but, as compared to the earlier *Dolphin*, she was twice as big, and doubly menacing. Rather than fight what she considered the inevitable, Kaahumanu immediately lifted the female kapu, and again ordered the stockade unlocked. Even with the harbor doxies free, she and the chiefs braced themselves for another ugly confrontation with a lewd and blasphemous American.

Commodore Thomas Ap Catesby Jones, U.S.N., commander of the more imposing warship *Peacock*, quickly discovered that it would necessitate a lot of fence-mending before the Hawaiian Alii were inclined to render the same trust and respect they automatically gave to the well-disciplined and courteous captains and crews of English vessels, or even those of the less popular French. Luckily the *Peacock* sailed into Honolulu harbor on a week day. She gave and took her gun salute without making an international incident of it. Commodore Jones kept the swimming prostitutes off the ship decks. The *Peacock's* sailors were forbidden to pursue the offering females to shore like hunters seeking quail.

Jones did not seek shelter with riotous foreigners, nor did he demand lavish shore quarters and attention from the Hawaiian government. He remained discreetly aboard his ship. He kept his disciplined crew under restraint while he petitioned king and chiefs for audience and rights of landing. The regents and chiefs, understandably, were slow about inviting another savage American into their dignified circle, nor did they want to repair walls and replace glass in Alii palaces so soon after the destructive assault on the house of the prime minister. But Jones was permitted to land.

While the commodore awaited official recognition of his mission, he spent considerable time interviewing and making friends with the people of Honolulu, both native and haole. He considered it important to hear firsthand the grievances of the natives against Americans, along with the haole side of the story concerning unpaid debts, and the insufferable restrictions American missionaries had foisted on the city through their over-zealous native converts. He realized, too, how much tact and diplomacy would be necessary before he could dispel the bad impression left so vividly by Mad Jack Percival. Unlike Percival, Jones paid little heed to complaints over Kaahumanu's female kapu. He considered this a matter to be decided by the monarchy in any way they chose. Hawaiian complaints about Percival were duly noted—for possible court-martial evidence against the *Dolphin's* obstreperous skipper.

For Commodore Thomas Ap Catesby Jones was in Hawaii as direct and personal representative of the United States President, John Quincy Adams. Even the commonest Hawaiian instantly recognized him as Alii. He possessed the stately, erect carriage, courtly manners, the large shapely head, and the noble brow—characteristics bred into the elect. Actually Jones *was* an aristocrat, born out of Virginia's cavalier ancestry. He had been educated in the highest tradition and, more than being merely an officer and a gentleman, he was a diplomat born and bred. His dark eyes, under shaggy brows, were kindly and understanding.

Jones instantly felt kinship with the smiling, beautiful Hawaiians. He had only to level his expressive eyes with the natives, to gaze into their generous hearts, to win their ready affection. Before Jones ever officially reached the Hawaiian court, the people were calling him *Ke Alii o Ka Maka Olualu*—"the Chief with the Benevolent Eyes."

When Commodore Jones finally entered the royal court, he came with highest recommendation—from the people themselves. Kaahumanu, by long experience, could instantly appraise a good man. But when she saw Jones she was so impressed that she all but forgot the hate that festered in her mind and heart against Percival.

Percival had reported that the American missionaries were seat of power in the Hawaiian monarchy; that they exerted influence with the Alii detrimental to Hawaiians and haoles alike. Shrewd and diplomatic, Commodore Jones now made his own quick analysis of the situation, and came out of it convinced that the mighty matriarch, widow of Kamehameha the Great, was the real and accepted power source. It was to Kaahumanu he paid his first state visit.

The complimentary gesture was not lost on the lonely old queen. Where she had been repelled by the crudity of Lieutenant Percival, she was charmed by the courtesy and flawless manners of the commodore. They were instantly attracted one to another, and Kaahumanu had visual evidence that what Hawaiians were already saying about this American envoy was truth indeed. Because he had the stature, the bearing, the looks, and the walk of Alii, Commodore Jones *was* Alii. This first meeting of the dowager queen and the distinguished American was to have far-reaching consequences in the rise of American prestige in Hawaii and the Pacific. The commodore's courtly manners were ever a delight to Kaahumanu. She had attended royal functions since the palace days at Kailua, and this man's intuitive feel for royal decorum, his attention to the niceties of protocol, marked him a man born high and elite.

While he paid her homage as true head of the kingdom, he was subtly flattering in other ways. He responded to her every wish; he never failed in his offering of those delicate personal attentions so important to women. All of this enchanted Kaahumanu who, in spite of her imperious nature, could respond with feminine charm when dealing with men. Jones, in turn, was thoroughly intrigued by this island Amazon. The stories told about the regal creature who had served as hostess to the court of Kamehameha during the visits of European notables had not been exaggerated.

Kaahumanu could not avoid comparing the commodore with the well remembered Lord Byron. And he lost none in the weighing. Lord Byron had been equally attentive, and equally charming, but the big queen had never been able to shake the feeling that Byron's closer interests lay in Boki and his beautiful wife Liliha—both of whom had visited London and had returned pro-British to the core. To be considered second place in any man's esteem and affection was an unforgivable affront to the proud Kaahumanu.

Commodore Jones, having won Kaahumanu to his friendship and goodwill, used diplomatic restraint in seeking court with the other Alii powers functioning during the young king's regency. He graciously accepted the dwelling Kaahumanu provided for his shore headquarters. Here he went about the pressing and mundane business of hearing out the complaints of haoles and natives alike, as to American problems, before requesting a full-dressed royal audience on state level.

The shippers, whose howls over desertion of American seamen had precipitated the two naval incursions into the islands, were heard out by the patient commodore. The runaway sailors truly were a problem, and he endeavored, insofar as possible, to also hear their story. Quickly he realized that many of the ship-jumpers were living as harmless and inoffensive beachcombers, practically adopted by the natives. Others had become farmers and shop owners, and were good and upright Hawaiian citizens. Only the hard core, dangerous and criminal escapees were marked for his handling. Of the latter, he and his marines rounded up about thirty. They were jailed in the Honolulu stockade, and turned over to departing whaleships, for deportation to the United States. Kalanimoku and Boki were pleased by this prompt riddance of the haole scum that had made life unbearable for many Hawaiians.

With the same attention and patience Commodore Jones listened to the heartbreak of the hundreds of natives who had fallen into the morass of debt to American shippers, shop-owners, and whiskey entre-preneurs. He realized that this happy, carefree people were victims of a system beyond their abilities to cope. When credit was offered, they took it. Whatever they saw in baubles or indulgences, they wanted. It had been too easy to accept the temptatious offers. But this bondage of debt was something the haoles themselves had brought to the islands. The commodore stood on the side of the Hawaiian natives in one valiant effort to clean the slate.

When it came to the larger obligation, incurred by the dead Liho-liho's profligacy for ships and luxuries, and the Alii's hunger for like goods in almost equal measure, Commodore Jones amazingly smoothed the way—through respect and close attention to Kaahumanu. His meeting with the king, regents and high chiefs, was nothing at all like that session of threat and coercion conducted by his predecessor. Be-cause he had already won over the most important woman in the realm, Jones was able to face the problem with these intelligent and kindly people in an atmosphere of tact, courtesy and goodwill.

Frankly and openly he acknowledged that grave mistakes had been made on both sides. Prices extracted by the American traders had been exorbitant. Desire for possessions and aggrandizement had trapped the late king and his national leaders. The total American claim was listed at more than half a million dollars, payable in gold or sandalwood. The commodore suggested that settlement could be made at much less, if it were agreeable to the chiefs and regents. He suggested that they forget they had unwittingly signed papers under duress of John Perci-val. He advised that they make their own reasonable offer for settle-ment. The main point was that, whatever the final figures arrived at, this obligation should be considered and accepted as a national responsi-bility of the Hawaiian kingdom.

Jones, ever the diplomat, did not press the matter. With genuine understanding of the Hawaiian temperament, he graciously allowed the decision to drag along for six weeks. When the chiefs called the commodore in for questions and suggestions, the high state get-togethers were carried on in an air of amiability and friendship. He had no difficulty whatsoever in winning an agreement from the Hawaiian government to pay one hundred and fifty thousand dollars for the total debt. Sandalwood, delivered to the beaches, was to be the medium of exchange.

With the mission which President Adams had directed, now suc-cessfully completed in almost every phase, Commodore Jones assumed a prerogative that was not part of his portfolio. He proposed a treaty between the Hawaiian kingdom and the United States of America. America, he said, would not ask for extraordinary privileges—only

"equal privileges with the most favored nations in time of peace, and
strict neutrality in time of war." He explained that he was in no hurry
for an answer to his unexpected suggestion but, again showing prescience for Hawaiian "talk-talk," suggested a month for them to think
it over.

The moment Richard Charlton, consul to His Britannic Majesty,
heard of Commodore Jones's proposal, he lodged diplomatic protest. He
reminded the Hawaiian king and his regents that their nation was
already a protectorate of Great Britain. They had no right whatever,
he declared, to sign an independent treaty with another nation. But
in Jones, Charlton met his equal. The commodore reminded Charlton
that his own commission as consul was open recognition of the fact
that he himself recognized the Kingdom of Hawaii as an independent
state.

Kaahumanu was entranced by the adroit manner Jones handled
himself in every situation. She now liked and accepted the American
religion, and Jones was a practicing example of it. She would readily
have married this Chief with the Kind Eyes were the opportunity
available.

The first treaty between America and the Hawaiian Kingdom was
signed December 23, 1826—in spite of protests of the British consul.
Signatories to it were Commodore Thomas Ap Catesby Jones, representing the United States. And, in behalf of the Hawaiian nation, it
was signed by Elizabeth Kaahumanu, queen regent; Kalanimoku, as
prime minister; the chiefs Boki and Hoapili; and chiefess Lydia Namahana.

The only ruffle to this masterful and idyllic visit of Commodore
Jones to the Sandwich Islands occurred just after Christmas, and only
a week or so before his departure for the United States. The matter of
the missionaries and their undue influence on the government through
"the old queen" still churned the nation. From talking with the foreigners Jones could not avoid the fact that Bingham and his longnecks
were considered the source of every woe. The missionaries themselves
provoked the matter to crisis by publishing a circular denying every
charge, open and snide, against them. Furthermore, to set every lie
and calumny at rest, they demanded full and public investigation of
their activities.

Honolulu's foreigners accepted the challenge with alacrity. Here
was opportunity to expose and discredit the longnecks once and for all.
The public hearing was held at the home of Boki, as governor of Oahu.
Commodore Jones reluctantly but graciously accepted the role of arbi-
trator of the dispute.

It was anticipated the session would be an explosive one. And it might well have been such under a less skillful hand. The missionaries were allowed to read their circular before their accusers. Those who had charges of malfeasance of any kind were challenged to make them public. As expected, Richard Charlton was first to speak to the issue. With anger and obvious hostility he accused the missionaries of interference with the lives and well-being of the natives. Longnecks had destroyed natives' freedom; had injured health by stuffing them into clothes that bundled them up, in the tropics, like the somber Puritans of Boston. By interfering with Hawaiian sports, and sealing natives into a rigid Sabbath, missionaries were changing a nation of carefree and happy people into the sad pattern of themselves. Worse, commerce and industry were stalled and stagnated because American Christians kept the populace constantly employed building churches throughout the land.

The most serious charge leveled was that the longnecks controlled the thinking and exerted undue influence over many of the chiefs and leaders in government. Not one of the Alii dared testify against the missionaries, simply because old Queen Kaahumanu had ordered them to keep their mouths shut on such matters. And the woman herself was under total dominance of Hiram Bingham.

Charlton was followed by other foreigners, who made the same charges or worse. As arbiter of a national ferment Commodore Jones was faced with a delicate and absolute task. Tactfully he questioned each accuser personally. When it came to placing the charges into actionable context, not one could present evidence of legal wrongdoing on the part of the longnecks. And they were forced to openly admit this fact. Astute probing of some of the haoles brought admittance that their hatred of the missionaries stemmed from warnings the missionaries constantly made to the natives that they were being exploited and overcharged by the shippers and shopkeepers. In this, after examining the public debt, Jones was forced to conclude it a Christian virtue rather than a vice.

When Jones requested the missionaries to make statements for their own defense, Bingham and his associates refused to do so. Every proof of their innocence was published in the circular, Bingham insisted. Let the circular be their defense. So the matter was left to the American commodore for decision. He asked for a few days to ponder the evidence.

The final statement of Jones came in full vindication for the longnecks, and a triumph for Kaahumanu and the more ecstatic native Christians. In public declaration Jones wrote: "Not one jot or tittle, not one iota derogatory to their characters as men or ministers of the Gospel was made against them."

To the disgruntled haoles the commodore's whitewash was merely another example of Bingham's manipulation of Kaahumanu. Apparently now it extended to coercion of the American envoy.

Commodore Thomas Ap Catesby Jones and his handsome warship *Peacock* sailed from Honolulu January 6, 1827. Although the treaty he had negotiated with such pains and care between the United States and the Hawaiian Kingdom was never ratified by the U. S. Senate, the mission in every other way was a brilliant success. He was one of those extraordinary men who, no matter how brief their appearance on the world's stage, leave an indelible imprint and an undimming recollection through personality, common sense, graciousness, and a proper timing with destiny. As a diplomat, this distinguished Virginian equalled, and in some ways surpassed, England's Lord Byron.

The Hawaiian people, long after he had departed their islands, considered him truly Alii born. He had worn every physical and mystical symbol associated with aristocracy as known and accepted by the Polynesians. With telepathic swiftness he had won the respect, affection and reverence of the Hawaiian people. More important, this man, and this man alone, laid the groundwork for the coming influence of America in Hawaii and the Pacific. As to actual physical possession of the islands, Great Britain had undeniable prior right. But an American commodore, because he was kind and attentive to a lonely old queen, changed history's course midstream.

VIII

AFTER DEPARTURE of the *Peacock* and Commodore Jones there was serenity in the island paradise. But not for long. Undercurrents of national erosion and divided loyalties still muddied the stream of Hawaiian life. Many a person longed for the old ways, and were confused and alarmed by the haole forces that were rooting out ancient customs and the very joy of living. They preferred the low, passionate moan of the conch shell to the metallic whang of the church and school bells that meant the new tabus of the Christians. Innately they loathed and resented the debauchery and commercialism that had come in with the foreigners, in spite of the *pule* and the *palapala* of the longnecks.

Within a year the dissidents found a leader in Boki. And the Oahu governor's thatched palace at Waikiki became the scene of fundamentalist revolt. Boki could never forget that he had been to London, and had observed Anglican worship as practiced in that great nation. He had been, like Billy Pitt, baptized into the Catholic faith, aboard the French ship *L'Uranie*, and, because he didn't like the longneck way of blighting Hawaiian spirit as requisite to conversion, he had come to loathe Hiram Bingham, his American toadies, and the way Binamu manipulated government through that mighty zealot Kaahumanu.

First thing the big woman had done, after the departure of Commodore Jones, had been to assign to Boki the responsibility of paying off the American debt on behalf of the nation. Being completely pro-British in sentiment and loyalty, it irked Boki to have to turn over to American shippers the best and last of the already scarce sandalwood.

To pay all that was owing would completely devastate the islands of their greatest single asset. The fact that king and chiefs had pledged the sandalwood without thought of its eventual depletion was not the whole point. That he should have to preside over this final debacle, to slight his British friends, to force the now rebellious islanders into the wet and cold forests for the high and occasional trees, was more than Boki could accept.

Worse, he had enormous debts of his own, mostly to British and French entrepreneurs. For personal relief, and to augment payments on the American debt, Boki decided to go into business for himself. Foreigners made vast profits selling liquor. He would open up a big grog shop in Honolulu, and gain some of those profits for himself. When Kaahumanu heard of it, she came at the hapless governor with scorching fury. Her Kamehameha had never allowed Hawaiians to traffic in the poison that destroyed. As regent, and in the name of the present king, neither would she. Boki's liquor store must close. As further reprimand, the leases he had made to haoles for the growing of sugar cane on crown lands, for the purpose of making rum, were immediately cancelled. With this edict went other grants he had made to favored British friends.

Boki could have weathered the loss, and tolerated the rebuke, had not the imperious old woman assigned other crown lands to the missionaries. He watched her command the Hawaiian nation to build two-story houses for the longnecks at each of these gift stations. The land she was so generously doling out to Americans was Kamehameha's own, tendered to the chiefs at his death as sacred gift. Boki deliberately made certain that the rumble of dissent among loyal Aliis sifted down to the angry cells of the commoners.

As Boki's business failures and debts mounted he grew more infuriated with Kaahumanu and the friends she was favoring. He began to see the Hawaiian kingdom as a nation defrauded; in the grip of forces both overwhelming and tragic. He remembered the old way,

before the haoles had cruelly despoiled it. There was a time when the
island kingdom had been a world of beauty, serenity and happiness.
Now greed and venality gripped everyone—Alii and commoner. And
sadness was everywhere.

When Kaahumanu revisited the island of Hawaii, and in touring
the seat of Kamehameha the Great, despoiled the holy of holies, Boki's
fury erupted like Mauna Loa. South of Kailua, at Honaunau, was the
City of Refuge, the *heiau*, and Hale-o-Keawe, the sacred necropolis
where were deposited the sacked bones of ancient chiefs. In the most
heretical act of her long history of heresy, the old queen ordered the
bones brought to Honolulu for Christian burial. Worse, she hauled
back with her, from the ghostly City of Refuge, a collection of the
carved images of the once sacred gods. These the old woman blithely
tendered to Mr. Bingham, with suggestion that Binamu work them
into cane handles and collection boxes. It took this final blasphemy to
turn Boki into a dedicated revolutionary.

He had plenty of support among the natives. There were chiefs
who seethed with like fury. All of them saw in Boki a leader to right
the wrongs; to obliterate once and for all this meddlesome and heretical
old woman. There were others who rallied to his support with less
violent thoughts. Some were only confirmed patriots who were frightened and disturbed because the kingdom was torn and festering with
the polarizing wounds of partisanship. They were convinced that anything less than national unity spelled eventual death for the nation.
To avoid Hawaiian destruction they hoped for an airing of the problems. With compromise would come a rebirth of island faith and
spirituality.

A segment of unrest lay with the older natives who still had tender
recollection of how it was before the foreigner had grubbed and clawed
his way into their culture. More than anything they wanted the island
paradise their ancestors had bequeathed them. They had grown weary
and disgusted with the tensions; the Christ-generated kapus; the endless clash of the present culture with the traditional ways. They wanted
return of the joy-filled yesterdays, when one didn't have to work for
the haoles; when there had been time for leisure, play, and contempla-
tion.

When the black-headed fiery-eyed Boki called a rump council at
his Waikiki yard and dwelling, every segment of protest was on hand.
Absent was the king, the regents, and the court sycophants who cared
more for Binamu and his longnecks than they cared for the nation they
were strangling. But Kaahumanu, through her loyal and discreet spies,
was fully aware of Boki's insurgency.

That the old queen was subject for discussion was inevitable. One wild-eyed nihilist suggested that control of the nation would never be restored until the American missionaries were driven from the land, and that bossy old woman was "disemboweled" on the *heiau* of her ancestors.

But to the old people, such barbaric dispatch of Kamehameha's queen was blasphemy. They arose to their feet in angry protest. With all her faults, they loved her. The trouble was not Kaahumanu. Look elsewhere!

And there was the problem of the king, one chief reminded. Kauikeaouli was now sixteen years of age. Were he unfettered by his Alii advisers, and missionary tutors, and could assert his rights—*he* would lead his people back to the tranquil nation his father had bequeathed. Let him not be like his profligate brother, Liholiho. Truly the king must be conscious of the ever-widening rift of his people?

Boki quickly explained that this was definitely so, but that the young man was bitterly torn between conflicting loyalties. The king was respectful enough to his father's queen and regent, Kaahumanu, but he, Boki, was proud to report that he held a deeper love and affection for Boki and Liliha.

Boki acknowledged one point of constant friction between himself and Kaahumanu—that matter of the young king choosing a wife, or wives. The governor frankly confessed that he, along with others of the older Alii, wanted Kaiukeaouli to marry his own sister, Princess Nahienaena. There was nothing wrong with a marriage between brother and sister. It was the old way—traditional—back to the gods. This, the *pi'oia*, was the sacred marriage of Alii royalty. Like the bond between Liholiho and Kamamalu, the young king had tenderest of thoughts for Nahienaena. He was writing *meles* to her. It could be that he was making love to her.

Like most orthodox Hawaiians, Boki could see nothing even remotely amiss in King Kauikeaouli marrying his sister. Why the suggestion of *pi'oia* should strike horror in the minds of Bingham and his longnecks was completely incomprehensible. Yet the longnecks, and now Kaahumanu, were standing implacably against a king's exercise of his own natural desires. It was wrong. Another evidence of foreign meddling in the affairs of the nation.

Boki's house and yard echoed to the angry cries of the extremists. Destroy King Binamu and Queen Kaahumanu! But once more the old people sprang to defense of the old woman. "The fault is not in Kaahumanu. The fault is with the haoles who deceive her."

The outcry remained unanimously insistent that the foreigners, good and bad, be ousted from the islands. Everyone agreed of this necessity before Hawaii could truly be returned to Hawaiians. But the intransigent fact remained, in spite of the seditious oratory, that the foreigners moved and manipulated with impunity the royal court of the nation. Boki himself had welcomed and defended British interests—as had his wife Liliha—as had his brother, prime minister Kalanimoku. Kaahumanu and her Alii retinue were enamored of Americans, and under almost complete dominance of Binamu. Again came scathing denunciation of that wicked and ambitious woman.

This time the old people were spared the necessity of rushing to her defense. The meeting was interrupted by arrival of High Chief Kekuanaoa,* former paramour of Kaahumanu, and he who had accompanied Boki to London as part of the ill-fated royal delegation. As a member of the pro-British circle, Boki warmly respected Kekuanaoa, and welcomed him as friend. But now, dispatched to the insurgent conclave by Kaahumanu herself, the high chief proceeded to put strain on that friendship.

His first utterance, as he strode to the front of the noisy gathering, was that he had come from Kaahumanu, and at her behest. She had heard that, as revolutionaries, they planned to assassinate her. Her message to Boki—to all of them—was that if such was their desire, they would find her alone in her home, unattended by guards, waiting and ready for their guns, knives, or poison.

"Kill her, if it be your wish!" Kekuanaoa shouted, flinging his arms dramatically. "Destroy her, if it be your desire! She awaits you willingly. It is for you to do as you please. But in her last words she begs of you not to set the nation against itself in war. Allow her to be the sacrifice! But please—in the name of the Christ she loves—do not push the nation into conflict!"

The assemblage was stunned to silence by the chief's operatic pronouncement. Then once more the old people were on their feet. They cried Kaahumanu's name. They blessed her enthusiastically. They begged that the mighty woman be spared—be loved—be adopted as the symbol of unity.

Kaahumanu's timing had been flawless. Not a soul now wished her ill, or wanted to do her injury. By the next morning the fire and fervor had gone out of Boki's seditious eruption, and the people were quietly trudging back to their homes. Older natives still clung to the hope that somehow, miraculously, the foreign influence would be removed, and the nation would sink back to its tranquil and mystic past. As for themselves, they no longer were anxious or ready to push things along with guns or knives.

*Ke-ku-a-na-o-a: *Kay*-koo-ah-nah-*oo*-ah.

Boki could not help but be stunned and crushed by the defeat. Broken in spirit, headed for complete oblivion and disgrace, he realized now that any further opposition to Kaahumanu and the longnecks was useless. There was no reprisal against him or his activities in fomenting a revolution. He remained in office as governor of Oahu. But in guiding the affairs of the nation, his voice now grew low, listless, and inert.

IX

KAUIKEAOULI, second son of Queen Keopuolani, and the second prince of the great Kamehameha to rule the Hawaiian kingdom, was now, at age sixteen, restless for the full authority that had been promised him as Kamehameha III. He was growing into a tall, reedy, handsome man—a replica of all that was physically symbolic of the best in Hawaiian aristocracy. He was as handsome as Liholiho. He possessed the same sensitive intuitiveness, and love of native land and people, that had so motivated his ill-fated brother. His shy gentility, perfect manners, and ever probing intellect, gave little hint in his earlier years of the strong will hidden beneath.

Unlike Liholiho, Kauikeaouli was a product of Christian training and British-American persuasion. Under Binamu and the longnecks his eager young mind had devoured everything they provided in the *palapala* and, not having been exposed to the earlier "heathen" worship that had motivated his mighty father, he accepted the *pule* without too much resistance. But, as with Liholiho, he was not averse to haole enticements of drinking and gambling, and, like a true Alii, was appreciative of anything that sensuously glided in lithe and alluring island femininity past his eager gaze. With these latter urges, Bingham and his missionaries had special problems.

He held in deep affection his sister, Princess Nahienaena, and Liliha, wife of the noisy and irascible Boki. Both were beautiful, vivacious, and utterly charming women. It was Liliha who guided the young king in building and furnishing his new palace at Waikiki. Unlike Kalanimoku, who had set his big dwelling at Pohukaina, on the southeast shore of Honolulu harbor—much too handy for the constant intrusion of favor-seeking and mischief-bent haole shippers, sailors and merchants—the king had honored the palm-studded stretch of sand at Waikiki with his royal enclosure.

The Right Reverend M. Russell, who visited the palace as guest of Bingham and the king, later described it in his book *Polynesia*, published 1849, in London: "The floors are covered with beautiful carpets suited to the climate, the large windows at either side of the room and the folding doors of glass at each end are hung with draperies of crimson damask; the furniture consists of handsome pier tables and large mirrors, and of a line of glass chandeliers suspended along the center of the ceiling with lustres and candelabra of bronze affixed to the pillars which line the sides of the apartment . . . A native lounge occupied the whole length of the apartment . . . In the center stood a rich couch of yellow damask, with armed chairs on either side . . . The portraits of the late king and queen, painted in London, are placed in the upper end in carved frames, richly gilt." A real blending of Kauikeaouli's "foreign" tastes, and Liliha's English observance.

Long before his maturity the young king had been irked and chafed by the rigid control of state by the regency, headed by the fanatical Kaahumanu. With the missionaries as his tutors and preceptors, he was practically forced to follow the big woman's lead in matters religious. But his deeper loyalties were for the discredited Boki, and the exciting Liliha. His constant preoccupation with Hawaiian tradition, nationality, and physical welfare of the brutally exploited natives, sprang from the British-nurtured and pro-Hawaiian thinking of the governor and his wife. When the young monarch, caught between two immense and smothering pressures, lashed out against the restraints that bound him, it was the aging Kalanimoku who acted as buffer and friend between the factions. At least old Billy Pitt was certain the sensitive and intelligent Kauikeaouli was prepared and ready to rule the nation.

After Kaahumanu had aborted Boki's "rebellion," the young king himself turned wildly against the oppressive dominance of the old woman and the missionaries. Wearing the sword presented to him by Lord Byron, and the feather that marked his royal authority, he took to the streets—mingling with the young folks of his age. Fortified by grog liberally supplied by the traders, he urged his enthusiastic friends to throw off the Christian tabus, return to surfing, racing, gambling, and the joyful abandon of the hula. Heeding his example, Honolulu and Waikiki suddenly became happy and cheerful once more—with the fun and freedom of old days. Kauikeaouli, to the young people at least, was proving himself a doggedly loyal Hawaiian—their idol—their king.

Mr. Bingham had eradicated from the young ruler's mind the foolish necessity of common people groveling before royalty. He had taught that only heathen Hawaiian ancestors practiced human sacrifice, and exacted death of commoners who stepped in the shadow of the Alii. Now Bingham found himself overwrought and alarmed at the antics of his star pupil. It was one thing to tolerate and understand the democratic ideal; it was quite another matter for a son of Kamehameha to fling aside Christian ideals, wallow in levity, and expose his royal person to constant danger of bodily harm and assassination. Frantically Binamu called on Kaahumanu, Boki, Liliha and Billy Pitt for conference on the matter of the monarch's deportment. This meeting, held in Bingham's missionary headquarters, was the first chance Kamehameha III had to share in the actual affairs of government.

Eloquently Kaahumanu pleaded for a return of Christian restraint instead of the wild, carefree participation in youth revolt. She commended Binamu and the longnecks for the greater joy in Christ they had brought to the islands. She recommended that, instead of an open return to "barbarism," that the nation more freely support the efforts of the missionaries by building more schools and churches for the people. The monarchy, she reminded, was solely responsible for the schools in which forty-six thousand Hawaiians were now enrolled in *palapala.*

Boki and Liliha likewise suggested less levity and more responsibility on the part of their young king, and hoped that he would, like Lord Byron, set an example in dignity and decorum. But they had little to say that was commendatory of Bingham and the missionaries. Kalanimoku took the floor, and told of the old days, and what it was like before the missionaries. He accepted the Americans, though he had been baptized by the French, as a Catholic. But what he wanted, was what the king wanted—a Hawaii for Hawaiians. He wanted a balancing of the old and the new. He wanted an end to the regency. In his opinon, the king should be allowed to govern in full force and right.

It was a needed and complimentary gesture, and Kauikeaouli responded gratefully. His decision, too, was to accept the missionaries. Much of what they said was good, and he gloried in the *palapala* and the wondrous things he had learned because he could read and write. The *pule* was a personal matter for those who wanted it—let each man accept or reject it as he wished. What he abhorred was the Christian kapus, the sorrowful Sabbaths, the restraints in clothes, acts and manners. Much of Hawaii's old ways were good. Let the people have at least some sense of joy and freedom, rather than the sad and somber conduct Binamu expected of king and people. He warned that in the future he intended to take a deeper hand in government.

Mr. Bingham had reason to be pleased. The royal council of elders seemed to have straightened out the thinking of Hawaii's youthful king. Kauikeaouli immediately issued a proclamation—throwing weight of the monarchy behind public efforts of the longnecks. He urged the Hawaiian people to support the *palapala* and the *pule.* And the results were miraculous. Natives, recognizing at last that there would never again be return to those ancient gods that the sons and wives of Ka-

HISTORIC KAWAIAHAO CHURCH
AS IT APPEARS TODAY

176

—Paul Bailey Photo.

mahemeha had destroyed, came forward willingly to accept Christianity as offered by the haoles out of New England.

At the dedication of Kawaiahao*—Honolulu's immense new church, built to seat three thousand, native style—King Kauikeaouli, Princess Nahienaena, and Queens Kaahumanu and Kinau,* all publicly participated. The church was packed with high caste Hawaiians. The crowds, unable to find sitting room inside, spilled out across the yard; congregating at doors, windows, or any spot where they might glimpse or hear the Alii who were sharing the services. Pew holders, and special guests, entered the building by long and colorful procession, with *kahilis* of every high chief's family borne in pride on this day of triumph. The king and his delicately beautiful sister were carried into the building, at the head of the procession, and seated on the rostrum amid flowers and their own towering royal *kahilis*.

It was the king himself who opened the services, with a speech of greeting and dedication to his people. It was the king and his sister who joined Kawaiahao's big choir in chanting the One Hundredth Psalm in the soft, liquid vowels and consonants of their own ancient tongue. It was the shy and lovely princess who offered the first public prayer in the new stone building. And it was the choir and the Alii present who sang out the First Psalm—again in the language of the people. When the service of dedication was completed, it was the young and formerly rebellious king who concluded it with the prayer of benediction.

American Protestantism had become the state church of the land. Only Boki and a few of the Alii intransigents refused to share in what they considered a betrayal.

Bingham and his missionaries were at last secure. They were riding the high wave of acceptance and popularity. But even in the aura of their victory, all was not well in paradise. On July 7, 1827 there came the Catholic priests to Honolulu—aboard the French ship *La Comète*. Leading the group, eight months out of Bordeaux, was Father Bachelot. With him—all members of the Congregation of the Sacred Hearts of Jesus and Mary—were Father Abraham Armand, Father Patrick Short, Choir Brother Theodore Boissier, Lay Brothers Melchior Bondu and Leonore Portal. They were welcomed ashore by Boki and Kalanimoku, both of whom had accepted Catholicism aboard the earlier French ship *L'Uranie*.

Kaahumanu, the zealot, was furious. Deeply resenting Boki's act as presumptuous and blasphemous, she ordered all the French priests and the ship's captain to appear before her. Boki told them to ignore the imperious demands of the old woman, and continued to entertain the

*Ka-wa-i-a-ha-o: *Kah*-wah-*ee*-ah-*hah*-oh.

*Ki-na-u: *Kee*-nah-oo.

Frenchmen in his home. Kaahumanu responded to this insult by ordering the *La Comète,* and its master, to take the unwanted and unwelcome
priests immediately out of the Hawaiian nation. The captain of the
ship ignored her commands. The *La Comète* sailed back to France
without them.

Boki, Kalanimoku, and a few Alii dissenters continued to harbor
and help the Catholics in getting an ecclesiastical start on Oahu. Father
Bachelot and his devout priests soon were making such progress as
to be a public embarrassment to the Protestant mission. For one thing,
Hawaiians were discovering that Christianity, Catholic style, had few
of the uncomfortable restraints so irksome to the buoyant and carefree
native spirit. In Catholic service, they were allowed to bedeck themselves with flowers. They were allowed to smile, laugh, go swimming,
and even smoke. In comparison to the joyless service of Christ among
the longnecks, this was "much betta." Even more important, there was
the elaborate ritual, abounding in symbolism, pageantry, mysticism
and color—the soul cry of all Polynesia. There was rhythmic singing
and chanting "alla same like" the mystic and ancient *meles* which extolled the glory of gods and people. Catholic priests were really being
accepted on Oahu.

But Catholic intrusion was heavy cross indeed for Kaahumanu, as
regent, to bear. One month after dedication of Kawaiahao, riding the
wave crest of Christian zeal, Kaahumanu issued an order forbidding
Hawaiian subjects to attend services at the Catholic mission. With the
same single-minded effort with which she had wiped out the gods and
priesthood of ancient Hawaii, she commenced a reign of terror against
the Roman Church and its troublesome priests.

Beatings, torture, and prison sentences at hard labor upon the
island roads and walls became price for native attendance and conversion to the Catholic faith. Exile to barren Kahoolawe became the lot
of intransigents who continued to listen to the exhortation of the priests.
But harsh as was Kaahumanu's edict, it failed to stop the spread of
this unwanted type of Christianity. In desperation she commanded all
members of the Alii to unite in ousting the French priests from the
islands.

Not all Alii supported her campaign of terror. Some preferred the
priests to the longnecks. Others refused to abuse and intimidate their
fellow Hawaiians for violating the religious kapus that were supposed
to have been abolished years ago by the same queen who now seemed
obsessed in setting new and equally burdensome measures of public
conscience. Kaahumanu's own brother, Kuakini, governor of the home
island of Hawaii, was extending protection to Catholics in his lands.
Boki and Liliha remained friendly and loyal to the priests. Their home

had become a refuge for converts; a shelter for clandestine meetings.

The young king, determined in his efforts to gain control of the nation, remained aloof from the religious struggle. To be scrupulously fair he withdrew his direct support from Protestantism, and ignored Catholicism. All he asked was that his people remain "lovers of the true God," but to keep their worship above petty sect or denomination.

It was inevitable that Kaahumanu, the indomitable zealot, should eventually run collision course with those Alii who preferred their personal lives less rigidly dominated. The long-standing quarrel with Boki erupted into a storm when Kaahumanu presented her plans for the chiefs' children's school before the grand council.

King and Alii were in agreement as to the necessity and desirability of the school. The big woman even forced the acceptance of Reverend and Mrs. Bingham as conductors of Hawaii's royal institution of learning. That Kaahumanu wanted it established on two hundred acres of Honolulu mauka land, known as Punahou (New Spring), was the real bone of contention. Punahou had been a gift to Liliha by her father, Governor Hoapili of Maui. Boki and Liliha were willing enough that Punahou be used for such a purpose, and would give the choice land for educational needs. Their objection was that Kaahumanu wanted the property placed in the name of Mr. Bingham.

The council seethed with hot words and acrimony. Boki once more denounced Bingham as a meddler. Again he warned against the increasing power of the longnecks within the government. But again Boki ran into the implacable will of Kamehameha's queen. While the land gift was bitterly deferred, Kaahumanu appealed to Governor Hoapili, who, in the end, induced Liliha to go against her husband, and turn Punahou over to the missionaries.

Boki howled out against Punahou's cession to Bingham, no matter how noble the purpose. He warned king and people that Punahou would never be used for benefit of the natives, that it was only another wedge being driven into the Hawaiian commonwealth for the use and aggrandizement of the haoles. In crass defiance of the tortured Boki, and as quickly as Punahou was secured to the Protestant missionaries, Kaahumanu ordered construction thereon of a large house for the Binghams, and another dwelling for herself nearby.

This defeat proved the absolute end for Boki. He announced that he was leaving the Hawaiian nation forever. A ship had arrived from Australia bearing the fortuitous news that great forests of sandalwood had been discovered on the island of Erromanga, in the New Hebrides group. Boki declared that he was removing himself to that island. Since the Hawaiian nation's supply of sandalwood was almost wholly depleted, he would seek a fresh life—and a new future—in Erromanga.

Everyone, including the king and Liliha, endeavored to dissuade the defiant chief from leaving Oahu. It was useless. Two ships were made ready—Boki's own barkentine *Kamehameha,* and the *Becket,* to be commanded by Chief Manuia. Ten ambitious haoles, and one hundred and fifty Hawaiians signed on to the *Becket* for the venture. Boki accepted only pure-blood Hawaiians on his *Kamehameha.* He had no difficulty in gathering a force of two hundred and fifty men loyal to the fiery and opinionated governor.

On December 3, 1829, at dawn, the two ships sailed off on the long voyage, exactly as had so many other audacious missions in earlier times. The *Becket* reached Erromanga, and waited five weeks for Boki and his *Kamehameha.* But Boki and his ship never arrived at the fabled island of sandalwood. They were never heard from again.

X

KAAHUMANU's crusade to save the people from evil contamination of the foreigners, and the consequence of sin, became Calvinism in its most repressive form. Laws and edicts flowed from the aging regent's lonely palace with a pace and fervor that was baffling and frightening. The deeper she immersed herself in the pattern of Christ, the farther the young king withdrew from the circle of moral strangulation preached and practiced by the longnecks.

With Boki gone, and his dissenting voice silenced, the Hawaiian brand of American Puritanism now had its day. The governor's palace, with the vivacious Liliha holding constant court to Charlton and the rich foreigners, remained Oahu's one hive of sedition. Unlike her lost husband Boki, Liliha was not a crusader. She was charming, she was sought after, she was beloved by the native people. But her stance was strictly personal and theatrical. She preferred a life of conviviality and joy.

The greater power, only moderately challenged by the regency-hampered king, remained in the fanatical hands of Kaahumanu. Her changing viewpoint as to the rightness of living was, for the first time, putting strain on the love and affection which Hawaiians themselves held for her. No longer could the native *olioli* and *mele* be chanted. Such ancient words were now, by law's edict, considered "foul speech." No longer could women swim in public places. It was sinful to thus display the female form. And that ended all sea sports for the lithe and graceful maidens of the realm.

Whiskey and gambling were outlawed. No more hula dancing—it was lewd, and sexually exciting. The word "adultery," heretofore unknown to the Hawaiian vocabulary, was a new and vicious kapu—

exceeding anything ever mouthed by the ancient priests. Hawaiians, born to the thought that the sex act, and coitive excellence, were the greatest gifts the gods could bestow, were baffled by the missionary claim that babies were conceived "in sin." They were shocked and frightened by constant pronouncement of the longnecks, and echoed in the edicts of Kaahumanu, that sexual fun and copulation were low and vile. Such crusade against maiden-tumbling was unbelievable and incomprehensible.

At first they considered the pronouncements as ridiculous and preposterous. They followed their own inner promptings in the matter. What they were totally unprepared for were the new and ferocious laws against "adultery." It was suddenly announced that all natives, not legally married according to the sacred rules of the church, were living in sin. The prosecutions, formerly meted out to foreigners who seduced native girls, and the native girls who were willing to be seduced, was now extended to all Hawaiians. Penal colonies were established on two islands adjacent to Maui. Men sex offenders would be banished to the rocky island of Kahoolawe. The women would go to lonely, but greener, Lanai.

There were a lot of puzzled Hawaiians in those first roundups—especially when the culprits were speedily dispatched to the two islands. According to Samuel Kamakau, respected Hawaiian historian: "Some died of starvation; some drowned themselves in the sea."

But nothing ever concocted in the haole mind offended the natives as much as this barbarous meddling in their personal lives and habits. Kaahumanu was shocked and surprised by the wave of resentment that spread across the islands. The new laws, which she had promulgated for the good of the people, were intensified. A greater, more thorough, hunt for sin was instituted.

One night, male prisoners from Kahoolawe, swam the shark-infested six miles to Maui. With the help of loyal and enthusiastic natives of Maui, canoes were filled with food, and the adulterous prisoners paddled on to Lanai. Here each of the men chose himself a woman prisoner—many of them their own wives without the benefit of clergy—and with the women, returned to Maui. Again the escapees were helped by the natives—proud to have hand in so noble a conspiracy. The adulterers were guided to safe hiding places high in Maui's mountains. To the end of their days these fugitives lived in hidden seclusion—in the free and ancient way.

When it was discovered that Hawaiians were the same good swimmers and ingenious humans they had always been, and that banishment was growing less effective, adulterers found themselves sentenced to something infinitely worse—hard labor. Untold hundreds of them were put in chain gangs, building island roads and walls. Kamakau records that: "If a man was caught in adultery he might be sentenced to stone breaking until he died." All of the island roads were constructed almost entirely by those natives who had attempted to accept nature's joys wherever they found them, but who had neglected to seek Christ for sanction.

"There were innumerable laws; laws upon laws; and there was no peace; there was bitterness everywhere," Kamakau wrote in lamentation. "There were many petty laws that demanded hard labor, and not even the king had the power to pardon."

Unquestionably young Kauikeaouli would have acted to blunt the headstrong and oppressive course of the regency—this unprecedented humbling of the flesh of his people, and in his name. The Christian oligarches who denied him the matings which were his right as granted by Polynesia's own gods and tradition, and who proscribed his own sexual conduct, had become as petty and as irksome to Kamehameha's son as they were to the lowest native doing penance for sin on the roadways of the nation.

Noting the monarch's unmistakable slide back to debauchery and the old Alii custom of plucking the most desirable flowers sexually, the missionaries and Kaahumanu urged an immediate royal wedding. The bride would be safely of their own choosing—Kamanele,* daughter of Governor Kuakini of Hawaii, and niece of the queen regent. Christians had long since set an insufferable kapu upon the time-honored practice of polygamy, and even more so on the sacred *pi'oia* with one's own kin. They had flung their arms in holy horror at suggestion he might wed his beautiful sister, or take on Boki's deserted Liliha. So His Majesty, in turn, just as summarily rejected the Christian selection of Kamanele.

Only the king dared rebuke Kaahumanu. Bitterly he informed her that he would choose his own wife. He alone would set the time for the selection. Kauikeaouli, plainly, was waiting out the days to his own majority, when he could royally kick the oppressive regency in its Christian teeth. He reminded the old woman that in the times when Hawaiians were free to live their lives in their own manner the nation had been happy and it had been great. In those lost days when men lived in the pattern of their ancestors, Hawaiians had been forceful in character, free, and their souls had soared in the sheer delight of living. He asked the big queen to examine Hawaiians under the yoke of Protestantism. People were sick, they were diseased, they were oppressed, and laughter no longer was heard in the land. He informed her he had made his own choice. He would turn to the old ways of happiness and freedom. If it were sin for a man to go in the way his flesh and thoughts

*Ka-ma-ne-le: *Kah*-mah-*nay*-lay.

dictated, then let the king too work at hard labor, along with his people.

The great problem was that the king, aside from repudiation of counsel as to monogamous and state marriage, was already seeking erotic pleasures. Mr. Bingham had whispered that Kauikeaouli's "show of recklessness" stemmed from his almost inseparable association with a handsome young man from Tahiti by the name of Kaomi. Born of a Tahitian father, and Hawaiian mother, Kaomi was a magnificent physical specimen of the best in the two Polynesian cultures. He was not an Alii, but he walked and moved like one, in the graceful, feline manner. The intellectual and moral spell he cast over people—men and women—amounted almost to an enslavement of body and soul. Already Kaomi had established a wide and loyal following among the young men at court. Worse, he appeared to be building an intimacy with the young king that sent shudders of apprehension through the devout mind of Mr. Bingham.

The king's rejection of moral advice, and the sure word of God, made him a sinner by default. Of that he was piously reminded. What worried the Christians was His Majesty's ready and unhesitating admission of sin.

It was not surprising that when public cattle ravaged the Punahou acreage and the yards of Mr. Bingham's new house thereon, a wall was decreed by the regency. The order for building the wall was issued in the name of the rebellious king—and sex prison-gangs would build it. Construction of the Punahou wall would require hundreds of captive laborers. But the surprising, unbelievable thing to Hawaiians was that their young monarch—dressed in the kapa *malo* of the shackled prisoner—turned out to lift and break stones for the wall being constructed by the adulterers.

It definitely shocked Mr. Bingham when the people of the islands discovered that one of the laborers muscling great stones to Punahou's wall was none other than their own divinely worshipped sovereign. The natives interpreted this unprecedented sight as proof positive that Bingham considered himself as Hawaii's ruler. He was publicly making a slave of the son of Kamehameha the Great. They gathered at the Protestant mission with the same anger and belligerency their grandfathers had accosted Captain Cook. It took a public explanation of the sweaty king to save Bingham from a like fate.

"I am not working at this wall by the command of Mr. Bingham," he told the rioters. "There is a law, issued under my name, which decrees hard labor for the sin of adultery. You, my people, are being punished because of it. But we are all Hawaiians, and all of us are alike under the law. If it is necessary for you to work on this wall, as punishment for breaking a law issued in my name, then it is just as necessary that I work beside you. I lift stones, because I too am an adulterer."

A shout went up—and it probably saved the life of Mr. Bingham. But, more than that, it made public hero of the king. He had wrapped his frustrated and unhappy people in his own cloak of protection, understanding and camaraderie. They loved him for his humble act. "This chief holds his people close to the heart!" they cried out.

Kaahumanu could not remain complacent to the fact that native resistance was continuing to build against Bingham and his missionaries. The control they assumed over king and regency, and the irksome tabus of their religion, were not being favorably accepted. Sadness and restraint of American Calvinism were making the less inhibited Christianity of the Catholic priests far more attractive by comparison. The big queen, however, was sincere in believing the course she was taking was the best way possible for her people.

Physically she was fading, growing older, more stubborn in her convictions. But her voice, in quiet talk, or in the booming thunder of declamation, remained the final word of authority. As "the massive, magnificent *tutu*" she ruled her family and her people with rod of iron, but with a heart everyone sensed was full of love. Her analogy was simple. The foreigners had brought the woes to the islands. The haoles had debauched, diseased, and enslaved the people. The way pointed out by the missionaries was the path back to virtue, universal love, and complete removal from the temptations and sins by which the foreigners had enslaved the nation. Acceptance of Christ, and the way of the missionaries, were best—even though there be grumbling and occasional defiance.

Removal of Catholicism, of course, was necessary. There is no evidence that Hiram Bingham had anything personal to do with the campaign of persecution which Kaahumanu leveled against Father Bachelot and his priests. But on Christmas eve, 1831, all the French priests were herded aboard the *Waverly*, by the king's troops, and were summarily deported to California. Kaahumanu went to her grave convinced that she had done a mighty deed for the Lord.

XI

BUT with all her high-minded zealotry this strange woman never quite succeeded in purging her nation of its sins, nor in unshackling it from a worse form of foreign bondage. Nevertheless, the mighty queen who had defied convention, who had wiped out her own native religion, died wholly "in the arms of Christ."

Manley Hopkins, in his book *The Sandwich Islands*, aptly summed up her life: "Kaahumanu was beloved for her own sake. She was a woman of remarkable character, with strong passions and great failings; but she was a fit mate for the warrior king and made no unworthy Caia to his Caius. During her long and intimate association with him [Kamehameha] she seems to have drawn in her husband's disposition; and when he died she reproduced his character, reflected from her womanhood. It was the moon 'taking up the wondrous tale' after the setting of her lord from whom she derived her light."

Even as Kaahumanu fought for breath and strength in her new Boston-style house, the fifth company of American missionaries were on their way to the islands, to aid in the mighty harvest she had so sedulously planted. Among this new crop, destined to join Bingham and his longnecks in the Lord's great work, were some who would embrace Hawaii with love and compassion, and others who would harvest much of the nation for themselves and their persistent heirs.

But not even Kaahumanu, sick or well, could win the vacillating king completely to Christ. Aware that when this autocratic matriarch departed the scene, took with her the unwritten power of Kamehameha the Great, and the regency would end, Kauikeaouli made ready to receive the kingdom—and with it the right to guide it as he pleased.

To the bedfast Kaahumanu came reports of the king's debauchery. There were whispers of parties wilder than anything Liholiho had ever concocted aboard the now decayed and dismantled *Cleopatra's Barge*. Guided by his attentive and constant companion Kaomi, Kauikeaouli had launched the secret order of *Lahui ka Hulumanu* (Birds of a Feather). Their circle advocated the ending of missionary rule, harbored the revolutionaries whose aim was to dethrone the longnecks and wipe out their kapus, and, as Kaomi declared, to "seek the pleasures of the world." Its overall objective was to restore the unrestrained joy, festivities, and dancing, of the old order, and to once and for all return full power and control to the sovereign.

Secret meetings of *Hulumanu* were packed with malcontents and royalists. The *Becket* had come back from Erromanga, its crew decimated by hostile natives, and ill with deprivation and thirst. They brought final sordid confirmation of the disappearance and loss of Boki and his *Kamehameha*. Liliha, never a missionary-lover, and completely irked by Kaahumanu's autocracy, now joined up with the royalists of *Hulumanu*. She quickly ceased grieving for Boki after sharing the revelry of the circle's young and carefree Alii. Princess Nahienaena returned from Maui to join the wild court of her brother. Once more there were rumors that the king might marry his sister, and maybe the beautiful Liliha, in the ancient way. Hiram Bingham, and the ill and helpless Kaahumanu, could only mentally writhe in apprehension.

Kaahumanu died June 5, 1832, surrounded by the missionaries who had become her companions, her solace, and her conscience. "She was unusually feeble and unusually affectionate," Mr. Bingham recorded. "The interests of the nation pressed upon her, and she turned with unwonted confidence to the aid supplied by our mission." Mrs. Judd appraised the magnificent matriarch, in her passing, as "more humble, more lovely, more affectionate than ever."

Like Keopuolani, that other sainted wife of Kamehameha the Great, she passed to her eternal reward confirmed in the faith, and staunch at the finish.

She did not die in the new Boston-style house at Honolulu by the sea. Her last earthly wishes were to be carried to her grass mountain-dwelling, far up Moana Valley. Dr. Gerrit P. Judd, in attendance, was certain her condition was not such as to withstand the trip. But the strong-willed old queen would not have it otherwise.

The big woman was toted—in her bed—by her faithful retainers—up the long trail. A canopy of palm fronds shaded the bed from heat of the sun. Her litter was made fragrant and beautiful with maile, ilima, and the brightest blossoms of the hibiscus. Behind followed hundreds of Hawaiian natives, chanting her *meles;* reciting her genealogy back to the gods.

The king, his sister, and Liliha, awaited the procession at top of the Moana. They, with others of the highest Alii, and Binamu, and Dr. and Mrs. Judd, kept vigil at the grass cottage until Kaahumanu breathed her last. There was no chanting, no joy, as the procession followed the queen and her deathbed back to the Boston cottage. The missionaries, led by Binamu and Dr. Judd, were in full control. They countenanced no wailing, no mourning excesses, no bodily mutilation as evidence of sorrow. In the frame cottage the dead Kaahumanu was prepared for burial, placed in a velvet-lined foreign casket, and made ready for Christian services.

Every attempt of the native populace to vent their grief in keening and excesses were, like every other ancient custom, declaimed against, or ruthlessly put down. The queen had died as a bride of Christ. The puritanical Protestants were masters of the situation. Everything that hinted of pomp and the splendid sorrow of royalty were dispensed with. The missionaries insisted there be "no rending of the air with heathen wailing . . . no libidinous and revolting customs of a pagan state."

The cortege traveled in stately silence to the big new Christian church of Kawaiahao. Only occasionally was the air of solemnity broken by some humble outcry of grief. "Oh, Kaahumanu! My Chief!

My Mother!" But, as wrote Mr. Bingham, "The missionaries preferred to move in silence."

The service, of course, was read by Hiram Bingham. Then to the slow and solemn tolling of the New England church bell, Kaahumanu was carried by her fellow Alii to the stone mausoleum housing the caskets of Liholiho and his Kamamalu. Many a Hawaiian, in this foreign usurpation of royal burial, felt betrayed and defrauded.

So the Christians entombed the most controversial queen in Hawaii's history—a leader out of the great and traditional past—an imperious but beloved ruler, whose acts and decrees had affected every human life on the islands. The bones of her beloved Kamehameha, in whose pattern she had molded her existence, lay secretly hidden somewhere on the genetical island of Hawaii. There is a native story, probably apocryphal, that her half-brother, Governor Kuakini of Hawaii, engineered a midnight coup. It has been said that, under the cover of darkness, Kuakini and his helpers removed Kaahumanu from the crypt, filled the coffin with bags of sand, and carried Kamehameha's queen back to the homeland. At Kailua, and at the sacred Hale-o-Keawe at Honaunau, a more suitable funeral was held, in the old way.

But there can be no question that Kaahumanu died a surrendered Christian. Even under analysis of that critical haole Henry A. Peirce came the prompting to write: "She died a *Christian*. It has always heretofore been my opinion that her adherence and adoption of the Christian religion was from policy . . . but I have lately been convinced from the piety displayed during her sickness and at the hour of her death that she really believed in and practiced the principles of the Christian religion."

XII

WITH Kaahumanu at last safely out of the way, the young king considered the regency as ended. He now made the move to claim every right and power of the crown. In this he ran into headlong opposition to the high chiefs comprising the council. They were reluctant and cautious about surrendering the nation wholly to a young man of vacillating character, and whose interests seemed almost wholly tied to pleasure. They did not challenge his right to rule—but insisted that it be under the joint safeguard of a *kuhina-nui*.

And the *kuhina-nui* they gave him was the staunch Christian, Elisabeta Kinau—another daughter of Kamehameha. Kinau was half-sister of Liholiho and Kauikeaouli. She had been a bride in royal marriage to the dead Liholiho. Now, as symbolic prime minister, she was joint ruler of the Hawaiian kingdom. This half-sister and royal widow was older in years than King Kauikeaouli, and there is no evidence that he ever particularly cared for her. In more ways than one, Kinau became the king's new thorn-in-flesh.

On July 5, 1832 the two rulers issued parallel proclamations:

The king: "I am superior, and my mother [in Hawaiian custom meaning Elisabeta Kinau, *kuhina-nui*] subordinate . . . She is my chief agent . . . We two have been too young and unacquainted with the actual transaction of business, now for the first time undertake distinctly to regulate our kingdom . . . Ye men of foreign lands, let not the laws be by you put under your feet. When you are in your own countries, there you will observe your own laws."

The new *kuhina-nui* declared: "The office which my mother [in Hawaiian allegory meaning Kaahumanu, who was never known to bear a child] held until her departure, is now mine. All her active duties and her authority are committed to me. The tabus of the king, and the law of God, are with me, and also the laws of the king . . . My appointment as chief agent is of long standing, even from our father [Kamehameha] . . . This is another point. I make known to you; according to law [meaning for violation of law] shall be the loss or dispossession of land. We are now endeavoring to make our minds mature."

It would appear that Kinau assumed her role with the imperious aplomb of Kaahumanu. It was clear, too, that she considered herself as having inherited the regency. This assumption the king bitterly fought. It was his contention that the regency ended with Kaahumanu. And for two years he stubbornly opposed Kinau.

His first confrontation with this second extension of petticoat government was occasioned when he attempted, as king, to purchase a royal shp for himself. His dead brother had owned and used *Cleopatra's Barge* as his floating pleasure haunt and capitol. Kauikeaouli could see no reason why, as Kamehameha III, he was not equally entitled to a ship—in this case a trim and coveted New England brig—and proceeded to negotiate for its purchase from the American ship owners.

Kinau, after consultation with her Christian mentors, utterly refused to co-sanction the purchase. She reminded Kauikeaouli that the government, already strained in the repayment of the American debt, was in no position to finance any such extravagance. The islands were almost denuded of sandalwood. No longer could sandalwood be used for the aggrandizement of chiefs and king. Kamehameha III was denied his ship.

Angered and disappointed, Kauikeaouli agreed to postpone his ship purchase to a later and more propitious time. But he answered Kinau, and the stubborn old chiefs, by calling the people together in Honolulu. As sovereign he was handsome, magnetic, and his vocal eloquence was improving with his years. "These are my thoughts to all ye chiefs, classes of subjects and foreigners respecting this country which by the victory of Mokuohai was conquered by my Father and his chiefs," he declared. "It has descended to us as his and their posterity . . . All that is within it, the living and the dead, the good and the bad, the agreeable and pleasant—all are mine.

"I shall rule with justice over all the land, make and promulgate all laws. Neither the chiefs nor the foreigners have any voice in making laws for this country. *I alone am the one!* Only three laws which were given out formerly remain still in force, *viz.*, not to murder, not to steal, not to commit adultery. Therefore govern yourselves accordingly."

The people were joyfully impressed. Here truly was a king in the old tradition. Here truly was a worthy and pugnacious son of the great Kamehameha. Here was a man who dared spit in the faces of the long-necks and their stifling rule. He had given the country back to its people.

But the victory was only outwardly. The missionaries, through Kinau, were applying the national brakes on Kauikeaouli even more effectively than through the regency of Kaahumanu. When the king awoke to the fact that the chiefs and the strong-willed *kuhina-nui* were not yet ready to deliver his country fully to him, he battled to get Kinau replaced by Liliha. When this failed against their implacable stubbornness, the frustrated king retreated to the gay circle of Kaomi. And younger natives—seeing that the king himself indulged in gambling, racing, dancing and debauchery—followed his example. None of Bingham's stern pronouncements and warnings had any effect on the two years of licentiousness that set itself upon the islands. As to effective government, there now remained only uncertainty and confusion.

To save Hawaii from utter chaos, both factions were forced eventually to yield. All attempts at maintaining a regency over Kauikeaouli were finally abandoned. At long last he was publicly proclaimed Kamehameha III, and his reign set up as an absolute monarchy.

Outwardly he had gotten what he wanted. Inwardly the victory was not so absolute. Surprisingly—either through his own volition, or from behind the scenes pressure—Kamehameha III still retained Kinau as his *kuhina-nui*. He still considered her a nuisance, and he had no love for her. Nor could he dodge the fact that Kinau continued to take her guidance from Binamu and the missionaries.

Actually the king was too erratic and vacillating to successfully reign as an autocrat. Chiefs, missionaries, and Kinau, apparently were fully cognizant of that fact. By 1835 Kauikeaouli was leaving most of the responsibility of government in Kinau's hands. Consul Richard Charlton wrote home to England: "Kauikeaouli . . . is now about twenty-three years of age and is possessed of more talent than almost any other native, but being of very indolent habits and excessively fond of pleasures he does not attend to the affairs of government, but trusts Kinau his half sister with the reins. She is entirely governed by the American missionaries who through her govern the Islands with unlimited sway."

By any standards it was bad government. The tug-of-war between Puritans and profligate could not long endure without driving the nation into revolution. The only ones gaining from this internal seethe were the foreigners. They moved relentlessly in their constant encroachment on the island economy. Internal pressure finally forced king and chiefs to draw up a fresh and more workable code of laws. At public assembly, on January 5, 1835, the king himself proclaimed a new basis for government.

Execution of the new laws were entrusted to Kinau. The penal code, in five divisions, was each officially signed by Kamehameha III. First chapter of the code dealt with murder and various degrees of homicide, providing penalties graded to each offense. The second was concerned with theft—a fine of twice the amount stolen, imprisonment, or lashing on the bare back; the number of strokes being proportioned according to the amount stolen. Third chapter was concerned with general lawlessness, illicit sexual intercourse, and divorce. The fourth covered fraud and false-witness. And the fifth finally got around to drunkenness, and offenses committed while under the state of intoxication. For these lesser crimes there were graduated penalties.

The new laws wore a lot more teeth than did the simpler platitudes of the Ten Commandments. The nation finally was coming to grips with its own internal problems—and none too soon. With some degree of unity the leaders could at last face and factor the greatest of all menaces—the foreigners—and the multiplicity of problems haoles had brought to the islands.

John Rives, the Frenchman who had been companion and confidant to Liholiho, and whom the surviving members of the royal Hawaiian mission had angrily dumped in London, had spent the intervening years in France promoting the idea of Catholic evangelization of the Sandwich Islands, and the opening up of the Hawaiian economy to trade with France. Rives had turned up in Honolulu with Father Bachelot and the French priests aboard the *Comète*. But the former official quickly discovered he no longer had influence with the Alii. The new king showed absolutely no interest in him, in Catholicism, and in French trade. The high chiefs ignored him. And Kaahumanu had despised everything French—including the priests.

Face to face with the firmly entrenched Protestants, and the American and British preferences and priorities, Rives was helpless. When the French priests were forcibly deported to California aboard the ship *Waverly*, Rives abandoned all his Hawaiian hopes, and departed for friendlier shores.

Arrival of the U. S. frigate *Potomac*, commanded by Commodore John Downes, found the pro-American Kaahumanu dead. Downes received considerably less warmth than Commodore Jones had known and reported. The new commodore announced that he was in Honolulu to insure the safety of American shipping interests, and to confer with government in the matter of the American trade debt. At conference with the king he took great pains to express his disapproval of the high-handed manner in which the nation had treated the Catholic minority. Since the king, engrossed in his own affairs, cared not a whit what happened to evangelists of any faith, and there was no booming voice of Kaahumanu to pontificate against Catholics in particular, the American commodore gathered neither argument, agreement, or protest.

In 1836 the Catholics returned to Hawaii—this time in the person of Father Arsenius (Robert A. Walsh). On the day that Father Arsenius landed in Honolulu, the *U.S.S. Peacock* again lay at anchor in the harbor. This time the familiar ship was commanded by Commodore E. P. Kennedy, on routine check of American interests. October 8, one day before the *Peacock's* departure, the French warship *La Bonite* dropped anchor. She was commanded by Captain A. N. Vaillant, belligerently anxious to return France to prestige and power in the Sandwich Islands. On October 24, the day of the *La Bonite's* sailing, the British warship *Acteon* also glided into Honolulu harbor. This ship contained none other than Lord Edward Russell, with an agenda of recrimination fed through the years by the unhappy reports of Consul Richard Charlton.

All through that fall and winter the grass palaces at Waikiki and Honolulu were scenes of heated and angry meetings in which representatives of three great powers chided Kinau and Kauikeaoli with breach of treaty, breach of faith, unfair denial of trade advantages, and enough charges to confuse and bewilder any little nation desiring only to preserve its independence, and keep at least a part of itself for the people who had inherited it.

Commodore Kennedy demanded clarification of the right of American residents to transfer real estate and properties without consent of the king. And there was the question, too, of American privilege to lease Hawaiian soil on a grand scale for agricultural pursuits. The king "argued, that if he yielded the right of free transfer . . . he virtually resigned his right to the soil, and thus he might be deprived of all his country . . ." Leasing of crown lands for the purpose of cultivating sugar, cotton, tobacco, or silk, was talked of. On this the king showed interest. But he made it very plain that, in recognizing the principle of lease, he felt no obligation or duty to grant lands to any or all who might apply.

Regardless of assiduous prodding and insistence, Kauikeaoli refused to furnish any consent in writing. Too much had already been signed away. Kennedy argued that the treaty of 1826 had pledged the Hawaiian government to allow American citizens to enter the country and engage in business and planting without royal permission. Kennedy's failure to pressure the king into full compliance of the trade agreements was blamed, by the islands' American entrepreneurs, on the influence of the missionaries. But the king, in graciously accepting Kennedy's long letter of advice, in lieu of a signed contract, was displaying a sudden new statesmanship. He at last was growing up to his responsibilities.

The French captain Vaillant, who arrived on *La Bonite*, unloaded a snout full of woes on the monarch and his *kuhina-nui*. The French nation was shocked by the treatment of Father Bachelot and his priests. French subjects must never be mistreated by Hawaiians, no matter on what pretext. France was mighty, and though its king desired friendly relations with Hawaii, the power and strength of Vaillant's great nation must never be underestimated. Kauikeaouli desperately tried to smooth the French captain's ruffled feathers. He even agreed to allow the priests to remain and operate, so long as they gave no "religious instructions to any native Hawaiians." This was not much of a concession, to be sure, but next year the persistent Father Bachelot and his priests were back once more in the islands.

Unlike his predecessor, Lord Byron, England's latest official visitor, Lord Edward Russell, blustered into Honolulu with a portfolio of complaints the moment the *Acteon* dropped anchor. First and foremost he demanded of the king that Father Arsenius (Robert A. Walsh), a British citizen even though Catholic, be allowed full security and freedom. The king, by now thoroughly surfeited by the parade of foreigners making demands on his government, promised Lord Russell that Walsh was free to remain in Honolulu so long as the priest obeyed the laws, and refrained from teaching his religion to the natives.

This half-promise infuriated Russell. He turned with open belligerence to the bundle of complaints Charlton had sent to London during the years of his consulorship. One protest was the matter of a house supposedly belonging to George Chapman, a British subject. The charge was that Chapman's house had been seized by Hawaiian authorities; had been partially destroyed. When the king and Kinau offered only to take the matter "under advisement," Richard Charlton stood with Lord Russell in declaring that if the Hawaiian government "would not accede to principles more liberal or adopt a policy more favorable to British interests he must declare that there was an end to a good understanding between the two governments."

Pressure upon the hesitant and slow responding Kauikeaouli soon turned to bald threat. The right of the crown to decide as to the sovereignty of Hawaiian soil passing to foreigners was no matter for simple or light decision. Of the affair, Rev. J. S. Green wrote from Maui to Boston: "The question of the political interests of this poor nation is a deeply interesting one. I know not but the fatal blow to all independence at the islands, independence of the chiefs, I mean, will be struck. One of his [Britannic] Majesty's ships of war is now at Honolulu threatening to blow down the fort unless the chiefs will give up their right of soil."

Faced with the possibility of war with the nation his father and brother had considered as the great protectorate, Kamehameha III was forced to the promise that he would restore Chapman to his house. He must rebuild it, and freely grant concessions to Britishers, no matter how trivial or unfair. On November 16, 1836 he signed a clumsy treaty with Lord Russell. It promised that "English subjects shall be permitted to come with their vessels, and property of whatever kind, to the Sandwich Islands; they shall also be permitted to reside therein, as long as they conform to the laws of these Islands, and to build houses and warehouses for their merchandise, with the consent of the king . . ."

The words "consent of the king" rankled Lord Russell. In the interest of England, it was not a good concession to make. Before he left Honolulu he forced through an amendment to the treaty. The revision conceded that "the land on which the houses are built is the property of the king," but clinched it by the promise that "the king shall have no authority to destroy the houses, or in any way injure the property of any British subject."

By the time he had been pushed and pommeled by the Americans, the French, and the British, Kamehameha III had lost much of his zeal for governing the Hawaiian nation as an absolute monarchy. Final blow came with return of the French priest Bachelot, aboard the brig *Clementine*, on April 17, 1837.

The *Clementine* was a British registered ship, owned by a French-man by the name of Jules Dudoit, and for the voyage to North America just concluded, had been chartered to an American merchant in Hono-lulu by the name of Hinckley. Mr. Hinckley, as soon as the *Clementine* had discharged her cargo, returned the vessel to Dudoit. On May 10, Dudoit chartered her to another American—William French. Under this charter the ship began loading for return voyage to the United States.

Unexpectedly and without warning, Kinau added to the ship's cargo, for the return trip to America, the two priests—Bachelot and Short—abruptly hustling them back to the vessel. A little war ensued, with the two Catholic Fathers protesting the forced deportation, along with the angry owner and the lessees of the ship. Dudoit hauled down the British flag from the brig's masthead. He dramatically abandoned his vessel. He carried its flag to Consul Charlton. The consul, declaring that England's flag had been violated by the Hawaiian government, publicly burned it in the street. The foreign factions quickly blew the affair into a national calamity, and both Dudoit and Charlton made public declaration that the Hawaiian government had forcibly seized and misused the *Clementine*. The government would be held liable for all losses of ship and shipping.

The king had no other course than to back the impetuous Kinau, although he endeavored to convince the angry foreigners that no seizure had been made. But Honolulu and Lahaina had become tension-charged cities. Foreigners of every nationality were arrayed against native Hawaiians and their tortured king and chiefs. The explosive situation continued until July when, on the eighth and tenth, two war-ships sailed into Honolulu harbor. The British war frigate was the *Sulphur*, captained by Edward Belcher; the French vessel, *La Venus*, was commanded by Captain A. Du Petit-Thouars.

These representatives of two mighty nations held stormy session with Kauikeaouli and Kinau, in which the law of the seas and rights of nations were laid down in two languages. A detachment of British marines were dispatched by Captain Belcher, to "recapture" the *Clementine* in the name of His Majesty's England. Fathers Bachelot and Short were brought ashore in triumph. The foreign populace cheered and shouted in joyous victory.

Since Lord Russell had forced a treaty of sorts upon Hawaii, it was only natural that Captain Du Petit-Thouars should exact a similar agreement from the cornered and harassed king. One clause of the document declared that "the French may go and come freely on all the states which compose the Government of the Sandwich Islands; they will be there received and protected, and they will enjoy the same advantages as the subjects of the most favored nation."

The king, weary of being browbeaten and threatened by enormous nations with ships, guns, and endless manpower, issued one more defiant proclamation before inevitable surrender. In it he displayed his father's courage and pugnacity, even though he had inherited a nation already dying from diseases and exploitation of the mercenaries. The royal edict was issued as "An Ordinance Rejecting the Catholic Religion." One of its more interesting parts reads:

". . . I, with my chiefs forbid . . . that anyone should teach the peculiarities of the Pope's religion . . . nor shall the ceremonies be exhibited in our kingdom, nor shall anyone teaching its peculiarities or its faith be permitted to land on these shores; for it is not proper that two religions be found in this small kingdom. Therefore we utterly refuse to allow anyone to teach those peculiarities in any manner whatsoever. We moreover prohibit all vessels whatsoever from bringing any teacher of that religion into this kingdom."

It was a gesture bald and reckless enough for any Kamehameha. But in effect it was as futile as a shorn bird beating wings against a hurricane. The longnecks were smug and secure in victory. America, England and France now trained their ships' guns on the fort and palace with impunity. The priests remained. Captain Du Petit-Thouars reported Kauikeaouli's intransigence to France. That nation, traditionally a defender of the Catholic faith, and on the move to plant it on every Pacific island, ordered Captain C. P. T. Laplace and his frigate *L'Artemise* to visit Honolulu; to teach its upstart rulers a salutary lesson in international manners.

By November, after the French *La Venus*, and the British *Sulphur* had departed with their bad reports of a quarrelsome and autocratic king, two more priests were landed in Honolulu from the French mission ship *Notre Dame de Paix*—Fathers Maigret and Murphy. They too remained.

Father Bachelot went aboard the *Notre Dame de Paix* for a missionary cruise to other islands of Polynesia. He died on ship, less than two weeks later. And with the similarly unexpected deaths of both Kinau and Kalanimoku, in April of 1839, Hawaii's fear of Catholicism grew less haunting as a national specter. But the final and most humiliating lesson against offending a stronger nation and its religion came with the arrival of France's war frigate *L'Artemise*, and its Captain Laplace. The ship dropped anchor in the center of Honolulu harbor on July 9, 1839, and trained its heavy guns on the palace, the governor's house, and the fort.

Laplace sent word that he was coming ashore to conduct a school for king and chiefs. The course of instruction would concern itself with the proper steps of how once more to attain the esteem of France, and the proper methods of allowing freedom of worship to Catholics. Tuition for this short course would be $20,000 in cash, payable in advance. Failure to pay, or attend the school, left only one alternative—immediate war.

Laplace was a good schoolmaster. His sessions were brief, and to the point. The king and chiefs attended. And with the warship's guns trained on them, they paid the $20,000.

Constant harassment of foreign emissaries and ships of war—insistent demands made by the foreigners—the strangling hold of the missionaries—were almost more than king and chiefs could bear. To the formerly carefree Kauikeaouli the role of absolute monarch now became a nightmare of frightening responsibility. Every step he made in dictating policy, his every move as to needs of nation and people, were invariably countered by some haole thrust that demeaned and ridiculed the ancient rulership he had inherited from his forebears.

He missed the strong-handed and strong-willed Kinau. Instead of *kuhina-nui* he should have made her his queen. At her death, because she had been a daughter of Kamehameha I and wife to Kamehameha II, as well as his own half-sister, Kauikeaouli now adopted Kinau's offspring into his own childless family. These royal children were Alexander Liholiho, Lot Kamehameha, and Victoria Kamamalu. In this accepted Hawaiian manner, even without marriage, Kamehameha III and Kinau were as one.

But as to the demands of foreigners, king and chiefs were constantly forced to give way. The blows they had already received made them painfully aware of their naïveté and lack of experience in dealing with the cunning and avaricious haoles. Kamehameha III, though he was now absolute ruler of all the islands, without even a *kuhina-nui* to strike his hand, had been made grimly aware that to stand up in dignity and strength to even a Christian from one of the three great powers was to make certain the facing of guns from their warships. His constant failure to govern Hawaii for Hawaiians had saddened and sickened him.

◁ *HAWAIIAN CHIEFS CONFERRING WITH CAPTAIN AND OFFICERS OF SHIP LA VENUS*
Lithograph by Masselot.
—*Bernice P. Bishop Museum, Honolulu.*

Before Kinau's death, David Malo, trainee out of the longneck *pule*, but emerging as one of the truly great Hawaiians, wrote to the impetuous woman who then served as co-ruler:

"I have been thinking that you ought to hold frequent meetings with all the chiefs . . . to seek for that which will be of the greatest benefit to the country: you must not think that this is anything like olden times, that you are the only chiefs and can leave things as they are . . . If a big wave comes in, large fishes will come from the dark ocean which you never saw before, and when they see the small fishes they will eat them up; such also is the case with large animals, they will prey on the smaller ones.

"The ships of the white man have come, and smart people have arrived from the great countries which you have never seen before. They know our people are few in number and living in a small country; they will eat us up, such has always been the case with large countries, the small ones have been gobbled up . . . God has made known to us through the mouths of the men of the man-of-war things, that will lead us to prepare ourselves . . . Therefore get your servant ready who will help you when you need him."

It took the deaths of Kinau, Boki, Kaahumanu, and Kalanimoku for Kamehameha III to realize how lonely and helpless he was. It took the loss and vanishment of these great Hawaiians before the floundering king fully and finally got the message.

XIII

In the dependence the groping chiefs placed upon the missionaries, it could be expected that the prime mover toward constitutional government should be a part of this dedicated group from America. Reverend William Richards was a member of the second wave of zealots out of New England. He had settled in Lahaina in May of 1823. Richards, like Bingham, was a good listener to Alii political problems. More than that, he had spent his years endeavoring, in every way he could, to coach them in the wise and mature handling of their political responsibilities. In filling this desperate need, he had gradually become their unofficial adviser. Constant foreign harassment, and the ferment within the nation itself, fed the need for a lot of advice.

At the death of Kinau, and at the behest of the battered monarchy, Richards gave up his task as missionary. Reluctantly he assumed the post of "chaplain, teacher, and translator for the king."

Educated Hawaiian young men, like David Malo, were coming out of Maui's Protestant school, established by the mission at Lahainaluna. They too were trying to persuade their rulers as to the hopelessness of the Hawaiian nation ever returning to its paradisaical past. Good or bad, the foreigners were here to stay. What was needed was the political sagacity to deal with them without the loss of one's sandals.

Richards was better versed in the scriptures than he was in political economy, but his first effort at court was to conduct lectures to the Alii on that very subject. For his seminar, conducted in the Hawaiian language, he used a borrowed textbook from an American professor. But through him, king and chiefs at last came wisely to grips with the frightening specter of the truculent foreigners, and the merciless thinning of Alii ranks by death.

They groped, they talked, and they were slow and uncertain in finding the way. But what they accomplished stands as "one of the most wonderful triumphs of good will recorded in the history of men." In June 1839 the Alii finally gave the kingdom its first Code of Civil Laws. With it came Hawaii's Magna Charta—a superbly assembled declaration of rights. "God hath made of one blood all nations of men, to dwell on the face of the earth in unity and blessedness," the code began. "God has also bestowed certain rights alike on all men, and all chiefs, and all people of all lands." Superbly, intelligently, it set forth those rights.

With a sharance totally selfless, Richards gathered in with the chiefs the intelligent and enlightened young Hawaiians emerging from the schools. The king, becoming wiser with age, surrounded himself now with such bright and energetic natives as David Malo, Timothy Haalilio, John Ii, and Boaz Mahune. These men worked masterfully at persuasion, and they handled the newly written language with Polynesian cadence and poetical nuance. Voluntarily the chiefs surrendered their rights in favor of the people. These rights, in noble phrasing, went into the declaration, and from there into the Constitution of 1840. Not only did the Alii yield power with admirable grace, but the new constitution guaranteed freedom "for all men of every religion in serving Jehovah according to their own understanding." More than that, it established a legislative assembly that would include representatives elected by the people

The king allowed Kinau's sister, Miriam Kekauluohi,* also a daughter of Kamehameha I and polygamous wife to Kamehameha II, to be named as *kuhina-nui.* Fourteen high chiefs were selected to serve in

*Ke-ka-u-lu-o-hi: *Kay*-kah-oo-loo-*oh*-hee.

the newly created House of Nobles: Kaheiheimalie,* Kuakini, Kekauo-noni, Kahekili, Paki, Konia, Keohokalole, Leleiohoku, Kekuanaoa, Ka-naina, John Ii, John Young II, and Timothy Haalilio. Kamehameha III would never again be alone in his decisions.

Hawaii's bloodless revolution, from which it emerged a constitu-tional monarchy, silenced the inner turmoil of wrangling chiefs, and strengthened and made real again the sagging ethos of the people. Enshrined in the new constitution, forever now constant to the eye and conscience, were the rights, aims and hopes of a little nation of souls who already had suffered enough. Their code of laws covered every-thing from murder to prostitution and the "regulation and sale of ardent spirits." It even set limits on the amount of encroachment allow-able to the clamoring and vindictive haoles.

But not even a constitution, and the shackling of a bellicose king, could silence the wants of the foreign residents. Eager for land, anxious for profit, endlessly hatching schemes for gain and exploitation, no law, however fair and well intentioned, could stop them. In Honolulu and Lahaina and Hilo, on the street corners and their own chauvinistic meetings, they bellowed out against king, chiefs, and their "lazy kanakas." While the consuls of the three great nations consistently meddled in Hawaiian affairs, and magnified every trivial occurrence into public outrage, their nationals worked and pushed toward the day their favored homeland would take over the islands from the bother-some natives who resisted them.

While it is true that William Richards was a bird out of the Ameri-can missionary nest, his entire life changed to one of dedication to the king and Alii. Like John Young and Isaac Davis, who so ably had served Kamehameha the Great, this remarkable man became in every sense a Hawaiian in guiding Kauikeaouli and his nation through these perilous and troublesome times. Unskilled in diplomacy or political science, he grew to greatness in his job. His was the wise and gentle voice that united king, chiefs and people into a workable and repre-sentative government. He told Hawaii's worried leaders that "the for-eign relations of this government must soon be placed on a more substantial basis, or the nation as such must soon cease to exist."

Another haole following Richards into government was Gerrit Parmele Judd, a medical missionary who had arrived with the third company of Protestants in 1828. Dr. Judd was one of those compulsive and tireless Yankees whose skills seemed endless. He could set a broken bone, suture a wound, set type, plow a field, or milk a cow with equal facility. He soon would show like adaptiveness in pioneering and man-aging a government. The chiefs made such call upon Judd's unassail-

*Ka-he-i-he-i-ma-li-e: *Kah*-hay-*ee*-hay-ee-mah-*lee*-ay.

able honesty and righteous judgment that by 1842 he finally left the mission to enter the official service of Kamehameha III. Mr. Richards created the constitution, but it was Dr. Judd who set up the mechanics of workable government, and endowed it with the stability that made its life and endurance possible.

At the suggestion of William Richards, and hopefully to gain worldwide recognition of Hawaii's sovereignty, Thomas J. Farnham was appointed minister-plenipotentiary to the governments of Great Britain, France, and the United States. Farnham, "famous American traveler and author," promised king and government a lot when he departed Honolulu. His appointment was an utter failure. Farnham did nothing whatever for Hawaii.

Undismayed, and still recognizing the rightness of Richards' advice, the king suggested the appointment of Peter Brinsmade to the office Farnham had failed to keep. Brinsmade had been one of the more friendly and cooperative haoles of Honolulu. He had come to the islands as one of the three founding partners of Ladd and Company. His firm, expanding and in search of capital, had decided to send him to the United States to seek financial help. When he left Honolulu, in 1841, he carried letters from Kamehameha III to President John Tyler, Queen Victoria, and King Louis Philippe, proposing treaties that might guarantee Hawaii's survival as a free and independent nation.

Brinsmade's audience with the American secretary of state, Daniel Webster, made official note of the king's letters, and the urgent plea for some guarantee of security. Webster filed them, and forgot them. The same thing occurred in London and Paris. Hawaii's predicament was not a matter for big governments to worry about.

But the king, ever hopeful, sought advice of Sir George Simpson, governor of British North America, and head of Hudson's Bay Company. Simpson, visiting his nephew Alexander Simpson in Honolulu, had turned a chat with the king into a round of advice and help. Cease all timorous wooing of indifferent bureaucrats, was Simpson's admonishment. Great nations should be approached boldly. Appoint accredited ambassadors.

Gratefully accepting the advice and help of Sir George Simpson, the king named this dynamic Englishman, together with William Richards, and Timothy Haalilio,* as joint ministers-plenipotentiary.

Sir George returned to Europe, by a route of interest to his office as head of Hudson's Bay—through Siberia. Richards and Haalilio sailed from Lahaina July 18, 1842. They would make an official visit to Washington before joining Simpson in London.

*Ha-a-li-li-o: *Hah*-ah-lee-lee-*oh*.

GERRIT PARMELE JUDD (1803-1873)
Judd, a medical missionary, arrived in 1828, with the Third Company.
He was an indefatigable exponent of constitutional government.

—Photo, Bernice P. Bishop Museum, Honolulu.

Richards proved to be as astute at diplomacy as he had been in guiding Hawaii toward a constitutional government. When he informed Daniel Webster that he was empowered to place the nation of Hawaii under British protectorate if its independence was not guaranteed, the American secretary of state came alive. There was a meeting of Richards and Haalilio with President Tyler. Two days later the Hawaiian ministers had their prize. The American president, in writing, assured the Hawaiian nation of recognition of its independence, and protection by the United States of America—without the immediate need of a treaty.

In London things were not so easy. Richard Charlton had already arrived from Honolulu with a dossier of complaints and charges against Kamehameha III and his government. Charlton had always been adamant about British claims on Hawaii, and for years had worked every device he knew to induce Britain to claim the Sandwich Islands as an outright possession—ahead of the United States or France. Departure of Richards for Washington had so convinced him of chicanery in that direction that the hot-tempered and volatile consul had taken the next ship for England.

In explosive resignation of his Honolulu post, Charlton had named Alexander Simpson as his successor. Alexander Simpson, though a nephew of Sir George, was a resident of Honolulu. He was a man as violently anti-Hawaiian and pro-British as Charlton, and even more determined to make Hawaii a British possession. This pugnacity had probably been aggravated by the fact that a suspicious Hawaiian government already had refused to accept young Simpson's credentials as British consul, even to fill the vacancy of the departing Charlton.

With former American missionaries carrying high appointments in Hawaiian government—William Richards, foreign minister, Gerrit Parmele Judd, official adviser to the king—both Charlton and Alexander Simpson were undergoing paroxysms of neglect and betrayal. Their charges and their petulant anger had spun the British colonists on Oahu and Maui into a state of fear and apprehension. Already acting under the complaints of Charlton and Simpson, Admiral Richard Thomas of the British Pacific fleet had dispatched a ship, and delegation. In Hawaii they would thoroughly investigate the deterioration of British affairs.

This British war frigate *Carysfort*, commanded by Lord George Paulet, dropped anchor in Honolulu harbor on February 10, 1843. Here Paulet listened well to Simpson and the alarmed Britishers. In his mind there no longer was doubt that Kamehameha III had abused and humiliated both Charlton and Simpson. Worse, British subjects appeared to be discriminated against, in favor of Americans. Missionaries or ex-missionaries, from America, alone were privy to the king. And it was their influence and persuasion that was guiding the island kingdom to a straight surrender and takeover by the United States.

Lord Paulet acted with British dispatch and efficiency. Like the French before them, the guns of the *Carysfort* were trained on the old fort, the palace, and the government buildings. In a blustery audience, Kamehameha III was presented with six demands and an ultimatum. There must be immediate and unquestioned acceptance of Alexander Simpson as representative of Great Britain, along with royal apology for the alleged mistreatment. The other demands were equally insolent and trivial, because they concerned claims and grievances of British nationals. The ultimatum—acceptance of all demands, or face immediate bombardment from the warship's guns.

To spare Honolulu, and in last desperate hope of preserving friendship with the nation from whom Hawaii had copied its flag, Kauikeaouli bowed his head, and accepted the humiliation.

But Simpson and Paulet were not through with Kauikeaouli. In a few days they were back—with new and impossible demands. This unabating insolence, instead of cowing the proud sovereign, now only infuriated him. "I will give no more," he declared, turning from them in disgust.

So Lord Paulet stormed Honolulu. Hawaii's king gave no order to fight the invasion. The fort did not fire on the British ship. England's sailors and marines, in battle gear, swarmed ashore. They paraded in strength through the sullen silence of the town. They marched to the old and crumbling fort. On February 25, 1843, to the music of the *Carysfort* band, and at the stiff attention of Lord George Paulet, Lieutenant John E. Frere, and the ship's gaudily attired officers, the flag of the Hawaiian nation was lowered. Up the fort's high staff went the flag of Great Britain.

XIV

UNTIL late July of 1843—while Richards and the king's envoys, blissfully unaware of the takeover, were seeking national recognition abroad—the Kingdom of Hawaii remained a part of the British Empire. Kauikeaouli, battered and bruised in his every attempt to rule in justice and honor, bitterly and sadly exiled himself to his palace, and surrendered once more to drunkenness. Lord Paulet ruled Hawaii under guise of a "commission." This governing panel was headed by His Lordship, Lieutenant Frere, and a resident national by the name of Duncan Mackay. The Hawaiian king, even though invited, refused to further degrade himself as fourth member of the commission and "representative of the people." Such dubious honor fell to the lot of his haole adviser, Dr. Gerrit P. Judd.

The armory, built by Kauikeaouli along the Honolulu waterfront, had already found eminent use for governmental deliberations, and as home for the newly created constitutional legislature. It now served Lord Paulet and his "commission" as seat of authority. From February 25 to July 31 of 1843—nearly five months—the British flag flew over this and other public buildings.

Three schooners belonging to the Hawaiian monarchy were seized by Paulet. Their Hawaiian names were stricken from prows, and they were renamed, in good Anglican, the *Victoria*, the *Albert*, and the *Adelaide*. On March 11 Lord Paulet dispatched the *Albert* (formerly the *Hooikaiki*) to San Blas, to carry the report of his coup, and the astonishing progress he had made in the name of Queen Victoria. Alexander Simpson was also put aboard the ship, as chosen envoy, to carry Paulet's triumphant story on to London. Included was Simpson's own dossier covering his personal energy and patriotism in behalf of the British nation.

Prior to confiscation of the *Hooikaiki*, the Hawaiian ship had been chartered by Ladd and Company for a voyage to North America. They had released their charter to Lord Paulet only under the proviso that their agent be included on the voyage to San Blas to pick up and return with a quantity of specie being forwarded to the American company. In allowing this, Lord Paulet made his one big mistake. Ladd and Company, long friends of king and chiefs, secretly suggested to the depressed and worried monarch that their agent might also serve as his agent in carrying Hawaii's version of the subjugation to high places in the outside world. The king accepted the offer with alacrity. A young American merchant by the name of James F. B. Marshall was chosen for Ladd and Company, and for the more delicate mission of Kamehameha III.

Marshall's commission as "envoy extraordinary and minister plenipotentiary" to Queen Victoria, to act in unison with William Richards, already in Europe, were prepared in utmost secrecy. Inside the royal tomb, using the coffin of Kaahumanu as writing desk, Dr. Judd prepared the documents in the name of Kamehameha III. When the *Albert* sailed out of Honolulu she carried her two messengers—Alexander Simpson, with one version of the story—James Marshall, with another tale of a small nation's betrayal. Eventually, after months of travel by sea and land, the two sets of documents landed on the same desk in the London foreign office.

Hawaii's five months as a possession of Great Britain were not without troubles for Lord Paulet and Lieutenant Frere. Dr. Judd was no easy man to work with. The American dissented vigorously on every point that invaded the rights and humbled the crown of the nation he had come to lovingly serve. Using the excuse of ill health, Mackay finally resigned from the commission in disgust, and was never replaced. Nationally, Hawaii's own laws were ignored, the bars to moral laxity were quickly brought down, and the waterfront brothels restored. His Lordship organized a body of native soldiery as "The Queen's Regiment," and a new police force was drafted. Dr. Judd was forced to pay the bills for Paulet's army and constabulary from the public treasury. Alii and people groaned under the humiliating burden foisted upon them by this pompous representative of the great nation they once had considered their truest friend.

On May 10, Dr. Judd reached the end of his endurance. He leveled formal protest, in the name of Hawaii's king, against the highhanded acts of the commission. Next day Judd too resigned as member of it—refusing to have any further part in its acts or its decisions. When Kamehameha III would not appoint anyone to replace Judd, the governing body consisted only of British officers Paulet and Frere. To forestall any attempt at forcible seizure, Dr. Judd hid all Hawaiian state documents and archival papers in the royal tomb.

On July 7 the United States war frigate *Constellation* sailed into Honolulu harbor. Aboard was Commodore Lawrence Kearney, commander of the American East India squadron. Seeing the flag of England flying over Honolulu, Kearney lodged vigorous protest. But without higher orders, he was in no position to launch a war. On July 24, a group of young Alii chiefs boarded the *Constellation,* carrying their own precious flag. Kearney ordered it hoisted to his ship's foremast. It was given full and formal salute. A band of the United States Navy played stately music in its honor.

Paulet was furious. He wrote a long and vigorous protest to Her Majesty the Queen. He trained the *Carysfort's* guns on the *Constellation*. Kearney swung his own ship into fighting position. For days on end the warships of two great nations sat poised and ready for a fight.

The least incident might have touched off a real war, had not the *Dublin*, flagship of Rear Admiral Richard Thomas of Her Majesty's Navy, suddenly appeared at Honolulu. Admiral Thomas had arrived with a burden on his soul. Upon news of Paulet's unprecedented seizure of Hawaii, he had set sail from Valparaiso direct for Oahu. Immediately upon arrival in Honolulu the Admiral sped a note to Governor Kekuanaoa,* asking that he quickly "obtain the honor of a personal

*Ke-ku-a-na-o-a: *Kay*-koo-*ah*-nah-*oh*-ah.

interview with His Majesty, King Kamehameha III" to discuss the impropriety of the cession.

Admiral Thomas, a sensible and sensitive man, required only two private audiences with the king to re-establish the respect and goodwill once held by Hawaiians for the great nation across the sea. Kauikeaouli willingly agreed to all that Thomas asked—a guarantee of the rights and privileges of British subjects in Hawaii, in accordance with the equality tendered other foreigners. In Richard Thomas the Alii were seeing another Lord Byron—an Englishman worthy of trust.

On July 31 on the plain east of Honolulu the Hawaiian flag, which long had carried the symbol of Great Britain, was once again raised. The ceremony was correct, formal, heart-warming. Before the people Admiral Richard Thomas read his nation's apology:

"The Commander in Chief of her Britannic Majesty's Ships and Vessels in the Pacific, for the reasons herein stated, and as the highest Local Representative of Her Majesty Queen Victoria, . . . hereby declares and makes manifest that he does not accept the Provisional Cession of the Hawaiian Islands made on the 25th day of February 1843; but that he considers His Majesty Kamehameha III the legitimate King of those Islands; and he assures His Majesty that the sentiments of his Sovereign towards him are those of unvarying friendship and esteem, that Her Majesty sincerely desires King Kamehameha to be treated as an *Independent Sovereign,* leaving the administration of justice in his own hands, the faithful discharge of which will promote his happiness and the prosperity of his Dominions."

There was public and precision salute to the Hawaiian flag by the sailors and marines from the warships. There was music from the bands. In the afternoon a service of thanksgiving was held in Oahu's beautiful new stone church of Kawaiahao. Here the handsome young king made formal declaration that the nation had been restored again to the people, and that henceforth Hawaii would be governed in strict conformity with its new constitution and its new code of laws. There was singing of Protestant hymns in Hawaiian words. There were prayers of thanksgiving. And the king proclaimed a ten-day holiday so that the entire community might surrender itself to festivity, feasting, song and dance.

After things had quieted down in Honolulu, and the warships had departed from her harbor, a British merchantman brought additional good news direct from London. Richards and Haalilio had achieved brilliant diplomatic success. The king's letters, through Marshall's astute mission, had counteracted the waspish accusations of Alexander Simpson and Richard Charlton. The Hawaiian envoys not only had won recognition of the Hawaiian nation by Great Britain, but had witnessed the signing of a joint declaration by England and France pledging them "reciprocally to consider the Sandwich Islands an independent state."

Richards and Haalilio had cannily played the declaration of President Tyler against the foreign offices of the European nations. It was fear of America's course which had impelled this mutual accord. But whatever means or motive, the results pleased Kauikeaouli and Dr. Judd. Hawaii could at last move with ease, and a sense of security.

XV

THE YEARS, and an increasing dependence on such advisers as Richards, Judd, and legislators, for direction and help, had made Kamehameha III over into a mild-mannered, almost gentle monarch. Increasingly his court became more European patterned. Its protocol, manners, and dress grew ever more glittering and stylized.

Kauikeaouli was a handsome king—a true Kamehameha in every sense. A little more darker-skinned than Liholiho, he wore his mustache British-styled—heavy, meticulously trimmed. By 1846 this mustache had drooped darkly down his firm mouth sides to join a sharp and closely cropped beard. Like most Hawaiians, his black hair remained thick and wavy throughout his lifetime. His eyes were dark brown, heavy lashed, and gently penetrating. His face, even in repose, was amiable, friendly, and appealing. He stood erect like an Alii. His people respected and loved him.

But his lifetime never ceased to be one constant harassment by the pushy and self-centered foreigners. Still, in spite of the trouble haoles caused him, he counted many of them as close and permanent friends. Time gave him sense and wisdom enough to use their sharpness and acuity to royal advantage. He drew into his orbit those American missionaries, Honolulu entrepreneurs, and business men whom he personally felt could be trusted. He chose discreetly and well. Few who were so favored ever betrayed his confidence.

Besides his ornate grass palace at Honolulu, he maintained a smaller house at Waikiki, on the beach front where now stands the Royal Hawaiian Hotel. Like his brother, he tried a floating palace—a rebuilt American brigantine—but the orgiastic parties of his earlier days had worn thin, and he opted in favor of a royal hideaway at Lahaina. In later years he constructed a more substantial abode of stone and wood in Honolulu.

Somehow he never too blatantly allowed his weakness for drinking and gambling to interfere with his more decorous appearance as king of the united islands. The years added to his gift of ruling well and sensibly, in spite of discreet intemperance and extra-marital love life.

He never did accept, as his queens, the women whom his Hawaii-minded chiefs had advocated. Caught up in the circles of Kaomi, and the *Lahui ka Hulumanu*, his earlier years were an almost constant round of dissipation and pleasure, with little attention paid to marriage of state—with sisters, half sisters, or with mana-loaded queens. But on February 14, 1837 he did take to wife Kalama—daughter of Iahuula and Naihekukui, and adopted by Charles Kanaina. Kalama had sterling Alii antecedents, and ample mana. But of the two children born to this rather unhappy union, both died in infancy. Kauikeaouli was never to father an heir to the throne.

For state purposes the problem of succession was handled with Hawaiian simplicity and directness. Kamehameha III adopted, or grafted in, the children of Elizabeta Kinau, as fathered by Governor Mataio [Matthew] Kekuanaoa. Kinau, as daughter of Kamehameha I and once a plural wife of Kamehameha II, became by royal proxy, after her death, under identical kinship status with Kamehameha III. Just as vitally important, even in so tangled a family pattern, she was Kaukeaouli's half-sister. And, up to her death, his *kuhina-nui*.

The family of Kinau and Kekuanaoa, in their new role as foster children of Kamehameha III, had left the house of the governor of Oahu to take up residence in the royal palace upon death of their renowned Alii mother. In the manner of Hawaiian adoption, little Alexander Liholiho, Lot, and Victoria became essential members of Kauikeaouli's household, and princes and princess of the realm. Photographs of the royal family, showing Queen Kalama, Kamehameha III, and their three children out of Kinau, began circulating as national daguerreotypes, and therefore history. In those pictures both Queen Kalama and King Kauikeaouli looked unusually stern.

To the childless Kalama, striving to maintain semblance of a home to the faithless and ebullient Kauikeaouli, the three handsome children were a godsend. They were given a real mother's love. They were educated in the Chiefs' School, and the best private tutoring available through Dr. Judd and the missionaries. Alexander was exceptionally bright and studious; with the ability to outstrip any of his young Alii companions in every class and in every phase of learning. As heirs-apparent to the crown of the Kamehamehas they were buds of great promise.

Kalama coached them in court manners and etiquette. In affairs of state they stood correctly in the margins, to observe and absorb all ways and functions which went with Hawaiian rulership. King Kauikeaouli, like his brother Liholiho, loved pomp and pageantry. Tutors were hired to coach the royal family, and the chiefs who surrounded them, in the protocol and niceties common to the courts of St. James and Versailles. But in the matter of raising finances to pay for this glitter and extravagance the king relied heavily on the advice and money-grubbing skills of the Americans.

It was Kalama who shielded her foster-children from the more private and exclusive court of the king—the palace area given over to Kauikeaouli's less mannerly and less glittering companions. Here there was carousing, gambling, music, noise, and plenty of the nationally banned hula dancing. But with all his excesses, Kamehameha III kept the private and state areas of his life forever separate. When his people and his court saw him, functioning in the capacity of judge and sovereign, they saw him impeccably attired, a six foot, handsome, and articulate king. They accepted his faults, forgave them, and loved him in spite of them. They respected and admired him for the finesse and positive way he played out his role. To them he was never less than a true and noble son of Kamehameha the Great.

The haoles had long ago learned to esteem this placid and intelligent monarch. In the matter of the welfare of Hawaii, and its people, he could never be pushed or coerced. He could explode upon them like a volcano when his fury was aroused. But the Americans whom he had drafted into royal service, like Richards and Judd, quickly realized Hawaii's internal chaos. Kauikeaouli was valiantly striving to rule a kingdom, built upon a stone-age culture, colliding head-on with an aggressive and unfeeling world of foreigners.

Both Richards and Judd had discovered that the nation existed without a system of bookkeeping. No accounting was made of taxes collected, or any record kept of money paid out. The kingdom of Hawaii, monetarily at least, was a mess. The king taxed the people. The chiefs, in their respective jurisdictions, taxed the people. But no one could give final answers as to how much, or how little. Administrative reorganization became the first and imperative necessity.

By joint act of king and *kuhina-nui*, on May 10, 1842, a "Treasury Board of the Kingdom" was commissioned. Appointed to it were Dr. G. P. Judd, Timothy Haalilio, and John Ii. William Richards, knowing he had served Hawaii with loyalty and genius, was now on greater mission, as foreign minister in Europe. On the day the treasury board took its office, a set of books were opened—the "first attempt of the Sandwich Island Government to keep anything like regular and systematic accounts," wrote Dr. Judd. Ably assisted by his two loyal and educated native commissioners, Judd attacked the immense and jumbled problem. "At that time, the Finances were a mass of confusion," Dr.

Judd confessed, "requiring great labor and patience to reduce them to any kind of order."

In the face of this crying need, one so able as the American missionary-physician could not help but be drawn ever deeper into the desperate necessity for orderly and efficient government. Five days after his appointment to the treasury board, Dr. Judd was named national translator and recorder. Over the signatures of king and *kuhina-nui* he was instructed "to aid Kekuanaoa [governor of Oahu, and true father of the crown heirs-apparent] in your official capacity, which relates to all business of importance between foreigners."

There was some basis for the constant furor foreigners made over the specter of the longnecks dictating monarchical policy. But there can be no question of the effort and dedication these Americans gave to the confused and faltering king and legislature in building a Hawaii capable of standing face to the avaricious haoles.

With a workable accounting system installed, the next and equally pressing problem was the delineation and recording of ownership of the nation's lands. Neither foreigners, chiefs, nor common natives would longer tolerate the claim that all islands and all land belonged in fee simple to the king. Before Kamehameha the Great, at each royal accession, there had been a redistribution of land to those chiefs loyal to the new regime. Down through the rulership of three kings there had been the clamor for a wider sharance of what the monarch claimed as his own.

At the behest of sovereign and legislature "The Commission to Quiet Land Titles" was created in December of 1845. John Ricord, James Young Kanehoa, John Ii, and Zorababela Kaauwai were commissioned to the board. At its first meeting, February 11, 1846, William Richards, now returned to the islands, was elected by the board members as president. Under able direction of Richards the commission plunged into a thorough study of the land system then prevailing. Their published report became the test for validity of all claims.

"The Hawaiian rulers have learned by experience, that regard must be had to the immutable law of property, and that the well being of their country must essentially depend on the proper development of their internal resources, of which the land is the principal," the commission reported. The most shattering of their conclusions was that the nation and its resources could not be orderly or even properly developed unless the common people shared in them.

The earlier declarations of Kamehameha III in which, through royal decree of his father, he had claimed all the nation's lands as his own, had brought plenty of foreign turbulence upon his head. Those haoles who had squatted upon, leased, or purchased land for business

or agricultural pursuits utterly rejected this insecure premise to their
holdings. Half of Hawaii's problems had been centered over disputes
of foreigners regarding island property.

In hopes of once and for all laying quietus to this concern, the
government's first step was a directive to all foreign landholders requesting them to enter into official written agreement to establish
metes and bounds of the lands they occupied. With it they were asked
for declaration of the length of time they wished to use the land, and
cooperation in establishing the annual rental for same.

The move quickly ended in failure. Foreigners, suspicious of the
king and his claims, demanded outright possession, not leaseholds.

By the time of this launching of his land commission, Kamehameha
III had mellowed in his autocratic claim of ownership. More than anything he wanted to heed the wishes of his people. If at all possible, he
would appease the raucous voices of the foreigners. But he was as
baffled as his commissioners when it came to the task of apportioning
Hawaiian lands fairly and honorably. The problem was eventually
solved through the borrowed skills and acuity of sharp Americans.

In setting up judicial courts to supersede the archaic and ineffective
chiefs' councils, and the erratic judgments of favored Alii, king and
legislature reached out to every American arriving with some background knowledge of courts and laws. First there was John Ricord, who
became the monarchy's first attorney general. As a semblance of magisterial sagacity emerged to take the place of the bans and pronouncements from such autocrats as Queen Kaahumanu, or King Kauikeaouli,
other American barristers were added to the new and more efficient
judicial system. Young haole attorneys, arriving in Honolulu, found
themselves quickly drafted into government as judges for a quickened
and forward-looking nation.

Lorrin Andrews was appointed, June 24, 1846, as one of the judges
of the original and appellate jurisdiction of Honolulu. William Little
Lee had scarcely stepped off ship in Honolulu when he found himself
a legal coordinate with Judge Andrews. The appointment of young
Judge Lee marked the beginning of a new era in Hawaii's judiciary.

It was Judge Lee who suggested a solution to the crisis in land ap-
portionment—the Mahele* Book. Let the king, suggested Judge Lee,
keep whatever land he chooses and needs, as personal property. Then
let the king divide all other lands in all the islands into three parts:
One part for the government, one part for the chiefs and Alii, one part
for the common people. Let the divisions be made honestly and accurately, and the holdings forever recorded in the Mahele.

*Ma-he-le: *Mah*-hay-lay.

The plan was adopted. And responsibility for sharance of the lands between king and chiefs was given to Kamehameha III, assisted by Dr. G. P. Judd, J. Piikoi, Mataio Kekuanaoa, and John Young II. Between January 27 and March 7, 1848 the Mahele actually came into being. A total of 245 chiefs appeared before the committee during that time, and voluntarily divided their fiefs with the king. The transactions were duly recorded in the Mahele Book. When this was completed, Kamehameha III solemnly separated his immense share of public domain into two parts. The smaller portion became "crown lands," or his own private property; the larger portion, labeled "government lands," the king gave "to the chiefs and people forever."

Within two years the commoners were issued, without cost, fee simple titles to the kuleanas,* or lands they lived upon and cultivated as tenants of the king, the chiefs, or the newly representative government. Town lots were not considered as kuleanas. Those natives with no claim to kuleanas were offered government land on all islands at fifty cents an acre. The success in lifting serfs to landholders was soon amply proven. In five years awards of land were made to 9,337 native owners. Thirty thousand acres of fine agricultural land passed into the hands of Hawaii's former peasantry.

This unparalleled example of a peaceful revolution, conducted with intelligence and dignity, was marred by the 1850 act of the Hawaiian legislature which granted full rights for foreigners to purchase and own land in fee simple. Some members of the government, including a few dedicated Americans like Dr. Judd, begged for restrictions on the amount of Hawaiian land that could be peddled to foreigners for money. They had long been aware of haole avarice and greed. But the suggested constraints were instantly branded as "iniquitous" by the land-hungry foreigners, and the necessary controls were omitted in the public law. With this concession, all hurdles were down.

From that point in his reign to the day of his death Kauikeaouli could do little to stem the phrenetic tide of events which shaped and changed the nation he had expected to rule. Like Mauna Loa's lava, relentlessly flowing downward into every crack and crevice, the foreign tide burrowed into the vitals of the common weal. Frantically Hawaii was reorganized, reoriented in its thinking, and modernized— in desperate hope of coping with the pressures bearing unceasingly upon it.

To counter haole influence in public affairs, the king and the confused legislature invited in canny and experienced haoles. The result changed an honest but primitive culture into a nation imitative of the best and the worst in nineteenth century nationalism. Through the

*Ku-le-a-na: Koo-lay-*ah*-nah.

next decade Hawaii would be as insecure and as bewildered as the day Kaahumanu had burned its idols and destroyed its ethos.

The Kamehamehas, and the Alii from whence they had risen, were in general, valorous custodians of their culture. The center core of this super family were, for the most part, loyal and pugnacious fighters for the grand concept of their heritage. But every move they made to preserve their nation, and their way of life, brought resistant and savage battle from the foreigners. Islanders had no choice other than to recognize and placate the haole. He was here. And he was here to stay.

While Dr. Judd, with his treasury board, struggled to make the islands' economy self-sufficient—while Judge William Lee and his fellow justices shaped Hawaii's jurisprudence haole style—the growing flood of missionaries were teaching everyone, Alii, commoner, and foreigners, to read and write. Dr. Judd, with New England business acuity, was collecting governmental taxes in cash—wherever possible. Penniless natives, however, were still permitted to pay their levies in produce, or in labor. Rents, sales of land, licenses, and business assessments accounted for a third of the public revenue. Customs duties on the flow of imports, and the commerce incident to provisioning the hundreds of visiting ships, accounted for the remainder of the taxes collected by the treasury board. The monarchy's gross income rose from $41,000 in 1842 to $323,000 in 1854.

In defining the rights of foreigners to own property, to acquire concessions, and to operate businesses without consent of the king, the door was opened to widespread exploitation. Ladd and Company, Honolulu owned and long favored by king and chiefs, quite naturally became the first of these concessionaires. Ladd's idea for promoting the nation's economy was simple. They asked only that the government grant them huge districts on the various islands to develop. Their promise was to return to the national treasury one half of the net profits realized from each such district. Native laborers would receive wages for their efforts, land for their homes and gardens, and free instruction in mechanical and agricultural skills. The company would provide public buildings, factories, schools, churches, teachers and medical services. But Ladd and Company were unable, through lack of finance (blamed on Dr. Judd) to get their grandiose scheme off the ground. Still the idea became pattern to later concessionaires, and forerunner of the future baronial plantations which, in the 1890s, would finally strangle the monarchy.

The first successful sugar plantation in the islands had started at Koloa, Kauai, in 1835—a Ladd enterprise. Peter A. Brinsmade and the longnecks had persuaded Kamehameha III that a leasing of 1,000 acres of crown land to Ladd and Company would be a good thing for king and economy. The chiefs of Kauai opposed it from the start, and native labor proved inept. But in spite of the obstacles, Koloa, within a year, boasted 25 acres of sugar cane, 5,000 coffee trees, 5,000 banana clumps, 45 taro patches, and 20 factory buildings. Mill power was provided by a rock-and-earth dam. For each day's labor, Koloa's workers received rations of fish and poi, and one hapawalu in Ladd's "Kauai money." An hapawalu was worth 12½ cents—good mostly at the company store.

With this beginning on leasehold lands, the sugar industry grew slowly but with unmistakable certainty in all the islands whose acreage was suitable to cane fields. Refineries were built with foreign capital and with constantly improved techniques in processing. When finally it became possible for foreigners to acquire public land by purchase, there was no stopping the advance.

At Waimea, Kauai, tobacco became an established and successful crop. The dry, sunny slopes of Kona, on the parent island of Hawaii, became host to coffee plantations. On this same island, where the first Kamehameha had built himself to greatness, and where Kauikeaouli had walked as a boy, the cattle which Vancouver had tendered as gift had—because they carried the king's kapu—increased to "ruinous" proportions. It was estimated that, by 1846, 25,000 head of cattle roamed the island, wreaking havoc in the villages, and devouring the lush flora of Hawaii. Repeatedly the king passed laws for fencing out the wild and pernicious beasts, especially after the haole plantation owners applied their pressures. Many enterprising natives had domesticated Vancouver's bovines, and were living well on milk and meat. The butcher shops of Honolulu and Lahaina now openly sold Hawaiian beef. Eventually Vancouver's largesse, and a lot of the ancestral land of the Kamehamehas would become the Parker holdings—one of the largest and most successful cattle ranches in the world.

Agriculture was now rising to compete with the whaling industry as the economic life blood of the nation. Sandalwood, now entirely depleted, turned no more money into Alii coffers. By now, too, whales were becoming less plentiful, with the ships forced to range ever wider in their search. When gold was discovered in California, Hawaii became more than ever the crossroads of the Pacific. Argonauts, traveling by sea, made Honolulu port of call in the great arc swing across the Pacific to the shores of North America. Not only were the islands host to thousands of travelers—with trade brisk and flourishing—but as California became more populous, Hawaiian exports in agricultural foodstuffs became ever more promising.

KAMEHAMEHA III (KAUIKEAOULI) IN 1853

—Photo, Bernice P. Bishop Museum, Honolulu.

This ended, however, when the residents of California and Oregon discovered the possibilities of their own acreage, and began raising food nearer home. In 1851 Hawaii dropped into a ruinous depression, and the lush days of agricultural trade were over. Hundreds of haole entrepreneurs failed. Crops rotted in island fields for want of market.

Only the cane and coffee growers remained optimistic. California and Oregon would never be able to grow either of these crops successfully and, on them at least, the islands could still look favorably to the future. But disappointment came, swift and sure. The United States levied a high tariff on Hawaiian sugar and coffee imports. From the Philippines, from Central America, better sugar and coffee came to San Francisco than Hawaii was exporting—and at cheaper prices.

Few of the original planters survived this disaster. Ladd and Company failed. Only those who improved their techniques, who moved toward the highest possible quality, survived the collapse of the booming fifties.

In other more tragic ways Kamehameha III realized he was ruling a dying nation. The foreigners were relentlessly gouging and devouring everything of value. Hawaii's greatest calamity stemmed from their appearance and presence. The native race was swiftly perishing. In 1778, the year of Cook's entry, there was a native population of 300,000. In 1850 only 84,165 natives remained. Wars, deprivation, exploitation and haole disease had wiped out almost two-thirds of Hawaii's people. As a king his sovereignty must now be tailored to meet the wants and tastes of two foreigners to every precious islander.

And fate of the survivors was not at all promising. In 1850 only 1,422 native children were born. White man's diseases and white man's ways made certain that three-fourths of these babies would die in infancy.

Dwindling of the labor supply, with fewer and fewer natives to work the fields and serve the foreign population, brought crisis of another sort. On January 3, 1852 a ship appeared in Honolulu harbor bearing workers from another land. Aboard the American bark *Thetis* were 195 indentured immigrants from Amoy, China. As answer to Hawaii's catastrophic loss in population, the *Thetis* would not be the last ship to concern itself with human traffic.

The Chinese brought their own strange religion. But the cause of Christ did not graph itself downward with collapse of the business boom. Protestant schools flourished, even with diminishing population. The Mission Seminary at Lahainaluna, Maui, was turning out educated Hawaiians. Punahou, under the direction of Rev. and Mrs. Daniel Dole, was providing natives and haoles with an educative pattern comparable to anything found in New England. Hiram Bingham had

retired back to his native American soil, but he had left a legacy of
devoted followers. Protestant churches and mission schoolhouses dotted
every island. And Rev. James Kekela had been ordained a minister in
the Congregational Church—the first but not the last native Hawaiian
to gain that post.

The Catholic faith, now that bans and hindrances were vanished,
was prospering and expanding across the islands. By 1853 they had
gained 11,401 converts, had built their impressive Cathedral of Our
Lady of Peace in Honolulu, and had set up numerous busy and efficient
schools.

On December 12, 1850 the Mormons arrived. Their mission was
headed by George Q. Cannon. When, in three years, their selfless elders
had garnered three thousand converts, even the haoles began to fight
them. Undismayed, Cannon, with the help of native converts J. Napela
and J. Kauwahi, translated the *Book of Mormon* into Hawaiian. And
the Mormons too remained and prospered.

But the king was unceasingly astonished by this ferocious war of
sects fighting for the last souls of the last Hawaiians. Other than that,
he no longer cared a seraph's feather as to who came out winner. Indifferent to the many mission schools and their devoted and accomplished instructors, he pushed wherever he could for government
institutions less tied to the salvation of Christ, and more concerned
with salvation of the people and his nation. The Chiefs' Children's
School, established solely for education of offspring of the Alii, and
operated by Mr. and Mrs. Amos Starr Cooke, was having its problems.
At Kauikeaouli's suggestion, it was renamed the Royal School. Somehow it survived the pressures of spoiled aristocratic students and the
pomposity and indulgence of their parents. By 1851 the government
had acquired, from the missionaries, both Lahainaluna Seminary and
the Oahu Charity School.

But this ever deepening penetration of Americans into the affairs
of the Hawaiian monarchy was not looked upon with equanimity by
Great Britain and France. Those of the American missionaries entering government service induced friends and relatives to Honolulu to
avail themselves of Hawaiian trade and commercial advantages. The
new haoles were often less nobly motivated than their longneck cousins.
Men like Charles Reed Bishop, who had entered Hawaii as friend of
Judge William Lee, and others like Dr. Robert Wood and Elisha Allen,
were now moving to the top of Hawaii's financial, social and political
circles. And already there was open talk in Honolulu, in California, in
Washington, D. C., of the possibilities and advantages of American
annexation.

All such favoritism, all such rumors, stirred unrest and apprehension in the legation offices of Great Britain and France. Once again Kauikeaouli caught the brunt of the international battle of greed being fought in his own front yard. The raucous clamor of foreigners was a plague to his life as real and certain as the chronic alcoholism he constantly faced. With both these insidious and destructive illnessses he coped bravely and unsuccessfully.

On August 22, 1849 a French warship entered the harbor. Once again guns were trained on town, fort and palace. Rear-Admiral Legoarant de Tromelin was wearied that French brandies, priests, sailors—and above all, Catholicism—were not as welcome in Hawaii as the American counterparts. He had decided that, with his flagship *La Poursuivante*, France should again teach the haughty Alii a lesson. There was no time to ascertain whether or not he was acting under official orders of his government. Backed up by the threatening guns of the big ship he presented the harried Kauikeaouli with a new set of French demands.

But this time the French naval officers caught the hung-over king in a foul mood. He not only refused to concede to the impertinent act, but blasted at the Frenchmen like a true Kamehameha.

So Tromelin proceeded with his international lesson. Marines from *La Poursuivante* seized the government buildings, Kauikeaouli's yacht, captured the poorly garrisoned fort, spiked its guns, dumped its powder and its shot. In drunken rage, Kamehameha III vowed that he would surrender his nation to the United States or Britain before he would again yield to the bald threats of France.

With final departure of the French man-of-war, he ordered Dr. Judd to visit the capitals of the three great powers, to lodge Hawaiian protest for the outrage, and once more demand for his nation the protection and equitable diplomatic treatment it deserved. On this journey, at the king's request, Judd took the two princes of the realm—Alexander Liholiho and Lot Kamehameha. They were old enough now to acquaint themselves with the world of trouble and hostility they would eventually be called upon to face.

While the three men followed the former mission of Richards and his Alii companions in seeking diplomatic consideration in the capitals of Paris, London and Washington, they faced a changed climate of nationalism. The French and British moves in Hawaiian waters had succeeded in spreading annexation fever throughout America. One exuberant politician, celebrating Franklin Pierce's election to the American presidency, had toasted Pierce with: "Cuba and the Sandwich Islands—may they soon be added to the galaxy of states." A San Francisco editor was calling Hawaii "a luscious pear," and urging

HONOLULU HARBOR IN 1853
Lithograph by Burgess.

—*Bernice P. Bishop Museum, Honolulu.*

Washington to "pluck" it. In August 1852, in the halls of congress, California's congressman J. W. McCorkle had rocked the chambers with his speeches advocating annexation. And, back in the islands, knowing the king's announced willingness to honorably surrender his nation, there was great worry and wonder among natives and haoles as to which big power—America, England or France—would be first the pluck the fruit.

Another danger was the possibility of a filibustering or freebooting takeover from those fiery caucuses out of California. These were the days of America's "manifest destiny." Expansion had become the holy cause. And within the islands themselves were Americans, secure and prosperous, working frantically against the monarchy, its legislature, and its chiefs. They were equally determined to turn Hawaii over to the United States.

Foremost of Hawaii's own internecine movements for annexation was a group of powerful haoles calling themselves "The Committee of Thirteen." Such men as William Ladd, long favored by the king, not only was a member of the committee, but had joined with others in plotting, by way of California filibusters, the forcible overthrow of the government. Even the frustrated monarch was said to have listened favorably to the persuasive arguments of these powerful Americans.

In May of 1853 the haole plague of smallpox hit Hawaii with a virulence that decimated the population. Natives were wiped away in tragic and fearful numbers. The pestilence, already raging in California, had crossed the Pacific barrier by some unknown ship, and had set its tenacious hold upon the vulnerable and helpless Hawaiians.

In name of the king, Dr. Judd called upon the doctors of Honolulu and Lahaina, and the medically trained missionaries, to aid the government in battling the scourge. The king appointed Dr. T. C. B. Rooke and Marshal William C. Parke to serve with Dr. Judd, as royal commissioners of public health. Isolation centers were set up. A courageous attempt to vaccinate the populace moved to action. With natives everywhere dying from the loathsome disease, the haoles, caught in midst of it, made screaming demands upon Judd for greater governmental efforts in fighting the epidemic. Judd was accused of parsimony in allocating funds sufficient to cope with the tragic situation. His difficulty was that little public money was available.

On every island the natives sickened and died. Those who surrendered themselves to the kahunas and witch doctors perished. Those who somehow were reached by the crude and hastily prepared vaccines of the haole physicians and missionary doctors were saved. But the death toll from the epidemic was appalling. On Oahu the natives died by the thousands. Sailors, imprisoned for Honolulu riots and criminal infractions, were forced by the militia to aid in burying the dead. Such missionaries as Dr. Dwight Baldwin, at Lahaina, kept the death rate lower by more carefully prepared vaccine, especially on Maui. But when the epidemic was finally conquered in January of 1854, it had wiped out six thousand of the nation's population—a catastrophe from which Hawaii never fully recovered.

The hue and cry against the king and his ministers were incessant for the "bungling" manner they had conducted the public fight against a calamity Hawaiians had never before known. The fact was that the king himself was appalled and shaken by the march of death across his nation. Mrs. Amos Starr Cooke wrote into her journal, in October 1853, that the king had been continuously drunk for several weeks. She mentioned that His Majesty's latest "paramour" had died of smallpox, and the king had hardly been sober since.

He sobered up, however, when the insurgent haoles confronted him with new demands, and more of their seemingly endless complaints.

They insisted on immediate dismissal from government of Dr. Gerrit P. Judd and Rev. Richard Armstrong. The Committee of Thirteen, through the public press, had already inflamed the populace into believing the smallpox epidemic could have been averted had it not been for the niggardly administration of the national treasury by Dr. Judd. It could have been stopped far short of disaster had not Armstrong, who as minister of public instruction, reputedly botched the vaccination program, in whose charge it had been placed. William Ladd, as active member of the Committee of Thirteen, now publicly laid blame for the failure of Ladd and Company upon the king and his "inept" ministers.

By September of 1853 the clamor against Kauikeaouli was enough to have driven even a Puritan to drink. Not until the Committee of Thirteen threatened to back and engineer a filibuster invasion from California, to topple the Hawaiian monarchy, did the sick and harassed king sacrifice his trusted and proven Dr. Judd, along with Richard Armstrong and other loyal haoles, to the traitorous and ambitious Americans working for his downfall.

After Judd's wise voice was silenced the Committee moved with heavy hand against the sovereign. Despondent, wasted, and physically ill, Kauikeaouli listened repeatedly to their persuasions. Finally, on January 1854, he instructed Robert C. Wyllie, his haole minister of foreign relations, to confer with Honolulu's U. S. Commissioner, David L. Gregg, on the matter of United States annexation of the Hawaiian kingdom.

Gregg, overjoyed at the prize in his grasp, drew immediate response from Washington. The United States Department of State authorized Gregg to negotiate a treaty of annexation with Kamehameha

III. By August Gregg passed to the king, for study and decision, a draft of the proposed treaty.

When England and France heard of the impending coup, their ministers descended upon Kaukeaouli like angry hornets.

But it was the quick support of these two great nations that rallied the king from his despond. With typical snap decision, he now rejected Gregg's efforts toward annexation. His new resolve was to keep his kingdom. His health improved. Once more he stood in Alii dignity— the master of his nation. Once more he battled against the pestiferous interference of foreigners in the affairs of state. But the web, through the years, had been carefully woven. No matter how bravely, frantically he struggled, he could never quite be free of it.

Haole vaccination had saved him from the plague which had wiped out six thousand of his kinsmen, but physical excesses, and mental travail, were proving fully as lethal. On December 15 of that mad year of 1854, Kamehameha III, last son of the Great One, finally gave up his kingdom by death. The Hawaiian people who loved him—strength and weakness both—tendered him a funeral of pomp and pageantry befitting the noblest of their kings. Their tears were genuine as they wept and chanted to "Ka Mo'i Lokomaika" — "King of Benevolence."

The brilliant and educated Alexander Liholiho, foster son of the dead king, who stepped into the loss as Kamehameha IV, summed up the reign of Kauikeaouli: "The age of Kamehameha III was that of progress and of liberty, of schools and of civilization. He gave us a constitution and fixed laws; he secured the people in the title to their lands, and removed the last chain of oppression."

But, more important, he died leaving his beloved islands still in the hands of Hawaiians.

KAMEHAMEHA IV (ALEXANDER LIHOLIHO)
WHO REIGNED 1854-1863

—Photo, Bernice P. Bishop Museum, Honolulu.

PART FOUR

The Last of the Kamehamehas
Alexander Liholiho (Kamehameha IV) and Lot (Kamehameha V), the Bachelor King

I

THE DAY they prepared Kamehameha III for the royal entombment, twenty-year-old Alexander Liholiho acknowledged his responsibility as the new king. He opened the orgy of public mourning with the cry of "E, alii, e!" "I have become, by the will of God, your Father, as I have been your Child." To his people he humbly pleaded: "You must help me, for I stand in need of help." And that was verily true.

Less than a month later, January 11, 1855, when the public wails were silenced, and the Alii *kahilis* were once more put away, Alexander was inaugurated as Kamehameha IV. This brilliant, handsome young man, triumphant product of the Chiefs' Children's School and the best American tutors, rendered his coronation address in flawless Hawaiian, and, to the foreigners gathered in Honolulu to watch his start, he delivered it in equally flawless English. "Today we begin a new era," he reminded his people. "Let it be one of increased civilization, one of decided progress, industry, temperance, morality, and all those virtues which mark a nation's advance."

To the haoles, in English: "The duties we owe to each other are reciprocal. I shall use my best endeavors to give you a just, liberal, and satisfactory government. I shall expect you in return to assist me in sustaining the peace, the law, the order, and the independence of my kingdom."

To natives and foreigners, it was an auspicious start.

Alexander's uncle, Kauikeaouli, after his one recorded marriage, without living issue, and his persistent disregard for Queen Kalama in the pursuance of his amours elsewhere, had satisfied the need for heir-presumptives by appropriating the family of Elisabeta Kinau, and her second husband, Governor Mataio [Matthew] Kekuanaoa. This Polynesian royal adoption was done at the time of Kinau's death. Kinau, being the king's sister, out of the blood of Kamehameha the Great, the

foster children—Prince Alexander, Prince Lot, and Princess Kamamalu
—were, according to Alii custom and tradition surrendered by Kekuanaoa to the king. Not only were they groomed for the throne of Hawaii,
but the three children had been universally accepted as the king's own.

On October 7, 1853, a year before Kauikeaouli's death, Alexander
had been proclaimed as heir-apparent to the throne of the Kamehamehas. "Aleck" had traveled the world with Dr. Judd, and had been
coached and polished for the throne by Robert Wyllie and the fashioning hand of the royal school. For Hawaii, this bright, witty and perceptive young king was a new product.

A year after his coronation, Kamehameha IV put end to all whispered speculation. At Kawaiahao Church, June 1856, he married
Emma—daughter of Fanny Young and George Naea. There were
whispers that the king was mongrelizing the sacred blood line by
marrying out of the Alii pattern of family kinship. But times were inexorably changing the Hawaii once known to the great god Lono.

Still the new queen possessed plenty of mana. She was granddaughter to a full brother of Kamehameha the Great, Keliimaikai. She
was also granddaughter to John Young, the first haole to enter the Alii
circle. She was foster daughter to Dr. T. C. B. Rooke, who had married
Grace Young, Emma's mother's sister. Emma had possessed more than
enough royal mana to gain her entrance into the Chiefs' School.

There the bright-eyed, wavy-haired student Alexander had met
her. Aleck, wildly in love with this luscious *wahine* out of two cultures,
had sworn he would someday marry Emma Rooke. And this he did—
publicly, and in lavish church ceremony. After the Reverend Richard
Armstrong had pronounced them man and wife, Emma's *mele* was
sung by an Hawaiian poet: "Bind thy rich hair with gems! Around thy
neck let glowing rubies shine! Thy lovely form support the feather'd
robes of royal state, bright with the spoils of twice ten thousand birds
robbed of their one sole treasure to form a mantle fit for thee! Stand
forth . . . queen of loveliness! Worthy to share the throne of these fair
Isles!" No royal couple could ever have received a more loquacious and
auspicious start.

Alexander commenced his reign as Kamehameha IV with enough
popular adulation to turn any lesser man's head. Haole tailors and
Alii court favorites kept him dressed in the latest European fashions—
English pantaloons of worsted wool, brocaded vests, waistcoats with
satin lapels. His black hair lay in tumbled wavelets, his dark eyes
were expressive, challenging, intelligently questive. He effected a lip-
lined mustache, burnsides, and a circlet of chin whiskers that wildly
charmed the females of his court—whether they be Alii born, foreign

QUEEN EMMA, WIFE OF ALEXANDER LIHOLIHO
(KAMEHAMEHA IV)

—Photo, Bernice P. Bishop Museum, Honolulu.

dignitaries, or the Anglo and American nouveau rich now dominating Honolulu's social world.

After the coronation, everyone in the islands breathed easier. For a king, young Aleck could easily have won a popularity contest as everyone's choice. Natives adored him because he was a true Kamehameha—straight from the loins of the Great. Foreigners were satisfied. He was Christian—Anglo and American tutored—had traveled to Europe and America—was seemingly unfettered by the inclinations and restraints of his forebears. What they did not realize was that Aleck was Hawaiian first. His thinking was always to remain that of an Alii. And the genes of Polynesia were stronger within him than the superficial veneer he had acquired from travel and culture.

He entered his reign shocked and shaken by the tragic wasting of his nation by the twin scourges brought to it by the foreigners— avarice and disease. On that day in 1855, when Kamehameha IV addressed his legislature for the first time, only 70,000 natives remained from the 300,000 population his grandfather had governed. He was still shattered and dismayed by the enormity of the smallpox epidemic. This catastrophe had left Hawaii a virtual abyss. "The decrease of our population is a subject in comparison with which all others sink into insignificance," he reminded the joint houses of the legislature. "Our first and great duty is self preservation. Our acts are in vain, unless we can stay the wasting hand that is destroying our people." His words were sharp with truth. They rang with cogency. He had visited the empty farms, the abandoned villages, and had keened his mourning songs in the crowded cemeteries.

From the legislature Alexander asked support for his plan to save the nation. It was vital, he told them, to encourage agriculture and commerce, to build and improve roads, to modernize the harbors of Honolulu, Lahaina, Kona and Hilo. Schools must be made available for every native, so that healthy Hawaiians could live and compete in the haole world. Hospitals must be erected to care for the sick and dying casualties of this same world. In forlorn appeal—a thing of shame and humiliation to Hawaiian pride—he proposed the importation of citizens from other Pacific islands, "to bring new vitality to the Hawaiian stock." Plainly the new king was something more than comely wonder boy.

Three years of service in the privy council of Kamehameha III had not only given Alexander an insight into governmental process, but had prepared him for the day he would come to grips with it. Now as monarch, he considered it wise and prudent to retain all the ministers who had served his uncle so loyally. Dr. Robert Crichton Wyllie remained as head of foreign relations; John Young II was retained as minister of the interior; Elisha Allen kept his post in finance; and Richard Armstrong was again sustained as minister of public instruction. As partial offset to haole dominance, Alexander's brother and sister received special appointment. He named Lot Kamehameha as commander of the Hawaiian army. Especially for Victoria Kamamalu, he again established the post of *kuhina-nui*.

Wyllie was dispatched to American commissioner David L. Gregg and instructed to tell him of the new king's "unalterable determination to put an end to the question of annexation." Wyllie was further ordered to demand of the French minister a revision of the obnoxious treaty wrung from Hawaii at gunpoint in 1849. On the belief that only when Hawaii was respected by the world powers could there be peace and prosperity at home, Judge William Lee was commissioned envoy extraordinary, to negotiate in Hawaii's favor with the great nations, and to try to wring a workable reciprocity treaty out of the annexation-minded United States. For six years Wyllie had haggled with the French consul-commissioner in Honolulu, Emile Perrin, for modification and accommodation with France's hard treaty. Not until 1858, and after endless wrangling, did Kamehameha IV sign a new pact. He did it reluctantly because, even in the new agreement, an aloof France had grudged Hawaii but little.

Still there was a general improvement in relations with the world powers apparent almost from the start. Alexander's other forward-looking hopes were slower in coming. Not until 1859 was he able to get his first hospital started. Honolulu's residents pledged $50,000 toward its construction, the legislature reluctantly provided government land of "equivalent value." The king himself was forced to personally solicit, notebook in hand, Honolulu's streets, shops, and stores, where he raised $13,000. The new hospital was named in honor of Queen Emma, and opened the same year in a building on Fort Street. Permanent structure was begun the next year, and Queen's Hospital received its first patients in December of 1860.

Importation of natives from other islands was a dismal failure. Disease and exploitation had made Hawaii unattractive to other Polynesians. Wyllie's wooing of Chinese immigrants as laborers was more successful. Two hundred Cantonese coolies had been brought to Hawaii in 1852, to serve as plantation laborers. Wyllie brought 183 more in 1855. The whole plan blew up when these people—strangers to both Hawaiians and haoles—refused to accept the servile pattern imposed upon them. Because they were completely misunderstood, animosity and abuse were theirs from the start. Nothing could keep the coolies on the plantations. They persistently fled to the cities and to the villages. There they remained, isolated and unassimilated by the general popu-

ALBERT EDWARD KAUIKEAOULI, THE PRINCE OF HAWAII
Son of Kamehameha IV and Queen Emma, he was the last child
born to a monarch of Hawaii. He died at age four.

—*Bernice P. Bishop Museum, Honolulu.*

lation. There, for a time, they lived in resentful vagrancy. Fearful of these strangers, Hawaiians and haoles blamed them for many crimes of which they were doubtless innocent. But the failure of all attempts at importation of native population halted for many years the announced policy of controlled immigration.

Then the king was suddenly confronted with a new threat—of tragic proportions. No one knows for sure how leprosy came to the Hawaiian Islands—whether from haoles or Asiatics—but by 1860 it was running rampant among the already decimated islanders. By 1863 Dr. William Hillebrand was warning king and nation of this new and fearsome scourge.

In 1865 the legislature ordered the board of health to establish and enforce a policy of segregation for victims of the disease. Kalawao, on the island of Molokai, was designated as the recipient for all lepers in the nation. In 1866 universal banishment of sufferers of the dread disease, to this lonely outpost, was commenced.

It had taken the "foreigners" only half a century to complete the defilement of an island paradise.

II

ALEXANDER LIHOLIHO and his beloved Emma were probably a near perfect example of royal happiness and domesticity—at least from the "foreign" eyes constantly and critically staring in on the drama of Polynesia. They resided at the palace, built at Honolulu, for Kamehameha III. This unpretentious bungalow with its spacious and airy lanais was now reduced—by comparison with the lavish dwellings of some of the haoles and ex-missionaries—to a rather humble and unostentatious abode for a king. Only at the court functions—modish, glittering, selective—were there comparative reminders of the pageantry and splendor of former days.

A later king, Kalakaua, would someday replace the king's dwelling with an opulent palace of stone and fine woods, and on the same spot. But for now a wise and serious young monarch conducted state business and social amenities from the modest edifice built for his uncle. Emma had inherited a more luxurious retreat at Nuuanu, from Keoni Ana II (John Young, Jr.). It became a favorite escape from Honolulu's pressures of work and duty.

On May 20, 1858, a royal prince was born to them. He was christened Albert Edward Kauikeaouli, and the nation rejoiced. The advent of this "Prince of Hawaii," born in love and promise, was accepted as an omen from heaven. Little Albert Edward stood as symbol that the

Hawaiian race still lived; that it no longer was dying. Christian training, by now, had weaned the Alii from what the missionaries had
preached as the monstrous sins of polygamy and polyandry. But with
abandonment of these royal prerogatives the chances for fertile pro-
creation had vastly diminished. For that reason alone, the birth of the
"Prince of Hawaii" was a joy shared by every islander.

The nine-year reign of Alexander as Kamehameha IV witnessed a
profound change in the image and life-style of the royal court. From
the beginning the dependence of king and chiefs on the patriarchal
sagacity of the American missionaries for decision and guidance had
irked the intelligent and independent-minded Aleck. His visits to
America and Europe had, in many ways, molded his thinking. America,
he had become convinced, was a land without joy or pageantry. Its
people were either meddlesome do-gooders, or business and political
sharpers. Now this paranoiac nation was in the act of tearing itself apart
in bloody civil war.

He hated France for its autocratic attitude toward what they considered the minor peoples of the Pacific Islands. Aleck was certain,
given least chance, France would set her colonial claws upon Hawaii—
exactly as she had seized and subjected other island peoples. What had
happened to the isles of Tahiti—motherland of Hawaii—stood symbol
of what possibly could befall the kingdom he had inherited.

But, like Kamehameha the Great, Liholiho, and even that tragic
zealot Boki, Aleck had become an Anglophile. In England he had found
a perfect balance of public conscience, wisdom, and the pageantry so
dear to every Polynesian. The royal court of England, with regal Queen
Victoria sitting in charm and beauty at its head, had become the dream
and model under which Kamehameha IV was striving to pattern his
household and royal circle at Honolulu.

Emma, from English kinship of the two John Youngs, possessed
nostalgic mind pictures common to any family of displaced Britishers.
Dr. Robert Crichton Wyllie, an Anglican Church communicant, and
closest confidant to the royal family, had profoundly reinforced Aleck's
shift toward England. American missionaries, who long had occupied
favored place in Hawaii's royal court, were soon painfully aware that
their expertise could be neglected and spurned. Dr. Gerrit P. Judd,
already turned out of government by court intrigue, was both censorious
and sympathetic toward the protégé he had guided and protected, as
prince of the realm.

By 1859 Alexander had grown utterly weary of American sectari-
anism. He'd had his fill of the trickery he had experienced in its statesmanship. He felt an impelling necessity to build back the once warm
ties with Great Britain. He instructed Wyllie to petition Queen Victoria

for the establishment of "an Episcopal chapel or church" in Honolulu. He offered a portion of his own land for a building, providing England would furnish a chaplain.

Dr. Samuel Wilberforce, Bishop of Oxford, answered the Hawaiian king's appeal by presenting him with an entire hierarchy of Anglican episcopate. This new brand of Christian invasion of the islands was headed by Dr. Thomas Nettleship Staley, his family, and two assistants—Rev. George Mason and Rev. Edmund Ibbotson.

The Episcopalian "pro-cathedral" commenced building on the land given by Alexander. Eventually it grew into the magnificent Saint Andrew's Cathedral. But by that time another king was reigning in the nation of its original sponsor.

Along with the help and impetus rendered by Kamehameha IV in establishing the Church of England in Hawaii, he licensed the episcopate to found Saint Alban's College in Pauoa Valley, and Saint Andrew's Priory as a school for girls. By now Alexander's kingdom had become the frenzied plucking ground for a multiplicity of sects—Congregationalists, Catholics, Anglicans, and Mormons.

Into Aleck's tranquil family circle, and his calm and steady national expansion, was suddenly plunged the callous hand of misfortune. It started with a royal holiday excursion to the island of Maui.

The happy and carefree group of young Alii had been personally selected by Aleck and Emma. From Lahaina harbor twelve yachts and outriggers, bedecked with Hawaiian flags and bunting, put out to sea, carrying the royal party. In rounding the island to Wailuku, natives waved to the king's entourage as it passed offshore like a nautical parade. From Wailuku the king's happy group climbed the extinct volcano of Haleakala, and camped overnight on its summit. Oddly, in this circle of royal vacationers, was Lydia Paki who, later, as Lilioukalani, would reign as Hawaii's last sovereign.

The king, not exactly noted for his temperance habits, had indulged copiously in ardent spirits. So had several other male members of his entourage. But next day, without incident, all returned to Lahaina. Some of the group, including Lydia Paki, returned to Honolulu, but the king and coterie of his friends remained at Lahaina to continue festivities. And there at Lahaina, impelled by a sudden drink-crazed fit of suspicion and distrust, Aleck turned a gun on a member of the party—his haole secretary, and trusted friend, Henry A. Neilson.

Many years later, long after Lydia Paki had become the deposed queen of Hawaii, she wrote in her memoirs of the shooting of Neilson: "There were causes which were apparent to any of our people for something very like righteous anger on the part of the king." The "causes" she enumerated were undue familiarity, absence of etiquette, and rudeness and disrespect to royalty. "To allow any such breach of good manners to pass unnoticed would be looked upon by his own retainers as belittling to him, and they would be the first to demand the punishment of the offender. It was in this case far too severe. No one realized that more than the king himself . . ."

How "severe" became apparent to Aleck after a sobering from drink and temper. For more than two years, while Neilson lay dying from the impetuous attack, Kamehameha IV lived through a hell of personal remorse. It took heroic measures on the part of his ministers and family to keep him from abdicating his throne. Every effort of the tormented monarch was directed toward making amends to the victim of the tragedy. Finally, with death of Neilson, Alexander turned frantically to the Anglican Church for moral strength and forgiveness.

But fate was not yet through with Aleck. Temper of the Kamehamehas had descended to his Prince of Hawaii, and at age four the lad was already displaying it. One morning, dissatisfied with a new pair of boots, the youngster burst into an uncontrollable fit of passion. Seeking to control the tantrum, Aleck like any less kingly father, attempted to cool off his hysterical and angry son by holding the boy's head under a spout of cold water.

It effectively cooled off the young prince, but later in the day, when the boy went into a fit of nervous weeping, with indication of great pain, Aleck, Emma and the attendants realized they had a truly sick child to contend with. Little Albert Edward Kauikeaouli, Prince of Hawaii, died August 27, 1862—of "brain fever." The king, and those close to him, blamed the child's death on the cold water immersion. It never occurred to Aleck that what had happened was pure coincidence; that he had not really killed his own son. But to Alexander and Emma, it was the final stark tragedy. The final devastation.

Death of tiny Albert Edward was a shock to native Hawaiians, who had fondly watched the growth and progress of the baby through the pictured likenesses now circulating across the islands. With the death of the nation's own little boy, went the last child ever born to a monarch of Hawaii.

Alexander's heart traveled to the grave with his son. From that time on he was a changed man. Under mask of smiling urbanity was a melancholia deep as the pit of hell. The death of Neilson, and the death of his child, were the tragedies which broke the heart and health of a king. From docility he became querulous, moody, and quick to anger. He drank more, ate less, and, with increasingly aggravated asthma, could scarcely breathe.

Finally, stricken by conscience, burdened by state affairs, and weakened by chronic asthma, Kamehameha IV died, on November 30, 1863.

The final attack had occurred early that morning, and in frantic effort to restore normal breathing to the choked and noisy lungs of the man she loved, Emma had laid beside Aleck, trying to breathe life, mouth-to-mouth, into the dying man. But in spite of every heroic effort, no human could save Kamehameha IV.

On December 1 the handsome king, still young in age, lay in state in Honolulu. The Church of England conducted the services and the burial. Village kahunas throughout the realm chanted his *meles* and added their own unique prayers for the soul of the Hawaiian they were sure had been a good king.

III

LOT KAMEHAMEHA, in his ascension to the throne of Hawaii in 1863, bore striking resemblance to the founder of the dynasty, Kamehameha the Great. In manners, culture, elegance and wit he suffered greatly in comparison to his brother Alexander. Not for him the high culture, social graces, and British-patterned court claques. Like Aleck, he had traveled the world, and had been educated in the fawning exactitude of the royal school. But little of this privilege and snobbery had rubbed off on Lot. By nature he was stolid, boorish, and strong-willed. William Synge, British commissioner, accurately summed up the new king in his report to London: "Inferior to his late brother in refinement, grace of manner, and general culture, he is I think superior in energy, per-severence, and strength of will." In his assumption of power, it was as though the Great One himself had come alive.

Lot was fully as conscious of the tragic decimation of native popula-tion, and the demeaning of Hawaiian culture, as Alexander had been. But he was not half as willing to ride the haole juggernaut onward to what he considered total oblivion. His first public act was complete refusal to take oath to maintain the Constitution of 1852. He allowed no public inauguration to mark his ascension to the throne.

Men in high places began to tremble when it was learned that the new king was, by nature, an unreconstructed autocrat; that he looked upon the hard-won progress toward universal suffrage as a direct threat to an effectual and workable government. His choice of ministers were not out of the circles of liberalism and democratic reform. His cabinet consisted of his true father, Governor Kekuanaoa, DeVarigny, Wyllie, Harris, and Hopkins.

Alexander, as king, had petitioned eight successive legislatures for the constitutional reforms he had deemed as vital to the very existence of the nation. Lot, as Kamehameha V, revealed no such patience or

KAMEHAMEHA V (LOT KAMEHAMEHA), THE BACHELOR
KING FROM 1863 TO 1872

Lot Kamehameha was an efficient and autocratic ruler.
Unmarried and childless, he was the last of the Kamehamehas.

compunction. In the summer of 1864 he summoned a convention of publicly-elected delegates and, in the matter of constitutional reform, he gave them their one chance. As usual the vociferous delegates argued for weeks. After they had vocally boxed themselves into deadlock, the king brusquely dismissed the whole convention. The assemblage was shocked and paralyzed by his announcement: "The Constitution of 1852 is abrogated." When pressed as to his intended course of action, he simply stated: "I, the king, will give you a constitution."

In one stroke Kamehameha wiped out the power core of the legislature, and by this sudden coup restored to the crown all the rights Kauikeaouli had, in 1852, surrendered. Once more it was the old pattern. Foreigners and natives came to quick realization that the king was supreme.

Lot ascended the throne unmarried and unencumbered by wives or children. Throughout his nine-year reign he remained a bachelor, with no discernible inclination toward acquiring himself a queen. But, while heir-apparent during the short reign of Kamehameha IV, he was known to have persistently courted the beautiful Bernice Pauahi,* daughter of Konia and Paki. Konia was granddaughter of Kamehameha I, and Paki was one of the high chiefs of Oahu. Lydia Paki, foster sister of Bernice, and who herself was to become Hawaii's last sovereign, had this to say of Prince Lot's choice in women: "She was one of the most beautiful girls I ever saw; the vision of her loveliness at that time can never be effaced from remembrance."

In her seventeenth year Bernice Pauahi Paki was betrothed to Lot Kamehameha. Since Prince Lot was in direct line of succession, hers was the distinct possibility of someday being queen of Hawaii. But in her eighteenth year she abruptly jilted the future king—to become the bride of one of Honolulu's American bankers, Charles R. Bishop.

Perhaps Lot never quite recovered from his loss and humiliation to the haole who so neatly had bested him in love. But Lot was definitely not the type of man to wear defeat and sorrow in public gaze. He entered his kingship a bachelor—and he remained a bachelor. The nation was forced to adjust itself to the singular experience of having a lonely autocrat as its sovereign. And, once king, Lot's preoccupation became an endless coping with the turbulent waves of growth, trade rivalry, and foreign interference—waves that broke fiercely, ceaselessly upon the islands.

By 1865 the United States had victoriously settled its bloody civil war. Yankees, once more preoccupied with international advantage, no longer could be flaunted nor ignored. Steamships were beginning to put into Honolulu harbor, but with sandalwood long vanished, the cry

*Pa-u-a-hi: Pah-*oo*-ah-*hee*.

was for Hawaiian sugar, molasses, rice, coffee, beef hides, and tallow. The whaling industry, which twice a year had brought up to half a thousand ships into Honolulu and Lahaina, already was in its fast decline. The great whales, scarcer and more difficult to find, required overlong cruises to kill and render down a cargo.

In November of 1871 Honolulu's newspaper *The Friend* announced the catastrophe which marked the beginning of the end to America's whaling industry. Far to the north, in the Arctic's Bering Straits, the American whaling fleet was caught helplessly in treacherous and sudden freeze. Thirty-three ships, from the already shrunken fleet, were crushed in the ice, and had to be abandoned. The few remaining vessels dumped 1,200 seamen into Honolulu as escapees from a disaster that had already claimed half an hundred lives. The decline in whalers making Hawaii its twice-a-year port of call, never ceased after that. America's whaling industry could not recover from the loss.

After demise of whalers as sustenance to the economy, other sources of income were necessary to feed insatiable demands upon the national treasury. The export of Hawaiian sugar, the multiplying of cane mills, and the spread of plantations across the islands, became the principal lifeline of Hawaii to its increasingly dependent outside world. In 1865 thirty-two plantations exported fifteen million pounds of raw sugar.

The grass shack and clapboard face of Honolulu was changing into brick fronts and shop buildings of a lively, growing city. Kamehameha V, much as he deplored the shrinking of Hawaiian native population, and regardless of his stubborn determination to restore his nation to the shape and form of its golden days, found himself constantly dealing, in affairs of state, with the ever-present citizenry of foreigners.

He and his privy council were persistent in their efforts to present a creditable and pleasing face to government in its contact with the sharp and canny emissaries of the greater nations. New and attractive government buildings were a necessity, now that Honolulu was the acknowledged and accepted capital of the nation. Along the shady green streets, and among the fragile native dwellings, and the claptrap store fronts of the foreign entrepreneurs, were rising new and handsome stone edifices to house government offices. Even the city's sprawling lumber structures were being built with taste and modernity. Slowly, abetted by the stolid will of Kamehameha V, Honolulu was showing a respectable and businesslike face to the world.

Despite slowness and reluctance of the legislature to appropriate funds for Lot's modernization campaign, fresh structures were started and completed. Honolulu's new post office, an imposing edifice of cut stone, with curved and lacy balustrades, was erected at Bethel and Merchant Streets. Hale Koa, later known as Iolani Barracks, was built under Lot's demands, to house his royal household guards. Under the king's urging, through his privy council, a suitable and beautiful royal mausoleum of stone, resembling an English cathedral, was started in 1863, and finished in time to receive Lot's own remains among the great kings and queens of Hawaiian history.

A spacious quarantine station, to more adequately process the flood of immigrants, was erected handy to the waterfront. An insane asylum was built as custodial to Hawaiians whose minds were cracking from the once unknown scourges of disease and stress. These, with the fine schools and hospitals already sponsored by Alexander and Emma, would have done credit to any city and any nation.

The ventures of Lot's autocratic government into private enterprise—a practice not at all unique to his regime—resulted in Honolulu's first efforts to accommodate the tourists who, by sailing ships and steamers, were streaming into the paradasaical islands the world had now discovered in mid-Pacific. The Hawaiian Hotel, whose balconied elegance had risen at a cost of $150,000 in government money, was popular and prosperous from the start. Not only did it fill a pressing need, but quickly became Honolulu's social center.

Lot made no effort to constrain his privy council in urging the necessity for a "suitable and creditable" stone public building for their lonely but popular king and his government. Magnificent Aliiolani Hale,* built from plans prepared by Australian architects, was barely started at the time of Lot's death. The bachelor king was never privileged to walk its spacious halls, or preside over sumptuous court in its public rooms. It emerged, on its finish in 1872, as Hawaii's government office building. It stands to modern days as monument to a king and nation valorously endeavoring to accommodate to history.

To sustain the economy, the export of raw sugar, coffee, and rice became an ultimate and compelling necessity. The island pattern was changing from its idyllic concept of woods, streams, and rolling hills, to the geometric patterns of vast plantations. In direct contradiction to persistent legend, Hawaiian natives were not lazy, nor unwilling to work. Haole bosses quickly realized that islanders, once properly trained, became valued employees. Their industry, dependability, and innate loyalty gave them preference over imported ethnic groups. But by now more than half the able-bodied native males in the kingdom were employed by sugar plantations. The bald and depressing fact was that there were just not enough native Hawaiians to begin to fill the ever-increasing demands.

*A-li-i-o-la-ni: *Ah*-lee-ee-oh-*lah*-nee.
*Ha-le: *Hah*-lay. Hale: Hawaiian for "house" or dwelling.

ROYAL MAUSOLEUM AT NUUANU

Built by Kamehameha V to house the remains of the kings and queens of Hawaii, it now serves as a small chapel in the royal cemetery, Honolulu. Hawaii's vanished royalty are now entombed in the national monument crypt to the rear of the chapel.

—*Paul Bailey Photo.*

Lot Kamehameha knew that depopulation of his kingdom could be laid directly at the doors of the foreigners. Like the kings before him, he hated the intruders for what they had done. After decimating the population with diseases fatal to Hawaiians, these same foreigners still marveled at the ease with which natives continued to die. A minor infection—laughed off by the haole—was speedy finish for a native. Foreigners persistently believed that Hawaiians actually willed themselves to death—a legend not without foundation. What worried the king, and his ministry of health, was the continued practice of contraception and *kahuna lapaau* abortions accepted by his people in the very face of a continuously falling birth rate.

In the still remembered days of island glory, living had been simple, food everywhere abundant, and there had been no such thing as struggle for the basics of life. Breadfruit, coconuts, roots, fish and clams, were within the reach of every man's hand. Children had been raised with complete indifference. They acquired instant dexterity at caring for themselves quick as they were weaned from their mother's nipples. To work for food, other than the simple effort of gathering it, was simply unthinkable. This indifference in caring for babies and children, and the abandonment of adults to the strange diseases they now acquired, still continued—until it had emerged as Hawaii's major problem. Worse, the new monogamous patterns of marriage, and the imposition of Christian "chastity," had brought endless unions of complete and tragic barrenness.

During the reign of Kamehameha V the native population dropped to 50,000—only one-sixth of what it had been in the times of Kamehameha I. Irritated by the necessity of governing his nation for the benefit of foreigners—Lot refused to budge from his stand of autocratic implacability when it came to his monarchy and its preciously few native subjects. For this gruff, sad king, it would be "Hawaii for Hawaiians" to the day of his death.

With all his effort, Lot's "Bureau of Immigration" succeeded in inducing only 126 natives of other Polynesian islands to settle in Hawaii. The bureau did better in Canton and Yokohama. Chinese and Japanese nationals were entering Honolulu at an accelerating rate. Quickly as they were cleared at quarantine of leprosy or other visually apparent diseases, the haole entrepreneurs moved them out to the coffee groves and cane plantations. For Lot, it was a sad and shoddy way to treat a national malady. And among the 50,000 natives of Hawaii, who were seeing their islands become havens to these strangest of all people, there was a growing core of resentment.

IV

THE CONSTITUTION which Kamehameha V had promised, in his assumption of 1864 was, in due course, given to the nation. It was anticipated that it would come forth bearing the heavy hand of the restored autocracy. But, other than some special articles of constrainment, mainly dealing with property and literacy qualifications as to voters and government representatives, it was not too obviously unlike that under which the nation had operated up to Lot's accession to the throne. Suffrage remained; so did the Hawaiian legislature. But essentially it still left no doubt—the king ruled.

The greatest fears were allayed when Lot's subjects came to realize that his sole interest lay in the preservation and wellbeing of his people. Their security as humans and as citizens were never endangered by the document, or by the king's acts. The stolid, aloof ruler, throughout his nine-year reign, managed his nation with firmness and with efficiency. He was truly the "last great chief of the olden type," and his subjects knew him as a just and honorable man. They never doubted his declaration "to maintain this kingdom, as an independent monarchy, in peace with all nations." He never wavered in his conviction that to make Hawaii less vulnerable abroad, he must strive always to strengthen it at home. He must face the hungry eyes and greedy talons of the big powers with firmness and with dignity.

His uncertainty as to the intentions and policy of the United States was a constant source of irritation. His petition for a reciprocal treaty, though endorsed by Presidents Johnson and Grant, was bandied around Washington through five sessions of Congress, and finally rejected in 1870. American ignorance of Hawaii, despite trade, tourism, and impertinent diplomats, was something Lot could not understand.

Relations with the United States seemed to be under constant strain, made doubly so by the letters mailed home by visitors, missionaries, merchants and opportunists. Washington was belabored by strange tales baldly recited by its congressmen regarding the Sandwich Islands and its aloof and implacable ruler. Envoys and reporters, some indifferent, some possessive, some belligerent, were problems that confused and worried. Never, during his reign, was Kamehameha V certain whether Hawaii would be abandoned or stolen by the American nation. Never did he feel confident or trustful with its politicians, emissaries, or missionaries. To the United States Lot was reported as anti-American and pro-British. Actually all he strove to be was loyal to his own nation and to his own people.

In 1866 the *Sacramento Union* sent a sharp-tongued reporter, under the pseudonym of Mark Twain, to Hawaii for a month—to tell its readers about the Hawaiian paradise and its boorish bachelor king. After four months of delightful dawdling, and after twenty-five sprightly "Letters from the Sandwich Islands," Mark Twain went home to greater literary heights, and a lifetime of nostalgia for the fair isles.

Queen Victoria sent her second son, the Duke of Edinburgh, on state visit to the court of the Hawaiian king. He was the first foreign prince to visit Hawaii. Through these and lesser visitors, went kinder words regarding the gutty little nation so far out in the Pacific.

But that did not prevent Britain and France from conducting occasional ship surveillance. Mainly, the visits were to keep state eyes on unpredictable America and her intentions, rather than to load a greater burden of harassment on Hawaii's king. The usual grumble resulting from these visits was for "equal privilege" in trade and concessions.

Lot, like his brother Alexander, had been impressed by Britain's military ostentation. He opted for gaudy dress for royal guards and Hawaii's tiny army. In 1870 the king ordered the formation of the Royal Hawaiian Band. The Prussian government furnished Captain Henri Berger to take charge of the island ensemble. This handsome and accomplished maestro remained forty-three years in Honolulu. Captain Berger created a band whose fame went through generations of Hawaiian life, to become an immortal and respected segment of its musical culture.

The nation down to its most humble village native worried about a king who preferred bachelorhood, and was providing no sons or daughters to rule the nation. In 1864 Lot Kamehameha, to make certain of succession, had proclaimed his sister Victoria Kamamalu as heir-presumptive. Two years later Victoria was dead. And the public again clamored to get Lot married.

Various eligible ladies of Alii lineage were proposed by his ministers—and in turn rejected by the stubborn king. Queen Emma, his brother's widow, was persistently suggested. It is alleged that Lot, for a time, showed willingness to accept this union, and actually favored it. But history was somehow never given so fortuitous a turn. Equal pressure was for him to name to successorshp one of the chiefs. For years the aloof and moody king dodged even this responsibility.

In the meantime he grew ever more fat and portly. In later years his obesity, worn on the frame of a physical giant, made it difficult for him to move about. When he grew so corpulent he could no longer ride a horse, he spent most of his time indoors.

In the ninth year of his reign, Kamehameha V was forced to abandon all physical activity and take to his bed. Court physicians diagnosed his illness as "dropsy of the chest." Growing steadily weaker, surrounded by anxious friends and retainers, the dying king made his final demands in phlegmy voice. First of all he insisted that high chiefess Bernice Pauahi Bishop come to his side. The young woman who had rejected him in favor of an American, was still vivacious and lovely. When Bernice arrived, she looked in surprise and fright at the huge man who once so desperately had loved her.

Weakly, hesitantly, Lot took her hand. "I have chosen you, oh daughter of Paki and Konia," he declared, trying to smile. "You, my Bernice, shall succeed me."

Bernice, thoroughly shaken, protested. "No, not me!"

"Yes, I choose you."

"Take Keelikolani!* Take Emma!"

"You have been chosen."

The king was firm in his decision. It was not, in his weary mind, to be the equally corpulent princess, Ruth Keelikolani, nor was it the dowager Queen Emma. Deliberately and consciously, he had chosen the young, fragile and beloved Bernice Pauahi.

December 11, 1872, a few mornings later, instead of facing the court party and feast in celebration of his natal day, Kamehameha V calmly announced it as the day of his death.

"It is hard to die on my birthday," he whispered.

His shocked and saddened friends protested such utterance.

The tired man, racked with pain, wearily shook his dark and massive head. "God's will be done," he said.

As was the custom for years past, the birthday guests arrived at the palace. This time they found Lot's house unlivened by dancers and musicians. Instead it was filled with wailing mourners.

The last of the Kamehamehas was dead — exactly as he had predicted.

*Ke-e-li-ko-la-ni: *Kay*-ay-*lee*-ko-*lah*-nee.

PART FIVE

The Short Reign of Lunalilo, and the Kalakaua Dynasty

I

DEATH of Lot, "the old bachelor," left the nation in a monarchical crisis, despite the fact that he had named a former sweetheart, Bernice Pauahi, as his chosen successor, and had mentioned the dowager Queen Emma as an acceptable candidate toward marriage. Both these women were high Alii, with legitimate claim, now that the primogeniture right had died out with the Kamehamehas.

But Bernice Pauahi, married to the American Charles R. Bishop, had drawn a built-in opposition from the chiefs. They feared, more than anything, a return of American dominance in government. It was Queen Emma, as living wife of Kamehameha IV, who had better claim. Had not loyalty to the dead Alexander and the scruples of the Anglican Church erected their own tabus when it came to marrying her husband's brother, she would have stood as indisputable successor. Princess Ruth Keelikolani was not entirely unacceptable. But Ruth was only half-sister to the dead sovereign, spoke only native Hawaiian, and, wholly dedicated to the "old way," had little interest in, and less knowledge of the foreigners whose counter-force in government must constantly be met, conquered, or placated. Too, it would have taken a real Polynesian "queen size" throne to have fitted her 400-pound bulk.

The one candidate Lot had not named, and whom he had died ignoring, was his cousin, William Lunalilo.* Historians have conjectured that the long hesitance of Kamehameha V to appoint a successor stemmed from Polynesian superstition that such act would, with certainty, hasten one's own death. Lot's household had operated on the more typical Hawaiian pattern. He consciously had spurned the complex aura of grafted-in Christianity. Always he had kept a kahuna in the palace—in the last years a female one—old Kamaipuupaa.* Many natives considered her the best in the kingdom. Even foreigners had rated her as "a nervous, magnetic woman, shrewd, intelligent, and adept to a wonderful degree." In affairs of state, Lot had used her, consulted the native star-gazers, and had not ignored the native shamans.

*Lu-na-li-lo: *Loo*-nah-*lee*-low.
*Ka-ma-i-puu-paa: *Kah*-mah-ee-poo-*oo*-pah-ah.

From the palace had often come the sound of ancient chants, the *meles*, and the terpsichorean thump of the hula. But it is doubtful that racial superstition was the real reason for the delay and confusion in Lot's naming a successor. He died knowing full well that William Lunalilo would be the next king. Willful refusal to acknowledge it was Lot's deathbed sign of disapproval.

William Lunalilo never forgot nor forgave the Kamehamehas for this slight. In a corner of Kawaiahao's churchyard stands the lonely mausoleum of William Charles Lunalilo. Above the door's grillwork of iron is graven, in bold letters, the words *Ka Moi* [The King]. His request was that, when he died, he be buried completely apart from the massive Nuuanu sepulchre housing the remains of the Kamehameha dynasty. Its last king had ignored and rejected Prince William.

Even Lot, who stubbornly ignored Prince William's claim that his grandsire was Kamehameha the Great, could not deny the bloodline legitimacy of this debonair and popular chief. Actually William was grandson of a half-brother of Kamehameha I. He was born in 1835. His mother was Miriam Kekauluohi,* niece, stepdaughter and daughter-in-law of Kamehameha I, plural wife of Kamehameha II, and *kuhina-nui* for Kamehameha III. Prince William's father was Charles Kanaina, a minor chief. Though high Alii indeed, he still was not, as he and his supporters claimed, a blood-true Kamehameha.

It wasn't the lack of Alii stature or mana that caused Lot's deliberate oversight. It wasn't William Lunalilo's stance as a legitimate Kamehameha. Prince Bill was tremendously popular with the people. He had endless friends among the haoles. Lot had refused to name him to successorship simply because he was convinced the man lacked qualifications of a sovereign. Though educated in three languages, intelligent, witty, and as handsome as Prince Aleck had been, he lacked the political acuity and statesmanship qualities of his uncle. Prince Bill had been utterly spoiled by doting parents. His frivolity, and monumental bouts with the bottle, were known to Alii and commoners alike. Though Lot had been perfectly aware that cousin Lunalilo possessed the best natural claim to the throne, he went to his grave without lending authority to the claim.

Throughout the noise and pageantry of public mourning, affairs in Honolulu were in a state of confusion. The ominous undercurrents had not been buried in the royal crypt with the king. The cabinet's first act was to call the legislative assembly into session. It met January 8, 1873, knowing that it faced the solemn necessity of electing a sovereign to the nation.

*Ke-ka-u-lu-o-hi: *Kay*-kah-oo-*loo*-oh-hee.

By now the newspapers of Honolulu—haole dominated—were advising and editorializing on the issue of succession. The *Pacific Commercial Advertiser* was denouncing the Constitution of 1864 as nothing but an autocratic decree of Kamehameha V; that it had died with its author; that the nation should now revert to and operate under the liberal and democratic Constitution of 1852. It claimed that the cabinet of the deceased king had no authority, and suggested that a convention be called by the people to not only choose a new sovereign, but to restore the old and liberal form of government.

United States minister Henry A. Peirce, and the British acting commissioner Theophilus H. Davies, wrote letters of warning to the cabinet. They both reminded of the danger of bloodshed and uprising inherrent in a prolonged interregnum of crisis and uncertainty. Both diplomats furnished their lists of Alii whom they considered best qualified to step into the breach. For once they seem to have concurred—at least in this choice.

Number one on their memorandum was William Charles Lunalilo. The popularity of this grand-nephew of Kamehameha the Great was growing hourly with natives and with foreigners. The "Missionary Party," a loosely-knit group of haoles and mixed-blood haoles—led by sons of the original missionaries, and including foreigners who had no ecclesiastical or family connections with the New England Calvinists, but who were desperately opposed to the "Royalists"—felt their interests would be safely served by Prince William. Ruth Keelikolani was also suggested, but only because she was half-sister to the dead king, a favorite candidate with the chiefs, and "because she would place several others in presumptive relation to the throne."

David Kalakaua made the elective list because he was genuine Alii. His blood line went back to the fierce and independent chiefs of Kona; was great-great-grandson of Kameeiamoku; had been tutored in the Chiefs' School, and, according to Peirce was "well educated, speaks English well, of polished manners and bearing." Davies appraised Kalakaua as "intelligent and well-educated, and mingling freely in general society." Bernice Pauahi entered the diplomatic suggestion only because both Peirce and Davies had been informed that the dying king had "pointedly designated" her, and that the cabinet was therefore bound to present Bernice to the legislature "as the formal nomination of the king."

It is significant that the representatives of both the great English-speaking nations requested warships of their countries be on hand to serve as "a steadying influence" during this unsettled and potentially

*Ka-la-ka-u-a: *Kah*-lah-kah-*oo*-ah. Popular usage: Kah-lah-cow-ah.

dangerous time. The *U.S.S. Benicia* made a most obvious appearance on January 3.

Popularity of Lunalilo soon reached the point that only he and Kalakaua remained as possible candidates. On December 16 Lunalilo issued his manifesto to the nation. In it he claimed direct descent from Kamehameha I. Unabashed, he stated that, "Notwithstanding that according to the law of inheritance, I am the rightful heir to the Throne, in order to preserve peace, harmony and good order, I desire to submit the decision of my claim to the voice of the people to be freely and fairly expressed by a plebiscitum. The only pledge that I deem it necessary to offer to the people is that I will restore the constitution of Kamehameha III, of happy memory, with only such changes as may be required to adapt it to present laws, and that I will govern the nation according to the principles of that constitution and a liberal and constitutional monarchy, which, while it preserves the proper prerogatives of the Crown, shall fully maintain the rights and liberties of the people."

Lunalilo's final request was that all male subjects throughout the islands go to the polls, January 1, 1873, and express their free choice for a king of the Hawaiian Islands. Result of this vote was to be certified to the legislative assembly.

The only adverse reaction to this lofty manifesto was publication of a widely distributed circular. This attack, sponsored by a group designating themselves as "The Skillful Genealogists," was mainly a refutation of Lunalilo's claims as to direct descent from Kamehameha the Great. While the circular was generally correct in its premise, it served only to anger Lunalilo's followers, and to drive them to even greater efforts in getting Prince William elected king.

Kalakaua was slower in getting his declaration before the public. Unlike Prince William's brash and forthright bid for popular support, the second runner's petition was couched in the alliterative and poetic style of oldtime Polynesia. His candidacy, Kalakaua stated, was based on the history of his fighting ancestors. He promised to obey the advice of "Kaeweaheulu, my grandfather, which he gave to Kamehameha I, to be a rule for his government: 'The old men, the old women and the children shall lie in safety on the highways.'" He promised "to pre-

HALE KOA, NOW KNOWN AS IOLANI BARRACKS
Finished in 1870 for the Royal Guards of the Household.

—*Photo, Bernice P. Bishop Museum, Honolulu.*

serve and increase the people, so that they shall multiply and fill the land." He would "repeal all the personal taxes, about which the people complain," and "put native Hawaiians into government offices, so as to pay off the national debt." He was for "amending of the Constitution of 1864. The desires of the people will be obtained by a true agreement between the people and the occupant of the throne." Finally, he warned the people to "beware of the Constitution of 1852 and the false teachings of the foreigners who are now grasping to obtain the control of the government if W. C. Lunalilo ascends the throne."

If Kalakaua had expected to sway the voters with his pronunciamento, the results were scarcely visible. The Missionary Party was overwhelmingly successful in selling Prince William to the nation. The plebiscite of January 1 went almost unanimously for this affable Hawaiian. Next question was whether the legislature would willingly accept the verdict, and confirm the victor as King of all Hawaii. The delegates met the day following the popular election, in a climate of tense anxiety. Natives from all over Oahu milled outside the doors of the new two-story stone courthouse of the Hawaiian kingdom while the final balloting took place. From them came noisy utterance and threats, promising everything from clubbing to strangulation for any legislator failing to mark his ballot for "King Lunalilo."

Of the scene, Queen Emma recorded: "Thousands of natives stood in one dense mass round the Court House, prepared to defy the voice of parliament if they decided contrary to the wish of the nation, and quite ready to proclaim Lunalilo King in spite of it. Hundreds awaited to tear to pieces [members] who were suspected of opposing Lunalilo."

The people were satisfied, and civil war doubtless averted, when the legislature voted unanimously to sustain the plebiscite. William Lunalilo was formally proclaimed Hawaii's king.

With all his background, and his promises, Kalakaua never had a chance against this first and spectacular popular election of a sovereign. Completely forgotten and sideswept along the way were the female candidates: High Chiefess Bernice Pauahi, dowager Queen Emma, and Princess Ruth Keelikolani.

Next day at noon, in Kawaiahao church, the new sovereign took oath of office before the people. The room was packed. The overflow filled the churchyard, and far out into the street. The choir sang a majestic Protestant hymn, keyed and worded to ancient Hawaiian. After the prayer and response, the handsome thirty-eight-year-old Lunalilo delivered two short addresses—one to the members of the legislature—another to the assembled populace.

The new king, personable, intelligent, educated, and witty, commenced his reign with most excellent inaugural speech. As expected,

LUNALILO (WILLIAM KANAINA), WHO REIGNED 1873-1874
Elected sovereign by popular vote.

—*Photo, Bernice P. Bishop Museum, Honolulu.*

he rendered tribute to his predecessor, thanked the people for their overwhelming confidence in him, and promised his greatest efforts toward the peace, happiness and well-being of the kingdom and its people. His remarks showed two points of unmistakable perception and understanding.

"This nation," he declared, "presents the most interesting example in history of the cordial cooperation of the native and foreign races in the administration of its government, and, most happily, too, in all the relations in life there exists a feeling which every good man will strive to promote."

To its citizens he acknowledged the nation's most overwhelming problem. "It is a fact, which oppresses my heart, that the Hawaiian population has been gradually diminishing for years. And I appeal to every Hawaiian, whether here or at his quiet home, to arise in full strength and stay this desolation. It can be done, but it will require the efforts of all who love Hawaii nei. Industry, temperance, and virtue, with a moral and religious education, will accomplish it."

After the public ceremonies, Lunalilo, King of Hawaii, walked across the street, through the throngs cheering themselves hoarse, and entered the royal palace—to the worries and travail of high office. That night Honolulu was illuminated, while the nation danced and sang.

II

EDUCATED and intelligent though he was, Lunalilo possessed little preparation for the role of sovereign. Spoiled in childhood, a hedonist by nature, he had served no important functions of government, and knew little of the grinding cares that went with the task of serving it. But, like all Alii, he was conscious of the overwhelming tragedies that were eating the life out of his nation, yet he was much too inexperienced and inept to effectively deal with them.

As expected, he quickly named his cabinet. And, as expected, they were all haoles. Charles R. Bishop became minister of foreign affairs; Edwin O. Hall was minister of the interior; Robert Stirling, minister of finance; A. Francis Judd (young lawyer son of Dr. G. P. Judd) was elevated to attorney-general.

No reign could have started with more promise. The foreigners, long held at arm's length by the irascible old Lot Kamehameha, were moving back into high places with confidence and with pleasure. In spite of all goodwill and favorable portents, however, the warships of United States and Britain were also moving into Honolulu harbor.

King Lunalilo started his reign with hope, confidence, and energy. He did not forget or put aside his promise of constitutional reform. Nor did he attempt to amend, erase or alter the constitution by monarchical fiat as had Kamehameha V.

To the legislature, which had remained in session, he delivered a message recommending changes, such as removal of the property qualifications for voters, return of Hawaii's little parliament to the British style of two houses—nobles and representatives—meeting separately, and equal in power. There were other less drastic constitutional changes proposed by the king. In all the 1873 special session of the legislature passed thirty amendments, which were referred for final action to the regular legislative sessions of 1873. If again adopted, Lot's constitution of 1864 would be reshaped and overhauled along promised democratic lines.

But not even this peaceful reform was allowed accomplishment without outside pressure. Hawaii's change of administration had occurred during a period of economic depression. Customs house reports for 1872, published three weeks after Lunalilo became king, showed a drop in sugar exports of nearly five million pounds. The plantations were in serious trouble. And, since sugar had become mainstay of Hawaiian economy, government and people were suffering. The year's cane crop was continuing to come up short, and prices offered by the shipping firms for sugar from Hawaiian docks were the lowest in years. Emergence of a new monarch was cue for resumption of the American ideas and pressures that so long had bedeviled the little nation.

Henry A. Peirce, United States minister to Hawaii, and Theo. H. Davies, commissioner acting for Great Britain, kept their government superiors fully informed as to progress of Hawaii's ship of state through the perilous waters of monarchical transition and economic struggle. On February 11, 1873 Davies confidentially reported:

"There are at present great depression and discontent amongst sugar planters and others, and they have long regarded reciprocity with the United States, on almost any terms, the great hope of deliverance.

"The transition from reciprocity to territorial cession, and thence to annexation appears so easy that the advocates of the first of a week ago, are today boldly urging the last, and there is a great feeling of insecurity, lest the King himself in a moment of weakness should be persuaded to sell his throne.

"Many Englishmen by birth are so enamored of the advantages of annexation, that they are ready to advocate for the sake of possible gain, transfer of this territory to the United States."

The English diplomat had reason to be alarmed. With demise of stubborn old Lot, and ascendancy of a playboy prince who not only spoke English but chose his convivial companions from among Honolulu's American haoles, the advocates of cession and annexation once again surfaced with loud and anxious voice. That King William had stuffed his cabinet with Americans was taken as an alarming omen.

Davies was especially apprehensive about the two American warships in Honolulu harbor. Aboard were a navy admiral, and two army generals. Davies tried to quiet his own fears with the thought that "Although Admiral Pennock and Generals Schofield and Alexander are doubtless interested observers of passing events, they make no demonstration of interest, and the movement for reciprocity or annexation has its origin entirely amongst naturalized Americans—doubtless encouraged by the presence of so many United States officials."

The *U.S.S. Benicia* had arrived January 3. The *U.S.S. California*, carrying Admiral A. W. Pennock, and flagship of the United States Pacific Squadron, arrived January 15. Aboard, ostensibly as passengers vacationing for their health, were Major General John M. Schofield, commander of the United States Army Military Division of the Pacific, and Brigadier General B. S. Alexander, of the Corps of Engineers. These men had no reason to enter publicly into the annexation and cession ferment of the islands. They were on a mission for their government, acting under confidential orders from the Secretary of War, W. W. Belknap.

According to Belknap's secret orders, their Hawaiian vacation was "for the purpose of ascertaining the defensive capabilities of the different ports and their commercial facilities, and to examine into any other subjects that may occur to you as desirable, in order to collect all information that would be of service to the country in the event of war with a powerful maritime nation . . . It is believed the objects of this visit to the Sandwich Islands will be best accomplished if your visit is regarded as a pleasurable excursion, which may be joined in by your citizen friends."

Schofield and Alexander toured and partied around the islands for two months. And, apparently, gathered all the information they were after. Their report would not be made public for twenty years, but when the story was eventually told, it would reveal that America had

ALIIOLANI HALE, THE GOVERNMENT OFFICE BUILDING
It was built, 1872-1874, from plans prepared by Sydney architects.

—*Photo, Bernice P. Bishop Museum, Honolulu.*

been made fully aware as to the size, value, and necessity for Pearl Harbor, and the best means for making it available for naval and commercial advantage.

Here was potentially the most strategic port in mid-Pacific. Here was the only natural harbor in the Hawaiian kingdom. In all the Pacific area there was nothing to match it. All Pearl Harbor needed, to make it pricelessly valuable to America, was the cutting away of the coral reef which obstructed its entrance channel, and the building of docking facilities, shops, and structures for storage and repair. This, of course, was beyond the capabilities of the Hawaiian government or its people.

Davies did all he could to counter the influx of American navy and army high brass. Her Majesty's Government had provided only one warship against America's two, but before the year was out, Honolulu hosted a steady stream of vesesls—British *and* American.

But with all his able and promising start, when Lunalilo, "the people's king," was finally confronted with the pressure of foreign demands, he was stricken with fright and paralysis. In the first month of his reign, Henry M. Whitney, Honolulu editor and journalist, confronted the new king with a document that suggested if Hawaii were to gain any treaty with the United States, either in protection or reciprocity, its sovereign must be prepared to offer some inducement in the form of a *quid pro quo*. Whitney's committee baldly suggested that the lease of Pearl Harbor to the United States, for a period of fifty years, might be considered an acceptable gesture.

The Whitney explanation to the tormented king was that it "will defeat and indefinitely postpone all projects for the annexation of these Islands to any foreign power, at the same time that it will secure to us all the benefits claimed by the advocates of annexation, and will guarantee our national independence under our native rulers as long as the treaty may continue." Lunalilo wavered between acceptance and rejection. Finally, in despair, mentally drowned the issue in ardent spirits.

Meanwhile the pressures for annexation, and the ceding or leasing of Pearl River and harbor to the United States, never relented. The bait was the promised treaty of reciprocity, so essential to getting the Hawaiian economy back to normal. King and ministers seemed to be unaware that most of the agitation along these matters were locally induced; that the great push was from the haoles of Honolulu itself. Charles R. Bishop, minister of foreign affairs, now worked closely and constantly with Henry A. Peirce, U. S. minister to Hawaii, to draft and present a petition to the United States Department of State for the needed treaty. Appended was an offer to lease Pearl Harbor—a supposedly necessary inducement to the American Senate for ratification of the desperately needed agreement.

It was October of the fateful year of 1873 before Peirce received American answer to the proposal he had forwarded on behalf of the Hawaiian nation. The new Secretary of State, Hamilton Fish, in his reply, perfunctorily and officially disposed of the matter. "It is possible that the acquisition suggested might in some respects be advantageous to the United States," Fish agreed. "No encouragement, however, can, under existing conditions, be given that the proposition will be accepted upon the terms proposed. There is full experience that a reciprocity treaty with the Sandwich Islands is not palatable to the Senate, and the expediency of acquiring further territory abroad is doubted by reflecting members of Congress, whose opinions have much influence." Since Fish already had in his possession the Schofield-Alexander secret report and survey on the strategic military and commercial assets of the islands, it would appear that he was waiting for a later more advantageous time to move America into thrust for the islands.

Another thing of which Fish probably was not cognizant was the backlash of Hawaiian public opinion against further giveaway to the insatiable greed of the foreigners. A mass meeting of "loyalists" had been held at Kaumakapili Church, in which young David Malo, son of the distinguished Hawaiian scholar, had driven his listeners to frenzy over the "trickery of the foreigners" in their attempts to cede the native land to America. One American, however, Walter Murray Gibson, through his own weekly newspaper *Nuhoa*, carried on the campaign against the Missionary Party's machination with such vigor and skill as to win their undying wrath and enmity. The nation had gone through a summer of constant parade of ships and military men. The little palace and the new courthouse never seemed to be free of foreign notables, paying respects, seeking information and favors, meddling officiously into Hawaii's affairs of state.

The king had fled into hiding. Indisposed, he kept himself in seclusion at the Waikiki summer palace for his "health." By September, a month before Fish's letter, the cabinet, assailed by the furious clamor of the citizenry, had the courage to withdraw Hawaii's offer to cede, or even to lease, Pearl Harbor.

The reforms which Lunalilo had launched with such vigor were slow in materializing. The speed and momentum of legislative effort had run down into inaction, resistance, and wrangling among the delegates. Few of the major problems besetting the nation had receded. with the change of kings. Leprosy, in spite of the heroic efforts at segregation and banishment eight years before, was still making inroads among the natives. Though only mildly contagious, and slow in ripening into immobility and disfigurement, the increasing number of cases frightened and panicked government officials.

Hundreds of lepers already had been banished to the settlement on Molokai, but it was still apparent that many afflicted with the dread disease were living among the healthy natives throughout the islands. Villagers seemed to have little fear of the disease the foreigners had brought, and allowed afflicted lepers to mingle freely among them. The king's newly appointed board of health moved rapidly to cope with the problem.

Dr. George Trousseau, member of the new board, advised immediate resumption of the segregation efforts. All persons having the disease, or suspected of having it, were ordered to report immediately to Kalihi hospital in Honolulu for examination. Of the 1,200 cases appearing for diagnosis, about half of them were discharged as free of the disease. From Kalihi and other detention camps, five hundred and sixty known lepers were discovered. These pitiable creatures—including half a dozen foreigners—were sent to Molokai.

The influx of patients at the isolation settlement at Kalawao, more than doubled its population of incurables. The island's already meager and primitive facilities for care of the patients was put to tragic strain. Victims of the dread disease were dumped from the boats, into the surf at Kalawao, and forced to swim ashore. Housing was inadequate; food and water were insufficient to the needs. No banishment could possibly have been worse.

The leprosy campaign became a time of sorrow and recrimination. "I never in my life had to witness more painful scenes of physical and mental suffering," wrote Dr. Trousseau. But the haole physician carried out his painful task fairly, and without fear or favor. "No consideration of fortune, rank or nationality" was allowed to interfere with the obnoxious obligation he had assumed. Through "prayers, threats and worse," the board of health continued at its chore. Among those sent to Molokai was a cousin of Queen Emma, Peter Y. Kaeo, a member of the legislative house of nobles. The letters of this high chief to the queen would later reveal the pathetic and insufferable conditions at Kalawao. The notable William P. Ragsdale, haole interpreter for the Hawaiian legislature, and inimitably portrayed in print by Mark Twain, was victim of the disease. Ragsdale served as superintendent of the settlement to which he was banished.

In time, more poi and better housing was made available to the leper colony. With arrival of Father Damien, the Catholic priest who voluntarily exiled himself to a lifetime ministry in the leper colony, and who himself would eventually die of the disease contracted there, conditions on that bleak island would improve for the unfortunate people who were forced to live in such terrible exile. Father Damien, the heroic martyr of Molokai, was born Joseph de Veuster, 1840, at Tremeloo, Belgium. He took the name of Damien when he became postulant. Among the world's self-effacing men of goodwill, he made that name immortal.

The king escaped leprosy, but through the early summer months his health was precarious from other causes. Illness forced him to shun the public in whose circles he once had walked with such grace and popularity. The summer palace at Waikiki kept him close to the ocean which he loved and used. He pared his court down only to consultant ministers, government heads, and those haole cronies from "Prince Bill's" earlier and more carefree days.

By the middle of August friends, officials, and Alii alike were despairing of the king's life. The attack, Charles R. Bishop explained, came about because Lunalilo "was imprudent and took a severe cold which affected the pleura and right lung." The imprudence was his mistaking the cold beach for his warm bed, and a twin soaking of rum and sea water. Dr. Trousseau, deeply worried, confided to Peirce that "he cannot live very much longer, unless he totally abstains from the use of intoxicating drinks." But Lunalilo slowly recovered from the pneumonia, only to end up, in his weakened condition, as victim of that other dreaded white man's disease, tuberculosis.

During the slow convalescence the royal cottage was visited by privileged guests only—all of them worried and anxious about their stricken king. On September 7 the royal guards, stationed at their barracks on Honolulu's Palace Walk, mutinied. The sixty tall and handsome native soldiers, hand picked for the duty by Lot Kamehameha, indicated they'd had enough of their imported Hungarian martinet and drill master, Captain Joseph Jaraczy, and their haole adjutant general, Charles H. Judd. They demonstrated their acerbity by thoroughly threshing the Hungarian. When John O. Dominis, Oahu's new governor, and General Judd, were called to quell the brawl, the angry troops swung their attack on Judd.

To the royal cottage sped three of the mutineers, to tell the king of their grievances. Jareczy and Judd must be removed, the household troops insisted, before they would return to their functions of parade and stations.

The sick and weary monarch, faced with another decision, ordered the mutineers to submit to authority. They must allow him time to ponder the matter. They must trust to his clemency. While the soldiers anxiously waited, Major William Moehonua was placed in charge of the barracks, and the mutineers unprotestingly followed his orders to stack arms. However, they ignored his order to go to their homes. Instead they stubbornly remained in the barracks.

A delegation of the mutineers again visited the king. This time Lunalilo, in writing, issued a decree not only for the disgruntled troops to go to their homes, but officially disbanded the royal guards, with the exception only of the royal band. Still peevish and dissatisfied, sensing they had been neglected and betrayed by their king, the men finally and reluctantly went to their homes.

The incident brought the people swiftly and thoroughly into sympathy with the little army. They protested the abrupt manner in which the troops had been turned out of office. Chiefs and Alii worried that the nation—its only defenders removed and disarmed—faced the grave danger of revolution and perhaps a coup. Kalakaua, who had lost in the race for kingship, was seen attending the various clandestine meetings of the rejected soldiers. The king was convinced that Kalakaua was plotting mischief.

But if Kalakaua still coveted Lunalilo's throne, he had only to wait with patience. The king attempted to stem the crisis by returning to palace and office in Honolulu, but it was plain that the pale and wasted monarch was a very sick man.

In November, after the mutiny was settled and the guards restored, Dr. Trousseau suggested that Lunalilo seek restoration of health on the big island of Hawaii. It was hoped the warmer sunshine and clear sea air at Kailua, on the historic Kona coast, would be beneficial to the king's lung congestion. But Kailua failed to restore any degree of health to the troubled king. His condition continued to worsen.

In January of 1874, when the steamer *Kilauea* brought Lunalilo back to the thronged wharf at Honolulu, the people were shocked at sight of the helpless invalid who was carried ashore.

Lunalilo lived a few weeks longer—his death occurring on the evening of February 3, 1874. He had barely passed his thirty-ninth birthday, and his reign had been a short one—one year and twenty-five days. As a kind and considerate high chief, he had wanted and desperately tried to magnify his office as king. Like all the other sovereigns before him Lunalilo had placed his people and their welfare ahead of the raucous wants of the foreigners who bedeviled him. It was haole disease and haole alcohol that had killed Lunalilo. But in his will, this tragic, short-lived "people's king" left his personal wealth to the establishment of a home for "poor, destitute and infirm people of Hawaiian blood or extraction, giving preference to old people." His monument—the Lunalilo Home—became an enduring part of Honolulu.

The other enduring monument to his memory is the handsome stone crypt on the grounds of Kawaiahao Church. Spurned by the Kamehamehas and their Alii, he requested no burial in their royal sepulchre up Nuuanu. The "people's king" and his family sleep quite apart from them—aloof and alone.

III

AGAIN a Hawaiian king had died—without wife, without issue. Like Lot Kamehameha, this second bachelor to ascend the throne had failed to name a successor. Once again the nation faced a painful and dangerous interregnum. And again chiefs and people attempted to popularly elect a sovereign.

During Lunalilo's short reign there had been frantic efforts to get him married, in the hopes of reestablishing once more an incontestable dynasty in the royal house. The respected and aging high chief, Paul Nahaolelua, on behalf of the worried Alii, had pressed Lunalilo for a decision on the delicate question of his personal life. Even the Honolulu newspapers, particularly the *Pacific Commercial Advertiser*, had called public attention to Lunalilo's single status, and had reminded the king's ministers that it was their duty to force him into a quick decision on the matter. During Lunalilo's September illness another public meeting of native Hawaiians was held at Kaumakapili Church— a church which also served the city as a forum and town hall—to discuss the problem of royal succession.

As personal and intimate as was the subject, the king received plenty of urging, and not a little advice. Ministers Charles R. Bishop and Edwin O. Hall, on behalf of the cabinet, called on the ailing Lunalilo and used every persuasive argument at their command. But the king, angered by public agitation over his private affairs, and the manner in which the subject of marriage was being pressed upon him during his illness, told them repeatedly that his mind was not made up, ". . . that he would not do anything about it until he was well, and could not say when he would do it." To Paul Nahaolelua, and other close Alii friends, he did disclose his willingness to marry Queen Emma, once he had recovered from his sickness, and should she be willing to accept such a match. And, to their own satisfaction, these Alii associates of the king ascertained that Emma was not averse to ending her widowhood by accepting Lunalilo. The problem was that Lunalilo never recovered from his illness. And, like Lot, left no successor to his name.

The election of 1874, hastily and frantically held within days of the king's death, brought again the Alii names of a year ago—David

Kalakaua, Queen Emma, and Bernice Pauahi Bishop. Kalakaua, known as "Taffy" to friends and associates, had spent a year preparing for chance to reverse the loss he had sustained at the hands of Lunalilo. On the surface he had accepted defeat of his bid for the kingdom with docility and grace, and had been rewarded by appointment to the winning king's staff, with the rank of colonel. Unlike Lunalilo, Kalakaua was already a seasoned hand in government. He had served Lot in establishing Hawaii's gaudily attired little military façade. As a member of the house of nobles, he had spent years as a legislator.

His campaign—already prepared—was swift, well tailored, and efficient. Since his previous rejection by the legislature he had played it cannily. This time there was no vacuous or flamboyant wording to his declaration of candidacy. It came as a straightforward request, insisting that he wanted everything done strictly in accordance with the constitution; asking the people to instruct their representatives in the legislature to vote him in as king. "My earnest desire is for the perpetuity of the crown and the permanent independence of the government and people of Hawaii, on the basis of the equity, liberty, prosperity, progress and protection of the whole people." Alii friends, and those within the government in position to know, saw through the humble naïveté of Kalakaua's appeal. In his year with Lunalilo, Taffy had pulled every string to secure the coveted spot for himself—from abetting mutiny within the troops, to overt and shrewd manipulation behind the throne.

Henry A. Peirce, the American minister, had already reported that Kalakaua was "active in the formation of a party to place him upon the throne" upon the death of the sick king. Kalakaua was energetic leader of the "Young Hawaiians," and had publicly made known that he accepted and backed the popular move toward "Hawaii for Hawaiians." The diplomatic representatives of both United States and Great Britain had forwarded to their respective governments the distrust and dislike they held for this ambitious young chief.

Whether or not Queen Emma would have accepted marriage to Lunalilo as a way to the throne, was never tested because of his death. But there could be no doubt, now that he was gone, of her serious plan to succeed him. During Lunalilo's terminal illness the sharp-witted and intelligent dowager queen had noted that "Taffy is forming a military company of young Hawaiians . . . the ultimate object is to secure their tickets at the next election for members opposing cession or annexation . . . the object given out thus is good . . . but I cannot help thinking more is at the bottom." Fearing Taffy's intentions, and the possibility of his effecting a coup, she bitterly resisted his bid for the throne. More than anything now, Emma wanted to succeed the dead monarch, as queen of all Hawaii. She had hoped and expected Lunalilo would personally have named her his successor.

Of the three candidates to Hawaii's highest office, Bernice Pauahi, in spite of her right through flawless genealogy, had the least chance of making it. Her handicap was that she was married to Charles R. Bishop who, though the most trusted adviser to the dead king, was also a rich young American. Everyone was of the opinion that, because of this marital link which marred her appeal to native Hawaiians, she would be friendly and partial to American interests. Haole residents would have been pleased to see the beautiful and talented Bernice on the throne but, since she made no public effort whatever to gain it, and the other candidates had announced themselves as totally pro-Hawaiian in principle, she quickly was outdistanced in the race.

Publicly there was great support for both Kalakaua and Emma, but with the groundwork already meticulously laid, the edge was definitely for Kalakaua. For months he had assiduously courted the friendship and support of native groups, the haole press, and the commercially-oriented "kingmakers." Up to the final and devastating intrusion of these special-interest partisans, both candidates had conducted their campaigns with such restraint and high manners as to have done credit to an English election. Now, throughout Honolulu, there arose an angry division of opinion—a sudden pervasive tension—ugly and ominous.

The diligent proselyting for support by David Kalakaua began to pay off. Honolulu newspapers, the *Gazette* and the *Advertiser* were as one in singing the praises of the popular and handsome young chief. The *Nuhoa*, owned and edited by Walter Murray Gibson, declared that only Kalakaua could save the Hawaiian race from extinction.

On the morning of February 8 the inter-island steamer *Kilauea* put into Honolulu harbor. Aboard were the legislative electors from the other islands. The haole "kingmakers" made certain that all delegates were properly met, escorted to one of Honolulu's haberdasheries, and each rigged out with high silk hat and cane. To make certain they were safely out of reach of Emma's partisans, the delegates were specially housed, fed, and treated to four days of *luaus*, hula and all the liquor they could possibly desire.

On February 12 they were hustled by carriage to the courthouse. By now they were wearing such alcoholic hangovers as to cause wonder even among the "kingmakers" whether they were sober enough to mark their ballots and get them properly into the box. The crowds shouting for Queen Emma were kept safely outside the courthouse, while upstairs the delegates were each handed their two ballots—the plain one for Queen Emma. The one with the large black heart for

WARSHIPS IN HONOLULU HARBOR

Trouble was expected at King Lunalilo's death, so the *U.S.S. Tuscarora,*

Kalakaua. The unsteady dignitaries managed to get their ballots safely into the box—but only with help from their friends and mentors. There could be no question as to how they were marked.

The counting showed thirty-six votes for Kalakaua—six for Queen Emma. From the courthouse door the tally was announced to the surging crowds outside. When the Emma partisans heard the verdict, all hell broke loose. "Down with the foreigners!" came the shout. "The true *makaainana* is our choice!"

Hundreds of Emma's supporters stormed the building. The native electors who had supported Kalakaua were severely beaten. A couple of them were tossed out second story windows. When angry and defiant mobs began ranging up and down Honolulu's streets, it took two hundred sailors and marines from the American and British warships to suppress the riot.

Not until the interior of the courthouse was reduced to rubble, desks overturned and broken, cabinets ransacked, papers scattered, and windows broken, did the mob meet its equal in the disciplined sailors from two navies, as it rampaged the streets of Honolulu. Carriages waiting outside to convey delegates from the building were demolished by the mob. Chunks of the vehicles, and spokes from the wheels, were used as clubs by the angered and fanatical Hawaiians. Kalakaua, his minister Charles R. Bishop, and Oahu's governor John O. Dominis, joined in requesting help from the ships. Influential haoles Charles C. Harris, Sanford B. Dole and George Dole were in the streets endeavoring to quiet and placate the murderous mob. Native police were useless. Many of them took off their badges and joined the crowd.

Next morning, after Honolulu once more was quiet and orderly under the vigilant American and British sailors, Queen Emma graciously accepted defeat. With supreme magnanimity she sent a message to Kalakaua acknowledging him as sovereign. From the porch of "Rooke House," Emma's Honolulu residence during her widowhood, she addressed the people in native Hawaiian—begging them to peacefully accept the new king, and to disperse quietly to their homes.

Externally at least, amicable relations were established between Emma and Kalakaua, when next day he paid formal visit to his defeated rival. But the struggle between Emma and the new royal family was never truly settled. It would endure to the final end of the Hawaiian monarchy.

Because of rioting and bitterness there was nothing gaudy, spectacular or flamboyant about Kalakaua's inauguration. Next day, after the electors had decided the issue, a small, quiet ceremony was held in the messy interior of the courthouse, before the battered and bruised members of the legislature, representatives of foreign governments, influential haoles, Alii, and prosperous Hawaiians. Before them Kalakaua took the oath, as required by the constitution. Simply, and without ostentation and fanfare, he stepped from Hawaiian chieftainship to king. Compared to the pageantry of Liholiho's assumption, it was the briefest and simplest inauguration in the nation's history.

The new king wasted no time in getting to the business of his reign. So there would be no doubt as to his intent, he immediately named his younger brother, Prince William Pitt Leleiohoku,* as next in line to the throne. In Kalakaua's reign there would be no further kingmaking by the public. Newspapers were quick to note that Kalakaua, in choosing his cabinet, recognized "the cosmopolitan character of the community." A native Hawaiian, former governor Paul Nahaolelua, was named as minister of finance; an Englishman, William L. Green, as minister of foreign affairs; a German, Hermann A. Widemann, would be minister of the interior; and an American, Alfred S. Hartwell, was chosen as attorney-general. Only the Chinese, who now were a substantial and loyal part of the citizenry, were slighted. Oddly the Chinese, prospering in business, and who, more than any other racial group, were marrying into Hawaiian families, were almost fanatical in support of the new king.

Since Hartwell and Widemann were both members of Hawaii's supreme court, the king appointed to that high bench, as replacements to them, Charles C. Harris as first associate justice, and A. Francis Judd as second associate. The supreme court, now, for the first time, was structured by men fully educated in the law.

The king's new team was well chosen, and promising. His inauguration had been quiet and conciliatory. In every way Kalakaua was evidencing a desire and resolve to serve his kingdom well. But his election had been a troublous one. His reign was destined to be equally turbulent.

IV

DAVID KALAKAUA was molded in the solid-fleshed, six-foot stature, of his forebears, the fighting chiefs of Kona. Their wilder propensities, however, were not a part of Taffy's makeup—unless it was his preoccupation with military display and participation. He modeled well in any and every uniform he wore. He made a handsome soldier—dark, wavy-haired, courtly—and he knew it. But beyond this permissive vanity, he was amiable, approachable, refined and intelligent.

*Le-le-i-o-ho-ku: *Lay*-lay-ee-oh-*hoh*-koo.

Certainly Kalakaua came to the throne better endowed for leadership than his predecessor. High rank as an Alii had assured him an excellent education in the Royal School. He was a voracious reader, naturally inquisitive, with a wide horizon in knowledge. This had been complemented by travel in America. Kalakaua was no stranger to politics and government. He had served, up to his assumption of the throne, as member and secretary of the privy council, had filled the office of chamberlain to Kamehameha V, was a commissioned colonel in the Hawaiian army, and, as a noble and Alii, had sat in every session of the legislature from 1860 to 1873.

David Kalakaua was a natural-born musician of great talent; a composer of Hawaiian chants and *meles,* and a master of almost any musical instrument he ever touched. This gift seems to have been a liberal endowment of other members of his remarkable family.

Charles Nordhoff, after a long visit to Hawaii in 1873, noted that "Colonel Kalakaua is a man of education, of better physical stamina than the late king, of good habits, vigorous will, and a strong determination to maintain the independence of the Islands." Nor was his Alii antecedents weak or questionable. His father, Kapaakea, was a great-grandson of the mighty Kameeiamoku. His mother, Keohokalole, was great-granddaughter to Keawe-a-Heulu, and second link to another fierce chief of Kona in the court of Kamehameha the Great. But there was nothing fierce about the refined and elegant Kalakaua.

Nor did he ascend the throne as bachelor and intestate, as had his two predecessors. In 1863 he had married Julia Kapiolani, granddaughter of Kaumualii, King of Kauai, and widow of Chief Benjamin Namakeha. He came to the throne with every right and privilege to found a high-right dynasty. But he came to the throne wearing the curse of so many native Hawaiians. His Queen Kapiolani was barren. As a royal couple, they were childless.

Like the kings before him, Kalakaua immediately faced the storms of foreign avarice, the yapping and howling for special privilege and favor, the pressures for American cession and annexation, the continuing battle of the "Emmaites" against him, and the absolute necessity for a reciprocity treaty with the United States. If Hawaii were to survive economically as a nation, the tariffs and discrimination against Hawaiian sugar and coffee must swiftly be removed. These unwarranted and unjust levies had strangled Hawaii's American market—had virtually closed this main and most essential pool for exports. So, like the kings before him, Kalakaua made another agonizing try for reciprocity.

One of his first acts was to dispatch Elisha Allen and Henry A. P. Carter to the United States, to present Hawaii's petition to Washington.

In his plea Kalakaua pledged that he would grant no other nation favored port privileges or partiality. Though he covertly avoided any direct mention of a cession of Pearl Harbor, he did honestly and humbly offer the United States every promise of preference short of cession or annexation, in return for the chance of an open market with that nation, unencumbered by manipulations and barriers of discrimination.

When Allen and Carter wrote that something more than talk and promise was necessary to win over a recalcitrant American Senate, they urgently suggested that a personal visit to Washington of His Majesty was not only necessary but imperative if a treaty were at all forthcoming. So, in November 1874, in the first year of his reign, Kalakaua went to America, aboard the *U.S.S. Benicia*, as guest of the American government.

As the first monarch ever to visit the United States, Kalakaua received royal honors everywhere he traveled. He and his stately queen thoroughly charmed America. President U. S. Grant, captivated by the cultured, educated, handsome king and his beautiful wife, insisted they be guests at the White House. The American press spoke favorably of the distinguished visitors from the exotic islands, and were editorially agreeable to what Hawaii asked of a beneficent democracy. Unquestionably, Kalakaua's presence on American soil influenced the Senate into swift ratification of a treaty of reciprocity.

The new treaty, to begin September 9, 1876, while saving Hawaii economically, was a greater gain for the United States. By this act, the nation captured virtual dominance over the islands, by a code of promises, and without the use of force. Hawaii was now an indentured and operative part of America's modern world. "Hawaii for Hawaiians" had vanished on the altar of expediency.

A measure of the accord's significance to Hawaii's future could be indicated by the fact that the very ship which brought word of congressional approval of the reciprocity treaty, brought also, as passenger, Claus Spreckels, California's shrewd and wealthy beet sugar magnate. Open and unrestricted trade with America meant open and unrestricted opportunity for wealth in Hawaiian cane sugar. By 1884, by acquirance of vast plantations, and as refiner, shipper, and banker, Claus Spreckels would be known as "ex-officio emperor," or "the other king" of the Hawaiian Islands.

◁ *KING KALAKAUA (DAVID KALAKAUA) REIGNED 1874 - 1891*
"A most elegant gentleman."

—*Photo, Bernice P. Bishop Museum, Honolulu.*

V

KALAKAUA ventured cautiously into his role as sovereign. The turmoil at his election, and the continuing resistance of the British-oriented "Emmaites," had left him unsure as to his hold upon national loyalty. Before elevation to the monarchy, Taffy had been mild-mannered, agreeable, and popular. Foreigners and political climbers who had known and associated with him in the earlier years imagined he was the same Taffy, now that he was king. His urbanity was mistaken for docility. His constitutional conformity, his winning of friendship and backing of the United States, and his alertness to the economic well-being of his nation, gave the haoles assurance and confidence in his stewardship.

A new wave of prosperity, and the king's continued and open concern for the welfare of native Hawaiians, soothed the wounds, and won support. Gradually the factions of Queen Emma ceased their open hostility and criticism of his every act. The elections of 1876 ended in such manner as to be a vote of confidence for his government.

The new word to the haoles was expansion. Island-born sons of the American missionaries spurned the austerity of their parents' circles. They seemed obsessed in gaining toeholds on wealth and privilege in the expanding economy of the nation. Missionary sons like Samuel T. Alexander and Henry P. Baldwin recognized the opportunities in sugar. Their beginning venture was a plantation at Haiku, on Maui. Eventually they were heading business firms throughout the islands. Their mighty commercial agency exists to this day.

The reciprocity treaty, in eliminating the American tariff, presented Hawaiian sugar producers with a bounty of more than two cents a pound. What was once small profit, was now the opportunity for great wealth. This had touched off what the Honolulu *Commercial Advertiser* called "a regular mania of speculation in cane-growing." By 1875, thirty-two island plantations had 12,230 acres of cane under growth, which exported to American market more than twenty-five-million pounds of sugar. Four years later, these figures had doubled.

◁   *QUEEN KAPIOLANI, WIFE OF KALAKAUA*
    She died June 24, 1899. One of the last of the great Alii.

    —Photo, Bernice P. Bishop Museum, Honolulu.

THE RECIPROCITY COMMISSION

(Seated), *Governor John Dominis (husband of the later Queen Liliuokalani, last monarch of Hawaii), King Kalakaua, Governor John Kapena;* (standing), *H. A. Peirce, Luther Severance.*

—*Photo, Bernice P. Bishop Museum, Honolulu.*

Since it required a ton of water to produce a pound of refined sugar, the great search now was for water sources sufficient to sustain this vast undertaking. Planters—now that the naturally watered fields had already been claimed and developed by earlier opportunists—went to fantastic lengths to procure and develop essential and needed water sources. Ditches, aqueducts, and stream diversion tapped the rain forests of the mountains. Deep artesian and pump wells went downward to the coral and lava cisterns under the islands. The once lovely rolling island terrain became endless cane fields—kapu to the once free roving natives, unless those natives were willing to accept the yoke-and-pittance servitude of haole masters.

Sons and relatives of the missionaries were already well entrenched where water was handy. But Claus Spreckels wasted no time in acquiring enormous areas of dry land on Maui. Aping Alexander and Baldwin's success, he somehow wrung from Kalakaua and the government the right to tap "all waters not heretofore utilized" between Maliko and Hana. His German engineer, Herman Schussler, supervised the digging of the Haiku irrigation complex, thirty miles long, which in two years, and at enormous cost, was delivering fifty million gallons of water a day to the cane fields of Spreckelsville and Puunene. On west Maui, Spreckels, with another big ditch was, a few years later, bringing more water from Waihee. The battlegrounds of Alipai and Kamehameha were now the treasure grounds of King Spreckels, sugar magnate from California.

Claus Spreckels, by every device, from purchase to governmental manipulation, acquired a total of 41,000 acres of beautiful Maui. In a town built by himself, and named for himself, he spent $4,000,000 to construct the largest and most modern sugar refinery in the world. By his example in providing his Hawaiian empire with towns, stores, roller mills, steam plows, and field railroads for his plantations, he not only set the example for other tycoons, but by his technical and industrial innovations, he revolutionized the sugar industry.

Vast acreage, and dozens of refineries throughout the islands to mill the sugar tonnage, created an equally vast demand for laborers. Kalakaua, much as he deplored the shrunken native population, could do nothing other than assent to the importation of Japanese, Chinese, Portuguese and Germans to fill the acute labor market. Robert Wyllie's frantic efforts to stuff the population gap with more desirable Polynesians, finally induced 2,500 natives from other Pacific islands to come to Hawaii for "a new life." Unfortunately, to be driven like animals by haole field and factory overseers, was much too new and strenuous for them. They soon departed for their kindlier homelands.

But the Asiatics, the Portuguese, the Europeans and, above all, the Americans, remained. The kingdom Kalakaua found himself governing had become a polyglot of nations. Actually, however, his government had little to do with the toilers in the fields. They were effectively and silently controlled by the business interests who hired and imported them. The king led, in actuality, only two visible cultural segments of the nation—the loyal but shrunken body of native Hawaiians—and the aggressive foreign entrepreneurs who were fast becoming the real owners.

VI

THE REIGN of Kalakaua is undoubtedly the most gaudy and colorful in the history of the kingdom. Pageantry and glory of Liholiho's court pales by comparison. The king, obsessed with military trappings, set the pace. The royal guards were revived as a unit, and refurbished. New military companies were formed and, though they had little to do other than parade, this they did with precision and éclat. Honolulu's police were gaudily uniformed. Iolani Barracks were completed and occupied. And the capital city was a constant scene of bright uniforms and glittering shakos.

The court functions, which were many, were resplendent with correctly gowned Alii ladies and the wives and daughters of favored haoles. Gold-braided, militarily attired, and liberally be-medaled males, made the palace as flashy and formal as St. James.

In the beginning there had been nine brothers and sisters to David Kalakaua. He and his brother, William Pitt Leleiohoku, were the only members of the large family who remained close to the household of his father, Kapaakea, and then only so long as the stern old high chief lived. In the complicated and typical Polynesian pattern, the children had been dispersed and adopted into other Alii families—becoming the same as natural kin to their foster parents, but with their genealogy and antecedents still fully defined and provable.

On Kalakaua's rise to prominence, and election to the throne, he gathered more closely into his court those of his brothers and sisters who were still living, even though their diverse rearings had cast them into roles more like friends and acquaintances than blood kin. Prince William Leleiohoku had been adopted by Princess Ruth, daughter of Pauahi and Kehuanaoa. His baby sister Kaiminaauao had been accepted into the family of Kamehameha III and his queen, Kalama—only to die in infancy. Likelike,* a sister of exceptional beauty, grew up in distant home in the Hilo area of the big island of Hawaii.

*Li-ke-li-ke: Lee-*kay*-lee-*kay*.

The remaining member of a once large family, Lydia [Liliuoka-lani], had been doled out at birth to Chief Paki, and his wife Konia. Foster-mother Konia was a granddaughter of Kamehameha I, and Paki was of the highest Alii. Their natural daughter, Bernice Pauahi, was joined by Lydia [Liliuokalani],* and to every appearance these two girls—both destined to shape Hawaii in the final years—were truly sisters.

The latter years of the Chiefs' Children's School—or Royal School—had seen enrollment of those children destined to be the great names in the closing drama of the monarchy. In this privileged training center, maintained and operated by ex-missionary Amos Starr Cooke and his indefatigable wife, were enrolled the four children of Kinau, daughter of Kamehameha I and highest ranking woman chief of her day—Moses, Lot [later Kamehameha V], Alexander Liholiho [later Kame-hameha IV], and Victoria, their princess sister. Along with Lunalilo and Lot, was Bernice Pauahi, who twice could have been queen, had she not chosen an American banker as life consort. Kalakaua's family was represented at Royal School by himself, Leleiohoku [later the heir-apparent], and Lydia Paki [destined to be the last of Hawaii's sover-eigns]. Other budding greats were Emma Rooke [who, married to a Kamehameha, would become the Queen Emma of history]; there too were Peter Kaeo, Jane Loeau, Elizabeth Kaaniau, Abigail Maheha, Mary Paaina, and John Kinau Pitt. Royal School—the Alii's closed circle of learning.

These were the figures who later would be drawn inexorably into Kalakaua's court circle. Aside from such Alii adornments, the king added plenty of strange and influential haoles. As grafted-in Hawaiians they would wield drastic powers in moving this ebullient monarch through an exciting and epochal reign.

First came that elected legislative delegate from the outer islands, the stately and handsome Walter Murray Gibson—surely one of the most colorful and controversial entrepreneurs ever to walk across the scene of the Hawaiian kingdom. Gibson already had gained himself a principality—on Lanai. His bizarre and adroit skill in its acquirance is probably without parallel in Hawaii's annals of opportunism.

Gibson's birth, according to his own flowery claims, occurred aboard a ship carrying British immigrants to America. He modestly claimed to have run away from his home in Virginia, at age twelve, to spend five years with the Indians in North Carolina. At seventeen he was married to Rachel Lewis, a fifteen-year-old bride, carefully chosen from Anglo parents in South Carolina. Rachel died giving birth to Gibson's third child—a daughter Talula. Leaving his family with his dead wife's

*Li-li-u-o-ka-la-ni: *Lee*-lee-oo-*oh*-kah-lah-nee. Popular: *Lee-lee-oh-kah-lah*-nee.

parents, and at age of twenty-one, he escaped to New York with full intention of making his fortune.

According to his own accounts, a series of fantastic inventions— culminating in a machine that marvelously separated gold from sand, and marketed among the argonauts in California—made him wealthy in the short space of five years. Whether true or not, there was no question that he moved in New York's elite circles, with a wit, charm and loquaciousness that kept him swimming in diplomatic and social circles. While his gold washers failed to operate successfully in California, his theatric gift of gab soon landed him appointment as consul general to Guatemala, San Salvador and Costa Rica. This post he resigned to become, in his own words, an admiral in the Guatemala navy. It didn't matter, apparently, that Guatemala had no navy. As a Guatemalan admiral, he purchased a ninety-six foot schooner, and began arming his ship for war. The U. S. government, however, put quick stop to Gibson's outfitting any ship for warlike purposes, in an American port. Reluctantly Gibson stripped the cannons off his boat, converted her into a yacht, renamed her the *Flirt* and, amid a scandalous attempt to include a prominent female socialite as part of his crew, he set sail for the South Seas. After many adventures Walter Murray Gibson landed in a Sumatra jail—where he languished in prison for a year for allegedly attempting to foment revolt of native Sumatrans against their Dutch masters.

He claimed to have escaped execution for his crime by boarding the British ship *H. B. Palmer*, bound for England. Once back in New York Gibson had the temerity to press formal claim on the Netherlands, through the U. S. State Department, for false imprisonment and damages of $100,000.00. Failing in this, he wrote his adventures into a fanciful book, *The Prison of Veltevreden*, and gained moderate fame through flowery and heroic speeches on the American lecture circuit.

In 1859 he was in Salt Lake City, pouring his charm on Brigham Young, along with a plan for moving the Mormon people from Utah— then under U. S. military assault in the "Utah War"—to the happier and less turbulent South Seas. Brigham, however, preferred to remain in his native country, even though he and his people were still under the muzzles of Johnston's Army. But there was no question about Gibson's talent and charm. Brigham instantly recognized the ideal missionary for converting the Pacific islanders to the one true church, and he suggested that Gibson join the Latter-day Saints, and face up to this greater mission.

In January of 1860 Walter Murray Gibson was baptized into the creed. His preliminary missionary "call" was to America's eastern states, but within six months he was back in Salt Lake City. To Brigham

Young, Gibson reported an incredible record of conversions. Among the successful accomplishments of the aborted mission was Gibson's claim to having interviewed the members of Washington's new Japanese embassy, "in their own language," and that they were not only receptive to the Mormon message, but had invited him to visit Japan in behalf of the church. Within a matter of weeks, Brigham Young, in the Salt Lake Tabernacle, had "called" Walter Murray Gibson to carry the word to the unsaved gentiles of the Pacific, with particular commission to open the Latter-day Saint mission to Japan.

On July 4, 1861, with daughter Talula, and two men he had converted aboard ship, Walter Murray Gibson arrived in Honolulu. That was as far as he got in carrying the gospel message to Asia. He liked what he saw in Hawaii, and was instantly convinced it was the more proper place for his persuasive talents. For one thing, the Mormon Church had already planted the seed, and much was ready and waiting to be harvested. On six thousand acres, in the crater valley of Palawai, on Lanai, was already established Mormondom's colony—called "The City of Joseph." In 1857, when the U. S. government had decided to declare war on Utah, all missionaries had been ordered back to America. The promising City of Joseph, and the entire Lanai project, had been left untended, except for a native or two in doubtful charge.

Gibson quickly filled the lack. Without hesitance he set himself up as head of the colony, acting in the name of God, and President Brigham Young. He organized the natives into the Mormon ecclesiastical pattern—with a few Gibsonese touches. Attired in a white robe, he took all power unto himself as absolute head of the "City of Joseph" and the Kingdom of God soon to be established. Surrounding himself with the pomp, ceremony, and mystic priestcraft that had gone out with Kaahumanu, he struck that instant chord of obedience and elation once so commonly known to Polynesians.

In April of 1864 an official five-man delegation from Salt Lake City arrived in Lanai to investigate the strange state of affairs prevailing in the Mormon colony. There was an immediate confrontation with "President" Gibson—and a demand for return of the church possessions. Shrewdly, Gibson put the controversy to vote of the island's native Mormon population. Without hesitance they chose Walter Murray Gibson over their visiting "authorities" from Salt Lake City.

Gibson took his summary excommunication from the Mormon Church with a tolerant smile. He could afford to. He now owned half the island of Lanai. And he no longer needed a priestly garb to hold it.

The Mormons were forced to seek out a fresh area for a colony—this time at Laie, on Oahu. Eventually many of the converted natives on Lanai regretted their allegiance to the power-hungry and defrocked

Gibson, and joined their brethren on Oahu. But Gibson kept the land, became wealthy, set up residence at Lahaina, got himself elected to Hawaii's legislature as a representative from Maui. By charm, pro-Hawaiian oratory, and unmatched persuasion, he became closest confidant of the king. In Honolulu he established and published *Nuhou,* a completely pro-Hawaiian semi-weekly. To the sensitive, artistic Kalakaua, Walter Murray Gibson remained a complex, stimulating, and dependable man. In 1882, Kalakaua named Gibson as premier of the nation. For nine years this controversial figure would dominate both king and government.

It was Gibson who decided that His Majesty must have a proper and lavish setting for home and court. All Kalakaua had asked was replacement of the decaying bungalow which had served his predecessors. Iolani Palace took more than $350,000 of governmental sugar profits before it was completed. Honolulu was refurbished with public buildings whose beauty and cost far exceeded the opulence Lot Kamehameha had visioned for his rejuvenated nation.

Under Gibson's advice and persuasion, new fire engines came to Honolulu, fancy uniforms and modern weapons came to the army and police. Kalakaua restored the hula as a nationally accepted institution, and the Portuguese-introduced guitar became the musical expression of an already musical nation—because the king was adept at playing foreign instruments. When Joseph Kehuka, at the Kamehameha School for Boys, discovered that, by fretting a guitar's strings with a sliding comb or pocket knife, the instrument could be made to whine and wail like an ancient *mele*, guitar picking quickly became a lap procedure. The Portuguese brought the stringed instruments to Hawaii. Their largest guitar, the *viola*, had the six strings of the new Hawaiian guitar; their five-stringed *rajao* became Hawaii's "taro patch fiddle;" the four-stringed Portuguese *braga* emerged as the Hawaiian ukelele. But it was Joseph Kehuka and his fellow students at Kamehameha School who, by sliding an object along the strings of a Portuguese instrument, launched the Hawaiian steeled guitar as a national expression.

The Royal Hawaiian Band became Honolulu's cultural institution, and everything musical or dramatic became the king's desire for his bright and happy city. Opera came to Honolulu, as did visiting musical aggregations from other nations. No longer were the haoles sole custodians of culture on the islands.

The poetic and musical nature of the Hawaiian people had been noted from the time of Captain Cook through every foreign visitor who had ever walked and talked with them. Their male voices ranged from lowest basso profundo to exquisitely pure tenor. Women's voices, equally pure, roved the scale from contralto to limpid and liquid soprano.

Their native history, from the time they had departed Tahiti in open sea—their tremendous ocean exploits—their wars—their victories—their complex genealogy going back to the godlike beginning—all had been set to music, and endlessly memorized down to the last shade of meaning. These chants and *meles* were a part of every honorary or religious function—at least down to the time the foreigners succeeded in perverting the culture and ethos of one of the earth's most talented and expressive people.

Joyous, generous, childlike, the natives through the ages had shaped their lives and told their story in song and dance. The hula was nothing more than their universal saga expressed in exquisitely graceful pantomime. Because this dance had been performed with exuberance and gayety, and because the hips of the young and agile performers—boys and girls—swiveled rhythmically and seductively, it had been one of the first targets of obliteration by the New England Puritans.

Earlier orchestrations to both song and dance had consisted mostly of primitive bamboo nose flutes, musical bows made from hardwood strung tautly with sennit, held in the mouth and hand plucked with a twisted piece of kapa. The drums were carved from a section of coconut log, with percussion heads of sharkskin. Large drums and low voiced conch shell horns were a part of the temple ceremonials. Smaller drums, hula sticks, bamboo pipes, stone castanets, and leg rattles of dog teeth, were additional orchestration to the wild and expressive native dances.

Never, not even up to the time of Kalakaua's reign, had any serious attempt been made to record in notes and bars Hawaii's already rich heritage in song. This Hawaiian king sparked and encouraged the sudden renaissance of island music. Just as abruptly had the native dances been contemptuously shoved aside as unworthy of a study, and a trifle too hot for good Christians to handle. It should have been significant that every king, from Liholiho down to Kalakaua, had secretly held "Hawaiian court" with their people and with sympathetic and understanding Alii. In them there had been plenty of native singing, and plenty of hula, no matter how meticulously the king had been coached in the more somber pattern and teachings of Jesus Christ. Not until arrival of the musical and exuberant Kalakaua, and his remarkable family, was the expressive heritage of Hawaii allowed to emerge once more from the dark corners of suppression. The happy and racially-sensitive monarch revived the *Ka Hale Nau-a* [The Temple of Wisdom], an esoteric society out of the mists of Polynesian antiquity, dedicated to the search for man's mysterious beginnings, with rituals geared to Hawaiian vocal expression and dance. Once more the native beat and rhythm was heard in the land—played now from haole strings, and instruments manufactured by the enterprising Portuguese nationals who had been brought to the islands for the heavier toil of harvesting sugar cane.

When Princess Liliuokalani, sister to the king, had been merely the schoolgirl Lydia Paki, she had made a discovery. Not only could she read haole music, sing it and play it from the cold score print, but she possessed the uncanny faculty of being able to turn the songs that sang so brightly in her own intelligent head, into the written notes and bars so others could enjoy her music with a degree of precision. Even as a young girl she had discovered her mind was a constant spring of new and beautiful tunes—which she could write, play or sing with equal ease.

In the early years of Lot's reign as Kamehameha V, he had gone to young Lydia Paki, with the request she compose for him a suitable national anthem. For years the British "God Save the King," with Hawaiian words, had been serving the purpose on high occasions. The people had no national anthem of their own. It was at his royal command that this schoolgirl composer tried her hand at giving Hawaii a national air. In a week's time Lydia completed her job. She notified the king that the music was written and ready. The king had sat at Kawaiahao Church, dubious, moody and critical, for a first public hearing of it.

Lydia being choir leader, young as she was, gave such able presentation of her "Hawaiian National Anthem" that even dour old Lot was impressed. He appreciated the native lilt of Lydia's music. Publicly and enthusiastically he noted the appropriateness and aptness of the Hawaiian wording the young composer had written into it.

For many years Lydia's composition was the anthem of Hawaii—played gloriously by the Royal Hawaiian Band, and sung enthusiastically and meaningfully by the people of the kingdom.

Not until Kalakaua, her brother, was well into his reign, and Lydia had become Princess Liliuokalani, was her "national air" discarded in favor of Kalakaua's own composition of the *Hawaii Ponoi*. He'd asked the maestro of the Royal Hawaiian Band to wrap this poem with music. The band leader had answered this royal command by digging up an old German air. Kalakaua, being a musician himself, could probably have done better with his song.

By then the basic music of Hawaii had become an obsession with the royal family. Kalakaua, beset with the pressures of state, his extravagant and festive court life, and his travels, was eventually forced to withdraw from participation and contribution to the revival of native song, though he continued to support *Ka Hale Nau-a*. Prince Leleiohoku, heir-apparent to the throne, Princess Liliuokalani, and her sister Princess Likelike, continued as lively participants and competitors.

The crown prince, with the same taste for social pleasures and festive conviviality as his brother the king, had a matching passion for Hawaiian poetry and song. To sing one's songs and one's compositions, Leleiohoku formed a club—requisite for membership being male voices of the purest and sweetest quality to be found among native Hawaiians. Competing with the prince were two other clubs, of mixed singers, male and female—one headed by Princess Liliuokalani, the other sponsored by Princess Likelike. Practically none of the music presented by these three clubs, no matter how authentic, or beautiful, had been reduced to writing. It was done in the old Hawaiian way—vocal memorization. Dozens of major compositions by this musical family, and at one time sung ecstatically throughout the islands by the appreciative natives, have been lost forever because they were never recorded the haole way. The participants were like the ancient bards, much of their contributions are gone and forgotten.

But the dance, the poem, and the song *were* seeing a revival—along with the foreign style of expression in opera, drama, bands, orchestras, and the haole way of dancing with arms entwined. The longnecks were still shuddering, but Honolulu, encouraged and abetted by the zest and extravagance of King Kalakaua, had become a city of festive recklessness.

Kalakaua, like all Hawaiians, was a lover of the sea, and gloried in the tradition of those masters of paddle and sail who had conquered the wide Pacific. His boat house *Healani* was not only the site of many of his extravagant parties, but his close link with the maritime and sea joys he so enjoyed and coveted. Highest honor to any island canoist was to be chosen a member of the king's own rowing team. At *Healani* His Majesty spent hours watching and coaching the superbly muscled men who manned his racing shells—sleek craft, patterned after the traditional canoes of Hawaii's history.

But, more than anything, Kalakaua wanted to mingle with the great people of the world. He had visited America. He longed, like Liholiho, and Aleck, to know and associate with the crowned heads and governmental dignitaries of other nations. So, while the new and spacious Iolani Palace was being finished, he laid plans to circle the earth; "to recuperate his health;" to find means for "recuperating his people."

But Kalakaua's extravagance had already plunged him personally into debt. He was now paying twelve percent to his creditors in interest for past loans, and was constantly in need of new funds. When Claus Spreckels offered him loans at seven percent, Kalakaua happily responded. A new tangle of debt, with the "sugar king," soon settled about his royal neck. Once Kalakaua was within his financial grasp, Spreckels never loosened the grip. From that point on the king was forced to grant practically every favor and concession this haole banker and industrialist demanded.

The king's projected tour of the world was forced into postponement when, on April 10, 1877, the popular and talented Crown Prince Leleiohoku died suddenly—of rheumatic fever. Once more king and ministers were forced to the necessity of choosing another heir-apparent. The prince, because he had loved the people and their vanishing cultural background, had been a great favorite with native Hawaiians. The haoles, viewing the lavish living of Kalakaua, and the prince's propensities for much of the same, had never been too sure about their chances should there ever come the prospect of Leleiohoku's assumption as king. But with all worries ended in his sudden death, they mourned with the nation when his body was consigned to the royal tomb. To Kalakaua and his sisters the loss was shattering.

But even with death of the one and only male heir, it had been assumed that Kalakaua's family was virile enough to assure proper succession and, in all probability, to hold the dynasty. Princess Likelike, though she had married the haole inspector general of immigration and customs, Archibald S. Cleghorn, had, on October 16, 1876, given birth to a child. The baby was but six months old at the time of Leleiohoku's death, and had been a girl child whom they had christened Kaiulani.* This new princess had been considered by many Hawaiians as their second hope—the only direct heir, by birth, to the throne.

Princess Ruth, daughter of Pauahi and Kekuanaoa, who had adopted Prince Leleiohoku in his earlier years, now made immediate request of Kalakaua that she, Ruth, be proclaimed as heir-apparent.

The grave matter of succession was laid before the king's ministers and counselors, and each right and claim soberly considered. The decision was against Princess Kaiulani. Even though the mother was true and legitimate Alii, the father was haole. To a people so fiercely proud of their ancestry it somehow had appeared unseemly to think of Cleghorn's daughter as an Hawaiian queen. Decision was also against the claim of Princess Ruth. The objection was that, should her petition be granted, then Mrs. Bernice Pauahi Bishop would be next in line to the throne. Since they were first cousins, the proper succession would then forever pass out of the king's immediate family.

At noon, on April 10, 1877, after long months of deliberation, Honolulu's cannon boomed, and her church bells rang. Princess Liliuokalani, once known to her school chums as Lydia Paki, was proclaimed the heir-apparent.

*Ka-i-u-la-ni: Kah-*ee*-oo-*lah*-nee.

King Kalakaua's announced tour of the world, delayed by his brother's death, now had to be further postponed because of internal problems. The king remained as reckless and ambitious in urging expenditures upon his government as he was in his own personal conduct. His building program, now changing the face of Honolulu, put severe strain upon governmental finance. Kalakaua wanted new ships to replace the aging steamer *Kilauea,* and the decrepit sailing schooners, now serving in inter-island service. At his insistence, the Hawaiian government contracted with Dickey Brothers, in San Francisco, for the first of a series of new steamships. Trial run, in California, of the initial vessel, August 2, 1877, gave real promise of comfortable and efficient travel facilities throughout the island empire.

When the ship arrived in Honolulu, she was christened by the king—*Likelike*—and people were ecstatic in her praise. "Her cabin accommodations are light, airy, roomy, handsome, and a vast improvement on those of the old *Kilauea,*" it was reported. The only difficulty was that a desperately strained treasury forced the Hawaiian government quickly out of the inter-island transportation business. The *Likelike* had to be sold to Samuel G. Wilder for $96,000—less than she had cost. Wilder generously paid an additional $5,000 for the old steamer *Kilauea,* which he took out of service. The only concession left to Hawaii was that the king and queen, crown princess Liliuokalani and her husband, Governor John O. Dominis, were entitled to free passage on the *Likelike.* And each of them could include five servants.

With this start, Samuel Wilder organized the Wilder Steamship Company. In the next few years he was operating a fleet of steamers. To compete with Wilder, now that the monarchy was safely out of the transportation picture, came Captain Thomas B. Foster, with his Inter-Island Steam Navigation Company. Foster's first steamer was the *James Makee,* also built in San Francisco. Between the two companies more than thirteen steamers efficiently served the nation until long after the monarchy had vanished.

Like everything else they attempted, the haoles did it well. But while they prospered, the nation and its ambitious king floundered deeper into the mire of debt.

It was easy enough for Kalakaua to tumble into the arms of Walter Murray Gibson. A free-swinger and persuasive, Gibson talked plans and dreams equal or surpassing those of the king. Somehow, the way Gibson presented a project, he made it sound not only possible, but profitable. Much of Hawaii's emergence from insularity into modernity came through the plunging financial adventures of Gibson, and the willingness of a captive king to travel with him.

WALTER MURRAY GIBSON

—*Bernice P. Bishop Museum, Honolulu.*

The difficulty with Kalakaua was that he apparently was never quite able to distinguish outright fraud and quakery from the sensible and the genuine. November of 1879, in the very midst of his plan for the world tour, there came to Honolulu Celso Caesar Moreno. The king granted this Italian-American entrepreneur an audience, and was promptly captivated by Moreno's personality and glib tongue.

Moreno laid before the dark and flashing eyes of Kalakaua the prospectus and plans for instant communication with America and Asia, through trans-Pacific cable. He had, in addition, a new projection for trade with China in which the king and his government would profit endlessly. The king was promised, were Moreno taken into his government, that Hawaii would embark on a veritable millennium of prosperity.

So, on August 14, 1880, against the solemn advice of Premier Gibson and Bishop, the headstrong Kalakaua dismissed a loyal and able cabinet. As new minister of foreign affairs, and as virtual dictator, he installed the talking virtuoso, Celso Caesar Moreno.

Honolulu's citizenry were shocked by this capricious act. They were furious about the strange new cabinet's "grotesque unfitness." A mass meeting of citizens was held at Kaumakapili Church. Angry businessmen—haole and native—met at Bethel Church. Moreno faced this public stir of antagonism by rallying his supporters at the business and market section of the city. The new United States minister, General J. M. Comly, hoping to avert another bloody and tumultuous uprising, made hasty call upon the king.

Worried by public calumny, facing an angry and agitated American minister, Kalakaua at last caught the message. Reluctantly he dismissed Moreno. In appointing a new cabinet, the king again liberally sprinkled it with faithful and dependable Americans, and he retained the indispensable Gibson.

At last, on January 20, 1881, the genial and optimistic Kalakaua sailed from Honolulu on the long-anticipated tour of the world. Included with him, as advisers and traveling companions, were Charles H. Judd as chamberlain, and W. N. Armstrong as minister of state and commissioner of immigration. Included also was a small retinue of secretaries and servants. Her Royal Highness Liliuokalani had been publicly named as regent. She would manage the kingdom in her brother's absence.

Not all public reaction to the king's prolonged junket was enthusiastic, understanding, charitable, or kind. Many accused him of indulgence in another expensive and unnecessary whim. There were openly expressed fears that the unpredictable monarch might diplomatically suffocate the nation with ill-advised treaties, or that he might, when

he reached Washington, sell his kingdom to the highest bidder. Yet even
if Kalakaua had been overtly compelled, or had planned the trip strictly
to feed his vanity, he could not have chosen a more opportune time.
Nor could he have conducted it with more dignity and finesse. He became the first sovereign to tour the world. He was as regal, correctly
clad, and as polished in speech and manner as any royal host and
dignitary he encountered.

In every country he was greeted with highest honors. Entertain-
ments, troop reviews, royal balls and glittering decorations were tendered this handsome monarch out of a storybook kingdom. In return,
Kalakaua carried with him a supply of equally glittering Hawaiian
decorations, which he graciously pinned and presented to his hosts from
the nations of the world. In all his hedonistic, carefree life, he had never
known a happier time. The impression he made on governmental peers
throughout the world was most excellent and sympathetic. No small
nation ever had a better salesman.

On October 29, 1881, the king returned from his triumphal tour—
to a public welcome of bands, music and martial parade unparalleled
in Honolulu's history. As regent in his absence, Liliuokalani was relieved and happy to see her brother's return.

Her brief reign in his absence had been a troubled one. It had been
no easy task to fend off and placate the haole sycophants and opportunists who clung about the king and his official favor like flies at a
cane press. In March, five tramp ships, loaded with a fair share of the
4,400 Chinese immigrants Armstrong had arranged as consignment for
plantation labor, had put into Honolulu. An unwanted part of the importation had been the smallpox that had come with the Asiatics.
Hawaiians, remembering the fatal epidemic of 1853, were frightened
into hysterics by this second incursion of the dreaded disease.

Princess Liliuokalani, as regent, had made immediate call on the
king's ministers to take every measure necessary to stop the inroads of
a sickness almost invariably fatal to Hawaiian natives. Even with
prompt medical control and ruthless quarantine the scourge again
spread through Oahu, with dreadful toll. By martialing every medical
man, with vaccination centers, the epidemic was confined to the island
of Oahu, and one district only of Kauai. But again Hawaii had made
another appalling count of her dead.

As if smallpox were not enough to harass the regency of Princess
Lil, Pele herself decided to chastise the big island of Hawaii. Never
in recollection had Mauna Loa gone on such a fiery rampage. For
months molten lava blasted out of the eastern flank of the volcano,
flowing to the sea in rivers of blistering heat and devastation. For weeks
the city of Hilo stood on the brink of imminent destruction while

Christians prayed, and natives called again upon the more sure and trustworthy kahunas and shamans to intercede with Pele before all was lost. The princess regent, as a true Hawaiian, went to Hilo to stand with her people in their intercession with the goddess of fire. By the time King Kalakaua returned from China, Siam, Europe, and America, Pele had heeded the cry of her own people. She had calmed her wrath. Hilo had been saved.

Upon his resumption of royal power, and Liliuokalani could again return to the quietness of private life and her music, Kalakaua had declared Walter Murray Gibson prime minister of all the realm. He had need of this dramatic and ingenious virtuoso with the noble countenance and gray beard. And Gibson's services had already earned him favor. Through his years of service in the legislature, Gibson had turned up a record of solid support for the king and the Hawaiian people. In his acquirance of the *Advertiser*, Gibson wielded a powerful voice in behalf of "Hawaii for Hawaiians." The newspaper was an oblique purchase through Fred Hayselden, son-in-law to Gibson, and husband of daughter Talula.

Kalakaua had spent a lot of money impressing the world's heads of states. He had, on personal account, borrowed heavily before leaving on the tour. He returned to find his kingdom in desperate financial plight. Only Gibson seemed to have ready and favorable answers to the national problem.

Iolani Palace, a magnificent structure of lacelike stone, was rushed to completion. Over it hung a colossal debt, and it still must be furnished with the taste and elegance to which the royal family was accustomed. Other building programs had swallowed the returns from public taxes, crown leaseholds and sugar royalties, as fast as they could be gathered by the hard-pressed treasury officials. Unabashed and unshaken by these facts, the exuberant and enterprising Gibson, as expected, announced plans for a new prosperity.

First he repealed the liquor prohibitions which the missionaries and old Queen Kaahumanu had saddled upon the people. Liquor would be government taxed. Soon every grog shop in town bore welcome signs for the natives so long denied. Whorehouses could now operate openly in the waterfront districts of Honolulu, Lahaina, Hilo and Kailua. Under crown levy, of course.

But that was only Gibson's starter. Wizard of finance though he was, and adequate match for the free-spending Kalakaua, Gibson could not turn the tax money, honestly or ignobly gathered, into the treasury fast enough to satisfy the needs of both government and an extravagant and theatric monarch. Necessity dictated borrowing. Once again Claus Spreckels, already holding Kalakaua captive in debt, offered Gibson and the king a loan of $2,000,000—at six per cent interest.

But Gibson went further. He authorized Spreckels to use a million dollars of the borrowed money to mint and print in San Francisco a complete monetary system for his satrapy in the islands. It proved a brilliant piece of teamwork. Monetization gave Premier Gibson the cash he needed. It tendered to Spreckels an instant profit of more than $100,000. And it gave a tremendous lift to the king's vanity.

Before Kalakaua's departure on the world tour, Gibson had personally tended to another kingly whim. Royal decorations were needed —to confer on kings, emperors and presidents, in exchange for the be-ribboned marks of honor Kalakaua might be expected to receive as King of Hawaii. Gibson had gotten the medals in time—they had been cast in San Francisco—and they were beautiful. Conspicuous, dazzling, artistic were the spangled Greek cross, star and crown motif of the royal baubles. Largest was the medal of the Order of Kalakaua. The Order of Kapiolani was a dainty and beautiful cluster hanging from a royal crown. The Order of the Star of Oceania was smaller, but no less impressive. Every important state leader or monarch whom Kalakaua visited could add one or more of these decorations from paradise to his collection.

The new money, when it arrived from America, was no less impressive. It started with an hundred dollar bill, as beautiful in design and execution as the fragrant, green islands themselves. The one dollar silver coin had a sideview likeness of the king, with "Kalakaua I, King of Hawaii," wrapped around it. The reverse depicting the Hawaiian royal seal, was worded in pure Hawaiian, and its value designated as "Akahi Dala." The half dollar, the quarter, and the dime, were similarly engraved, and just as attractive. It was the five cent piece which raised the ire of the natives, and caused them to shun this governmental offering. In minting it, some idiot in San Francisco had given it the hated haole inscription of "Kalakaua, King of Sandwich Islands."

Postage stamps, bearing the king's and queen's likeness, which Gibson likewise ordered from the United States, put the final touch of modernity to the "reborn" nation. They were as attractive and artistic as the medals and the money.

It was fitting that such a nation honor its past, so Gibson—with Kalakaua's full approval—ordered a statue of Kamehameha the Great. It was designed by the eminent American sculptor T. R. Gould, and was bronze-cast in Italy. It would be placed, forever mindful, in front of the new and beautiful Aliiolani Hale, or government office building.

Plans were set for reception and unveilment of the bronze likeness—but on its long journey to Hawaii, the ship bearing it sank near the Falkland Islands. Undaunted, Gibson ordered a duplicate cast of the heroic memento. And on February 14, 1883, this second edition of Kamehameha I was duly unveiled in Honolulu.

To commemorate this event King Kalakaua ordered two weeks of public festivity, replete with picnics, parades, military marching, concerts by the Royal Hawaiian Band, and culminating in a grand and expensive luau, underwritten by the king, and with the public as his guests.

The original statue of the Great Kamehameha was later retrieved from the bottom of the sea, and now stands on the sea side of Kohala. But the expected prosperity, predicted by Gibson, was never brought up from its own ocean of debt.

VI

WITH the Hawaiian nation pointed toward modernity, Kalakaua's wants for it were insatiable. In history's all too familiar repetition, the first necessity was a real army to replace the ragtag ensemble of previous rulers. Hawaiian men made natural soldiers, bold and fearless, and those bearing Alii strain were six feet tall and over. They accepted a national militia with alacrity. And the royal guard of Iolani Palace was increased to five companies, uniformed as the king had studiously observed in London, and precision marched to the new and resurgent island music, in the tonal brass of the Royal Hawaiian Band.

Kalakaua's navy was not quite so flashy, or as useful. The *Kaimiloa*, a decrepit copra ship of 170 tons was purchased by the king for his government, at a bargain price of $20,000. She was a three-master for sailing, with a one-stack boiler and propeller to keep her moving when the trade winds failed. The boys' reformatory school furnished her with able seamen. Her officers, more experienced, were drawn from Honolulu's and Lahaina's waterfront haunts. It cost more than $50,000 to fit the *Kaimiloa* up for war.

Unabashedly Gibson now inflamed the king with a new dream. It would be "The Empire of Oceania," with Kalakaua, of course, heading this farflung kingdom of the sea. Gibson, in 1883, had already announced the new doctrine of Hawaii's expansion—"Primacy of the Pacific." Kalakaua, fresh from his world tour, had observed his brother sovereigns of Europe in expansionistic mood. He could not fail to see the advantages of being king over Oceania—or at least over all Polynesia.

KAMEHAMEHA STATUE, AS IT NOW STANDS IN FRONT
OF HISTORIC ALIIOLANI HALE, HONOLULU

By 1887 Kalakaua was ready to pursue the dream in earnest. To impress and intimidate King Malietoa and the warring chiefs of Samoa with Hawaii's new might, he dispatched his navy, the *Kaimiloa,* to these essential islands of his projected Oceania. A traveling embassy, to sit and function at various ports, was headed by John Bush, as envoy extraordinary, and Henry Poor, as legation secretary.

The uniforms of Hawaii's "diplomats" were the equal of anything ever witnessed at the court of St. James. The flashy and determined legation, installed aboard ship, were charged with the responsibility of inviting all Samoa's warring chiefs into the new "political confederation." With expected initial success, they were to similarly approach all other island governments. On the *Kaimiloa,* in council houses, and huts of jungle thatch, they began holding conference with King Malietoa, and enough rival monarchs and chiefs to baffle anyone but a Polynesian.

It was the mighty Bismark, in far off Berlin, who yanked the kapa mat from under Kalakaua's aspirations. His roars over this unwarranted intrusion into Germany's colonial preserve was heard throughout Europe. When Washington began receiving Bismark's angry tirades, the American state department took up the cudgel. Kalakaua was ordered to cease and desist from all inflammatory acts in other island territories.

Fearing an American confrontation far more than a German one, Kalakaua was finally forced to watch the crumble of his dream of might and power. With sadness and utmost reluctance he brought the *Kaimiloa* and his haole dominated legation back to Honolulu.

Kalakaua's compulsion for aggrandizement, and his sedulous copying of the glitter and pomp of Britain's royal circle, were problems that worried his ministers, his treasury, and the haole taxpayers who were footing the bill. He seemed obsessed with the necessity of making his court the equal of anything he had observed among the older, richer nations of the earth.

To his ministers and closest advisers he constantly deplored the fact that his election to kingship had been humbly and stormily accomplished, and without the fanfare of the Kamehamehas. After nine years of brooding over the slight, he ordered a lavish—though late—coronation for himself and the new dynasty he had founded. In explanation he claimed that he wanted to heal the wounds of his troublous inauguration, and to "awaken in the people a national pride."

A special domed and louvered pavilion was erected in front of the main entrance of his freshly new Iolani Palace. On February 12, 1883, within this pavilion, and witnessed by government officials, high Alii, foreign diplomats, and eight thousand less opulent spectators, Kalakaua

and Kapiolani were formally crowned King and Queen of Hawaii. The Reverend Alexander Mackintosh, after prayerfully blessing the event, lifted the twin crowns, both of fine gold bejeweled, both fashioned for the purpose in England, on the heads of Kalakaua and Kapiolani.

The royal pair had been dressed for the spectacle in regality and magnificence—Kalakaua in the white uniform of the King's Guard, with white helmet, and plume of red, white and blue, and enough gold braid and medals to dazzle everyone from attache to peasant; Kapiolani, her Alii figure secure in white satin, priceless lace overlay, and an eight-foot train of satin and ermine. Not for this coronation the traditional feathered cape and head-piece.

Then the Royal Hawaiian Band, and a special choir of matched voices, topped the event with a new and beautiful composition "Cry Out, O Isles with Joy!"

It was in the new throne room of Iolani Palace, before high and special audience, that Kalakaua more traditionally joined past with present. Here he accepted the precious and beautiful feather coat of Kamehameha the Great, the ancient white feather *kahili* of Pili, the *pulo'ulo'u* symbol of rulership, and *lei niho palaoa* of his Alii ancestors. Then, with even more pride, he received the standard regalia of the world's monarchies—the sword, the ring and the scepter. Public festivities to honor the belated coronation lasted two weeks—with luaus, parades, hula dancing, and fireworks—all a drain on Hawaii's battered treasury.

On November 16, 1886, Kalakaua's fiftieth birthday—the "Taffy" of his intimates, and the "merry monarch" of the people—honored the event with a jubilee celebration that topped all others. Again Honolulu was treated to an orgy of presentation ceremonies, military spectacles, parades, illuminations, fireworks, public feasts, and unbridled hula.

Taxpayers, especially the foreign-born taxpayers, were by now protesting the king's extravagance with enough noise to be heard even at Iolani Palace. Spreckels had managed, by his series of shrewdly placed loans, to thoroughly trap Gibson, political cohorts, and finally a resentful king. Whatever Spreckels now wanted by way of favor or concession was his—immediate and undenied. Few indeed were the incor-

◁ KING KALAKAUA AND HIS STAFF, ON STEPS OF THE ROYAL PALACE

(Left to right), J. H. Boyd, Curtis P. Iaukea, C. H. Judd, E. W. Purvis, King Kalakaua, G. W. Macfarlane, Gov. J. O. Dominis, A. B. Haley, J. D. Holt, Jr., Antone Rosa.

—Photo, Bernice P. Bishop Museum, Honolulu.

ruptibles who dared stand up to Premier Gibson and the Spreckels-backed faction.

Death was fast making inroads on the last little coterie of great Hawaiians. Bernice Pauahi Bishop, the last of the Kamehamehas, died October 16, 1884. Queen Emma, a thorn in the flesh of Kalakaua and his family, died a year later, April 25, 1885. On February 2, 1887, it was the turn of Princess Miriam Likelike Cleghorn to go. Her daughter, Princess Kaiulani—the only child heir born to Kalakaua's dynasty, had been sent to Harrowden Hall, in London, to be educated by "conscientious Christian ladies" in the high and special life which was to be hers.

While Kalakaua, through his own extravagance, and through the events of destiny over which he had no control, was being driven to the wall by debts and betrayals, his Queen Kapiolani, his sister, Princess Liliuokalani and their own entourage, were in England, as honored guests at Queen Victoria's empire-wide jubilee. It was probably well that these ladies, so deeply a part of Hawaii's final destiny, were not on hand for the last and ruthless breaking of a sovereign who had started his reign with such promise.

Outwardly Honolulu basked in the peace and beauty of a port of call whose romantic fame had already spread worldwide. Inwardly it seethed with hate, uncertainty, and enough intrigue to stuff a dozen books.

Kalakaua may have overspent, but he had beautified his cities with landmark structures that would last far beyond his day. From the stone filigree of Iolani Palace's wide verandas, the lonely and worried monarch could look out across the green and spacious acres of the palace grounds to a city that Kamehameha Paiea would never have recognized. It now had mule-drawn tramcars on its streets. From a comfortable porch chair the king's gaze could sweep across the guard area of his dwelling, to the stately new concert hall—out beyond that to the line of busy ships, Kalakaua's ever-poular boathouse, and the lighthouse that marked the harbor entrance. He would have liked to have been known as a man of the sea. It was in his blood. But in that he had not altogether failed.

Where he had really failed was falling into the trap so enticingly spread by the foreigners. Once in, not even a king could squirm himself out—except in chunks ripped and severed off by merciless barbs of the entrapment. Appeasement and placation had been his mistake. The way haoles offered help, and the ease with which they made it available—that was the bait. Once he'd become their quarry, the friendly faces were no more. Kings had been assassinated for lesser burdens than those with which he was saddled.

He had probably listened too willingly and too often to Gibson. And yet the loyally pro-Hawaiian Gibson had been the one needed crutch to his own ambitions and his own weakness. From the beginning, and to bring Hawaii into the modernity every chief craved, he and his nation had needed money. Earning money, creating money, lending money were haole specialties. The ingenuity and endless artistry of Gibson in tapping coffers of the foreigners were the very gifts and skills Kalakaua considered essential for the good of country and as aid to himself.

What he had not anticipated was the corruption and greed of his ministers, his legislators, of an hundred other public servants down to the tax collectors and customs agents at the wharves. There had been no public objection when the legislature granted Chinese brothel owners the right to sell opium on a flat cash basis of $30,000 per year. But why must it be the king's own agent, who in crafty and repeated sale of the same permit, had raised $125,000 on the side? That unfortunate swindle had blown hell across the pages of Honolulu's newspapers. Kalakaua had realized scarcely a token from this double-dealing with the Chinese. Righteous merchants accused him of taking it all. Now it seemed that everyone in his beautiful city was clamoring for his abdication.

While the queen and his sister regaled themselves in faraway England, as jubilee guests of Queen Victoria, affairs in paradise came to unexpected climax. The year 1887 had scarcely opened when four hundred of Honolulu's haole businessmen banded themselves together under the title of "The Hawaiian League." Every available gun and knife in the city was purchased or borrowed by the leaguers or their followers, until armed haoles far outnumbered guards and militia. Worse, the league was headed by actual scions of the missionaries— Sanford Dole, Lorrin Thurston, W. R. Castle, and others. But the league proved anything but Christlike in the relentness and efficient way it moved against Hawaii's king.

First the Hawaiian League announced, in Honolulu's newspapers, that it intended to dethrone Kalakaua—and that it had the armed might to do so. Under the ubiquitous façade of the "Committee of Thirteen," the "Honolulu Rifles" were organized, each member provided with a gun, seventy-five rounds of ammunition, and marched to the chambers of the legislature. "This is not a meeting to kill natives," Colonel V. V. Ashford, their commanding officer, shouted from the platform. "We are after the king!" Quickly as King Kalakaua, Premier Gibson, and all their unholy allies were turned out of office, and banished, other speakers assured, Hawaii would either become a republic

**PRINCESS BERNICE PAUAHI BISHOP,
LAST OF THE KAMEHAMEHAS**

*This great and remarkable woman, married to an American, en-
dowed schools and institutions for her beloved Hawaiian people,
including the Bernice P. Bishop Museum. She died Oct. 16, 1884.*

—Photo, Bernice P. Bishop Museum, Honolulu.

in its own right—or the islands—all of them—would be presented to the United States of America.

The impact on Iolani Palace was as though a bomb had already been exploded. Realizing that the Hawaiian League was not bluffing, and completely unsure of the loyalty of his own troops and office holders, Kalakaua, alone, with his family across the sea, sweated out an ultimatum that could cost him his throne, and perhaps his life. On June 28, under the threat of armed insurrection, Kalakaua was forced to oust his premier of the realm, Walter Murray Gibson. Every hated member in the cabinet of this dapper, bearded man was turned out of office. All other officials whom the haole insurgents considered unpopular or unwanted were summarily removed from their posts.

For Kalakaua, it was a miserable capitulation. In return for this drastic housecleaning, he was allowed to keep his job as king. But the humiliation of the next two months was almost more than a proud man could bear. Under coercion and threat, the new cabinet—hand-picked by the League and a frightened legislature—were forced to scrap Hawaii's own constitution, and replace it with one more in tune with what the rebellious haoles considered the nation should have. Kalakaua, in accepting and signing Hawaii's new "bayonet constitution" in order to preserve his own skin and crown, suffered the most humiliating defeat of his life.

The great Gibson had become the target of universal hate and ridicule, but that was only prelude to what his fellow haoles had in store for him. Gibson's unpardonable crime had been his undeviating loyalty to the king, and the fact that in aiding and guarding Kalakaua through the stormy years, he had placed the fealty of his calling consistently ahead of the foreigners who claimed special privilege as vested right. His health gone, and reduced to a coughing skeleton by the endless toil and anxiety of his office, Walter Murray Gibson had already paid a price. But for his crime of endless loyalty to king and country, Premier Gibson, and his son-in-law, Fred H. Hayselden of Lanai, were seized by an armed mob composed of the "missionary party." They were prodded by the "Honolulu Rifles" at gunpoint down the streets of Honolulu to the wharves. Throughout the demeaning march their tormentors were in ugly mood, foul-mouthed, and anything but respectful of the gray-haired man who for years had occupied the second highest post in the nation.

One of the mob, a son of a missionary, could not wait to get "Old Gibson" to the waterfront. While his cohorts howled approval, he knocked off the premier's high hat, and endeavored to punch some of the dignity out of Gibson's pale and haggard face. Eventually the noisy

ONE OF KALAKAUA'S FIVE MILITARY COMPANIES, AND
BAND, AWAIT HIS REVIEW

Behind is Iolani Palace, built for Kalakaua, and completed in 1882.

—Photo, Bernice P. Bishop Museum, Honolulu.

mob shoved and dragged the two men to the harbor; to a warehouse on the wharf. Hanging there, conveniently, were two ropes, with nooses open and ready. Another of Honolulu's public figures, a man of widely known missionary ancestry, led out with the cry of "String them up!"

While the mob was dealing with Gibson and Hayselden, another group, led by one more son of America's missionaries, forcibly entered Gibson's home at Kapiolani Park, roped the single occupant of the house, Gibson's daughter Talula—Mrs. Hayselden. After threatening to also drag her through Honolulu's streets, they kept the woman helplessly tied while the intruders ransacked the Gibson home. When this mob finally departed, the terrorized Mrs. Hayselden was left alone to fret and wait for return of her menfolk. But the menfolk did not return.

Fortunately for Hawaii, Gibson and Hayselden were not hanged. Intervention of the British consul saved them before the nooses were irreparably tightened. But on that fateful and lawless July 5 of 1887, they were dragged around Honolulu until Gibson was able to escape his tormentors only by agreeing to banishment aboard the sugar ship *J. D. Spreckels,* bound for California. Not until the vessel had put to sea did the noisy mob disburse.

Though Walter Murray Gibson had narrowly escaped being lynched in Hawaii, he died soon after his arrival in San Francisco. At St. Mary's Hospital, the already sick man succumbed to the effects of his brutal treatment and public humiliation.

Walter Murray Gibson had vanished forever from Hawaii's strange lexicon of history, but Fred Hayselden was furious and stubborn enough to remain in Hawaii with his distraught wife. When Liliuokalani became queen, she would reward his loyalty by naming him sheriff of Lanai. But when it too became time for Hawaii's last sovereign to face the fire that had all but destroyed her brother, Hayselden was turned out of his humble office by a new crop of haole usurpers— on the specious charge of being "a friend of the queen."

Between 1883 and 1887, the reciprocity treaty had neither been terminated nor renewed by the United States. The Senate had, at first, been in mood to scrap it, but the state deparment, worried over Britain's and Germany's high interest in the Pacific, had insisted on keeping the vacuous treaty alive. Suddenly now, after Kalakaua had been ignobly driven to corner, the United States asked for renewal of the agreement. This time it formally demanded cession of Pearl Harbor to the United States. This time—insistently prodded by the reform cabinet—the chastened and worried king signed a new and changed state document.

The exuberant, fun loving, intelligent Taffy, who had so wanted to bring his kingdom and his people up to the lush and happy level of modernity had, instead, by his reckless and plunging efforts, brought himself and nation to very brink of the abyss. All of Hawaii's kings, himself included, had cherished the persistent dream of "Hawaii for Hawaiians." But now the pitiful remnants of a once great people had been shoved aside in favor of the greedy and raucous-voiced foreigners. He had not meant to be the means of their ignominious betrayal. That all this indeed happened, crushed the sensitive Kalakaua. For the remainder of his short life, the king was a changed and silent man.

VIII

THE REFORM CABINET snatched back the reins of government that assertedly had been usurped and misused by the king and his free-wheeling premier, Walter Murray Gibson. Iolani Palace, under the austerity budget of the economy-minded revolutionists, and a legislature packed with haole candidates of the new National Reform Party, was no longer the lively social center of Honolulu. The king, reacting to criticism and humiliation, was moody, withdrawn, and certainly not the uniformed and dashing figure of former days. In brooding sorrow, he now spent most of his time at his boathouse at the harbor, or at his more modest frame cottage at Waikiki. Queen Kapiolani came back from England to find her husband sick and aloof.

Lavish spender though he was, Gibson had been penurious and negligent about taking care of the financial demands of public education in Hawaii. Along with other titular honors, Gibson had been named as president of the board of education, but he had devoted small attention to this the most minor of all his jobs. Schoolhouses were in a state of disrepair. Teachers had left their posts because public money for their salaries had been siphoned by Gibson into maintaining the opulent façade of king, court, and crown schemes.

The reform cabinet was public-minded enough to name the faithful and conscientious Charles R. Bishop as new president of the board of education. The board's equally new inspector was English-born Alatau Atkinson. These men went swiftly and creditably to work. They ordered immediate repair of old schoolhouses; they built new ones; they raised teacher's salaries; they hired new educators from America. Native and foreign children were soon back in classes.

The three Hawaiian youths Kalakaua had sent to Italy for special education at state expense, were ordered home, and their lush and promising scholarships cancelled. Instead of being cultured heroes upon their return to Honolulu, they found themselves snubbed and neglected by the new crop of officials now running affairs.

One of the youths, Robert Kalani-Hiapo Wilcox—born of American father and Hawaiian mother—had spent six years in Italy, where he graduated in engineering and military science from the Royal Military Academy at Turin. There he had married Gina, daughter of Baron Lorenzo Sobrere, and had hoped to return to a place high in Hawaiian government. Summoned back to rejection and virtual disgrace, Robert Wilcox laid bitter plans for revenge. Heading a secret group of young revolutionaries—150 armed and reckless men—he made one brave and foolhardy attempt to overthrow the reform government that had throttled and humiliated his beloved king. But the men in power, being smart and clever revolutionaries themselves, crushed the Wilcox revolt in a single day. Unhesitatingly they jailed this fiery protégé of Kalakau.

In 1888 the famed author, Robert Louis Stevenson, after a long visit in the Marquesas, settled down at Waikiki for a six months' try at recouping his health under the mild skies of Hawaii. He, like so many before him, was seeking the old, idyllic Polynesia—but, along with the search, he was burdened with the frantic necessity of ridding himself of the tuberculosis which had clutched itself upon him. His explanation for choice of the Pacific Islands as a place to finish out one's life was that he was forsaking "the dingy, ungentlemanly business" of civilization in favor of the simple, healthful beauty he had found throughout Polynesia.

While at Waikiki the great writer not only completed his book *The Master of Ballantrae*, but discovered King Kalakaua and his family. Out of it came a true and lasting friendship. Stevenson was entranced with the brilliant, artistic king, and the king's amazingly gifted sister, Princess Liliuokalani. Since the royal family spent more time now at the Waikiki beach house and harbor boathouse than they did at the opulent new palace, Stevenson and his family not only were neighborly visitors but hosted luaus and informal parties for one another at Waikiki, or at Honolulu's Hawaiian Hotel. When Robert Louis Stevenson finally set sail for Samoa—and his own rendezvous with death on another Pacific island—it was the last time he ever saw his good friend, Kalakaua.

The equally ill, and far more discouraged King of Hawaii, likewise sought a voyage in quest of health and peace of mind. And, like the writer, it too was destined to end in death.

On November 25, 1890, Rear-Admiral George Brown prevailed upon the ailing and despondent king to come aboard his flagship the *U.S.S. Charleston* and, as his guest, and America's guest, take the sea voyage to California and back. The recuperative rest, it was suggested, would do the king great benefit. And the public acclaim Kalakaua had experienced on his previous visit, would be like restoration's tonic to the dispirited monarch.

It is significant that Kalakaua went aboard the *Charleston* without bands and without public fanfare. Instead of gaudy uniform and gold braid, he wore a straw sun-hat, civilian coat of black, and white sailor's trousers. For a king, his retinue was absurdly small. He carried only a modest store of cash — Hawaiian money, with his face stamped thereon—certainly not enough for lavish public display. There were no cartons of medals of the "Order of Kalakaua," the "Order of Kapiolani" or his ill-starred "Order of the Star of Oceania." Pinning ceremonies on this trip would be few, if any. From his California visit Kalakaua asked only rest and healing. But once again in America, he found himself still tremendously popular. Invitations to social functions came from every part of the state.

There were few of these social affairs that he could physically manage. The years of easy living, and the terror of political upheaval, had taken their toll. On January 20, 1891, in San Francisco's Palace Hotel, Kalakaua "the merry monarch" unmerrily turned his dusky face to the wall and died. Dr. Woods of the *Charleston* attributed his death to Bright's disease. Among those at his deathbed were Admiral George Brown, Charles R. Bishop, and Claus Spreckels.

The *Charleston*, true to Admiral Brown's promise, brought the king back to his Hawaii. Honolulu had already arrayed itself in welcoming bunting for a happier return. When the people learned that a casket was aboard the ship, rather than their once lively king, the weeping natives hastily changed the gay streamers to mourning crepe. "Nalohia ka Makua" the people cried in Honolulu's streets, and on up the concourse to Iolani Palace. "Gone is the Father! Gone is the Father!"

PART SIX

Queen Liliuokalani
"Aloha Oe" to the Hawaiian Monarchy

I

IF, IN DEATH, Kalakaua were somehow able to view his "putting away," he would not have been displeased. The most somber, shocking portion would have been the simple military escort of the casket from the hold of the *Charleston* to Iolani Palace. American sailors and marines led and followed the caisson up the streets, the ship's band supplying the brassy dirge to this, the second Hawaiian king to come home in a box.

But after Hawaii's initial shock, the Polynesian mourning process gained momentum. In the luxurious throne room of the palace, scene of many glittering spectacles of the past, the king lay in state, surrounded by the tall *kahilis* testifying to his royal lineage, and those of the Alii families who had possessed sufficient virility to survive from the historical past to the turbulent present. The guards of honor were made up of chiefs, the sons of chiefs, the pick of the king's own troops, foreign diplomats, and the haoles who now had vested interest in the kingdom.

The mourning excesses of ancient times where, amid shrieks of sorrow, the chiefs knocked out their own teeth or mutilated their flesh to prove their grief, had no part in this Christian and decorous wake. There were sobs from friends and relatives, and special plush seats about the ornate rosewood coffin for those of royal rank to sniffle and whisper about His Majesty's sudden and unexpected demise. The grief naturally was heaviest among those who had grown up with Taffy and remembered him back to the time when he was Honolulu's amiable bon vivant, or those who had loaned him money as a king, and now had no hope of posthumously collecting their debts. The most truly sad of all was Kapiolani, his queen, and Liliuokalani, his sister—both stately, magnificent women; both honestly grieving because in Kalakaua's death they had lost a loved one.

In death, the king was back in uniform. And, as in life, no man ever filled one more fittingly, or more regally. At his side were his sword and scepter. Across the tunic of his rich blue livery flowed the gold braid, and the array of medals and decorations he had garnered from nations across the earth. Over the coffin, symbol of everlasting right to reign, lay the gorgeous feather cape that Kamehameha the Great had worn before his people.

When it came time for interment, the Royal Hawaiian Band was followed by the king's own troops from Iolani barracks. Two hundred of Honolulu's citizenry—native and haole—formed the double line to draw the catafalque from palace to royal mausoleum. Between these twin roped lines walked the mourners of the royal family, the governmental ministers, and those high enough in acceptance to be included in the queen's invitational list. No longer were there prostrations and obsequies at sight of an Alii death march. It had taken less than a century to educate the masses out of the old ways. Now the thousands passively lined Honolulu's streets and sidewalks as the royal band, the American naval band, Hawaiian troops, American sailors, and the last of the Alii, walked Kalakaua to his grave.

But in most ways it was a splendid show. No king, not even Kalakaua, could have asked for more.

II

Sudden as was the national bereavement, Kalakaua went with no uncertainty of succession. He had already named the last surviving member of his family, Liliuokalani, as heir-apparent. There was no necessity to submit the question to popular vote. Even as the funeral progressed, the cabinet and the legislature had unanimously confirmed Liliuokalani as sovereign of all Hawaii. And one of the first responses the new queen made was to name Princess Kaiulani as her own heir-apparent. The beautiful Kaiulani, daughter of Likelike, was being schooled in England, but no matter, even this moot question of royal succession had been quickly and tidily arranged.

Unlike the stormy uprisings at the time of Kalakaua's accession, there was no sign of organized popular opposition to the new queen. Naturally, as with any change of government, there were conjectures and apprehensions, voiced and written. But, in general, the foreigners— irrespective of their vested interest in Hawaii—raised no objection whatever to "Queen Lil" as the new monarch. The native population, with whom she was already popular, rendered unquestioned fealty. Foreigners, remembering that her brother had been putty in their hands, and, knowing that the new queen was married to the son of an American sea captain and trader, leaned back and waited for another round of national plunder.

Honolulu newspapers supinely reflected the haole attitude toward Her Majesty. The new queen was described to readership of the *Pacific Commercial Advertiser* as "a lady of culture and shrewd observation, with abundant good sense." In ascending the throne of the Kamehamehas she had "every presumption of a long, peaceable and happy reign . . . with the sanction of the constitution [meaning the new 'bayonet constitution'] and with the approval of her people and with a plainly marked path of duty stretched before her. To reign, and not to govern . . . the duty of a modern constitutional sovereign."

In his popular Honolulu publication, *The Friend*, Sereno E. Bishop commented: "Our good Queen Liliuokalani takes the throne under circumstances most favorable, if wisely used, for a happy and prosperous reign. She enjoys in a high degree the affection of her Hawaiian subjects, and their confidence in her attachment to their welfare. Her gentle and gracious demeanor, her good sense, and her fine culture, have also commanded the high regard of the foreign community . . ."

General thinking of the haole population was revealed by the same article in *The Friend:* "It can hardly be doubted by any one that this kingdom is advancing through a period of transition from monarchy to government by the people. The nation is slowly ripening for the ultimate change."

From far-away San Francisco, Claus Spreckels was quoted in a newspaper interview as saying that Hawaii's new queen "is a shrewd, sensible woman [who] understands the conditions upon which she is permitted to rule . . . Of course, as is natural, she may wish to assist her friends, but she will never go the length of setting up her will against the constitution . . ."

Theophilus H. Davies, guardian of Princess Kaiulani during her stay at school in England, sized up the new female sovereign to a member of the British Foreign Office: "The new queen . . . has always mixed freely in society in Honolulu, is dignified and sensible, and endowed with more ability and principle than her late brother, who was deficient in both . . . I believe that Hawaiian interests [British] are much safer under the present sovereign than they have been under either of the last two kings . . . Queen Emma, Mrs. Bishop, and now Queen Liliuokalani, have always shewn leanings to England, and I know that it is because they trust England's loyalty to the independence of Hawaii . . ."

Support of the native population came even more willingly, and with no price tags attached. Natives had no means of putting their love and respect into widely circulated print. As plain Lydia Paki, as princess, as regent, this wise and beloved woman had traveled the islands and associated with her own. Instinctively Hawaiians knew and trusted that their queen would never place political expediency ahead of the rights and obligations toward her own race. The foreigners—especially the American capitalists and the firmly entrenched and avaricious generation born of the missionary incursion—had, after wheedling high privilege out of her brother, destroyed him as a sovereign. In Liliuokalani, the natives uncannily sensed, there would be no betrayal.

The *Charleston* had glided into Honolulu harbor, bearing the remains of King Kalakaua—her yards cock-billed, in token of mourning. Before Kalakaua could be removed to the palace, and long before his burial, the "reform" cabinet demanded the appearance of Liliuokalani before them. When she acceded to this unprecedented command, they insisted she take immediate oath of office as queen, and in their presence. Unnerved by events, she remonstrated, and begged for time to collect her shattered composure. But the haole justices of Hawaii's supreme court, and the haole cabinet ministers, were adamant. Without realizing the consequences, or the effrontery of the dead king's political advisers, Liliuokalani reluctantly bowed to the demands. Frightened and coerced, she took her oath of office in chambered privacy. By act and token she had accepted and submitted to that same "bayonet constitution" that had brought humiliation and ultimate death to her brother.

With this matter taken care of, the star court was dissolved, and all members of cabinet and privy council adjourned to the Blue Room, to offer their finely balanced words of congratulations and condolences to Hawaii's new queen. The first in line was Chief Justice Judd, who followed his own voiced joy and sadness with the whispered suggestion that "Should any of the members of your cabinet propose anything to you, say 'yes.'" Before the queen could answer the syrupy riddle proposed by this son of a missionary, and a man long tagged in her chamber of hate, he had moved on, to make room for the others in line to complete their bows, and say their pieces.

Long after the privy council and guests had departed, the cabinet members lingered on—until they were alone with the hapless queen. John A. Cummins, minister of foreign affairs, came quickly and bluntly to point. He reminded Her Majesty that, as a cabinet, he and his fellow members were to remain in office. Godfrey Brown, minister of finance, rushed to his aid with the explanation that under the new regime, no changes could be made in the cabinet except by act of legislature. To this Arthur P. Peterson, attorney-general, suggested that the queen should understand the situation, and accept it.

The queen did understand the situation—far more than these haoles realized. And she did not accept it. She'd grown weary of being pushed around. With fire in her dark eyes, but with the graciousness with which she was adept, she informed the cabinet that she had no intention of discussing the "situation," or anything further pertaining to it, until after the funeral of the King of Hawaii.

Promptly, on the day following final obsequies, the cabinet called a meeting to force royal approval of their job perpetuation. One hour before the ministers were to arrive at Iolani Palace, Mr. Cummins, minister of foreign affairs, was on hand, and demanding audience with the queen. His first question was aimed at finding out the plans and purposes of Her Majesty in regard to the impending meeting. The queen's answer was simple and quick. She wished his resignation as minister. In return for his resignation, she offered the post so long held by her husband, General John O. Dominis, as governor of Oahu. His answer to the governorship offer was an immediate "no." He preferred to remain in the cabinet. When the queen asked him as to whether any others of the cabinet expected to remain in power, he smugly replied that he had no doubt of it.

The meeting was duly convened. The queen opened it with a query as to the business of the day. The attorney-general demanded that the queen sign the assembled ministers' commissions without delay, so that they might get on with the duties of their offices.

"But, gentlemen," the queen replied, "I expect you to send in your resignations before I can act."

Faced with emphatic demurrence, the queen explained her position. If they were *now* cabinet ministers, why should they appeal to her to appoint them to the positions they already claimed to occupy? "If you do not resign, I do not see how I can issue you new commissions."

It was totally unexpected any sister of Kalakaua would have insight and knowledge enough to fight on points of law and order. In fact they had not anticipated she would fight them on any issue. All they wanted was her royal signature. Now they were sitting perplexed and uncertain before Liliuokalani, the "gentle and loving queen."

She prodded them—never relinquishing the pressure. Since they would not, or could not, agree with her in the matter, it was her suggestion that the affair be referred to the Supreme Court for interpretation and decision. To this, Chief Justice Judd was reluctantly forced to agree.

After days of anxiety and worry to the queen, it was finally announced by the same chief justice, that a decision had been found in her favor. The court had concurred that the commissions of present members of the cabinet truly had expired with death of the king. That neither queen nor legislature could rightfully appoint anyone to office until that post was officially declared vacant.

Liliuokalani had not been bluffed. And, to her, it was a relief to turn the "reformers" out of office. Even a "constitutional" sovereign ought to have the right to choose one's own advisers. The haoles were mystified and worried about this new and "rebellious" trait in Queen Lil.

But she had come a great distance from her giddy girlhood in Honolulu. She had read much. She had observed much. She knew a lot more about her nation than did the haoles. She was cognizant of its tragedies, its failures, its lost opportunities. She knew its history, its unique culture, and the kind and generous hearts of its people. Her growing up had been a long and sometimes painful experience. To Hawaii she wanted only to be a good and understanding mother.

III

IN GIRLHOOD she was known as Lydia Paki because her foster-mother, Konia (a granddaughter of Kamehameha I) was married to High Chief Paki. The natural daughter of Paki and Konia was Bernice Pauahi, the last high chiefess of the Kamehameha dynasty. Bernice had been Lydia's foster-sister. In the warmth of Polynesian kinship they had grown up as true sisters. Lydia's actual father was Kapaakea, and her true mother was Keohokalole—the blood parents also of King David Kalakaua, and Princess Likelike, who also claimed separate foster-parents. The real mother of the royal family had also filled an Alii function as one of the fifteen counselors to Kamehameha III who, in 1840, gave the first written constitution to the Hawaiian people. Their right to rule had been made abundantly clear.

At four years of age Lydia had been enrolled in the Royal School. This school, conducted by Mr. and Mrs. Amos S. Cooke, missionaries, besides grounding its high Alii crop in Christian fundamentals, had given Lydia a chance to know her brothers and sister as something more than strangers. Too, it had served as host to that coterie of youngsters who would grow up into the vital and turbulent history of the Hawaiian nation. In the school were four children of Kinau, daughter of Kamehameha I—Moses, Lot (Kamehameha V), Alexander Liholiho (Kamehameha IV), and Victoria. Another future king was William

Lunalilo. There was Bernice Pauahi, highest ranking princess, and foster-sister to Lydia. And Lydia's family was represented by herself, Kalakaua, and Leleiohoku—two of these three destined to ascend the throne. Here also, among a dozen other high Alii offspring, was Emma Rooke, who married the tragic Kamehameha IV, to become the endless and uncomfortable thorn in the path of Kalakaua and Lydia.

Eventually Mr. Amos Cooke severed all connections with his missionary board, and gave up the most famous school in Hawaiian history, to go into the mercantile world of Honolulu. Like that of so many other ex-missionaries, his firm of Castle & Cooke prospered. There was more money to be had in selling goods for profit than in trying to cram learning and the word of God into the heads of the sons and daughters of Hawaii's chiefs. From Cooke's boarding school, Lydia was handed over to the new academy of Rev. Mr. Beckwith—another Christian institution headed by an American missionary.

But from the beginning, in every classroom she ever attended, Lydia proved a lively, alert youngster of superior intelligence. The acquirance of knowledge became for her an obsession that lasted to the end of her days. In music she could, in her earliest years, read notes, and transcribe tones to notes. She sang in, and led, the Kawaiahao Church choir. Song welled out of her soul—original, brilliant, old and new.

Her foster-sister Bernice was an entirely different personality. Her beauty became the talk of all Hawaii. She was courted by wealth and royalty, from the time she was fifteen years of age. Finally betrothed to Prince Lot, grandson of Kamehameha the Great, she blithely jilted a future king to marry, in her eighteenth year, the handsome American, Charles R. Bishop. The rejected and saddened Lot went into his reign as Kamehameha V, and Bernice sidestepped her rights to the throne. But marriage to her haole proved an happy one.

Bernice moved from the big house of Paki and Konia to Bishop's cottage on Alakea Street. Lydia continued to live at the Paki home (later known to Honolulu as the Arlington Hotel), until the wheel of fate drastically changed the direction of her life.

But, like her foster-sister, Lydia herself became engaged to a future king—Prince William Lunalilo. In this short betrothal she had lively competition with the Princess Victoria. The off-again-on-again proclivities of the wild and dashing Prince Bill finally decided the issue with the proud Lydia Paki—that and his fondness for ardent spirits. In the end, Prince Bill failed to make the grade even with Victoria. As king, he, like Lot, entered his reign as a bachelor.

There were other and varied opportunities for royal and Alii marriage which Lydia narrowly averted. But in the wings, waiting patiently for his chance on stage, stood the ever faithful John Owen Dominis. John was the son of a sea captain who, in his voyages around the Horn to Asia, had decided that Honolulu, most salubrious and beautiful of all ports of call, would be his home. He visioned profits in shipping to both China and California, by way of his own offices, and without the long and lonely months at sea. Captain John Dominis, shrewd in his appraisal, and successful in the ginseng traffic between China and New York, remained in Honolulu—and built himself an elegant home, known as Washington Place.

Ancestors of Dominis were entirely Italian. But he had married an American woman from Boston—a descendant in true-blue fashion from America's earliest English settlers. And to Washington Place, in the Pacific Islands, he brought his wife and son.

Lydia could not avoid the slender and reedy youngster who was later to be her husband and prince consort. John was enrolled in the Johnston Day School, in the building adjacent to the Royal School for privileged Hawaiians. Among the curious and obstreperous haole boys who climbed the brick wall separating the two institutions of learning, and who sat thereon to observe and heckle the Hawaiian pupils, was John Owen Dominis. The equally precocious Lydia fascinated the boy from Washington Place. And Lydia, seeing in his face the sensitivity and culture she so admired, liked John Dominis, Jr.

As the two youngsters grew into their separate maturities—Lydia into the increasingly glittering and lavish court circles, as an high-born prize among the Alii—and John Dominis among the favored haole fringe upon which the royal families so depended for advice and favors—they were never completely out of contact as friends and acquaintances. When Prince Lot, as military commander-in-chief to King Alexander, deemed it necessary to upgrade Hawaii's military, he commissioned young John Dominis a full general, and appointed him to his staff. In spite of the fact that John's more than average height, and willowy slenderness, gave him the appearance of a rather wan and sickly general, he was seldom again seen out of uniform.

A skin, pale and waxy, made John's abundantly thick black hair, burnsides, short cropped beard and carefully nurtured mustache, compellingly alert. It was a patrician, handsome head that peered out of the high collars of his uniforms. With plumed shako, shoulder boards of braided gold, sash and sword of his generalship, this young haole could not avoid being watched and sought after by the rising crop of *wahines* who enhanced the court of King Aleck. Dominis was too aesthetic and preoccupied to be considered dashing. But he wore his own brand of charm in his impeccable manners, thoughtfulness, and fund of useful knowledge.

When, in the second year of his reign as Kamehameha IV, Alexander married Emma Rooke, it was the greatest social event in Honolulu up to that time. Bridesmaids for the affair, at the great new Kawaiahao Church, were Princess Victoria, Lydia Paki, and Mary Pitman. Groomsmen were Prince Lot, Prince William, and David Kalakaua—all destined to walk across Hawaiian history as kings. A round of picnics, royal parties, luaus and balls filled the weeks after the marital solemnization. These affairs extended across Oahu, to which the traveling court joyously moved from place to place.

The king, in returning from Moanalua after one of these socials, was escorted by a noisy and carefree cavalcade of two hundred—horseback and in carriages. Riding with Lydia Paki was John Owen Dominis. A too exuberant horseman in the party somehow forced his mount between the animals of Lydia and John. The General lost both dignity and seat when his frightened mount pitched him off to the roadway. With a broken leg the young man somehow hauled himself back aboard his horse. And in an amazing display of grit and fortitude, he escorted his lady companion back to the Paki mansion.

But at Washington Place, when it became necessary for General Dominis to dismount from his saddle, it took two friends and a number of servants to lift him to the ground and carry him to his bed. By now the leg was so swollen that it was difficult to set the bone. And it was months before he could again pay attentive court to Lydia.

Emma Rooke had been Lydia Paki's adversary since school days. Now that she was Queen Emma, and even though Lydia had smilingly served as bridesmaid to the match, the enmity was never any the less. To begin with Lydia, along with a number of other Alii genealogists, were never sure that Emma possessed enough genetic mana to qualify her as bride to a king. On hearing of the intention of King Aleck to marry Emma Rooke, the king had been immediately waited on by a committee of high chiefs. They had wasted no time in begging the monarch to change his mind. When Aleck asked "Why should I?" they solemnly answered: "Because, Your Majesty, there is only one other equal to you in birth and rank—the adopted daughter of Paki." It was the king's angry rejection of this proposed match, and his abrupt ordering of the solicitous chiefs from his presence that forever rankled Lydia Paki. It had sorely wounded her pride.

Even when she herself was queen, Lydia continued to point out that Emma was descended only from a half-brother of Kaliopuu, the latter being only first cousin to Kamehameha the Great. Queen Emma lived a long life, but not quite long enough to see the feisty Lydia elevated to the throne. Had Emma done so, she would probably just as aptly reminded Lydia that she at least had *married* a king.

But Lydia remained an essential and decorative part of the court of Alexander and Emma. In 1859 she shared the royal entourage in its joyous excursion to the outer islands. Both Lydia and her foster-sister Bernice Pauahi were inseparably a part of the royal parties. The main point of interest, this trip, were the active volanoes so much a part of the land mass of Hawaii's big island.

She was also included in that more tragic royal excursion to Maui. There the happy and carefree party had been shocked by the act of the hot-tempered king. At Lahaina, over some unacceptable remark of his secretary, Henry A. Neilson, the king had shot and mortally wounded this trusted haole. The suffering and death of Neilson had been one of the tragedies that closed off Alexander's reign.

Lydia had observed that the equally tragic death of Aleck's only child, Albert Edward, Prince of Hawaii, followed as the final blow that unhinged his kingship, and sped the once buoyant and personable sovereign to his grave.

Through these giddy, exciting years, General John Owen Dominis had patiently waited out the time of Lydia's engagement to Prince Lunalilo. After that affair was shattered by Prince Bill's indiscretions, and after a couple of other of Lydia's Alii romances rose and fell, he doggedly pressed for her hand in marriage. The betrothal, no hurried thing, lasted two years. On September 16, 1862, Lydia married her haole. He took her to the Washington Place mansion, to share the big house with his widowed mother.

And then suddenly Lot was King of Hawaii—as Kamehameha V. As reward for long and loyal service, the bachelor king appointed General Dominis as governor of Oahu.

IV

WITH THE LAST living male of the Kamehameha dynasty sitting on the throne in non-productive bachelorhood, the presumptives with less definable claim to direct blood line moved tighter and closer into the royal circle, especially when the failing health became pronounced and noticeable with King Lot. Reticent about naming his own choice as heir-apparent, those chiefs most deeply concerned grew increasingly restive and apprehensive as King Kamehameha V grew ever closer to his inevitable time.

Lydia Paki Dominis watched with mixed feelings the phrenetic scramble for power as the choice of sovereign was thrown upon the people, the legislators, and the pressure groups who had special interests to appease. It was nothing like the old days, when the Alii themselves settled the problem of rulership in their own clearly defined ways. It angered her to witness the demeaning process of public election of a sovereign. The fact that the three active candidates were William Lunalilo, David Kalakaua, and Queen Emma—and that Prince Bill won the throne, and her brother David lost it in the election— were prime reasons for her dejection and disturbance.

She and her Governor Dominis stood among the royal select while William Lunalilo was crowned King of Hawaii. Lydia pondered the fact that had she married this man, instead of her faithful foreigner, she now would have been queen. But there were other compensations. Prince Bill's habits were so erratic—up to the very day of his election— that Charles R. Bishop, as family-appointed guardian, was forced to limit his personal allowance to twenty-five dollars a month, most or all of which went for whiskey. As to Queen Emma, her failure in the election process was perfectly agreeable to Lydia Paki Dominis.

The time of perturbation was small. Lunalilo's reign was short. As governor of Oahu, and general in Hawaii's little army, John Dominis had plenty of duties to fill the time. An ardent and dedicated Freemason, an haole activity strictly male, Lydia could only approve and not share. Another divisive fact to her life was Mrs. Dominis. The former New England socialite, of now faded beauty, refused to yield motherly dominance of her son to the wife John Jr. had brought to Washington Place. But Lydia had her music, which was her own haven of glory and comfort when life refused to yield to her will and direction.

With sudden death of Lunalilo, Hawaii was again torn apart with the necessity of electing and confirming a king. Since her brother, David Kalakaua and Queen Emma had strongest claims to succession, they were final candidates. This time Kalakaua won—handily and overwhelmingly—but the civil riots which followed were something new and fearful.

The followers of Queen Emma proved hard losers, and the queen herself never forgave the new family who had gained the highest and most coveted post in the nation. The bloody assault on the courthouse and legislators for sustaining the claim of Kalakaua, and the specter of foreign navies putting down native protestors was a dismal cloud for any king to face in his first days in office.

But, with her brother safely on the throne, no longer was she Lydia Paki Dominis. Her younger brother, William Pitt Leleiohoku, was a new and actual heir-presumptive. She was now, to the nation, Princess Liliuokalani; and her beautiful younger sister was now the Princess Likelike. King Kalakaua, and his Queen Kapiolani took up residence at the national palace, but Liliuokalani continued to live at Washington Place.

For a time it was wonder and joy. As a princess, Liliuokalani's every move was accepted with respect; with a new and delicious aura of worshipful interest and adulation. The happy musical circles which she and her brothers had shared became more stiff, formal, and custom laden. But her geniality, and her love of people, broke through the barriers, and Hawaiians adored her because she never let height destroy her perspective as a human.

But in time even the scintillating wonder of elevation to royalty became the accustomed thing, and commonplace. There were still worries, and there were myriad problems. Kalakaua's reign continued to be a troublous one. Her Royal Highness Liliuokalani watched with uneasiness and concern the ever-increasing swing of Kalakaua deeper into the orbit of the American opportunists. Taffy had always been respectful of her general knowledge and political acuity, and even now he occasionally consulted her in affairs of state.

He had inherited a world of pressure with the crown. American businessmen were once more talking annexation to the United States. Would be filibusters were surfacing with their panacea of revolution and new government. None of them seemed in the least disturbed that they were traitors; that they talked treason. The cry once again was for a reciprocity treaty with America. And the planters were beseeching king and ministers for the importation of foreign labor to work their acres and to supplant the dwindling native population.

Kalakaua's all-haole cabinet pleased everyone but his sister. Asked for advice, she spoke out against the sending of Allen and Carter to Washington to beg for reciprocity. When the king's diplomats failed, as she predicted they would, and Kalakaua announced his own intention of traveling to America—in the very first year of his reign— she tried to persuade him to remain at home and more deeply consider Hawaii as for Hawaiians. But the king, growing ever more important in his own eyes, was determined to show himself off to America.

So Kalakaua accepted passage on the American warship *Benicia* in November of 1874. To his sister the only sensible thing about it was inclusion, as adviser and privy member of his suite, of General John Dominis, her husband. The other companion, equal in power and responsibility, was Henry A. Peirce, United States minister to Hawaii. Crown Prince Leleiohoku was proclaimed regent during the king's absence.

While Kalakaua was feted and lionized in America, and especially in Washington, while he was gaining certainty for eventual American accession and the reciprocity treaty, his regent brother, and his popular and winsome sisters, were deep in their beloved music. Their time went mostly to this, and the social whirls of Honolulu.

The king returned—his mission an utter triumph. He was friend of the haoles. He was champion of the sugar interests. Behind him came Claus Spreckels and his counterparts of the money world to "invest" in Hawaiian plantations and water rights. It had taken only one year for Kalakaua to set the noose to his own shoulders. And all of it turned out exactly as his sister had predicted.

Another year, and the handsome and talented Prince Leleiohoku was dead. In midst of her grief, Liliuokalani was named heir-apparent to the throne of Hawaii—as her Royal Highness, the Princess Liliuokalani. In the usual manner, and in the old way, she and her now extensive retinue toured all the islands, to meet and talk to her people. Even the "Emmaites" in political persuasion met with her cordially, and vied with one another to make their dances and luaus worthy of a gracious princess of the realm. In getting close to this final remnant of a great culture—her own people—she smiled to their faces, because she loved them—she wept in her personal solitude, because of the same abiding concern.

In 1878 Princess Lil, for health reasons, and at the advice of her physician, made her first visit to the United States. She, and her ever faithful John Dominis embarked on the steamer *St. Paul,* and in nine days arrived at San Francisco. After touring the western part of the great nation that evoked such terror and wonder in the minds of native Hawaiians, and after a remarkable recovery of her health, the royal party returned to Honolulu on the steamer *Wilmington.*

In the same year the king, in private consultation with Liliuokalani, announced to his startled sister his intention of naming Charles H. Judd as his chamberlain. Worse, Judd was to be special agent for the management of crown lands—an office held efficiently and honestly by John Dominis since the time of Kamehameha V. The sister, knowing the invidious political maneuvering of this son of a missionary, and stung by the humiliation of such divestiture upon her husband, was indignant. As sop for this relinquishment to the king, Dominis would be appointed governor of Kauai, in addition to his governorship of Oahu.

Judd's elevation, at the sacrifice of John Dominis, was only the beginning of the long series of strange appointments Kalakaua would make that would eat away the sovereignty to which he had been trusted.

It started with Judd. It ended with Moreno, Gibson, and the "reform cabinet."

In 1881 came Kalakaua's dramatic tour of the world. In this, and his numerous other public demonstrations of pomp and power, Princess Lil had little criticism. Her objections were mainly concerned with the granting of power to haoles, at the expense of Hawaiians. That haoles were footing the bills for the king's displays of grandeur, seemed never to be the issue.

"In nothing has my brother been more grossly misjudged and even slandered by those whose interests he had at heart than in this journey," Liliuokalani later wrote of the world tour. "Probably he did have some love for travel, some sense of pleasure in visiting foreign lands . . . Why should he not have felt this interest? But the master motive for this enterprise was the good of the people of the Hawaiian Islands over whom he had been called to rule."

This time it was Her Highness who was appointed regent during Kalakaua's long absence from his nation.

While Kalakaua searched favor among the nations and rulers of the earth, the princess regent loyally and energetically tended to matters closest to home. She defended her brother against the carping and slander of taxpayers who resented his extravagance and ostentation. She saw no wrong in showing the good front of Hawaii to the world. Her resentment centered on the phase of the tour which most pleased the haole planters and industrialists—the search of the king for emigrant labor to fill the acute want occasioned by the dying out of the natives.

In Japan, China, India and Siam, word came of Kalakaua's talks with their kings and emperors in behalf of the planters and factory owners. Theory was that these nations could best furnish laborers because their climatic range was very similar to that of Hawaii. Other than being royally and regally entertained, Kalakaua was successful in selling his recruitment only to Japan and China. Siam and India never responded to the wholesale emigration of their nationals.

As regent, Princess Lil was confronted with unexpected problems. Kalakaua went from Asia on into Europe. But at home, along with the earliest shiploads of Chinese nationals came that second scourge of smallpox. The prompt and heroic battle the regent organized and led, saved the nation from another lethal tragedy.

And then came that unprecedented eruption of Mauna Loa. With the city of Hilo expecting momentary burial under the rivers of fiery lava, Princess Lil voyaged to the big island of Hawaii to be near her people in their travail. She, and that mighty Hawaiian, Princess Ruth, joined the natives in public prayers to God, and in more fundamental supplications and appeasement to the goddess Pele. When the laval holocaust stopped just short of Hilo, she joined with them in thanksgiving. Here on the big island Liliuokalani found the greatest concentration of pure Hawaiians—so far untainted by haole and Asiatic interbreeding, and not yet crowded out of their villages and off their land by the coolie importation of the planters.

In Kohala and Kau she found people still living and thinking as they had in the dear dead days of the first Kamehameha. She talked with them, listened to them, ate with them, and fondled their babies and their children. Her brother was known to consort too much with foreigners, but the people knew his royal sister to be all Hawaiian—true, pure and loyal. When the time came to return to Honolulu, they gave her their hearts, and they gave her their love.

Her major encounter while at Hilo was with the landholder—Samuel Parker. Parker, himself half Hawaiian, was raising beef cattle—from the wild animals delivered by Vancouver, and long kept kapu to natives by royal decree—and from the importation from America of improved beef strains. At first Parker had hired cowboys and vaqueros from America and Mexico—until he discovered that native Hawaiians, once they could master a horse, were even superior at the task. The princess regent, and her sister Princess Likelike, were lavishly feted at the home and table of the Honorable Samuel Parker. Later, when she became queen, Liliuokalani would name Parker to her cabinet.

On her return to Honolulu the princess regent was faced with accumulated responsibility. At Kinau Hale, she conferred the Order of Kalakaua on two distinguished members of the Roman Catholic Church—Hermann, the Bishop of Olba, and Father Damien, the leper priest of Molokai. A grimmer task, which haunted her for weeks, was the distasteful necessity of signing the warrant of execution for a convicted murderer. Not until magisterial pressure became unbearable could she bring herself to seal even a murderer's life in death.

The state trip around Oahu, which Kalakaua's cabinet had scheduled for the regent, was far more palatable. Princess Lil enjoyed mixing with the people. They invariably seemed happy with her presence.

On the Oahu circuit, with the Princess Likelike and her child-princess Kaiulani, and a gaggle of retainers and attendants, the royal party made it as far as Waimanalo. Here, at the estate of John A. Cummins, minister of foreign affairs, they were entertained as befitted royalty. They departed the lavish Cummins luau, and their carriages took the road to Maunavili and the country estate of Mr. and Mrs. J. H. Boyd. There the party remained overnight.

Next morning, as the happy group headed toward Kaneohe, the princess regent found herself pitched unceremoniously to the hard and unyielding roadway. Joseph Heleuhe, expert horseman, was in the driver's seat of Liliuokalani's carriage. A lead horse had tangled its reins in the bit of one of the other horses, and the frenzied animal soon had the carriage rolling downhill in a runaway. The princess was catapulted out of the seat with enough velocity to clear the wheels, but only to hard land between two rocks.

From the Boyd estate the unconscious and badly injured Liliuokalani was carried by stretcher all the way to Waimanalo. Urgent messages were dispatched to Honolulu, and to those who were still expecting to entertain the princess regent and her retinue. Carefully, tenderly, the injured woman was carried aboard the tiny steamer *Waimanalo* (owned by Mr. Cummins), and the craft made top speed for Honolulu.

It was nine p.m. before the steamer pulled into wharf. Waiting, solemn and anxious, were John Dominis, government officials, and a detachment of soldiers. Princess Lil was carefully placed in a light delivery wagon, and Hawaiian natives grabbed the long ropes to pull the vehicle. While Governor Dominis walked beside the wagon and his injured wife, the people silently and sadly hauled it toward Washington Square. Under full military escort, the strange procession moved through the night-darkened streets of Honolulu.

Medical examination revealed that her back had not been broken, as was feared, but internal injuries were such that it required many weeks, helplessly bedridden, before recovery slowly returned. Here, in the old way, with Alii bed watches divided around the clock, and with her *kahilis* rhythmically and endlessly waved over her, the princess regent battled her way back to health.

But she was still convalescing from the accident, and bedfast, when her regency ended, and Kalakaua returned. She rode in carriages and was carried in the olden manner, through the lavish ceremonies of Kalakaua's triumph. The city was decorated as never before. The new Iolani Palace was not yet finished, so King Kalakaua and his Queen Kapiolani temporarily occupied the more modest Hale Kinau. Here, though unexpectedly cramped for entertainment facilities, the king led a week of parties, parades, music, dancing and fireworks.

After the wild and noisy festivities of her brother's return, Liliuokalani finished out her convalescence in her own beach cottage at Waikiki. It had been a tumultuous year.

V

TO THE princess heir-apparent the gray-bearded and dapper Walter Murray Gibson never reached the ogreish stature of those other haole dictators—the planters and the newly rich sons of the once humble American missionaries. As premier, Gibson was obsessed with buildup of the monarchy to the pomp and regality it deserved. Since he always, somehow, managed to get money to do it, Liliuokalani had no criticism.

With the completion of the palace, in all its sugar-loaf beauty, with the coinage of Hawaii's own money, with the exciting glitter of newness upon Honolulu, the king decided to stage his official though belated coronation. Princess Lil voiced no objection to Gibson's turning the affair into a theatrical wonder.

Two crowns—of gold—studded with precious gems—were fashioned in England, along with a stately and ornate throne and golden scepter. A pavilion worthy of a potentate of India was erected on the grounds of Iolani Palace. Though nine years late, Princess Lil could see no harm in the coronation jubilee. She accepted Kalakaua's declared need to soothe the hurt of his troubled inauguration, and to stir a national pride once again in the people.

From England came the coronation gowns for Kapiolani. The finest dressmaking establishments of Paris furnished those for Liliuokalani. Her costume for the day ceremony was of gold and white brocaded silk. For the *soiree* and royal ball, it was of crimson satin. All the Paris creations were heavily embroidered, fantastically expensive, and the most elegant examples of Parisian fashion ever seen in Hawaii. Her sister, the Princess Likelike, utilized the official persuasion of her husband, Archibald Cleghorn, to procure the most beautiful pearl-trimmed gowns out of San Francisco, fashioned of the finest Chinese silks, complete with jeweled tiara. For the gorgeously uniformed king, and the splendidly attired females of his court, the coronation and jubilee were social triumphs to remember.

Long years later Liliuokalani wrote of it with fond remembrance: "Promptly at the appointed time His Majesty Kalakaua, King of the Hawaiian Islands, accompanied by Her Majesty Kapiolani, his queen, made their appearance. I give the order of the procession to the royal pavilion. Princess Likelike, bearing the royal feather cloak, and with her the Princess Paamaikalani; then the Princess Likelike, with the child-princess Kaiulani, and her father, Hon. A. S. Cleghorn; Governor Dominis, and myself; we were all attended by our *kahili* bearers, and

KALAKAUA'S CORONATION PAVILION
Palace Grounds, Honolulu.

—*Paul Bailey Photo.*

those ancient staffs of royalty were held aloft at our sides. Then followed Prince Kawananakoa, bearing one of the crowns, and Prince Kalanianaole bearing the other crown, succeeded by two others of noble birth and lineage bearing insignia of royalty of either native or traditional usage, the tabu sticks, the sceptre, and ring.

"Then came Their Majesties the King and Queen, attended by their *kahili* bearers, who, stationed themselves just inside the pavilion . . . The long and handsome train of Her Majesty's robe was carried by two ladies of high rank and noble lineage, Keano and Kekaulike."

Even the sharply observant Liliuokalani could discern, in this pompous show, the strange amalgamation of an ancient culture with the worst features of Nineteenth Century snobbery. That it should be opened by Christian prayer from the Reverend Mr. Mackintosh, instead of a blast from a conch shell, and the equally regal theatrics of a Hawaiian temple priest or high kahuna, was an anomaly the eager heir-apparent skirted with ease. Like any other Christian seeking a sign, she found it in the midst of opulence. "In the very act of prayer, just as he [Mackintosh] put forth his hand to lift the crown, before placing it on the brow of the king, a mist, or cloud, such as may gather very quickly in our tropical climate, was seen to pass over the sun, obscuring its light for a few minutes; then at the moment the king was crowned there appeared, shining so brilliantly as to attract general attention, a single star . . . A murmur of wonder and admiration passed over the throng."

If the gods meant the sign to be a good omen, heaven itself must have been confused. For Kalakaua, and for his princess sister, it never quite worked out that way.

Three years later the royal family walked through another social triumph with enough flash and glitter to plot a light opera. This time it was the fiftieth birthday of the "merry monarch." And again Honolulu was a tableau of parties, parades, public feasts and illuminations. Then followed, like an evil whiplash, the unexpected death of Bernice Pauahi Bishop, Liliuokalani's foster-sister, and last of the Kamehamehas. Next to go, and equally sudden, was the Princess Miriam Likelike Cleghorn. "I was tenderly attached to my sister, so much so that her decease had an unfavorable effect on my health," Princess Liliuokalani recorded.

Her brother, the king, came most opportunely to the rescue. Would she accompany Hawaii's Queen Kapiolani to England, to the Grand Jubilee in honor of the fiftieth year of good Queen Victoria's reign? Liliuokalani, sensing a rare chance to shed sorrows and benefit her health, accepted Kalakaua's offer with alacrity.

The royal party consisted of Queen Kapiolani, wife of the reigning sovereign; the heir-apparent, Princess Liliuokalani; General J. O. Dominis, governor of Oahu; Colonel C. P. Iaukea; Colonel James H. Boyd; each of the notables with from one to four personal attendants. Since Kapiolani had endless difficulty with every language other than native Hawaiian, the choice of the facile and completely anglicized Princess Lil was wise and fortuitous. The inclusion of Dominis and two other military men were more in the nature of guardianship and security, rather than any felicitous sentiment on the part of Kalakaua for his sister. The ever willing, ever handy Dominis could be depended on to vigilantly tend to the interest of Hawaii's two highest ladies.

On April 12, 1887, after she had "bade an affectionate adieu" to her mother-in-law, Mrs. Dominis, at Washington Place, Liliuokalani and John were taken by royal carriage directly to the Honolulu wharf, and the steamship *Australia*. The royal party, including the queen and her attendants, and the other aides and functionaries were already aboard. Waiting to bid them farewell were King Kalakaua and Walter Murray Gibson. After the martial and theatrical leavetaking, the king and his dignitaries went ashore. From the wharf the Royal Hawaiian Band played Liliuokalani's "national air," and, while the *Australia* was nudged out to her sea lane by the tugboats, the immense crowd tossed their *leis*, their paper ribbons, and shouted themselves hoarse.

On the third day at sea, chronic arthritis had put John Dominis to bed. But the sea was like a way of life to the Junoesque Alii ladies, and they thoroughly enjoyed the food and fun of the *Australia's* grand salon. It took seven days to reach San Francisco, and Dominis was reduced to the ignobility of having to be carried ashore on a stretcher. His travel to the Palace Hotel was by horse-drawn ambulance.

While waiting for John to recover from his arthritis sufficiently to entrain for their triumphal tour across America, Princess Lil made the acquaintance of two charming princesses from Tahiti. She was amazed that the language of Tahiti, as spoken by Princess Moetia and the Arii Manihinihi, was intelligible to a native Hawaiian, and not too different from that spoken in her own islands.

In a week Dominis had recovered enough for them to begin their train tour. And Liliuokalani stored in her mind recollections of America that would never be erased by time and tragedy.

Sacramento, and the public amenities . . . the winding crawl of the train through the snowsheds and steep grades of the Sierras . . . the plunge downward through Nevada . . . the pleasant stopover in Salt Lake City . . . where they were feted and entertained by the Mormons and their dignitaries . . . the church and people of her deep interest . . .

the meeting with the many Hawaiians who had been converted and had migrated to Utah . . .

As the royal party crossed America, Princess Lil was struck by the fact that even in April the trees of America were without leaves or blossoms, and only faint signs of spring green were apparent to eyes long accustomed to the endless verdure and color of a paradise that knew no seasons.

Washington . . . the visit, with Her Majesty, to the White House . . . the endless attention of President Cleveland and his beautiful young wife . . . the state dinner, tendered by the president and first lady . . . the surprise that a queen and princess out of Hawaii could stand socially triumphant in the grace and elegance of satin, brocade and lace.

John Dominis, and the royal lady consorts, honored by the Masonic Order . . . the Supreme Council of thirty-second degree Scottish Rite . . . the scrolls and certificates presented by General Albert Pike . . . the courtesy boat trip provided by the American government and its navy, down the Potomac . . . the tours and social affairs of Washington . . . the fawning attention of congressmen and their wives . . .

Boston . . . the Parker House . . . Deer Island . . . Waltham watch factory . . . the gathering of the Dominis relatives and eager friends . . .

New York . . . naval honors by Admiral Gherardi's great warship . . . the wild and noisy city . . . the concerts . . . the mayor with his courthouse welcome . . . the *City of Rome* at the wharf . . . largest steamship Liliuokalani had ever seen . . .

A mighty ship, shoving out to sea . . . the people, the noise, the bands . . . a thousand passengers aboard . . . notables, social climbers, singers, musicians . . . in sheer ecstasy the writing of two more songs.

In five days, it was England, and Liverpool.

Immense bouquets of British roses, delivered to the *City of Rome* while she still stood offshore . . . in the ship's grand salon, at dockage, Davies, British consul to Hawaii; Armstrong, Hawaiian consul to London; Rt. Rev. Staley, former Anglican bishop of Honolulu; high men in charge of British shipping interests . . . all bending the knee and kissing the hand of the Hawaiian queen . . .

Escort of one hundred soldiers . . . welcome by the Lord Mayor of Liverpool . . . Hon. R. T. Synge, of the foreign office, assigned by the Crown as British aide to the Hawaiian party . . . the train of carriages to the Northwestern Hotel . . . theatre . . . lord mayor's breakfast . . .

The train to Norwich and London . . . the already stirring immensity of Victoria's jubilee . . . royal suites at the Alexandria . . . suites housing the Prince Komatzu of Japan . . . the brother of the King of Siam . . . the Prince of India . . . the Prince of Persia . . . tomorrow

QUEEN KAPIOLANI, PRINCESS LILIUOKALANI, IN ENGLAND
While they participated in Queen Victoria's Jubilee, in London, the Kingdom of Hawaii was being stolen from King Kalakaua.

324

afternoon, felicitation to England's queen, in person at Buckingham . . .

Officer escort to the palace . . . Queen Kapiolani . . . Princess Liliuokalani . . . attendants, Colonel Iaukea and Mr. Synge . . . first greeting,
Lord Salisbury, premier of England . . . Lord Lathom, and Honorable
Secretary Ponsonby, holding their batons of office, leading the Hawaiians to Her Presence . . . Kapiolani, attended by Colonel Iaukea . . .
Liliuokalani, accompanied by the Honorable Mr. Synge . . . followed
by the ladies-in-waiting . . . the man in satin pants, at the doorway . . .
baton lifting for Hawaiian royalty to enter . . .

In one chair the squat and dumpish Queen Victoria . . . at the
windows H.R.H. Duke of Connaught and T.R.H. the Prince and Princess Henry of Battenberg . . . Victoria kisses her fellow sovereign
Kapiolani on each cheek . . . for Liliuokalani, one kiss on the forehead
. . . the two queens on the sofa, their fatuous felicitations translated
by Colonel Iauke . . . Princess Lil in one of the chairs . . . saved in
conversation by the Duke of Connaught . . . at last Victoria levels
attention at Liliuokalani . . . asks about the schools in the "Sandwich
Islands" . . . and Victoria introduces her two "children."

And then it was over . . . kisses as before . . . and they were moved
along to make room for other jubilee greetings with other sovereigns.

That evening the grand reception at the foreign office . . . gowns,
jewels . . . kings, queens, princes, princesses of the blood and of the
privilege . . . this time with John Dominis, saluted at the door as
"governor of Oahu." It wouldn't have mattered where Oahu was.

The jubilee day of days . . . Westminster Abbey . . . royal procession led by the Prince of Japan, followed by Prince of Persia, Prince
of Siam, and Prince of India . . . next the Queen of the "Sandwich
Islands," and the Crown Princess of the same nation . . . with escort
of Her Majesty's Life Guards . . . at the door of the Abbey, Lord
Lathom and Sir Henry Ponsonby . . . escort to the seats reserved on
the dais, already loaded to capacity with the stuffily dressed sovereigns
of the world . . .

Bugles and "God Save the Queen" as England's royal family entered
and took their assigned places . . . the big fanfare when Victoria ascended the dais and took seat in St. Peter's armchair . . . mousy looking
in her black dress and bonnet . . .

Prayer by the Archbishop of Canterbury . . . *Te Deum* . . . organ,
choir, anthems, a gawking of heads and necks . . . and the ancient
church had rocked to another historic occasion . . .

Back, through the streets of London, to Buckingham Palace . . .
Duke of Edinburgh for Princess Lil . . . Prince of Wales for Queen
Kapiolani . . . the long table inviting with food, rare china, rare silver

. . . from the banquet hall to another spacious room where all foreign guests could watch the naval parade through the windows, as weary men executed their last steps and turns before returning to ships . . . then the display of presents sent to Victoria for her jubilee . . . none more beautiful than Kalakaua's gift from Hawaii . . . the frame sat on an easel, in the center of an embroidered piece, the letters "V. R." worked in the royal feathers of the rare and almost extinct *mamo* bird, the frame studded with diamonds . . .

More dinners, more balls, more events in which to see and to be seen . . . endless rounds of honorings, social events and theatricals . . . the great garden party hosted by Victoria for her world menagerie of illustrious guests. This time it was singers, actors, actresses—souls who had achieved, and could spice a party with grace and accomplishment beyond having been accidentally born to the blood. To Princess Lil, everything about the jubilee was fascinating. As a musician and composer, the garden party became her rare opportunity to meet and speak to the great musical artists of the day. She returned to the hotel, convinced that this had been the best of all events.

With ending of the historic jubilee came the added happy prospects of a royal tour of the continent of Europe.

But while waiting and planning at the hotel, came also the somber news that changed all. Foreigners of Hawaii had revolted. Walter Murray Gibson had been driven from the islands. King Kalakaua, in order to save the throne, had bowed to the haole insurgents. While his queen and the crown princess had consorted with royalty from all the world, their own kingdom had gone into jeopardy. In Honolulu, on the other side of the world, the anguished Kalakaua was already surrendering to the humiliation of the "bayonet constitution."

Before the week was out Hawaii's jubilee representatives were on the Atlantic, sailing for home and the trouble sure to come.

VII

LILIUOKALANI, fresh from the London triumph, considered the denigration of Kalakaua as much an affront to herself as to the king. Kapiolani, proficient only in the Hawaiian tongue, and shielded throughout her life from the duplicity and greed of foreigners, could move only mutely and bewildered through the tragedy that had come to the kingdom in her absence. But Kalakaua and his sister, both haole educated, both trained in the customs and thinking of America and Britain, could not be anything but shaken and appalled by the treachery of those whom they once had considered as friends.

Liliuokalani found the usually jovial and happy king a hollow-eyed and haunted man. When he recounted the events of those black days, with their assassination threats and attempts, the driving out of Gibson, the stripping of the sovereign of all vested power of the crown, and the final degradation of the farcical "constitution," the gentle Princess Lil answered back with the ferocity of old Queen Kaahumanu.

"For years the 'missionary party' had, by means of controlling the cabinets appointed by the king, kept itself in power," she later wrote. "Its leaders were constantly intriguing to make the ministry their tool, or to have in its organization a power for carrying out their own special plans, and securing their own personal benefit. And now, without any provocation on the part of the king, having matured their plans in secret, the men of foreign birth rose one day *en masse*, called a public meeting, and forced the king, without any appeal to the suffrage of the people, to sign a constitution of their own preparation, a document which deprived the sovereign of all power, made him a mere tool in their hands, and practically took away the franchise from the Hawaiian race.

"This constitution was never in any way ratified, either by the people, or by their representatives, even after violence had procured the king's signature to it. Contrary entirely to the intent of the prior constitution drawn by a Hawaiian monarch (under which for twenty-three years the nation had been conducted to prosperity), this draft of 1887 took all power from the ruler, and meant that from that day the 'missionary party' took the law into their own hands."

Realization that Kalakaua had been forced to sign this perfidious document only because of threats on his life, with alternative of forced abdication, and the shattering realization that half his trusted friends had been traitors, stoked Liliuokalani's fury. She resolved to fight this infamous coup to the end of her days.

No longer could there be a settling back to the old normalcy at Washington Place. Mrs. Dominis was ill. John, always overly attentive to the demands of his mother, gave more and more of himself to the task of keeping her alive and placated. Always he had kept himself serenely above the politics and turmoil of Honolulu. But reduction of the king to a mere rubber stamp of the reform party, and the necessity of operating Iolani Palace on the penurious and grudging allotment of the new minister of finance, was apparently insufficient victory for the more revolutionary haoles. Nothing but complete ouster of Kalakaua would ever satisfy them.

"During the session of the legislature for the year 1888," wrote Liliuokalani, "Mr. James I. Dowsett, Jr., a young man, came to my house at Muulaulani, Palama, to inform me that he had been commissioned by those members who belonged to the missionary party to inquire if I would accept the throne in case my brother should be dethroned." The crown princess, shocked by the bald and crude proposal, responded with fury and indignation.

A week later, while still resident at Palama, where she had gone during the illness of Mrs. Dominis, Liliuokalani was visited by William R. Castle, American sugar magnate, pertinent to the same subject. "He announced to me that he had come to propose that I should accept the throne, to which I should at once ascend, and receive the support of the missionary party. I demanded of him how my brother could be dethroned. Did they mean harm to his person? He [Castle] denied that there was any such intent, but declared that King Kalakaua must retire, and that I should assume his position as the reigning sovereign." Was the Princess not an exemplary Christian? Did she not support every Christian charity? Did she not maintain a pew at Kawaiahao Church? Was she not friendly to the haoles? They, in turn, needed the loved and respected Liliuokalani.

"I told him with firmness and decision that I would have nothing to do with them in this matter. Seeing that I firmly declined the proposal, Mr. Castle retired; and as that was the last I heard about it, I infer that, having made their plots, they lacked the courage, or the heart, to put their plans into execution."

Also to the Kalama residence came Robert W. Wilcox, that wild-eyed zealot from the Hawaiian pasture. Robert had been chosen by King Kalakaua to go to Italy, to be educated for a state career. With the expulsion of Gibson, and the coup against the king, the scholarships and expense accounts of all Hawaiians studying abroad had been abruptly cancelled. Unlike other king's protégés, Wilcox had returned immediately to Hawaii, bringing back with him his Italian bride, the beautiful Countess Sobrero. He came back to Honolulu passionately loyal to his benefactor, the king, only to discover that the once open-handed and generous monarch no longer controlled either the right to provide careers in government, or the wherewithal to pay for such hoped-for services.

For a time, while striving for some governmental appointment, young Wilcox and his bride lived at the Arlington Hotel—until funds ran out, and he was forced to turn to Princess Liliuokalani for help in his desperation. She gave Wilcox and his bride a comfortable apartment at the Palama residence, hoping their fortunes might turn for the better. But the reform party, now running the government, had no place for any protégé of Kalakaua, no matter how talented. Eventually, with the help of Princess Lil, the Wilcoxes were able to leave Hawaii for America. In San Francisco, the countess found a position teaching and tutoring Italians, and Robert Wilcox accepted a job as surveyor.

But in a matter of months Wilcox was back in Honolulu—without a wife—more than ever determined to enter Hawaiian politics. He would, somehow, right the wrongs of the king who once so generously had befriended him. Again Liliuokalani graciously allowed Wilcox to live at Palama. A decision she later had reason to regret.

When it was apparent Mrs. Dominis was not likely to survive her illness, Princess Lil moved back to Washington Place, to be with her family through its travail. In April of 1889 the old lady breathed her last. After tearfully putting her away in the haole cemetery, John and Liliuokalani surfaced out of sorrow to realize that, for the first time, beautiful Washington Place was now altogether theirs.

With events moving inexorably toward climax, the tranquility they sought and hoped for in the cool and spacious old house continued to evade them. Liliuokalani, regardless of her betrayal and maltreatment by the "missionary party," and her disappointment in Christian gratitude for favors past, still busied herself in the endless charities with which she was associated. And, worried about the reduction of the King of Hawaii to puppet sovereign in the service of haole big business, she traveled much that summer—among the island people—listening to their complaints—sampling the pervasive heartbreak of a proud and once happy race. The sound she heard was the death rattle of their betrayal.

John Dominis, as governor of Oahu and Kauai, did his best to attend to official duties, but he was now practically bedfast with the arthritis that seemed to have painfully and relentlessly set itself upon the frail and reedy man immediately after his mother's death. It was a most difficult summer for both of them.

*   *   *   *   *   *

The revolt was no secret to Liliuokalani. It began when an almost hysterical Robert Wilcox presented himself at Washington Place. To Liliuokalani he brought the startling news that on that very night he and his men would storm Iolani Palace and the government buildings— oust those who had betrayed the king—and restore His Majesty to the position of honor and power he once possessed.

"He told me in a few words that he was ready to release the king from the hated thraldom under which he had been oppressed, and that measures had already been taken," Liliuokalani later explained. "I asked him at once if he had made mention of so important a matter to His Majesty. He replied that he had not."

Liliuokalani begged him to do nothing, attempt no coup, engage in no hostilities without first disclosing his intent to Kalakaua. But the man was afire with determination. Wilcox refused to tip his hand to the king until the revolt was secure, and its beneficiary could accept the fruits of its victory without having to be a party in its accomplishment. What Liliuokalani could not explain, then or ever, was how Wilcox managed to foment, plan, and equip his uprising from her Palama summer residence without her having the least inkling of what was going on.

The revolution occurred as timed and planned. It so happened that Kalakaua and Kapiolani were that night at the boathouse—as the summer sailing races were in full swing, and the king enjoyed sleeping near the water he so loved. Princess Lil was with her sick husband, at Washington Place, when the shooting started.

By stealth, and surprise, Wilcox and his forces took full possession of Iolani Palace during the night. Next morning Liliuokalani looked out on Iolani barracks to a scene of confusion. Government troops and a few palace guards were frantically regrouping in their move to oust the invaders.

Apparently even the guards on residential duty had revolted and joined Wilcox in his insurrection, and the problem of loyalty was on the mind of every militiaman as he hurried to the armory at Punchbowl Street to arm himself for the attack. Militia rifle companies stationed themselves in firing positions at the concert hall, opposite the palace. Liliuokalani, concerned for her brother's safety, sat in terror as noise of gunfire came at sporadic intervals throughout the day.

But the coup, no matter how well intended and courageous, was doomed from the start. The palace guards quickly deserted the wild-eyed Wilcox when mortar blasts from the streets began demolishing the bungalows and fringe buildings on the palace square. Wilcox had insufficient zealots enlisted to the foolhardy cause to sustain a revolution without outside help. Before nightfall Robert Wilcox had surrendered. When all was quiet and peaceful once more, the king came back to the palace. His sister, knowing that enemies would somehow link her to the aborted struggle, retired to another restless night.

Wilcox went to jail, the reform party pulled the noose tighter upon the sad and discouraged monarch, and liberation seemed more than ever far away.

With the approach of winter, it was apparent to friend and foe that the king's health was failing. Liliuokalani was not surprised when, in December of 1890, Kalakaua announced the trip to California as a frantic attempt to recoup his energies and his strength. The perceptive

Princess Lil was certain that the king would never be allowed the journey by his dictatorial ministers, were there not some motives present whereby the haoles of Hawaii would benefit. But Kalakaua was truly ill, and needed help. Even under reform party hypocrisy, California would be good for him—as it had been good for her.

A little probing uncovered the principal motivation for the journey. The McKinley Bill had just passed the American congress. In it were influences dangerous to the interest of foreign businessmen in Hawaii, and destructive to the profits of the plantation owners and sugar industrialists. The king, irrespective of his sagging health, was to contact the Hawaiian minister at Washington, Henry A. P. Carter, and attempt with all power at his command to nullify the adverse effects of McKinley's misguided legislation.

"Three days before his departure the king came to see me, Liliuokalani confessed. "I did all I could to dissuade him from the journey . . . His only errand at this moment was to notify me that I was appointed regent during his absence . . .

"So the king went cheerfully and patiently to work for the cause of those who were his enemies . . . With an ever-forgiving heart he forgot his own sorrows, set aside all feelings of animosity, and to the last breath of his life he did all that lay in his power for those who had abused and injured him."

The last breath of his life came on this trip. On January 20, 1891, in San Francisco, King Kalakaua gave up the struggle.

"If ever there was a man who was pure in spirit, if ever there was a mortal who had perfect charity, he was that man," Liliuokalani wrote of him. "In spite of all the revilings uttered against him, he never once opened his lips to speak against another, whomsoever it might be. And so my poor brother said good-by to us all, and bade farewell to his beautiful Islands, which he was never to look on again."

VIII

THE NEW Queen of all Hawaii—the stately, gentle, cultured musician —proved a shattering surprise to the haole insurgents who so successfully had extinguished the flame of her brother. The lessons these all-powerful opportunists had brought Liliuokalani were not the lessons they had taught poor dead Kalakaua. From the moment she took the sudden oath as sovereign, she faced the rapists of her nation in the regal and pugnacious stature of the ancient queens. Hawaii had a female ruler on its hands as imperious as Kaahumanu. Quickly she made plain her determination to restore the royal power so ruthlessly stolen. "Onipa'a! Stand firm!" was her motto. Courageously she spat the battle cry of King Lot at the haoles: "Hawaii for the Hawaiians!"

Without hesitance she dismissed the cabinet of Kalakaua—even though they insisted on remaining in office for his sister's reign. The problem she faced, of course, would be the difficulty of naming successors who could be fully sustained by the legislature. Under the "bayonet constitution" the sovereign could choose his or her ministers—but always subject to approval of the haole-packed "democratic process."

The new queen insisted and got a full state funeral for Kalakaua—and in the ancient way. The casket of His Majesty was laid on the hallowed cloth of royal feathers, on a table platform in the center of the red chamber in Iolani Palace. Guards were detailed around the clock. Bearing aloft the royal *kahilis* were twenty men, chosen from the Alii, who, in shifts of four hours kept the plumes of state constantly high above the fallen king. Queen Liliuokalani, in finding men whose ancestry went back to the ancient chiefs, discovered how few of them were now high in state. Unable and unwilling to compete with the sharp and avaricious foreigners, many great families had been reduced to poverty and peasantry. In threadbare clothes they now again proudly stood honor for a Hawaiian king.

At the royal casket some sang the death wail, or the *meles* belonging solely to the family of their deceased fellow chieftain. Younger attendants, but still impeccably Alii, composed dirges and chants in more modern lyric form, and sang them—because they knew their new and gracious queen would approve. Among second line guards of honor were representatives from the consular offices of various nations. American businessmen who had so deeply profited through the acts and generosity of the dead king, and even the Masonic fraternity, of which both Kalakaua and John Dominis had been practicing members. The foreign death watchers were less vocal in grief.

Death and burial of a sovereign in Hawaii had never been a trivial matter. But for Kalakaua the new queen demanded full and honorable treatment. Perhaps she had presentiment that this would be the last of such in her beloved islands. She insisted on the time-honored three weeks of obsequies, before final interment in the royal crypt. This gave sufficient pause for natives from other islands to assemble at Honolulu and vent themselves of the grief which tore at her nation. All through this period, in defiance of the haoles who controlled her government, she refused to transact any state business, sign any documents, or make any of the decisions they pressed upon her.

When the hour came for the state funeral, each dignitary assembled in the palace red room. Each took his or her assigned place, according to rank. His Lordship, the Bishop of Honolulu, fully enrobed for his office, began the ritual for the burial of the dead, according to the prescribed form of the Anglican Church. Queen Liliuokalani thought on how it would have been in olden days. Instead of the Church of England, there would have been the priests and the mystics. Instead of formal mourning attire, the high chiefs present would have been spitting blood from where their teeth had been clubbed out as a true sign of grief.

Now, at the proper time, each person moved to his assigned position for the procession which would travel in colorful pageantry from palace to royal mausoleum up Nuuana Valley. Behind the black and shiny carriages of the royal family walked Kalakaua's cabinet, still smarting under the threat of abrupt dismissal by the new queen. Behind them followed the attending members of the diplomatic corps, the muffled-drum band, and the military. On each side of the bier marched the *kahili* bearers, holding aloft those ancient feathered symbols of sovereignty.

On arrival at the royal mausoleum the casket was gently settled to the center of the tomb. Last prayer for the deceased was offered by the Anglican bishop, backed by the clergy assisting his lordship. Liliuokalani knew that, in the old days, Kalakaua's flesh would have been stripped from his bones and offered to the fire. And that the bones would have been laced in sennit, and placed in the ancient depository at Hale-o-Keawe, or hidden away like those of Kamehameha. Her Christian training, in this respect at least, was comforting. Kalakaua could lay with royal dead, in a prettier place—and wholly in one piece.

The Masonic brethren, representative of every lodge in Honolulu, and clothed in the regalia of their order, made an impressive sight as they stood in silence about the casket. Upon it was placed the ceremonial fittings worn by Brother David Kalakaua, and a scroll recording his various ranks as a Freemason. Each of them laid a sprig of green pine on the box as they retired. When they were gone, the tomb was closed off for a last moment of mourning for the royal family. Two queens—Kapiolani, his wife; Liliuokalani, his sister; vented their grief in sobs and little words of intimate remembrance.

The guns of the military escort, in three volleys of musketry, were fired above the mausoleum. The procession again formed. The *kahili* bearers held aloft their insignia to the new queen. And, after leaving Kalakaua to the cold crypt, the people marched slowly back to Honolulu.

IX

Now THAT the "time of mourning" was definitely and finally over, Queen Liliuokalani no longer could beg time or further stall the hard-nosed Americans. They had expected her accession to open the final door to complete dominance, and her instant defiance had for a moment thrown them off balance—but only for a moment. They used the interim of the state funeral exactly as did the equally tough-minded queen—to martial strength and set stance for inevitable struggle.

The first act of the queen was to officially accept the resignation of Kalakaua's ministers—exactly as she had demanded before interment of the king—even though they continued to insist on remaining in office as her cabinet. In foisting them on the unhappy Kalakaua, the reformists had failed to plug one important loophole. The sovereign could still appoint his or her own ministers, and there had been nothing written to cancel the fact that their official duties to that sovereign ended with his or her death.

Hoping to gain time in the battles ahead, and to enter her reign on a note of tolerable appeasement, Liliuokalani—much to the disappointment of the few remaining chiefs—did appoint a mixed haole cabinet. Samuel Parker, friendly cattle baron from the big island, became minister of foreign affairs; Charles N. Spencer was minister of the interior; Herman A. Widemann, minister of finance; William Austin Whiting was the new attorney-general; James W. Robertson filled the office of Hon. George W. Macfarlane, who was absent to the United States; Charles B. Wilson, close friend of the new queen, became marshal. Though most all of them were Americans, and only a few of them boasted Hawaiian blood, the stubborn Queen Lil had made certain they were not ex-missionaries, nor the sons of missionaries.

She was not unmindful of the possibility that the legislature, when it convened, would wrangle long and hard over her appointments. But until officially dismissed or rejected by that body, they could function—perhaps slightly in her behalf.

While this matter was pending, arrangements were made for a special convening of the legislature's House of Nobles. They would pass on the queen's nomination for heir-apparent to the throne—Princess Victoria Kaiulani, daughter of the dead Princess Likelike and the honorable Archibald S. Cleghorn. For consideration, too, would be the appointment of Governor John Dominis as prince consort to the queen.

On March 9, 1891 both appointments were accepted and confirmed by the House of Nobles. In recognition of the young and beautiful Kaiulani as heir-apparent to the throne of Hawaii a salute of twenty-one guns was fired from the United States ship-of-war *Mohican*. That John Dominis was now prince consort received considerably less recognition from busy Honolulu. He was bedridden with arthritis.

The queen made but slight progress in behalf of her people during that turbulent spring and summer of the first year of her reign. But neither did she lose ground in the battle. In line with ancient custom, and as new sovereign, she toured the islands of her realm—meeting her people; listening to their thoughts and problems. John Dominis, as prince consort, was recovered enough to accompany her. The Honorable Samuel Parker and the Honorable William Austin Whiting, of her cabinet, were a part of the grand tour. This friendly, politically-charged visit covered the islands of Hawaii, Maui, and Molokai. It was the return to Honolulu, preparatory to their travels to Kauai, that problems developed.

By now John Dominis was utterly fatigued and ill from the strenuous journey, and was forced to drop out of the official party. He chose to return to his bed at Washington Place rather than the cold and ornate luxury of Iolani Palace. By now, also, dozens of other notables were clamoring to join the royal tour—native Hawaiians as well as rich and influential haoles. When the steamer *James Makee* left the docks of Honolulu, bound for Kauai, the complement of dignitaries had grown fourfold. The new queen and her entourage were hospitably and almost hysterically received by the kind and gentle people of Kauai. From there the steamer took them to the last little island of Niihau. The tour was an utter triumph for Liliuokalani.

Upon her return to Honolulu she hurried to Washington Place, to find her John still completely bedfast, and still unable to finish with her the last segment of the state visit—the circuit of Oahu itself. This leisurely journey, with its continuous feasts and functions, took a week. When the queen finally reached Honolulu again, even her own robust Alii constitution had had enough.

She faced a John Dominis of strange grayish color. He moved with a feebleness never before apparent. Worried and alarmed, she remained constantly with him to the morning of his death. And she was at bedside when her kind and gentle prince consort breathed his last.

The ministers of Liliuokalani's cabinet agreed with her that John Dominis, even though a haole, deserved and would get a state funeral. No native Hawaiian could have worked more zealously for the nation. Here was one American who had stood shoulders high above greed

KAIULANI, THE LOVELY PRINCESS
She died March 6, 1899

—Photo, Bernice P. Bishop Museum, Honolulu.

and corruption. The evening of his death, the slender and wasted body of Governor Dominis was removed to the palace, and laid out in the red room. The only time John actually had sojourned there.

As with the so lately remembered Kalakaua, there were the military guards, the watchers from the Masonic fraternity, the lady mourners bearing their sweet-scented flowers. There were even attendants managing the royal *kahilis*. And on the day of the final ceremonies, John Owen Dominis was borne, with like honors accorded the late king, to his final resting place in the royal cemetery.

X

THE DEATH of John Dominis was an overwhelming tragedy to the impetuous and impatient queen. Never was she in greater need of his calm and seasoned judgment. The haole criticism and slander which followed his passing prompted her to move immediately against them, rather than sit out the fates for a more strategic time. They accused her of complete neglect and contempt for her American husband, once she had climbed the heights to the throne. The poor man had died, unattended, outside the palace, they claimed. The only time the prince consort had been allowed to sleep in Iolani Palace was when he was safely in his coffin. The fact that John could not climb the palace stairs to his bedchamber, and preferred sleeping in one of the service bungalows on the palace grounds, was interpreted by her calumniators as a complete palace lockout. Never again, from that point on, did Liliuokalani bow gracefully to the hard fist of haole authority.

With the palace bungalow untenanted, and the man who would have sojourned there no longer alive, the queen offered the house to her marshal, Charles B. Wilson, and his wife Eveline. Mrs. Wilson, a friend from childhood, became one of the queen's ladies-in-waiting— even more than that, a confidential companion.

The queen and her husband had taken Charles Wilson and pretty "Kitty" Townsend, who became the bride of Charles, into their home along with the coterie of young people with whom they had surrounded their lives. The youngsters, many of them musically inclined, had kept the royal household a happy and lively place. It seemed natural and right that Charles, the protégé, should be the queen's retainer, not only at Washington Place, but in the luxurious and spacious palace. "Kittie" Wilson, now favorite lady-in-waiting, was a product of Liliuokalani's love and mothering.

Presence of the Wilsons at the palace would have gone unnoticed were it not for the fact that their bungalow on the palace grounds became the center for Queen Lil's push to recapture Hawaii for Hawaiians. Frequent visitors to the cottage were John E. Bush and Robert W. Wilcox. Both these men were known royalists, fanatically determined to restore the monarchy to the power and prestige it had known under Kamehameha V.

Bush had served both as minister of foreign affairs and minister of finance under Gibson's premiership. He now published a royalist newspaper, the *Ka Leo o ka Lahui*. Wilcox, lately released from prison after his abortive revolution for the name and sake of Kalakaua, was universally popular with the Hawaiian natives and the Hawaiian mixed-breeds. All of them totally endorsed Liliuokalani and her strivings in their behalf. Both these leaders sought political appointments by the new queen. Both were intensely loyal. But the new sovereign, realizing these turncoat haoles had little chance of surviving a government dominated by the American "missionary party," wisely passed them over as appointees.

But within the palace bungalow, encouraged by a queen as determined as old Kaahumanu, a new constitution was being secretly written. The great hope was that it would replace the questionable document forced at gunpoint on Kalakaua and his Hawaii. The queen remained unmoved and unimpressed by the general belief that constitutional reform must come through the legislative process, and with the blessing and cooperation of the nation's supreme court. She considered the whole "reform" movement a dishonest usurpation of power; that every haole manipulator was a thief and pirate.

Several drafts by various participants in the clandestine effort, were read and debated in the queen's presence. No attempt was made to consult her cabinet and the ministers regarding the embryo document, nor did the queen discuss with them the secret moves being made toward its adoption. But now Liliuokalani, like her brother, was discovering that spies and traitors were among those most closely trusted. Bush jumped the gun by hinting of the document, and hammering editorially in his pro-Hawaiian newspaper for the necessity of a new constitution. Someone, very close to the queen, was feeding drafts of the great effort to the top haoles in government. Charles Wilson was bragging that he was closest confidant to the queen; that she sought his advice in every governmental matter; that he guided her hand in shaping policy.

So blatant became these rumors that Samuel Parker, the queen's minister of foreign affairs, felt the necessity of calling at the palace to bluntly ask Her Majesty as to the truth of these allegations. "I answered Mr. Parker that I consulted no one outside of my cabinet, and that no measures had ever been consummated excepting such as had been advised by the ministers," the queen declared. And in a major sense this was so. Her planning was for the future. She was not yet secure enough to move in the direction that obsessively motivated her. Mr. Parker, convinced by her direct answer, passed it on to the other worried ministers.

But such mysterious political machinations could not forever be cloaked in silence—especially with politically oriented informers working within the very circle itself. Never did Lydia have greater need of good and dependable John. Had he lived, the final tragedy might have been averted.

Wilson, Bush and Wilcox—all three—betrayed the queen's confidence in their eagerness to remake Hawaii's political structure. Wilson's tongue and inflated ego were not exactly assets to a court intrigue. And at the very time they were laying plans for the 1892 general elections and aiding the queen in drafting a new constitution, supposedly to be presented to the legislative assembly of that year, Bush and Wilcox were openly criticizing their trusting sovereign. Their questionable comments were published in the columns of Bush's royalist newspaper.

The queen's zeal in behalf of her people was weakened by a persistent refusal to utilize and trust her own hand-picked cabinet in planning and promoting such drastic reforms. Remembering Kalakaua's repeated betrayals by his ministers, she dared not, in the beginning, take them into confidence. When the time came that she desperately needed their help, the hostile legislature arbitrarily took her ministers from her. Yet they could never have betrayed her as thoroughly as did her covey of trusted friends.

The year of 1892 opened with political madness. The election was scheduled for February 3. Many diverse political parties had entered the fray, touting their candidates for the general assembly and house of nobles. By the first of the year it was settled into a titanic struggle between two major parties—both confederations of smaller groups of like political and patronage leanings. The National Reform Party had now emerged as a conglomerate of the old Hui Kalaiaina, which in the election of 1890 had been the political umbrella of native Hawaiians, the Hawaiian Political Association, and the. Workingmen's Political Protective Association. In this campaign, the Reform Party, through its still active core of Hui Kalaiaina, was the administration or government party. It had the blessing and support of the queen.

The other party, the Liberal Party, housing the segments of the haole groups who had immobilized Kalakaua, emerged as the party of opposition. Its orators and editors mounted a continuous and endless barrage against Liliuokalani, her cabinet, and her marshal, Charles Wilson. By now, Bush and Wilcox, unsuccessful in gaining governmental appointments as reward for their cooperation with the nation's militant queen, had reversed their stance completely.

The speeches of Wilcox now abounded in reckless and defamatory statements. In one of them he justified his reversible politics by explaining that "in times gone by he had been a staunch royalist, today he was in that same degree a Republican. He was a strong believer in freedom and justice and was in favor of a government *of* the people, *by* the people, and *for* the people." He had been pardoned as a convicted revolutionist. Now all he wanted from the people of Hawaii was election to the post of premier—as once held by the expelled and disgraced Gibson. That Liliuokalani could still countenance Wilson as her confidant and marshal brought malevolent accusations of the queen's "utter misgovernment of affairs at home. Ignorant fools are conducting the Government. A 'blacksmith' [Wilson] is very influential with the queen . . . It is a standing disgrace to the Hawaiian nation . . . "

The Liberals consistently pointed to the fact that Marshal Wilson was not of Hawaiian blood, but was half Tahitian and half British (which was true). Bush claimed that Liberals were gaining favor even among native Hawaiians because of "the present rotten condition of officialdom."

Strangely, in the confused issues of this most decisive Hawaiian political campaign, it was the Liberals who advocated a completely new constitution, to replace the hastily and strangely contrived document that had been forced on Kalakaua. But, since the National Reform Party too advocated a thorough revision of the document, the queen realized she must be ready and fully prepared to make certain that her own constitutional return of "Hawaii to Hawaiians" would be the instrument adopted. She was convinced the people would rally behind her. A petition asking for constitutional reform had been circulated by the Hui Kalaiaina among Hawaii's nine thousand five hundred eligible voters. Six thousand five hundred—or two-thirds—had signed and forwarded the petition either to the queen or to the Hui Kalaiaina.

But on the election, February 3, the Liberal party was defeated. A few of their candidates edged into office, but Bush and Wilcox had gained little in their noisy try. Though the victory was for the conservative forces of the kingdom, it produced a legislature, in both houses, blurred by no clearcut majority for either the original Reform Party, the National Reform Party, or the Liberals.

Not even the election silenced the attacks on the queen, her cabinet, and her alleged failure as a sovereign. The matter of annexation to the United States, the inability of a female to effectively rule, and the governmental stiffening against haole privilege, were constantly threshed in the newspaper columns of Honolulu. Bush, in his reputedly pro-Hawaiian journal, continued to lash out at the government that had rejected him. "We do not have any fear as to the result of any agitation that interested parties may make in favor of annexation or republicanism," he editorialized. "Either one of these two conditions is earnestly desired by a large number of people of this community from several causes." As summer waned, Bush was painting glowing pictures of what Hawaiians would enjoy "under the *stars* and *stripes.*"

The determined battle for the people's minds was by no means confined to newspaper columns. Pamphlets were privately circulated by the thousands. Wherever people congregated, or an audience could be cajoled into assembling, the silver-tongued pro-American orators—many of them mixed breed Hawaiians—were there to down the monarchy, sell the idea of a republic, or declare the benefits of direct and immediate annexation to the United States of America.

For Liliuokalani it was a bitter and difficult time. Because she stood exactly opposite to the treason-mouthed haoles who were determined to wrest her nation from her, she looked at the sons of the missionaries, the planters, the bankers, and all American entrepreneurs as her enemies. She deplored the necessity of allowing these insidious traitors a hand in the affairs of government. She would fight them to the end.

When Wilcox and his friends organized "The Hawaiian Patriotic League," and promoted drill teams and rifle companies, the queen's cabinet ordered that sand-bag barricades be erected on the makai and Punahou sides of Iolani Palace. The *Pacific Commercial Advertiser* ridiculed such protective measures by the queen's royal guards. But never, during that turbulent spring, summer or fall was Honolulu free of verbal threat, pari-military and marching townsmen, or the constant and menacing picture of American warships in Honolulu harbor.

After the sand-bag affair Wilcox and Bush made public disclaimer of any intention of resorting to arms against the queen and her government. Their "Hawaiian Patriotic League," they averred, was strictly a group pledged to "equal rights." "But if our queen continues to follow the idle advice of a few moneyed men, trouble might follow," Bush told a Liberal Party meeting. At another affair he unabashedly declared, "I favor federal governments. We can divide Hawaii into four states, and call them the United States of Hawaii . . . Who should be our first president?" The audience screamed: "Wilcox!"

At another meeting the attack was more venomous. "A half-Tahitian blacksmith [Wilson] and a half-caste cowboy [Parker] are running the government; but they are pitiful specimens of ignorance. If we are ready to revolutionize our government, I have been informed that America will recognize our new government . . . The power of casting off monarchy is in your hands, and you may do as you choose."

The vituperative attacks and the military posturing of the Hawaiian Patriotic League finally proved too much for Marshal Wilson. He infiltrated the organization with spies. The seditious evidence they gathered was presented before the cabinet ministers. After some hesitation the government decided to take action. United States Minister John L. Stevens and British Commissioner James H. Wodehouse were informed that warrants were being sworn out against R. W. Wilcox, V. V. Ashford, Lot Lane, J. W. Bipikane, and fourteen others. These suspects were arrested on a charge of treason and lodged in the Honolulu jail.

On May 26 a preliminary hearing was held before Judge Sanford B. Dole. On basis of the evidence presented, twelve of the defendants, including Ashford and Bipikane, were discharged on hte grounds of insufficient evidence. Six others, however, including Wilcox and Lane, were committed for trial before the supreme court.

None of them were ever actually brought to trial. But on supposition that there possibly was movement toward revolution and annexation, Commissioner Wodehouse requested that a British warship be stationed in Honolulu. By summer, the queen could look out on the *H.M.S. Champion* as a nesting threat in addition to the armed might of America.

XI

THE 1892 SESSION of the Hawaiian legislature proved to be the longest and most chaotic in the history of the kingdom. Not any one of the three major parties could mount a decisive majority and, because of it, the wrangling and recriminations stalled or drastically altered much desperately needed legislation. Inadvertently it set the scene for the tragic revolution of January 1893. The session opened on May 28, 1892 at a time when the nation was seething with internal problems and in depths of an economic depression brought on by America's McKinley tariff act. This suddenly foisted barrier to Hawaiian sugar and coffee exports had nullified every advantage gained by the reciprocal trade treaty, and had plunged the island nation once more into business chaos.

Queen Liliuokalani, opening the sessions with her speech from the throne, tempered her pro-Hawaiian remarks with a pointed reminder of the adverse effects of the depression and the desperate need for economy and retrenchment on the part of the nation's lawmakers. Her minister of finance, in his report to the body, warned that receipts of the government for the ensuing biennium would be at least $800,000 less than the preceding period. In his budget proposal he suggested the necessity of raising at least $900,000 additional revenue to finance public improvements and governmental necessity. It would have to be done by the sale of bonds, or the finding of additional tax base.

As the sessions moved ponderously and tediously through the weeks it became increasingly apparent that it would take more than governmental economy to stave off the eroding tide of depression. The Hawaiian Postal Savings Bank, the safe haven for the savings of the little people, was suffering a reversal in the flow of funds. When withdrawals reached $400,000 more than deposits, everyone—government and people—knew that prosperity in Hawaii was gone. The government had to borrow heavily from the bank of Claus Spreckels and Company to save its own postal bank. And in the closing months of the legislature's marathon session, an act was passed authorizing a national bonding of $750,000 to cover make-work projects such as harbor improvements, roads, and needed public works.

Blame for the nation's woes, of course, was foisted by the haole dominated legislature upon the queen and her hand-picked cabinet. In midst of governmental floundering over various means to raise money and plug the leaks in the economy, Robert W. Wilcox had been released from his jailing as a revolutionary, and suspected traitor. The moment he took his seat in the legislature, a long and bitter struggle against Liliuokalani and her cabinet began. The man whom the queen and her dead brother so generously had befriended turned in vindictive hate to the task of dismembering Her Majesty. His special venom was directed at the queen's ministers, and Marshal Wilson whose personal charges had brought about his incarceration.

On July 13 Wilcox introduced a resolution of want of confidence in the cabinet. The Wilcox resolution was defeated 32 to 14. The vote was not so much an approval of the queen and her ministers as it was disapproval and distrust of the noisy and erratic author of the measure.

The queen might have ridden the crisis to victory had it not been for a minor altercation within her cabinet. Attorney-General Whiting resigned because of a trifling dispute with Premier Samuel Parker. The queen was suddenly confronted, in the midst of a balancing act over the political chasm, with the necessity of appointing another minister to fill the Whiting vacancy. She was determined, against all opposition, to hang on to Wilson as marshal. But since the office of marshal was a subordinate position under the attorney-general—to insure Wilson's tenure, the queen asked for the appointment of a man she could depend on, Arthur P. Peterson. The appointment was doubly crucial for her because she had become obsessed with the idea of a national lottery to raise needed money for the nation. Not all her cabinet looked with

QUEEN LILIUOKALANI (LYDIA PAKI)

This brilliant woman, a gifted composer and musician, reigned
from 1891 to 1893, and was the last of the Hawaiian monarchs.
Imperious as Kaahumanu, her "Hawaii for Hawaiians" infuriated
344 *the haoles and cost her the throne.*

—Photo, Bernice P. Bishop Museum, Honolulu.

favor on the scheme. An enterprising and persuasive American visitor had succeeded in selling Liliuokalani on the plan.

Other ministers of her cabinet objected to the appointment of Peterson, and so plainly stated. Their choice and preference for attorney-general was Paul Neumann, a member of the house of nobles. The queen reluctantly agreed to Neumann's appointment, but only under the condition that Wilson remain as marshal; that they introduce the lottery bill in the legislature; that they throw their weight behind its passage.

The problem now was that Neumann was anathema to the Reform Party, there was plenty of opposition to the lottery scheme, and even Liberal Party members were ready to regurgitate at thought of Wilson's continuance at the right elbow of Queen Lil. When William White, backed by the queen and several loyal members of her cabinet, introduced the lottery bill to the Hawaiian legislature, the war was on.

The act would grant, to a group of five men, including three Honolulu residents, the exclusive franchise to establish and maintain a public lottery for a period of twenty-five years. The grantees would be required to pay to the Hawaiian government $500,000 each year—the money to be used in subsidization of an ocean cable connecting Honolulu to the American coast, the construction of a railroad around Oahu, another railroad along the Hilo coast of Hawaii, for harbor, roads and bridge improvements, and encouragement of industries and tourism.

On the day the queen's lottery bill was introduced, Representative S. K. Pau presented a resolution denouncing C. B. Wilson, and demanding his immediate removal from office. The resolution was duly entered on the calendar for early consideration. In the afternoon session, Representative W. C. Wilder submitted a second resolution of want of confidence in the entire cabinet of the queen. Her ministers, it charged, lacked the ability to cope with economic crisis, or to carry out laws necessary for the advancement and development of the nation. The cabinet, the resolution averred, operated entirely without policy, and "followed a weak, shifting and vacillating course, derogatory to the dignity of the office and injurious to the public interest."

After angry debate, and before the day was ended, the Wilder resolution was adopted by a two-thirds plurality vote. The queen's ministers promptly and publicly resigned.

Liliuokalani, in midst of preparation for the elaborate court celebration of her fifty-fourth birthday, was crushed and shaken by the sudden turn of events. Every move she made in behalf of her people and their betrayed nation seemed stopped and blunted by the haole jackals who hated her. She pleaded with her ministers to retain their portfolios until after the celebration, and a new cabinet could be formed.

In an earnest attempt to present a slate of ministers who might be acceptable to friends and enemies alike, she called in trusted legislative aids. Working with them she named, as her new cabinet, Edward C. Macfarlane, premier, and minister of finance; Samuel Parker, minister of foreign affairs; Charles T. Gulick, minister of the interior; Paul Neumann, attorney-general. This cabinet lasted only five weeks of heat and criticism. On October 17 they too were turned out of office.

Two weeks later the queen made another attempt. Her cabinet of November 1 consisted of William H. Cornwell, minister of finance; Joseph Nawahi, minister of foreign affairs; Charles T. Gulick, minister of the interior; Charles Creighton, attorney-general. Quickly as these ministers took seat in the legislature, Noble Thurston introduced his resolution, which briefly and simply stated: "Be it resolved that the Legislature hereby expresses its want of confidence in the present Cabinet." The vote that followed destroyed another crown cabinet. After this impudent gesture toward the queen the legislature adjourned until November 17.

Time after time Liliuokalani exercised her constitutional right to appoint the ministers—her free choice guaranteed. Just as regularly did the legislature exercise its constitutional right to reject the ministers she had appointed. The impasse was generating ugly rumors. The queen, dedicated to constitutional reform and the return of Hawaii to Hawaiians was said to be plotting a coup. On the other hand, the American ministerial attache, it was said, was conniving with the United States naval officers with the idea of immediate intervention. Neither of these rumors were true, but Honolulu was edgy and nervous.

For her final attempt in fashioning an effective and acceptable cabinet, the queen chose the most respected men she could find in the community. George N. Wilcox was named as minister of the interior and premier [not Robert Wilcox, the revolutionary]; Mark F. Robinson was minister of foreign affairs; Peter C. Jones was minister of finance; and Cecil Brown was attorney-general. All of the new ministers were widely known, and reputedly incorruptible. Three of them had been born in Hawaii; the fourth, Jones—an American—was a long time resident, and a member of the firm of Brewer & Company. Robinson was of British and Hawaiian ancestry. The parents of Wilcox were American missionaries. The appointment of this cabinet—all four members of the Reform Party—was considered as complete acceptance by the queen of haole dominance in the nation, and final capitulation of the sovereign.

Although she stubbornly clung to Wilson as her marshal and confidant, it was the deepest concession Liliuokalani had yet made to her enemies. She wondered what Lot Kamehameha would have said to this surrender of crown rights. She wondered if Kamehameha the Great could possibly recognize the Hawaii of 1892—beset by financial panic, torn by revolutionaries and annexationists, dominated by greedy and implacable foreigners.

But in spite of all the queen's concessions there still was carping criticism of the new ministers, of Charles Wilson, and the queen's stubborn refusal to change from her nativistic stand. Like an unhealable ulcer, there remained the constant gabble over Pearl Harbor, annexation, national depression, and the lottery and opium bills. But somehow this compromise cabinet survived the 1892 legislature to its bitter and turbulent end.

In the closing weeks of December a bill relating to the regulation of Chinese immigration was passed. A new appropriation package, calling for national bonding and new taxes, cleared the legislative hurdles. The matter of a constitutional convention was set forward to December 27 for debate. It met an impossible impasse by the divided delegates, and was finally tabled. The opium license bill, introduced by Representative C. W. Ashford, which put the government's hand directly into the lucrative traffic through the door of taxation and licensing, was passed on December 23. It had unexpected support— from the opium ring, respected citizenry, and even the queen herself, who had openly favored it along with the undecided lottery bill.

Not even the eight-month marathon had been sufficient to dispose of the contentious problems that had so preoccupied this unprecedented session of the Hawaiian legislature. And December slipped into January with its work unfinished. The Bush faction of the Liberal Party was still challenging and criticizing the queen's new cabinet. But her cabinet had survived. Then, quite without warning, Liliuokalani herself turned against the ministers she so carefully had hand-picked.

She had never been too pleased with its haole countenance. But one of her personal advisers had informed her that the cabinet was closeting with American Minister John L. Stevens. She was certain a coup for annexation of Hawaii was in the offing. Aside from the concessions she had been forced to make to gain legislative approval of these appointees, she had been anything but happy when all of them had voted against the crown in the matter of constitutional amendment by convention, and the lottery bill. Now, hearing that they were overly friendly and cooperative with the American minister, she had come to distrust them.

The wrangling legislature had already gone nearly a week into January of the new year. The delegates were weary. There was absenteeism. Over all hung a general anxiety to get the acrimonious and muddled session of lawmaking over and on into adjournment. Bush, true to form, again presented a "no confidence" resolution against the queen's cabinet. Even though she made no effort this time to save their collective skins, it was narrowly defeated.

The legislation accomplished was desultory, and mostly a cupboard cleaning before adjournment. Robert Wilcox had earlier introduced a reckless and wild resolution that Hawaii pay $200,000 in bonds to any company that completed the Panama Canal. Joseph Nawahi had proposed that Hawaii lead the way in enlistment of other countries toward the laying of a desperately needed undersea cable to America and Asia. On January 5 and 6, after prolonged debate, it was decided that conferral of these matters with Washington be tendered to "a royal commission, to be appointed by the cabinet and approved by Her Majesty the Queen. Said commission to consist of five persons, three of whom shall be members of the legislature." The commission was never appointed. The revolution, now only ten days away, would end all state functions for Liliuokalani, Queen of Hawaii.

On January 7 the weary and exhausted legislators, after passing the bill authorizing the nation's borrowing of $750,000 in additional funds, informed Liliuokalani that the legislature would be ready to be prorogued by her into adjournment on January 12. She proposed Saturday, January 14, at noon, as a better time for the ceremony.

But, while she made plans of her own, to fit around this always colorful event, the legislature had two more days for their own brand of mischief. In final gesture, they passed into law the controversial lottery bill which the queen, in spite of opposition from every quarter, had sponsored and defended. They also, and finally, passed a resolution against her cabinet. The entire Wilcox group were forced to resign.

The queen was not at all saddened by this turn of events. She quickly appointed a new cabinet consisting of Samuel Parker as minister of foreign affairs; John F. Colburn, minister of the interior; William H. Cornwell, minister of finance; and Arthur P. Peterson, attorney-general. On Saturday morning, January 14, the legislature held its final short session. Peterson, the new attorney-general, announced that the queen had signed the opium and lottery bills. Queen Lil may have been pleased by her progress against obstinacy, but the buzz and gabble following announcement of the crown's stand and attitude on these controversial matters, should have been her warning.

At Iolani Palace, after making the dogged sponsors of these bills, Joseph Nawahi and William White, Knights Commanders of the Order of Kalakaua, the queen readied herself for the trip across the street to Aliiolani Hale, and the waiting legislature. Precisely at 12 o'clock the stately sovereign and her *kahili* bearers marched across the green to the prorogue ceremony. Behind followed her new ministers, and the brilliantly attired retinue. The legislators forgot their bitterness as they stood before Her Majesty. In colorful and impressive ceremony the queen officially closed, on January 14, 1893, the "1892" session of Hawaii's legislature.

It was following the prorogue ceremony that Liliuokalani made her fatal mistake. Within two hours the queen called a select session to the throne room of the palace. Before them she bluntly and defiantly announced her new constitution for Hawaii. This she intended to sign as the sovereign. It would proclaim to the world Hawaii's new and fair basis for law. The paper she waved before her startled listeners was the document which, in draft after draft, she had long labored. Believing in her divine right as sovereign, recognizing the failure of representative government to amend or supersede the vicious document foisted on her brother, she had taken her cue from Lot Kamehameha. Necessity was being accomplished by royal proclamation.

Of this historic and surprising event Liliuokalani later wrote: "The members of the diplomatic corps had been invited; also the members of the supreme bench and members of the legislature, besides a committee of the Hui Kalaiaina. The latter were invited to be present because it was through them that many petitions [for a new constitution] had been sent to me."

The whole affair was probably the most shocking and traumatic in Hawaii's turbulent history. A determined queen stood before the startled dignitaries in the magnificence of Iolani Palace. "Mr. Parker and Mr. Cornwell had given me assurance of their support before their appointment as ministers," the queen later explained, "while Mr. Peterson understood that such was my intention, and although I had not mentioned it to Mr. Colburn, he had heard of it already from Mr. Peterson."

Captain Samuel Nowlein, head of the household guards, and Marshal Wilson were fully aware of the stratagem, and had helped their queen prepare the stage. "They assured me they would be ready, and I gave strict injunctions of secrecy." On her way back to the palace, after proroguing the legislature, she had met Marshal Wilson at the entrance to the blue room. "I went up to him and asked if all was ready. He replied, 'Yes.' "

The devastating surprise to Liliuokalani was that the new and supposedly loyal cabinet flatly refused to endorse the document with her. Consternation really broke out in the palace when all of them, including Wilson, disavowed any part of the transaction. With crass lack of chivalry, they left their queen to muckle through the problem alone. To her it was unmitigating evidence that no haole, no matter how favored, could be trusted.

The queen, the ministers, the legislators, left the throne room to its chattering and worried guests. Closeted in the blue room, a determined sovereign railed out at her betrayers. Only after they had literally forced her to the wall, did Liliuokalani agree to postpone the matter for two weeks. Then all of them repaired to the waiting audience in the throne room—to explain a sovereign's defeat and embarrassment.

But this time the enemies of Liliuokalani were not through with her. Within a week of that ill-fated Saturday, United States naval forces would be landed. The revolutionists at last were united against her. And Liliuokalani, the last monarch of Hawaii, would be forced from her throne. With this militant and courageous woman would go the last hope of "Hawaii for Hawaiians."

XII

HONOLULU was turned into a cote of gabble and intrigue. As this fateful Saturday wore along, it became clear that the forces set in motion were considerably more than the initial shock and surprise engendered by the queen's unprecedented actions. It mattered not that she had backed away from the promulgation of a national constitution by royal fiat; had accepted postponement and public debate. To the revolutionists and the annexationists the queen herself had provided a near perfect excuse for action. Nothing she now could do would stop their relentless march toward complete deposition.

The law office of William O. Smith, near the corner of Fort and Merchant Streets became, as though at a signal, the downtown center for the gathering of malcontents. Here, far into the night, moved a steady flow of government officials, politicians, and haoles of every strata of interest. Before the afternoon was over the noisy visitors had organized themselves into a quorum, with Henry E. Cooper as chairman, and William O. Smith as secretary. Smith recorded that "It was voted that a committee of thirteen be appointed to form plans for action . . . and be called a committee of safety . . ." When the Annexation Club joined the meeting, they quickly seized the initiative, and apparently, through the crucial days ahead, directed the course of events.

The Committee of Safety, as appointed, consisted of H. E. Cooper, chairman, F. W. McChesney, T. F. Lansing and J. A. McCandless— all Americans. Its W. O. Smith, L. A. Thurston, W. R. Castle and A. S. Wilcox, were Hawaiian born, of American parents. Its W. C. Wilder, American; C. Bolte, German; and Henry Waterhouse, Tasmanian; were naturalized Hawaiian citizens. Andrew Brown, a Scotchman, and H. F. Glade, a German, had never been naturalized, and had no intention of being so. Later, through resignation, Glade and Wilcox were replaced by Ed. Suhr, a German, and John Emmeluth, an American.

Quickly as the Committee of Safety was appointed, it went into prolonged deliberation. At its first session, on Saturday, the meeting lasted until long into the night. Preliminary thesis was that the queen herself was revolutionary; that she would undoubtedly persist in her irresponsible course; that intelligent and concerned citizens must take matters into their own hands, and establish and maintain law and order. "That steps be taken at once to form and declare a provisional government with a view to annexation to the United States."

A committee was delegated to make an early Sunday morning call on United States Minister John L. Stevens, to ascertain his views and seek his help. The Committee of Safety was then adjourned until next day—to reconvene at the residence of W. R. Castle.

The delegation found Stevens most interested and receptive when they called at his home to "acquaint him with the situation, and ask him if he was going to support the queen against the cabinet and the citizens." Mr. Thurston, committeeman, duly reported back that "Mr. Stevens replied to us that on three occasions he had been applied to by those representing the queen for support against those who opposed her, and that he had always given her assurance of such support as lay within his power.

"But in this case he considered the position taken by the cabinet and people a just and legal one, and the attempt made by the queen a revolutionary one. If asked by her for his support he would not give it; and on the contrary he should recognize the cabinet as the supporters of law and as possessing the authority of government so long as they were supported by any respectable number of responsible citizens. If they called on him he would give them the same assistance that he had always been afforded to the Hawaiian Government by the United States representatives."

With so generous a proffer of help, the Committee of Safety wasted no time availing itself of the good office of envoy Stevens. That pivotal Sunday wore itself out with meetings at the Castle home, conference with Liliuokalani's worried ministers, selection of speakers to harangue the growing crowds on the streets and waterfront, and a general call for a gigantic mass meeting Monday afternoon, at the Honolulu Rifles' armory. Before Sunday was out the city was saturated with posters calling for assemblage.

Even though the cabinet had opposed the queen and her constitution, and by divisive opposition had precipitated the mass hysteria now gripping the city, the Committee of Safety were not able to completely win them to their side. Realizing the danger and the damage, the crown officials promoted a counter mass meeting, to be held at Palace Square, under sponsorship of the "Committee of Law and Order." But their placards did not reach the streets until late Monday morning.

The city was treated to two desperate public gatherings, held simultaneously, deadly intent on capturing the people's minds. The Committee of Safety had planned well. Chairman for their meeting was William C. Wilder, and the armory was filled with nearly all of the "male white foreign element in the city." Speaker after speaker drove the crowd into frenzy with diatribe against the queen, advocacy of revolution, and the screaming promises of annexation.

At Palace Square the royalists meeting drew less than a thousand darker-skinned natives, abetted by little clots of interested bystanders. Oddly, among the orators appearing in behalf of the beleagured sovereign were such intemperate hotheads as Antone Rosa, Robert W. Wilcox, John E. Bush, Joseph Nawahi, and William "Oily Bill" White. Pushed aside and unwanted by the Safety Committee, they now had changed flags. Unflapped and unabashed, they now extolled Liliuokalani, and asked their listeners to support the monarchy while its problems were resolved.

This time they were extremely careful not to inflame the natives, or to risk the chance of precipitating a fatal riot. But even at Palace Square they found little enthusiasm for the queen's attempted coup. After a resolution was read to the audience, in which Her Majesty publicly made assurance that she would no longer endeavor to change fundamental law by revolutionary means, the meeting disbursed, quietly and orderly.

But before the listeners from either assemblage could reach their homes, John L. Stevens had contacted American Consul-General H. W. Severance, and together they had ordered Captain G. C. Wiltse to land the sailors and marines from the United States warship *Boston*. Fully armed, and in force, the navy paraded up Fort Street and Merchant Street, to take battle station at Arion Music Hall, adjacent to both the palace and the government buildings.

The Committee of Safety, deliriously happy and encouraged by these developments, set Thurston to work drafting the proclamation that would put end to the monarchy. Frantically Marshal Wilson, and the queen's ministers, pleaded before them. But their frenzied appeals had no effect whatever in staying the precipitous course—now that Stevens was cooperating, and the United States military might was on display for all to see.

Liliuokalani, sensing all power and influence as a sovereign ebbing relentlessly away, moved, shocked and listless, from her palace office to palace chambers. There were loyal ones who clung to her presence. A tenuous liaison was still mantained with her equally bewildered ministers. Through it all, like a true Alii, she bore her problems without panic or fear. When mood of loss overwhelmed her, she would retreat to the privacy of her apartment. When fury and outrage no longer could be contained, she fought back, gave orders, and railed out at "the missionary traitors," and their conniving American diplomats.

After it became abundantly clear that American troops had actually landed, Liliuokalani's brother-in-law, Governor Cleghorn, with ministers Parker and Colburn, went immediately to the office of John L. Stevens, to make formal protest to the United States minister for his unwarranted meddling in the nation's affairs. Parker verbally insisted to Stevens that the queen's government could provide protection to everyone, and could contain or suppress any or all rebellion, without United States aid. Colburn bluntly asked Stevens if it were his intention to annex Hawaii. Stevens disclaimed any such motive; that his naval help was for "the community at large." When it was made unmistakably clear to Stevens that the queen's government did not want the troops ashore, Stevens blandly suggested that they put their protests in writing. If their demand was in friendly spirit, he said, he would answer the same way.

Hawaiian protests were put in writing.

Next day the queen's emissaries were back for answer. When the replies coming from Stevens were even more ambiguous and meaningless than his oral answers of the night before, Cleghorn reported to the queen that he was certain that the Committee of Safety had taken over everything, were backed by Stevens, and "our independence is gone."

By eight o'clock Monday evening, the Committee of Safety had hammered out the outline of a new government—entirely haole in staff, and pro-American and annexationist in concept. The advisory and executive councils for a provisional government had been named. A finance committee had been set up to purchase additional arms and ammunition, should the queen and her palace guards attempt to resist. Judge Sanford B. Dole was asked to serve as president, and John A. Soper was to command the new government's military forces. Dole, reluctant at first to assume so heady a request, was perfectly willing that the queen should go, but argued for the naming of Princess Kaiulani as successor, under a regency. From the committee he drew neither support nor sympathy. The monarchy, he was told, must forever be ended.

All inter-island ship transportation was halted. Sanford B. Dole sent his resignation as associate justice of the supreme court to the queen's cabinet. The steamship *Claudine* was impounded by the new provisional government, and made ready for quick trip to the United States. Dr. William D. Alexander, writing of those fateful days, stated: "To judge from their conduct, the Queen's Cabinet were overawed by the unanimity and determination of the foreign community, and probably had an exaggerated idea of the force at the command of the Committee of Safety. They shrank from the responsibility of causing fruitless bloodshed, and sought a valid excuse for inaction, which they thought they found in the presence of United States troops on shore, and in the well known sympathy of the American Minister with the opposition."

Certainly the cabinet members were guilty of a deep disservice to their queen. Without their consent and backing she was as powerless to move against the revolutionists as she had been in proclaiming a new constitution. While they vacillated, argued and pleaded with the determined opposition, and the queen fumed alone and helpless, the takeover moved relentlessly toward fulfillment. When Stevens bluntly told the queen's ministers that the United States troops not only would not come to the assistance of Liliuokalani's government, but would intervene if the insurgents were attacked by the queen's troops, the ministers finally got the message. After Stevens further declared that he would recognize and support the new provisional government on request, they knew they and their queen were finished.

Marshal Wilson had watched, indignant, while John Good, the Committee's new ordnance officer, and his assistants, busied themselves collecting loads of arms and ammunition from Honolulu stores, under the very eyes of the United States military. When some of his police finally attempted to interfere with a wagon loaded with ammunition, as it left the store of E. O. Hall & Son, one of his police was gunned down by Captain Good. While this street altercation drew public attention, the new officers of the provisional government moved with speed and determination. Amply backed by their armed volunteers, they took summary possession of Aliiolani Hale, the seat of government.

President Sanford Dole, in a letter to his brother, described the momentous grab: "We found an almost deserted government building; we enquired for the Cabinet, they were absent when we demanded the possession of the building from Hassinger [Chief Clerk, Interior Department] who politely gave it up. The proclamation was then read at the front door to an increasing audience of Hawaiians and foreigners; we then moved into the Minister of Interior's office and began business, issuing notices, orders &c. Our soldiers began to arrive before the reading of the proclamation was over and before long we had a strong force in and around the building. We proclaimed martial law on this Island, demanded the station house which they (the Royalists) held in force, and by dark it was surrendered, the Queen giving up her authority under protest . . ."

Without hesitance Stevens, in behalf of the United States of America, accepted and acknowledged the provisional government as the lawful government of the nation of Hawaii. Marshal Wilson, recognizing that all was hopeless, finally yielded the police station.

The scene with the queen was stormy, and a bit more difficult.

It took a lot of persuasion by friends and confidants before the haughty Liliuokalani would bow her proud head to the foreign opportunists who had stolen her nation. Her capitulation, drafted with the assistance of Justice Paul Neumann, is a masterpiece of protest. Not even in these last words would she surrender to the haoles who had betrayed her. In it, she shrewdly yielded only to the authority and strength of the United States of America.

"I, Liliuokalani, by the Grace of God and under the Constitution of the Kingdom, Queen, do hereby solemnly protest against any and all acts done against myself and the constitutional government of the Hawaiian Kingdom by certain persons claiming to have established a provisional government of and for this Kingdom.

"That I yield to the superior force of the United States of America, whose minister plenipotentiary, His Excellency John L. Stevens, has caused United States troops to be landed at Honolulu and declared that he would support the said provisional government.

"Now, to avoid any collision of armed forces and perhaps the loss of life, I do under this protest, and impelled by said force, yield my authority until such time as the Government of the United States shall, upon the facts being presented to it, undo the action of its representatives and reinstate me in the authority which I claim as the constitutional sovereign of the Hawaiian Islands."

At seven that evening Sanford Dole accepted the queen's blistering protest; apparently without reading it. It seems incredible that he would neglect to challenge the queen's declaration that she was surrendering to the "superior forces of the United States." His failure to notice that she was in no way capitulating to the provisional government was a mistake for his later clarification. Probably relieved at receiving any kind of abdication document without a fight, Dole endorsed it. "Received by the hands of the late cabinet this 17th day of January A.D. 1893."

Before the steamship *Claudine* was allowed to sail for the United States, she was carefully searched to make certain there were no royalists or queen's advocates aboard. The deposed Liliuokalani was allowed to send her own written appeal to President Benjamin Harrison. Any personal representatives to plead her cause at Washington were forced to await the next Honolulu sailing, which would be February 2. But there was no dearth of provisional government spokesmen aboard the *Claudine* when she departed the islands bearing the news of Hawaii's revolution.

Before another ship left harbor, the humiliated and defrauded royalists had plenty time to prepare a petitionary dossier for presentation at Washington. The queen named Paul Neumann and Prince David Kawananakoa* [uncle to Kalakaua and Liliuokalani] to speak for her. Archibald Cleghorn, with the help of friends, sent Finance Minister E. C. Macfarlane to protect the interests of the heir-apparent, Princess Kaiulani. By the time the royalists reached Washington, however, Grover Cleveland was once more in the presidential chair—and the treaty, recognizing the provisional government, had already gone to the Senate.

XIII

Liliuokalani now had plenty of time and leisure to mull over the crimes with which the new government had charged her, and the fantastic series of events which, in the space of a week, had cost her the kingdom and the throne. Her great hope was that a wise and benevolent America would repudiate the outrageous acts of its Hawaiian representative, reject the Dole government, and return the sovereignty to her.

She would never believe that her attempt to promulgate a new constitution represented an act of malfeasance, or a matter of wrong. "It is alleged that my proposed constitution was to make such changes as to give the sovereign more power, and to the cabinet or legislature less, and that only subjects, in distinction from temporary residents, could exercise suffrage," she wrote in retrospect. And she answered affirmatively to this uninhibited effort to restore some of the ancient rights of her people.

"But, supposing I had thought it wise to limit the exercise of suffrage to those who owed allegiance to no other country; is that different from the usage in all other civilized nations on earth? Is there another country where a man would be allowed to vote, to seek for office, to hold the most responsible of positions, without becoming naturalized, and reserving to himself the privilege of protection under the guns of a foreign man-of-war at any moment when he should quarrel with the government under which he lived? Yet this is exactly what the quasi Americans, who called themselves Hawaiians now and Americans when it suits them, claimed the right to do at Honolulu."

*Ka-wa-na-na-ko-a: *Kah*-wah-nah-nah-*ko*-ah.

She never ceased to maintain that the right to grant a constitution to the nation was a basic prerogative of the Hawaiian sovereigns, and had been so from the beginning. "The constitution of 1840 was drawn at Lahaina by a council aided by missionary graduates, but promulgated by the king without any appeal to other authority." She cited the constitution of 1852, drawn up by Dr. Judd, John Young II, and Chief Justice Lee. "It was submitted to the legislature, not to the people, and, as amended by the members, became the law of the land."

The constitution of 1864, and its enactment by decree of Lot Kamehameha, had been the basic model and precedence for her own bold attempt. As Kamehameha V, Lot had "dissolved the convention, because dissatisfied with its inaction, and in a week's time declared the former constitution abrogated; and, without asking a vote from anybody, gave the land a new and ably drawn constitution, under which the country was prosperously ruled for twenty-three years, or until it was overthrown by aliens determined to coerce my brother. Then followed their own draft of 1887, which also was never ratified by any deliberative assembly."

She was equally vehement in defense of her support of the other two measures which had contributed to her downfall—the lottery bill, and the licensing of the opium traffic. As to the lottery act, which she so willingly had sponsored and signed, "No one would have been more benefited than my accusers. The government of Hawaii was to take no part in the lottery, but was to receive a fixed and openly stated sum for its charter. Among the advantages guaranteed was that the projectors should build a railroad around the large island of Hawaii, thus employing the people and benefiting landholders."

She was just as pragmatic in defending the opium bill. "I proposed to issue licenses for the importation and sale of opium. I did think it would be wise to adopt measures for restricting and controlling a trade which it is impossible to suppress. With a Chinese population of over twenty thousand persons, it is absolutely impossible to prevent smuggling, unlawful trade, bribery, corruption, and every abuse . . . The statute proposed among the final acts of my government was drawn from one in use in the British colonies; yet I have still to learn that there has been any proposition on the part of the pious people of London to dethrone Her Majesty Queen Victoria for issuing such licenses."

When President Cleveland immediately dispatched Congressman James H. Blount to Hawaii for full and impartial investigation of the Hawaiian revolution, and the petitions for American annexation, both Honolulu political factions made every effort to do him honor and court his goodwill. Because Blount was chairman of the house committee on

foreign affairs, both the queen and Dole strove to ingratiate themselves in a shower of comfort and courtesy.

Blount, recognizing that both parties had a desperate case to present, kept his head, and took his depositions with accuracy and candor. Mr. and Mrs. Blount accepted the queen's floral tributes, but politely declined the services of the queen's chamberlain and carriage during their stay in Honolulu. Dole and his representatives of the provisional government fared no better. The Blounts accepted neither the tendered furnished house, nor the free government transportation. They took up residence in a cottage at the Hawaiian Hotel and, before he was through, Congressman Blount had accumulated enough affidavits and statements pro and con to fatten a congressional handbag.

By now the provisional government had most of the haole legal and political minds working for it, and the case for the Dole regime was presented with more than adequate finesse. When it came time to interview the queen, she furnished the American government one of its most eloquent and readable declarations of outrage. She placed blame for the revolution squarely upon the American business interests, missionaries, annexationists, and the candid statement that she would still be sovereign of her nation were it not for moral and military backing of the Committee of Safety by the American minister, John L. Stevens. She viewed Stevens' show of military force as unnecessary meddling in the affairs of another nation, and in his instant recognition of the provisional government as evidence of bias and support for the revolutionaries.

The problem from the queen's standpoint, unfortunately, was that Blount's voluminous notes landed too late in Washington to do her any good. The skilled haole lobbyists, dispatched by Dole and the committee, had already carried their persuasive talk from President Cleveland down to the lowliest newspaper reporter anxious to pump up the story of America's "manifest destiny"—operational now as far west as mid-Pacific.

"After the so-called provisional government had been recognized by Minister Stevens, and I had referred in writing my case to the United States, there was no more for me to do but retire in peace to

◁ EXECUTIVE COUNCIL OF THE PROVISIONAL GOVERNMENT
ALL AMERICANS
(From left), James A. King, President Sanford B. Dole,
W. O. Smith, and P. C. Jones.

—*Photo, Bernice P. Bishop Museum, Honolulu.*

my private residence, there to await the decision of the United States government," the queen later wrote. "Before stepping out of Iolani Palace, however, I . . . cautioned the leaders of my people to avoid riot or resistance, and to await tranquilly, as I was doing, the result of my appeal to the power to whom alone I had yielded my authority."

However, Mr. Stevens was not awaiting things with such tranquility. He had arranged with "President" Dole to fly the American flag over Hawaii's government office building. When Congressman Blount discovered this inexcusable affront to Hawaii, had watched the brown faces of the natives standing sad-eyed and heartbroken on the building's steps, staring up at the strange device which had supplanted the flag Vancouver had given Hawaii, he acted with admirable dispatch. At his orders the stars and stripes were hauled down. Once more the flag of Hawaii, with its union jack design, went back to where it belonged.

There is evidence that Blount was more than displeased with Stevens and the unwarranted role he had played through Hawaii's mortal troubles. But he could never have been as devastated as was the deposed queen. Liliuokalani never forgave America's envoy, and later wrote: "But of Minister John L. Stevens it must be said that he was either mentally incapable of recognising what is to be expected of a gentleman, to say nothing of a diplomatist, or he was decidedly in league with those persons who had conspired against the peace of Hawaii . . . His official despatches to his own government, from the very first days of his landing, abound in statements to prove (according to his view) the great advantages of an overthrow of the monarchy, and a cession of my domains to the rule of the United States . . ."

After Blount—his portfolio fat with charges and countercharges—took final leave of Honolulu, Stevens followed not long after. A congressional committee, and the state department, had decided to make closer examination of the Hawaii affair, and the part Stevens and the American military had played in it. When President Cleveland expressed sympathy and concern for Liliuokalani's plight, and with the arrival of a new minister in Hawaii whom, rumor insisted, had secret instruction to restore the throne and kingdom to the queen, she felt revenge and vindication were near, and took heart.

There is no question but what Minister Albert S. Willis brought with him a course of action which President Cleveland and his Secretary of State Walter Q. Gresham believed might undo the mischief "the Stevens government" had piled up to the embarrassment of the United States. Willis, of course, had not expected nor anticipated the implacable attitude of the American annexationists, their provisional government, or that of a stubborn and determined queen. He arrived on November 7. After presenting his credentials to Dole's government, and after a slow and methodical study of the background of the revolution, it was November 13 before Willis sought audience with Liliuokalani.

His first mistake was in summoning Her Majesty to the American legation office. A rule of Alii was that no one ever summoned royalty. One petitioned the sovereign for audience. In spite of the obvious denigration to her high office, the queen swallowed her pride and paid the command visit to American Minister Willis.

With Liliuokalani before him, Willis wasted no time in getting to the core of his thesis. First he officially made known to her the personal concern of President Cleveland. He conveyed to her the president's sincere regrets that, through the unauthorized intervention of the United States, she had been obliged to surrender her sovereignty. It was the president's hope that—with her consent and cooperation—the wrong done to her and her people might be redressed.

To this the queen graciously and solemnly bowed.

"I then said to her," Willis reported in his own version of the interview, " 'The President expects and believes that when reinstated you will show forgiveness and magnanimity; that you will wish to be the Queen of all the people, both native and foreign born; that you will make haste to secure their love and loyalty and to establish peace, friendship, and good government.' To this she made no reply."

The dark-skinned, immaculate and stately woman coldly scrutinized the officious little haole. To her Willis was the epitome of the ten thousand other foreign-born creatures who, in less than a century, had despoiled an island paradise.

The report, prepared for the American state department, and to forestall later argument, indicates a quality of frigid officiousness in Minister Willis: "After waiting a moment, I continued. 'The President not only tenders you his sympathy but wishes to help you. Before fully making known to you his purposes, I desire to know whether you are willing to answer certain questions which it is my duty to ask?' She answered, 'I am willing.' I then asked her, 'Should you be restored to the throne, would you grant full amnesty as to life and property to all those persons who have been or who are now in the Provisional Government, or who have been instrumental in the overthrow of your government?'

"She hesitated a moment and then slowly and calmly answered: 'There are certain laws of my Government by which I shall abide. My decision would be, as the law directs, that such persons should be beheaded and their property confiscated to the Government.' I then said, repeating very distinctly her words, 'It is your feeling that these people should be beheaded and their property confiscated?' She replied, 'It is.'

"I then said to her, 'Do you fully understand the meaning of every word which I have said to you, and of every word which you have said to me, and, if so, do you still have the same opinion?' Her answer was, 'I have understood and mean all I have said, but I might leave the decision of this to my ministers.' "

Willis claimed to have been "surprised and disappointed" with the interview. Reportedly he was puzzled that an Hawaiian queen of the nineteenth century would deliberately insist on upholding some ancient Polynesian precept—when her every hope for the future rode on the urgently needed help of the nation he represented. He strove to explain that she no longer had ministers, or even a recognized cabinet. In desperation he queried: "If you were asked to issue a royal proclamation of general amnesty, would you do it?"

And Willis recorded another forthright answer. " 'I have no legal right to do that, and I would not do it.' Pausing a moment she continued, 'These people were the cause of the revolution of 1887. There will never be any peace while they are here. They must be sent out of the country, or punished, and their property confiscated.' . . ."

If Liliuokalani ever had the chance to return to her throne, she blew it in that hour. There was no doubt in the mind of Willis that, once restored to power, heads would roll and blood would flow. Never in his life had he met a more obdurate woman. What he had learned would please neither Cleveland nor Gresham.

Later, when the Willis version of the interview was made public, Liliuokalani vehemently denied she had ever used the term "behead" as suitable disposal of haole usurpers. But Willis claimed he had confronted the queen with the written report of the interview, as prepared for Secretary of State Gresham. After it was read aloud to her, he asserted, complete with the repeated statements as to the proper way to liquidate traitors and revolutionaries, she had acquiesced to the wording of the strange document. Her belated defense was that in capital punishment at the hands of the Hawaiian Alii, beheading was a form absolutely unknown, never practiced, and therefore impossible for her to have mentioned.

The confrontation with Sanford Dole and the officials of the provisional government went just as unrewarding. They made it plain to Willis that they had no intention of yielding any of their newly-won power to the queen. They neither sought her amnesty, nor expected she would be called upon to use it.

The stalemate was duly reported back to Washington. Congress, unexpectedly, failed to pass favorably on the annexation initiative, and the mission of Willis, no matter how noble in concept, was a total failure. Some of Liliuokalani's friends and close advisers, devastated by her intransigent and vindictive attitude, prevailed on her to reconsider her inflammatory statements to the American representative. Once again she bowed her proud head in defeat, and promised amnesty to her mortal enemies. And, confronted with a workable basis for action, Willis made formal demand on Dole and his government to step down and allow the queen to be restored to her throne.

But by now it was far too late. The provisional government defied Willis. They utterly refused to budge from their control of Hawaii. And, as for the United States, if it could not recognize and grasp an annexation opportunity when it saw one, they would proclaim Hawaii an independent republic.

Six months after Albert S. Willis had carried his portfolio of failure back to Washington—on July 4, 1894—the Republic of Hawaii was duly proclaimed. The new nation inherited the same cast of political characters gathered by the Committee of Safety. Liliuokalani was definitely and positively left out of it.

It took six years of oratory, political jugglery and debate before the United States finally picked up, by annexation, the precious prize that had been laid at its feet. But that did not mean it was not guarding the offering. In 1894, the same year Queen Lil's kingdom was named a republic, the U. S. Senate passed its first resolution warning all foreign states that intervention in the political affairs of the Hawaiian Islands would be considered an unfriendly act toward its guardian nation. The cry for annexation and "manifest destiny" was still loud enough and clear enough to make certain that the prize must be America's to have and to hold.

XIV

LILIUOKALANI, fifty-six years of age and no longer the ebullient Lydia Paki of so long ago, waited bitterly and silently for the restoration which "righteous" members of the United States government had promised would come when that nation stretched its strong arm in her behalf. She never lost faith in President Grover Cleveland, and the concern he had expressed over the Stevens-backed revolt.

The problem now, however, was that the American Senate had taken matters completely out of the president's hands, and had set up their own independent investigation of Hawaiian affairs. Before them the entire dossier of the Safety Committee and the provisional government had spread their vicious and biased testimony, either by personal appearance, or by affidavit. The only voice allowed to speak for the queen and her government was the testimony of Blount, which he forthrightly and courageously presented.

WASHINGTON PLACE, AS IT LOOKS TODAY

The former home of Queen Liliuokalani is now the governor's mansion of the State of Hawaii.

364

None of the mountainous defense the queen had sent to Washington, none of the anguished petitions of her people, nor the energetic and legally-framed testimony of Paul Neumann, were allowed even passing consideration by the Senate board of inquiry. Its final conclusion was that, rightfully or wrongfully, Hawaii's native monarchy had been overthrown. The parties who succeeded in the coup had been acknowledged as a government by the previous president, Benjamin Harrison. Therefore, the question would not be reopened nor the facts reviewed by the United States. Liliuokalani's hopes for intervention by the United States in her behalf had completely and unalterably vanished.

Lonely, sad and embittered, the queen retreated to Washington Place—to her neglected music, to her journals, and to the growing manuscript of the book she planned. She intended the book as a worldwide appeal in behalf of her people—now reduced by foreign disease and avaricity to 29,000 population. Deposed, widowed, and shoved into obscurity, she would never stop pleading—not in her own behalf, but for a nation reduced nine-tenths in less than a century, and now wiped out by rapacity of the scavengers who had fattened from it. No longer would she beg understanding for herself. The one great thesis of her life was Hawaiian autonomy.

In any country, in any age, Liliuokalani would have measured as an outstanding woman. Hers was a most complex personality. Stubborn, imperious—she was also warmhearted, cultured, modest, supremely gifted, and devout. But never for a moment did she doubt her divine right to rule. To her that meant a monarchy—benevolent—but absolute in power. It never occurred to her that the Hawaiian monarchy might also be an anachronism in a world where small states could not possibly compete with, or prevail over, the great powers who were growing ever greater.

Here was Queen Liliuokalani, a woman of Victorian times, born in a tiny Pacific kingdom, educated in its missionary-inspired schools, at a time when her own language had been written but twenty years. Out of it she attained a high level of competence. From the most inauspicious of beginnings she acquired worldwide knowledge, unmatched accomplishment, and a depth of understanding that was both her glory and her downfall.

Retired at last to the Washington Place that was constant reminder of her widowhood, she kept herself tirelessly alive in the projects which, as reigning sovereign, she had been unable to find time to enjoy. No longer, at Sabbath, was her stately presence seen at the special and ornate pew which Kawaiahao Church had provided for her royal worship. Because this church represented the American missionaries—the once-welcomed longnecks, whose sons and relatives had, as the "missionary party" stolen the nation from herself and her brother—she no longer, in conscience, could give herself to it. Her deep interest in the humbler creed of Mormonism waned in the undeniable fact that this odd and satisfying religion had also come out of America. Not even the all-understanding Christ Himself could be palatable if He wore the cloth and creed of the nation that so grievously had wronged her. In the end she moved her worship to St. Andrews, of the Anglican Church. What was good enough for the beloved Queen Victoria, was good enough for her.

But within a year of her exile, Dole and his provisional government, had cut all ties and all hopes from America, by proclaiming Hawaii a republic. Bitterly, unhappily, the deposed queen watched a new nation emerge from the shell of the old. The same opportunists and "traitors" were in control. With Sanford Dole as the republic's first president, the strange new nation was, to Liliuokalani, the haoles' final affront.

XV

LILIUOKALANI, even in her forced seclusion, never doubted that behind her lay a vast reservoir of strength. The native population, though outwardly easy-going, and apparently indifferent to haole-dominated "New Hawaii," were royalists to the core. They still recognized their queen as rightful head of the nation. Many royalists wore Anglo names, but were half-breed and quarter-breed Hawaiians—products of eager foreigners, sailors, traders and missionaries, and the amiable and cooperative native women. Oddly, too, there were Englishmen, Frenchmen and even Americans who deeply resented the provisional government's takeover, and the ousting of the queen from power. When the tenuous government went into a "republic," the royalist bloc was still large enough and active enough to worry President Dole and his uneasy officials.

The Citizens' Guard—a well-armed militia of haoles—was formed, and drilled against the possibility of insurrection. The army was increased in numbers. The royal guard was changed to an alert and tough constabulary, guarding all public buildings, and the police department was reorganized. As it became increasingly apparent that the United States had washed its hands of any effort to restore Liliuokalani to power, the royalists became just as assiduous as the Citizens' Guard in acquiring and hiding weapons and ammunition for the great day of their eventual triumph.

The loyal opposition, at first, was only a passive and sullen move on the part of angry Hawaiians, who resented their betrayal. At first it was inchoate and undirected. Then, out of the sultry past came Robert Wilcox—that protégé of Kalakaua—the same young man Liliuokalani had once protected and defended. He had led one abortive revolution, and had landed in Honolulu prison for his pains. He had stood with Bush, and their "Equal Rights League" in opposition to the reformers and the queen. Instead of appreciation for the woman who had defied the world to save her people, he had slandered her in public print, and had shown himself as a devious politician at a time when she could have desperately used him.

In spite of his unpredictable and erratic behavior, when Robert Wilcox again came secretly to Washington Place, and revealed his plan for a military takeover of Honolulu, and a return of the queen to Iolani Palace, the bereft and lonely Liliuokalani forgave him his trespasses. Once more he received her full support. This time in a most dangerous venture.

Wilcox made a good case for the revolution. His talk was winning and persuasive. Many haoles who had sworn allegiance to the new Republic of Hawaii were bitterly regretting their misplaced allegiance. Too late they realized they had made a mistake in supporting the Committee of Safety, the provisional government, and now a nation run by American opportunists. As little businessmen they had been in comfortable circumstances before the fall of the monarchy. Since then the American "new deal" had wiped out their savings, and had reduced many of them to penury. They were more than willing to support anything that might right the wrongs of the nation.

The queen, telling of the overt and clandestine support of haoles and natives, and without openly admitting her own part in the revolt, later revealed in her book: "Weary with waiting, impatient under the wrongs they were suffering, preparations were undoubtedly made amongst some in sympathy with the monarchy to overthrow the oligarchy. How and where these were carried on, I will not say. I have no right to disclose any secrets given in trust to me. To the time of which I now write their actions had been peaceful, out of respect and obedience to their queen. If, goaded by their wrongs, I could no longer hold them in check with reason; if they were now, by one accord, determined to break away, and endeavor, by a bold stroke, to win back their nationality, why should I prohibit the outburst of patriotism? I told them that if the masses of the native people chose to rise, and try to throw off the yoke, I would say nothing against it, but I could not approve of mere rioting."

The revolt never got as far as "mere rioting." Either the royalists underestimated the calculating shrewdness of Dole's government, or Wilcox had again badly planned. The movement apparently was liberally infiltrated with government spies, and its every intent had become state secrets. January 7, 1895 was the day set for the revolution. Wilcox had a well-trained and well-armed assault force of two hundred men, poised and ready for the strike. Let the Hawaiian flag once again be raised over Aliiolani Hale and Iolani Palace, and he was certain that royalists everywhere would carry their guns into the streets. The republic, he was convinced, would topple just as quickly and just as easily as it had been set into power.

The tragedy was that all this was known to the adversary. On January 6—one day before the revolt—the government police and guardsmen moved on the insurgents. Surprised and unprepared, they were arrested by the score, and hauled off to jail. For a week the national guardsmen and one thousand armed citizens pursued the rebels across Oahu—until all of the Wilcox company, including the leader, and all suspected townsfolk, were safely behind bars.

Without deference or compunction, Washington Place was ransacked for arms. It was publicly reported that, when the gardens were dug up, plenty of rifles, pistols and ammunition were unearthed from their temporary hiding. On the sixteenth of the month, Liliuokalani went back to Iolani Palace—but not as a queen reinstated to her throne. She went as a prisoner, under arrest. There she was delivered over to Colonel J. H. Fisher, who escorted her upstairs to the heavily guarded apartment set aside for her incarceration.

"There was a large, airy, uncarpeted room with a single bed in one corner," Liliuokalani wrote. "The other furniture consisted of one sofa, a small square table, one single common chair, an iron safe, a bureau, a chiffonier, and a cupboard . . . . There was, adjoining the principal apartment, a bathroom, and also a corner room and a little boudoir, the windows of which were large, and gave access to the veranda."

For a prisoner of the state Liliuokalani, of course, was faring far better than was Wilcox and his co-conspirators.

Night and day she could hear the monotonous and incessant thump of footsteps as the republican soldiers walked their beat in the hallway outside her door, or up and down the palace's wide veranda.

The morning after her arrest and seizure the faithful Charles Wilson brought news that the forty retainers at Washington Place had been jailed and, in addition to another diligent search and dig for hidden arms, the mansion itself had again been thoroughly ransacked. All private papers and manuscripts belonging to Liliuokalani and her deceased husband were confiscated. Judge A. Francis Judd had, without search warrant, supervised the seizure. To the end of her days the queen accused Judd of invading her study, taking all papers from her desk and safe—including her diaries, and the letters and petitions she had received from her people. They were, she claimed, "swept into a bag, and carried off by the chief justice in person."

On the fourth day Paul Neumann, once staunch friend, called on the distraught queen. His query was brief and pointed. In the event it was decided that all principal parties to the revolt were condemned to death—was the queen herself prepared to die? "I replied to this in the affirmative, telling him I had no anxiety for myself, and felt no dread of death. He then told me that six others besides myself had been selected to be shot for treason . . ."

Again it was Charles Wilson who, on January 22, presented to Liliuokalani the proposed document of abdication—worded and drawn up for the republicans by their own Justice Alfred S. Hartwell. The queen was furious and insulted by the paper, and refused utterly to consider it. When it was explained that by accepting a legal renouncement of all claims to the throne of Hawaii—confirmation of a condition already thoroughly established—"all the persons who had been arrested, all my people now in trouble by reason of their love and loyalty towards me, would be immediately released."

Stipulation was that signing of the document must be of the queen's free will and choice, in the presence of, and witnessed by close friends and associates. The bait, of course, overpowering and compelling, was that it would save the loyal but jailed conspirators—including herself—from imminent death. Faced with no choice, other than an ugly and useless blood bath, Liliuokalani asked that the official copy of the pernicious document be brought to her.

On January 24 the formal draft was carried to the queen's cell by Charles Wilson. Behind him followed an audience of witnesses—all friends, of royalist leanings—William G. Irwin, Herman A. Widemann, Samuel Parker, S. Kalua Kookano, and Paul Neumann. The queen lost some of her regal composure, and her heart was heavy and her dark eyes wet with tears as she bent to sign the document that forever ended the Hawaiian monarchy. At their insistence she signed the paper as "Liliuokalani Dominis." The friendly witnesses, including Charles Wilson, scratched on their signatures, and legal acknowledgment of the signing was verified and noted by W. L. Stanley, notary public.

"To myself, my heirs and successors, I do hereby and without any mental reservations or modifications, and fully, finally, unequivocally, irrevocably and forever abdicate, renounce and release unto the Government of the Republic of Hawaii, and its legitimate successors forever, all claims or pretensions whatsoever to the late Monarchy of Hawaii, or to any part, or to the existing, or to any future Government of Hawaii, or under or by reason of any present, or formerly existing

Constitution, Statute, law, position, right or claim of any and every kind, name and nature whatsoever . . ."

There was no question now. Liliuokalani had truly stepped down.

XVI

ABDICATION brought no end to the troubles of Queen Liliuokalani. On February 5 she was brought to trial for treason. Humiliation of the Hawaiian queen was complete when, like her friends in the aborted coup, she stood in Honolulu court and heard the wrath and fury of her enemies translated into cruel and wounding legal verbiage.

Fully cognizant of their prize exhibit, the Dole government utilized the former throne room of Iolani Palace as the scene for Liliuokalani's trial. Justice William Austin Whiting presided. Her former Majesty was represented by Paul Neumann. And Justice A. Francis Judd, son of a missionary, was the first to outline the state's charges against her. His attack on "the prisoner" and "that woman"—mouthed with utmost contempt, was almost more than any proud Alii could stand.

But stand it she did—before an audience of newsmen, diplomats, religionists, haole republican dignitaries, a scattering of darker-skinned and weeping Hawaiians, and even the poet Joaquin Miller. The trial lasted until February 27. At 2 p.m. on that day, sentence was passed on the last sovereign of Hawaii—the extreme penalty for "misprision of treason"—$5,000 fine, and five years' imprisonment at hard labor.

With the government's case now completely successful, Liliuokalani was sent back to durance. No attempt was ever made to collect the $5,000 fine. And certainly the deposed monarch did little of the hard labor imposed by the sentence. While she languished as a prisoner, her people sent her flowers, or stood mournfully on the palace grounds.

On September 6, 1895, even the republicans grew weary of holding in tight security "the stubborn old woman," and she was paroled.

As a private citizen, now freed of all responsibility and duress, Liliuokalani returned to Washington Place. With her music, her writing, and her loyal friends, she divided her time between the home she had shared with her General John and his mother, and her cottage on the "queen's beach" at Waikiki.

Four years later, Kaiulani, "loveliest of princesses," and last legal claimant to the vanished throne, died suddenly. The Dole government, and the annexationists, no longer had worry from that quarter. Three months later Queen Kapiolani, Kalakaua's widow, was dead. Out of all the great Alii, only three now remained alive—and Liliuokalani was one of them.

Not until that fateful day when the United States openly and cleanly annexed Hawaii as a part of her national territory, did Liliuokalani give up the battle for restoration, and the struggle to make the world cognizant of the plight of her defrauded and dying race.

She had anticipated the move by making an extended visit to America, where she pleaded her cause before friendly newsmen, congressional committees, and the American president himself. Everywhere she was received—not with the pomp and ceremony of a visiting sovereign—but as a gentle, cultured woman of astonishing intelligence, deep racial conviction, and persuasive and winsome personality. Her battle for complete release of the Blount report, and for inclusion of her own ministers' testimonies into the biased hearings that had followed her downfall at the hands of the provisional government, was acknowledged for "further study." The pleasant side of her tour was to hear her music being sung and appreciated by the great haole nation, and to find herself courted socially once more. But when President McKinley was inaugurated, to supersede the loyal and friendly President Cleveland, she returned once more to the islands, knowing that she and her cause had become an anachronism to history.

She turned now to the task of completing her memoirs, a remarkable and moving book, which was, after Hawaii's ignoble annexation, published under the title of *Hawaii's Story, by Hawaii's Queen*. It turned out to be much more than the compelling and tragic story of the last years of the Hawaiian monarchy. Her final words were told in pride for her royal predecessors, pride for her remarkable people, an inescapable testament for what she considered a world calamity. The work was delightfully colored by her deep loyalty to her beloved Hawaii and the native race who once had owned the little nation.

During imprisonment she had nearly completed translation of an ancient poem which had been handed down exclusively through the generations of her Alii family. While in the United States she finished it, wrote out its moving Polynesian music, and it was published by Lee & Shepard of Boston. "It is the chant which was sung to Captain Cook in one of the ancient temples of Hawaii," she explains. "It chronicles the creation of the world and of living creatures, from the shellfish to the human race, according to Hawaiian traditions." It was only one of several Polynesian *meles* she recorded for posterity.

She headed up, as patron, the Polynesian Society, an organization headquartered in New Zealand, devoted to the study of languages, literature, folklore, and all things having to do with the inhabitants of that vast and extended island world of the Pacific which Kalakaua had hoped to consolidate as Oceania.

Her music now, because of its haunting beauty, had become a demand item among peoples who had little knowledge of the native roots from whence it had sprung. One of her last acts was to gather up what she could of the songs, chants, and pieces she had written or translated over her past twenty years. These she bound into two fat volumes—one presented to the Library of Congress at Washington, D. C.; the other sent abroad as Liliuokalani's gift to England's Queen Victoria.

But strangely, up to the day of her death in 1917, Liliuokalani was known and revered as the Queen of Hawaii—even by a younger generation of haoles who knew little of her nation's story and cared less. When this regal and majestic woman—sculptored amazingly to the Alii pattern—entered a room in Honolulu, people rose to their feet in her honor. Let the Royal Hawaiian Band, or any other musical aggregation in Hawaii play her hauntingly lovely "Aloha Oe," and audiences automatically and spontaneously stood to it as though it were the national anthem.

In 1911, at the opening ceremonies of Pearl Harbor as United States naval base, she witnessed the celebration from the deck of the *U.S.S. California*. Seated beside the queen was her successor and once archenemy Sanford B. Dole. Time had mellowed the both of them. They now could talk amiably. She lived long enough to witness the United States enter World War I, as an ally of her fondly remembered England. By now the inevitable had truly been accepted, and to the first Hawaiian chapter of the American Red Cross she personally presented the Red Cross flag. Then, for the first time in her life, Liliuokalani went home and ordered the Stars and Stripes to be hoisted at Washington Place. It was a belated gesture of acceptance and loyalty. But whatever Queen Lil did, she did it honestly, sincerely.

In Hawaiian the word "aloha" is both farewell and greeting. Her immortal song "Aloha Oe"—["Farewell to Thee"]—could be the measured last chant of the incomparable and majestic Hawaiian Alii. For certainly, in all history, there is nothing quite like the kings and queens who so long ruled paradise. Their tragedy was that the island kingdom they so loved and so zealously guarded was equally desirable to a world of avaricious people who outnumbered them.

Once Cook and Vancouver made known this island gem of beauty and opportunity to a world far less happy, and vastly more numerous, history could only move toward its tragic, inevitable end.

But while the Alii lived and functioned, they truly were something special. It was mystically appropriate that Hawaii's last queen should have written her "Aloha Oe." And, since "aloha" in Hawaiian is a term for both end and beginning, it remained for Queen Liliuokalani to aptly and unforgettably phrase it.

SUGGESTED READINGS
IN HAWAIIAN HISTORY

ADLER, JACOB and BARRETT, GWYNN (Eds.). *The Diaries of Walter Murray Gibson*. Honolulu: The University Press of Hawaii, 1973.

ALEXANDER, W. D. *A Brief History of the Hawaiian People*. New York: American Book Co., 1891.

ANDREWS, LORRIN. *A Dictionary of the Hawaiian Language*. Tokyo: Charles E. Tuttle Company, Inc., Tokyo, Japan and Rutland, Vt., re-issue, 1974.

BEAGLEHOLE, J. (Ed.). *Journals of James Cook*, 3 vols. Cambridge: Harvard, 1955-1967.

BRADLEY, HAROLD W. *The American Frontier in Hawaii*. Stanford: Stanford University Press, 1942.

BUCK, PETER H. (Te Rangi Hiroa). *Arts and Crafts of Hawaii*. Honolulu: Bishop Museum Press, 1964.

BUSHNELL, O. A. *Ka'a' Awa*. Honolulu: University Press of Hawaii, 1972.
———. *The Return of Lono. A Novel of Captain Cook's Last Voyage*. Boston: Little Brown Co., 1956.

COLUM, PADRAIC. *Legends of Hawaii*. New York: Ballantine Books, 1973.

COOK, JAMES. *A Voyage to the Pacific Ocean . . . for Making Discoveries in the Northern Hemisphere*. 2 vols. London: Hughs, Publishers, 1785.

DAY, A. GROVE. *Kamehameha, First King of Hawaii*. Honolulu: Hogarth Press, 1974.

DANIELSSON, BEGT. *Love in the South Seas*. Family and sex life of the Polynesians. New York: Reynal & Co., Inc., 1956.

FORBES, DAVID. *Queen Emma and Lawai*. Honolulu: Kauai Historical Society, 1970.

373

GREER, RICHARD A. (Ed.). *Hawaii Historical Review: Selected Readings.* Honolulu: Hawaiian Historical Society, 1969.

HOLT, JOHN DOMINIS. *Monarchy In Hawaii.* Honolulu: Hogarth Press, 1971.

II, JOHN PAPA (translated by MARY KAWENA PUKUI). *Fragments of Hawaiian History.* Honolulu: Bishop Museum Press, 1963.

IRWIN, BERNICE PIILANI. *I Knew Queen Liliuokalani.* Honolulu: 1960.

JOESTING, EDWARD and BUSHNELL, O. A., edited by FEHER, JOSEPH. *Hawaii: a Pictorial History.* Honolulu: Bishop Museum Press, 1969.

JOESTING, EDWARD. *Hawaii, an Uncommon History.* New York: W. W. Norton Co., Inc., 1972.

JUDD, GERRIT P. *Hawaii: an Informal History.* New York: Collier Books, 1961.

KAMAKAU, SAMUEL M. *Ruling Chiefs of Hawaii.* Honolulu: Kamehameha Schools Press, 1961.

KUYKENDALL, RALPH S. *The Hawaiian Kingdom.* Vol. I, 1778-1854, *Foundations and Transformations,* 1938. Vol. II, 1854-1874, *Twenty Critical Years,* 1953. Vol. III, 1874-1893, *The Kalakaua Dynasty,* 1967. Honolulu: University of Hawaii Press.

LILIUOKALANI. *Hawaii's Story, by Hawaii's Queen.* Boston: Lee and Shepard, 1898. Tokyo: Reissue by Charles E. Tuttle Co., Inc., Rutland, Vt. and Tokyo, Japan, 1964.

LOOMIS, ALBERTINE. *Grapes of Canaan: Hawaii 1820.* New York: Dodd, Mead & Company, 1951.

MALO, DAVID. *Hawaiian Antiquities (Moolelo Hawaii).* Honolulu: Special Publication 2, translated from the Hawaiian by Nathaniel B. Emerson, 1898. Bishop Museum Press. Reprinted 1971.

MELLEN, KATHLEEN DICKENSON. *An Island Kingdom Passes.* Hawaii Becomes American. New York: Hastings House, 1958.

———. *The Lonely Warrior: Kamehameha the Great of Hawaii.* New York: Hastings House, 1949.

———. *The Magnificent Matriarch: Kaahumanu, Queen of Hawaii.* New York: Hastings House, 1952.

MERRILL, SIBLEY S. (Ed.) *The Kahunas, Magicians of Hawaii.* Boston: Brandon Press, 1968.

MORGAN, THEODORE. *Hawaii: A Century of Economic Change, 1778-1876.* Cambridge: Harvard University Press, 1948.

PUKUI, MARY KAWENA and ELBERT, SAMUEL H. *Place Names of Hawaii.* Honolulu: University of Hawaii Press, 1966.

WHITNEY, HENRY M. *The Hawaiian Guide Book.* 1875. Tokyo, reissued: Charles E. Tuttle Co., Inc., Rutland, Vt., and Tokyo, Japan, 1970.

INDEX

Pele (goddess), 23, 45, 147, 286, 287, 317
Peleioholani, 29
Pennock, Admiral A. W., 255
Percival, Lieut. John, 153-161, 163, 165
Perrin, Émile, 229
Peterson, Arthur P., 307, 343, 345, 348, 349
Petit-Thouars, Captain A. Du, 194, 195
Pierce, President Franklin, 219
Piikoi, J., 213
Poor, Henry, 291
Portal, Father Leonore, 177
Provisional Government, 358, 359
Puna, 39, 46
Punahou, 179
Punahou School, 179, 183, 217
Purvis, E. W., 292, 293
Puukohola, 44-46, 53, 92

Queen's Hospital, 229

Ragsdale, William P., 258
Reciprocity Commission, 272
Reform Party, 339, 340, 345, 346
Richards, Rev. William, 150, 198-201, 203-205, 207, 208, 210, 211
Ricord, John, 211
Rives, John (Ioane Luwahine), 108, 114, 116, 119, 190, 191
Robertson, James W., 334
Robinson, Mark F., 346
Rooke, Dr. T. C. B., 221, 226
Rosa, Antone, 292, 293, 352
Royal Hawaiian Band, 243, 278, 280, 293, 304, 372
Ruggles, Mrs. Samuel, 94
Ruggles, Rev. Samuel, 86
Russell, Lord Edward, 191-194
Russell, Right Reverend M., 317
Russia, 120

Saint Alban's College, 233
Saint Andrew's Cathedral, 233, 366
Saint Andrew's Priory, 233
Samoa, 291
Sandwich, Earl of, 31
Sandwich Islands, 29, 31, 32, 39, 47, 86, 88, 94, 105, 116, 119, 121, 142, 148, 149, 166, 190, 193, 194, 210, 243, 257, 325
Schofield, General John M., 255, 257
Schussler, Herman, 273
Severance, H. W., 352
Severance, Luther, 272
Ship
  Acteon, British warship, 191, 192
  Active, British warship, 139
  Adelaide (Hooikaiki), 205
  Albert, British warship, 205
  Almira, 138
  Australia, 322
  Balena, 109
  Becket, 180, 185

Ship (*Continued*)
  Benicia, American warship, 249, 255, 269, 314
  Blonde, British warship, 121, 139, 141, 143-148
  Boston, American warship, 352
  California, American warship, 255, 372
  Carysfort, British warship, 203, 204, 206
  Champion, British warship, 342
  Charleston, American warship, 301-303, 306
  Chatham, 46
  City of Rome, 323
  Claudine, 353, 355, 356
  Clementine, 193, 194
  Constellation, American warship, 206
  Daedalus, British warship, 46
  Daniel, 150
  Discovery, British warship, 31-34, 36, 46
  Dolphin, American warship, 153-156, 159-163
  Dublin, British warship, 206
  Eleanora, 40
  Endeavour, British warship, 29
  Equator, 109
  Fair American, 40, 41, 45, 59
  Flirt, 276
  Ha'aho o Hawaii (Cleopatra's Barge), 107, 108, 111, 114, 121, 126-128, 130, 132, 153, 185, 188
  Hooikaiki (Adelaide), 205
  Jackall, 50
  James Makee, 283
  Kaimiloa, Hawaiian warship, 289, 291
  Kamehameha, 180, 185
  Kilauea, 260, 263, 283
  L'Aigle, 113-116, 121
  L'Artemise, French warship, 195
  La Bonite, French warship, 191
  La Comète, 177, 178, 190
  La Poursuivante, French warship, 219
  Lelia Bird, 59, 124
  L'Uranie, French warship, 73, 75, 110, 169, 177
  LaVenus, French warship, 194-197
  Likelike, 283
  Mohican, American warship, 335
  Notre Dame de Paix, 195
  H. B. Palmer, 276
  Peacock, American warship, 162, 168, 191
  Peru, 138
  Portsmouth, American warship, 264
  Potomac, American warship, 191
  Prince Lee Boo, 50
  Resolution, British warship, 31, 32, 34-36
  J. D. Spreckels, 299
  St. Paul, 315
  Sulphur, British warship, 194, 195
  Tenedos, British warship, 264

BOOKS OF THE WEST . . . FROM THE WEST